T0257939

Ubiquitous Computing and Intelligent Systems

Ubiquitous Computing and Intelligent Systems

Edited by **Boris Vega**

New York

Published by Willford Press,
118-35 Queens Blvd., Suite 400,
Forest Hills, NY 11375, USA
www.willfordpress.com

Ubiquitous Computing and Intelligent Systems
Edited by Boris Vega

International Standard Book Number: 978-1-68285-276-7 (Hardback)

Printed in the United States of America.

Contents

Preface

This book aims to highlight the current researches and provides a platform to further the scope of innovations in this area. This book is a product of the combined efforts of many researchers and scientists from different parts of the world. The objective of this book is to provide the readers with the latest information in the field.

Ubiquitous computing is an advanced field of study in the discipline of computer science. It deals with the concept of pervasive computing, i.e., allowing users to use any device or any location for computing data. This book is compiled in such a manner, that it will provide in-depth knowledge about the emerging theories and applications of this field. The chapters included herein are a valuable compilation of topics like wireless sensor networks, wireless devices, framework and genetic algorithms for ubiquitous computing, etc. The book aims to shed light on some of the recent researches and unexplored aspects of this field. Students and professionals will find it an invaluable source of knowledge.

I would like to express my sincere thanks to the authors for their dedicated efforts in the completion of this book. I acknowledge the efforts of the publisher for providing constant support. Lastly, I would like to thank my family for their support in all academic endeavors.

Editor

Enhancing Wi-Fi fingerprinting for indoor positioning using human-centric collaborative feedback

Yan Luo[1], Orland Hoeber[2] and Yuanzhu Chen[2,3]*

*Correspondence: yzchen@mun.ca
[2]Department of Computer Science,
Memorial University of
Newfoundland, St.John's, NL,
Canada
[3]Department of Computer Science,
The University of Regina, Regina, SK,
Canada
Full list of author information is
available at the end of the article

Abstract

Position information is an important aspect of a mobile device's context. While GPS is widely used to provide location information, it does not work well indoors. Wi-Fi network infrastructure is found in many public facilities and can be used for indoor positioning. In addition, the ubiquity of Wi-Fi-capable devices makes this approach especially cost-effective.

In recent years, "folksonomy"-like systems such as Wikipedia or Delicious Social Bookmarking have achieved huge successes. User collaboration is the defining characteristic of such systems. For indoor positioning mechanisms, it is also possible to incorporate collaboration in order to improve system performance, especially for fingerprinting-based approaches.

In this article, a robust and efficient model is devised for integrating human-centric collaborative feedback within a baseline Wi-Fi fingerprinting-based indoor positioning system. Experiments show that the baseline system performance (i.e., positioning error and precision) is improved by collecting both positive and negative feedback from users. Moreover, the feedback model is robust with respect to malicious feedback, quickly self-correcting based on subsequent helpful feedback from users.

Introduction

After over a decade of research and development, location-aware services have gradually penetrated into real life. They assist human activities in a wide range of applications, from productivity and goal fulfillment to social networking and entertainment. Traditionally, location-aware applications have been confined to outdoor environments. Relatively less research has explored the potential applicability of similar services for indoor settings. However, in large indoor environments such as airports, libraries, or shopping centres, location-awareness can increase the quality of service provided by these facilities.

Large scale deployment of indoor location-awareness is much more difficult due to two technical challenges. First, GPS can not be deployed for indoor use because GPS signals can not reach indoor receivers. Second and more importantly, due to complicated indoor environments such as building geometries, the movement of people, and the random effects of signal propagation, triangulation-based approaches are much less effective [1]. In addition, interference and noise from other devices can also degrade the accuracy of positioning. On the other hand, such challenges provide researchers with great opportunities for innovative indoor positioning techniques. Some early indoor positioning technologies used infrared, laser, and/or ultrasonic range finders, yielding fairly good system performance in field tests [2]. The disadvantages of such an approach are its size, complexity, and cost, which render it infeasible for mobile devices.

A number of researchers have been working on using Wi-Fi infrastructure for indoor positioning, even though it was not specifically designed for this purpose [3]. Due to the infeasibility of indoor triangulation, most of these systems use a fingerprinting approach based on the Received Signal Strength (RSS) transmitted by nearby Wi-Fi access points [3]. Typically, such an approach consists of a training phase and a positioning phase. In the training phase, each survey position is characterized by location-related Wi-Fi RSS properties called *Wi-Fi RSS fingerprints* [4]. During the positioning phase, the position likelihood is calculated based on the current Wi-Fi RSS measurements.

For Wi-Fi fingerprinting, fine-grained system training is normally required to achieve high accuracy and resolution. This results in significant costs in terms of initial configuration and ongoing maintenance in order to continuously adapt to environmental changes and Wi-Fi infrastructure alterations. Such alterations are not uncommon due to system malfunctions, equipment upgrades, or simply turning on and off Wi-Fi access points controlled by individual users. A great deal of effort has been made by researchers to reduce such costs. A potentially effective way is to let users provide feedback to facilitate the construction and continual maintenance of the RSS fingerprints database.

In this article, we propose a Wi-Fi based indoor positioning system that includes an integrated human-centric collaborative feedback model. In the proposed prototype, we define an efficient and robust user feedback model, where the initial likelihood distribution calculated by the positioning system will be compensated before being presented to the user. Further, the user can participate in how the compensation works in the future by providing feedback.

The rest of this article is organized as follows. An overview of the related work is provided in Section 'Related work'. In Section 'Baseline Wi-Fi fingerprinting indoor positioning system', we describe a baseline Wi-Fi fingerprinting framework. The details of the proposed user feedback model are explained and discussed in Section 'Human-Centric collaborative feedback model'. This user feedback model is tested and evaluated in comparison to the baseline method in Section 'Evaluation'. This article concludes in Section 'Conclusions and future work' with a summary of the primary contributions of this work and an overview of future work.

Related work

The Wi-Fi-based positioning technology has a very promising application prospect mainly because of the ubiquitous and inexpensive nature of Wi-Fi infrastructure. Also, Wi-Fi is widely used and integrated in various electronic devices. Thus, the Wi-Fi based positioning systems can also reuse these mobile devices as tracking targets to locate users, which is a less intrusive way to provide location-aware services.

Wi-Fi fingerprinting-based indoor positioning

Due to the infeasibility of signal propagation model-based distance estimation, more and more researchers have employed a Wi-Fi fingerprinting-based approach, which is more robust, accurate, and cost-effective in real indoor environments. However, its system performance is highly dependent upon the elaborate training process and ongoing maintenance efforts. Also, in the positioning phase, random propagation effects of signal propagation introduced by complex indoor environments may result in large RSS fluctuations or access point (AP) loss [5] (i.e., APs which cannot be heard), which could cause the fingerprints in the database to become inefficient and result in large positioning errors. These shortcomings not only imply a high system overhead and training cost, but also vulnerability to environmental alteration. However, if such a system is enhanced with a self-learning ability adapting it to the environmental changes, such inaccurate positioning outcomes can be compensated. For mobile devices carried by people, such a self-learning capability and positioning compensation could come from end users for free. Users could provide feedback to the positioning service based on their knowledge of the surroundings. They may choose to accept, reject, or supply specific information (i.e., their known location) to modify the system results after being given the estimated position.

Human feedback to fingerprinting-Based positioning process

Active Campus [6] is an early system integrating user feedback. It allows users to update the training data incrementally for future use. When the system location is incorrect, users can click on the correct location and suggest new positions. Similarly, Redpin [7] uses a "folksonomy"-like approach, where many users train the system while using it. Gallagher at el. [8] focus on the adaptation of Wi-Fi infrastructure alteration. They investigate a new method to utilize user feedback as a way of monitoring changes in the wireless environment. Users are prompted to send their RSS measurements to a remote positioning server. The server can then update the Wi-Fi RSS fingerprints in the database based on the observations from the users.

Park et al. [9] propose a user promotion mechanism. They argue that in a human-centric positioning system, it is useful to only prompt users for their location when the system error is large. They propose a mechanism to convey the system's spatial confidence in its prediction based on a *Voronoi Diagram*, and the system only prompts users whenever its confidence falls below a threshold. Therefore, the size of the Voronoi cell naturally represents the spatial uncertainty associated with prediction of the bound space. Once the size of the current Voronoi cell is beyond a threshold, the system will prompt users to provide feedback.

The above approaches refine the existing Wi-Fi RSS fingerprint-based positioning system with the integration of human-centric feedback. However, a potential pitfall is that the model constructed during the training phase could also be negatively affected by unreliable or misleading user feedback. Thus, it is crucial that the feedback from users should be given proper weight or credibility, rather than blind acceptance or rejection. Hossain et al. [10] propose a simple credibility rating. In their system, a user's estimation is given a higher credibility weight if the suggested position has a small discrepancy with the system. In fact, according to the observation of our preliminary experiments, the system results are mostly close to user's true position. However, they are occasionally very far away from the true position due to insufficient Wi-Fi RSS data or large variance. In that case, if user's feedback follows the system's estimation and is assigned a high weight, it in fact becomes an outlier feedback and could bring large interference to future positioning queries. Such negative effects from outlier user feedback should be eliminated. A straightforward solution could be using clustering algorithms to filter outliers [9].

In this article, we will discuss a more general and efficient framework using a wider variety of user feedback. Such a framework is endowed with a high degree of system robustness when a large number of users provide correct feedback. Even when incorrect feedback is provided, the system is able to quickly recover by incorporating subsequent corrective feedback.

Baseline Wi-Fi fingerprinting indoor positioning system

We start by first introducing a baseline Wi-Fi fingerprinting system. The implementation of this baseline system is similar in many respects to the systems in the literature [11]. However, it is also refined to be more robust and suitable for integrating and processing user feedback.

Training phase

The system training is conducted for each survey point in a two-step process. The first step is to collect multiple Wi-Fi scans in order to stabilize the average of RSS readings and calculate the variances. The variance is used to detect the environmental interference level, where a large variance tends to cause unreliable positioning results. The following step utilizes the information collected by these Wi-Fi scans to generate an RSS fingerprint for each survey position.

Collect raw Wi-Fi RSS data

At each survey position, system administrators use a mobile device to scan for the beacon frames transmitted by nearby Wi-Fi APs. In each Wi-Fi scan, beacon frames from different APs are received and converted to a list of 3-tuples, which contains the MAC address of an AP, the RSS in dBm, and timestamp. Note that a single scan may not be able to capture beacon frames from all nearby APs due to the different beacon frame broadcasting periods or severe signal fading. Also, the collected RSS values have a natural variation when indoors, which is unavoidable. To compensate the RSS fluctuation and obtain complete AP information, a sufficiently large number of scans is needed to create an RSS fingerprint. As a result, in a given period of sampling, the device logs a time series of RSS vectors. These vectors are then used to construct the Wi-Fi RSS fingerprints for each measured location in the training grid.

Generate system anchors

The statistics are extracted from the raw Wi-Fi measurement data to generate an Wi-Fi RSS fingerprint for each survey position.

A Wi-Fi RSS *fingerprint* is defined as a vector of 5-tuples (i.e., *MAC, Timestamp, RSS Mean, Count,* and *RSS Variance*), describing a set of APs. The definition and explanation for each field are given as follows.

Given the i-th AP in a Wi-Fi RSS fingerprint, each AP determines one dimension of such a vector:

- *MAC*: The MAC field contains its MAC address, denoted as M_i.
- *Timestamp*: The time of creating the fingerprint is stored in the Timestamp field, denoted as t.
- *RSS Mean*: The RSS Mean $\bar{r}_i$ is an average of the Wi-Fi RSS over the sampling period.

- *Count*: The value of Count is the number of occurrences of the AP during the sampling period, denoted C_i, which is a very important indicator for the reliability of this AP. For a fixed number of Wi-Fi scans, a large Count value means that the AP can be heard for most of the time, indicating that the AP will have a more reliable estimation of its RSS value.
- *RSS Variance*: RSS Variance contains the variance of the measured RSS from the AP, denoted σ_i. The fluctuation level of the current Wi-Fi environment at a certain survey position can be estimated by analyzing the Wi-Fi RSS fingerprint. Each AP has its own mean and variance, which can not provide a global description about the current Wi-Fi environment. In order to estimate the fluctuation level of the entire environment, we use the weighted average of RSS Variance for each AP. The occurrence or the value in the Count field for each AP is utilized as the weight. The collective RSS variance for this fingerprint is defined as

$$\sigma_{F_s} = \frac{\sum_{i \in F_s} \sigma_i C_i}{\sum_{i \in F_s} C_i},$$

where F_s is its RSS fingerprint.

At the end of the training phase, each survey position is associated with an RSS fingerprint containing APs that describe the specific location. For each survey position $\mathcal{P}_s$ in the system, we define a *system anchor* A_s as

$$(\mathcal{P}_s, F_s)$$

The system anchors are reference points to determine the positions of mobile devices.

Note that it is quite possible for the RSS measurements to vary throughout the day, based on cyclical activities such as the number of people within the building, their use of electronic devices, etc. In order to carefully explore the benefits of the core contribution of this work (i.e., the inclusion of human-centric feedback within the positioning process), we found it necessary to simplify the problem domain and assumed that the RSS measurements are stable over time. As a result, we conducted all testing and experimentation at a consistent time of day to avoid temporal-based variances in the RSS measurements. A further discussion on how to extend this work to the more realistic situations of time-varying RSS measurement is provided in Section 'Conclusions and future work'.

Positioning determination phase

In the positioning phase, live Wi-Fi measurements will be collected and used to query the fingerprint database. Using only a few Wi-Fi scans during the positioning phase may generate a large error due to lack of informative RSS data. For experimental purposes, the prototype implementation allows for a variable number of Wi-Fi scans to evaluate system performance (Figure 1).

Suppose the total Wi-Fi scan number is S and the i-th scan will generate an RSS vector $R_i, i \in \{1, 2, 3, \ldots, S\}$. Given N system anchors, when the first RSS vector is formed, we use it to calculate the likelihood $L_j, j \in \{1, 2, 3, \ldots, N\}$ of it matching the fingerprint for each system anchor. Each subsequent scan should lead to a cumulative estimation result with a decreasing error. As such, the estimated result will become more and more reliable as more RSS vectors are used.

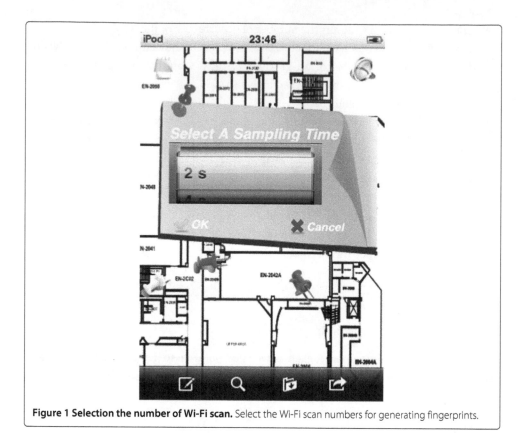

Figure 1 Selection the number of Wi-Fi scan. Select the Wi-Fi scan numbers for generating fingerprints.

Position likelihood distribution

In terms of our baseline system, we use sparse vectors containing all n APs and a Gaussian kernel to calculate the likelihood for each system anchor, which is robust and efficient according to the results of our preliminary experiments.

The Gaussian kernel method was originally used in support vector machines (SVM) to classify data [12], and has also been found to be very efficient for RSS vectors likelihood calculation [11,13,14].

Given an RSS live measurement (observation) vector generated at location $\mathcal{P}$ as $R_{\mathcal{P}_s}$, the resulting likelihood estimate between $R_{\mathcal{P}_s}$ and fingerprint F_i in system anchor A_{s_i} is the sum of n equally weighted density functions

$$L(R_{\mathcal{P}_s}, F_i) = \sum_{k=1}^{n} K_G(r_{M_k}; r_{F_k}),$$

where r_{M_k} is the RSS of k-th AP in the live measurement vector $R_{\mathcal{P}_s}$ and r_{F_k} is the RSS Mean of k-th AP with the same MAC address in fingerprint F_i. Note that when r_{M_k} or r_{F_k} is an impossible value (e.g., -100 dBm), we just ignore this dimension. K_G denotes the Gaussian kernel or radial basis function (*Gaussian RBF*), whose value depends on the distance from the centre. It is given as

$$K_G(r_{M_k}; r_{F_k}) = \frac{1}{\sqrt{2\pi}\delta} exp\left(-\frac{(r_{M_k} - r_{F_k})^2}{2\delta^2}\right),$$

where δ is an adjustable parameter that determines the width of the Gaussian kernel and the centre is r_{F_k}.

In terms of Wi-Fi RSS, whose value domain is $[-90dBm, -30dBm]$, δ less than 0.05 or greater than 0.5 could lead to a weak discrimination ability of Gaussian RBF. In the particular environment, we have to tune the δ value in order to archive adequate system performance.

After the likelihood calculation, each system anchor has a likelihood for being the true position of the device. Instead of just returning a single estimation, the system selects the top-k system anchors as candidates in order to provide redundant true position information. The main reason is that the true position may not always be in the system anchor with the highest likelihood. The next step is to choose a representative from these top-k candidates as the system's estimation of the position.

Position selection

A naïve approach would be to use the weighted mean of the top-k anchors as the estimation for the position. However, if one or more outliers exist, the weighted mean position could be pulled far away from the cluster formed by other system anchors. As a result, this mean position could be a meaningless point in the physical space.

Instead, we can use an approach to the vertex p-centres problem [15] to determine the representative of the top-k anchors. It is a computationally expensive problem for general k. However, in our case, we only consider the case of $p = 1$, i.e., the 1-centre problem. Since the value of k could be very small (less than five), we do not analyze the algorithm complexity at this point.

In particular, the vertex 1-centre for our positioning system is the system anchor point that minimizes the maximum distances from itself to the other top-$(k-1)$ anchor points. These distances are weighted with the likelihood estimated as above. For two indices $i, j = 1, 2, \ldots, k$, we minimize the following over all values for i

$$\max_{j \neq i} \frac{D(i,j)}{L_i},$$

where $D(i,j)$ is the Euclidean distance between anchors A_{S_i} and A_{S_j} and L_i is the likelihood of A_{S_i}. By choosing the vertex 1-centre, the resulting anchor takes advantages of both its likelihood and the positioning information shared by other top-k anchors.

Human-Centric collaborative feedback model

Before discussing the user feedback model in detail, it is useful to begin by identifying three types of user input that can be collected within a human-centric collaborative feedback system:

- *Positive feedback* is generated when users reject the estimated position and suggest a location based on their knowledge. In such a case, the system can accept the updated information from the users. The result is that the system may create new anchors from the users' suggestions, called *user anchors*.
- *Negative feedback* indicates that the users do not believe the estimated position, and are unable to make any suggestion as to their current location. In this case, the system should reduce the positioning likelihood of the returned location in the future.
- *Null feedback* occurs when users choose not to provide any feedback. The assumption here is that the estimated position is accurate, and that there is no need to make any modification to the positioning model.

Next, we will present the general idea of our user feedback model. Assume that the model has N (system and user) anchors, and the likelihood of the i-th ($i = 1, 2, \ldots, N$) anchor is denoted as L_i. Before ranking these anchors based on the likelihood vector L, our user feedback model compensates each L_i with two factors, α_i and β_i as

$$L' = \begin{cases} \beta_i L_i & \text{if } A_i \text{ is a system anchor, } and \\ \alpha_i \beta_i L_i & \text{if } A_i \text{ is a user anchor} \end{cases}$$

Due to the temporal or permanent random interfering factors of complex indoor environments, the reliability of system anchors will be reducing. In order to solve this problem, we design the β factor to gradually reduce the likelihood of system anchors as negative feedback is received. As mentioned before, the system estimation is provided by the vertex-1 centre of top-k anchors. However, if this estimation receives negative user feedback, this means that the user believes that they are not near this location which is an indication that the data stored for these top-k anchors may not be accurate. As a result, the model reduces their likelihood by updating the β factors for these top-k anchors. If more and more users provide negative feedback on a system anchor, it may never be selected as one of the top-k anchors. The β factor thus gives the system an ability to forget outdated or unreliable knowledge.

On the other side, new knowledge (user anchors) will be added into the database via positive user feedback. However, when a user anchor is first created, its likelihood is reduced by the discounting effect of the small initial α value. The rational is that the system can not assess the reliability or credibility of a newly created user anchor (which may be from a malicious user). However, as more and more similar user anchors are generated to confirm it, its α factor will be increased. Once some user anchors become sufficiently reliable, they may appear to be within the top-k anchors to affect the system estimation. Also, the β factor could affect user anchors should they receive negative feedback. The user anchor and α factor enable the system to absorb new knowledge about the Wi-Fi environment.

As such, future users can take advantage of the knowledge shared by previous users. Also, they are encouraged to provide feedback to benefit subsequent users. As a result, the positioning model can be consistently updated via the user feedback model thus designed. Later in this section, we will explain how to calculate the α and β factors in detail.

Positive feedback

Suppose likelihood calculation is finished, and each system anchor $A_{s_i}, (i \in \{1 \ldots N\})$ has a likelihood value L_i. For positive user feedback, users try to tell the system their estimations by providing suggestion positions. Note that these estimations could be close to the true position (accurate feedback) or still far away from it (inaccurate feedback).

Whenever the system receives a user-suggested location associated with its current RSS measurement, denoted as *user fingerprint*, the system creates a temporary user anchor (A_u). If this anchor is sufficiently similar to an existing user anchor in the model, it is merged with it, and the α factor is updated. Otherwise, it becomes a new user anchor, with the associated α factor set to a very small initial value. It indicates that the newly create user anchor is not as reliable as system anchors at the beginning.

Temporary user anchor

Since a user's suggested position could be arbitrary, saving these suggestions separately would bloat the model significantly. Therefore, we use discrete locations by dividing the study area into an $m \times n$ grid. That is, any position within a grid cell is represented by the centre of the cell. This grid-based selection of the position is enabled directly in the user interface provided to the user (Figure 2).

Note that the resolution of this grid could be different from the resolution as used in the training phase. We can set smaller grid space because the system training from users is cost-effective. This helps to efficiently reduce the grid space between system anchors. Thus, the resolution of entire system could be refined.

Within each grid cell, its geometric centre is used to represent the positions of all temporary user anchor points falling into it.

We thus define the user anchor A_u as:

$$A_u = (\mathcal{P}_u, F_u),$$

where $\mathcal{P}_u$ is the grid cell centre that contains the user suggested position and F_u is the user fingerprint summarized from the current Wi-Fi RSS measurement.

Anchor merge

A newly generated positive feedback could be either converted to a new user anchor point or merged with an existing user anchor point based on their similarity. As mentioned

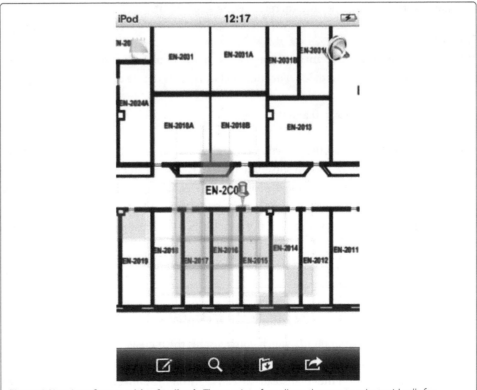

Figure 2 User interface, positive feedback. The user interface allows the user to select grid cells for positive feedback, confirming this choice with a double tap.

before, we believe that positive feedback represented by a user anchor point should gradually become reliable if more and more similar user anchor points are generated to confirm it. Before we discuss how to update the reliability of user anchors, we define the similarity between two user anchor points.

Given user anchor points A_{u_i} and A_{u_j} $i \neq j$, their similarity is determined by two aspects:

- *Wi-Fi RSS fingerprint similarity*: A natural measurement mechanism is the cosine similarity in the range of $[0, 1]$. Thus, the Wi-Fi RSS fingerprint similarity F_u is given as:

$$s_{F_u} = \begin{cases} 1 & \text{if } \cos(F_{u_i}, F_{u_j}) > a \\ 0 & \text{otherwise} \end{cases},$$

  where F_{u_i} and F_{u_j} are Wi-Fi RSS fingerprints of user anchor points A_{u_i} and A_{u_j} respectively. They are all sparse vectors of n dimensions; a is the threshold for Wi-Fi RSS fingerprint similarity.

- *Physical position similarity*: If two user anchor points share the same geometric centre of a grid as their position. They are considered as similar in position.

As a result, we claim that two user anchor points are similar if they satisfy both of the two similarity conditions above.

A temporary user anchor A_{u_i} is thus merged with the existing user anchor A_{u_j} in the same cell if their fingerprints are sufficiently similar. If multiple anchors already exist in the same cell as A_{u_i}, we only consider the most similar one, denoted A_{u_j}. If the similarity between A_{u_i} and A_{u_j} is greater than a threshold, the temporary user anchor is regarded as the same as the existing one, and therefore is merged with it.

The α factor

Whenever a temporary user anchor is merged with an existing user anchor in the system, the associated α factor is updated. For user anchor A_{u_i}, we define α_i as

$$\alpha_i = \frac{1}{a + e^{-x}}, \text{ with } x \geq 0 \text{ and } 0 < a \leq 1,$$

where the variable x has a cumulative effect and a is a parameter controlling the initial and maximum values of α_i. When a user anchor A_{u_i} is first created, its original likelihood will be reduced by a small α. As more positive feedback is provided in support of it, its α factor gradually increases until it reaches an upper limit.

Thus, the magnification capability of the α factor is $\frac{a+1}{a}$. The increment of x is defined as

$$\Delta x = \frac{\frac{T}{T_s} + e^{-\sigma_F}}{b} \text{ with } b > 0.$$

The pace of the increase of x is controlled by a few aspects:

- An independent parameter b, which compensates the increasing velocity of x. When there are many users (e.g., in a large shopping centre), we may not want to trust their individual estimation much. Instead, we can reply on the convergence effects of large amount of users to evolve the mode. However, when there are only a few users (e.g., in a depot), we assign each individual feedback a much higher weight.

- The variance of the current RSS fingerprint, σ_F. The user feedback generated in the environment with small RSS variance will have a greater influence on the evolution speed of the model.
- If T is the number of Wi-Fi scans used in the positioning query and T_s is the number of Wi-Fi scans used during system training, their ratio $\frac{T}{T_s}$ also reflects the credibility of this positive feedback.

As a result, the α factor increases fastest with the first few instances of the user anchor, becoming stable once a sufficient number of feedback events are received. The rationale for this design is to allow the system to quickly adapt to new information provided by the users, but without this feedback overpowering the system.

Negative feedback

Suppose the system delivers a position from the top-k anchors according to their likelihood ranking, but the user believes this location to be incorrect and cannot provide any further information regarding the actual location (Figure 3). The negative user feedback to this estimated position can also provide valuable information to the system.

Typically, when a user rejects the position estimated by the system, the reason could be that the user is nowhere near any of the anchors known by the system. In this case, none of the top-k anchors would truly represent a good estimate. Therefore, we should try to decrease their likelihoods simultaneously.

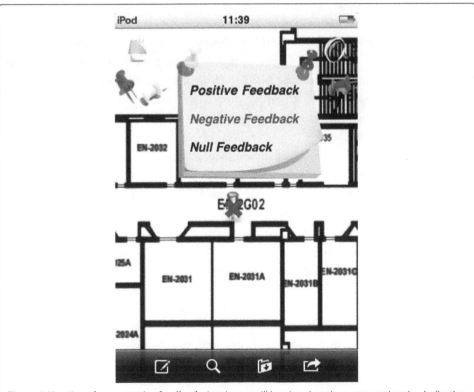

Figure 3 User interface, negative feedback. A red cross will be placed on the system estimation indicating a negative feedback.

Given an anchor A_i, we use a negative user feedback factor β_i to reduce its likelihood according to the accumulation of negative feedback received. Similar to the positive feedback model, the negative factor model also has fast adaptability. Accordingly, we define β_i as

$$\beta_i = e^{-x}.$$

When an anchor is given a negative feedback, we give x in above formula the same increment Δx used in the positive user feedback.

The value of β is inversely related to x, such that β will decrease from the initial value 1 to its limit zero as x increase from zero to infinity. As a result, if more and more users reject the same set of anchors, they will not be chosen as the top-k due to the small value of the β factor.

Evaluation

Experimental settings

The system evaluation consisted of two phases. The first phase was to analyze the performance of the baseline system without user feedback in field tests. The accuracy and precision of the baseline system was calculated. By analyzing these two performance metrics, we can determine whether or not our baseline system is suitable for comparison purposes. During the second phase, we explored how the proposed user feedback model improved the system performance.

Experiments and evaluations with this feedback model were conducted in an complex indoor office environment, which is the part of the 2nd floor of the Engineering Building at Memorial University. The reason we chose this experimental field is that we can fully control our evaluation process under this environmental setting. The space was divided into a grid using a 3×3m cell size. 33 positions were selected within the hallways for training the baseline system (denoted the *training area*), and an additional 20 positions were selected as untrained positions for testing purposes (denoted the *non-training area*). A diagram of the setting is provided in Figure 4. System anchors were created in the training area only. Note that the non-training area lacks valid system or user anchors. It can be treated as an area that is the result of environment alteration, a new Wi-Fi coverage area, or a region that was neglected in the training of the system.

The prototype system was developed for iPhone OS 3.1.2; experiments were conducted using the Apple iPhone and iPod Touch devices.

The system training was conducted during semester break (April, 2010). Each RSS fingerprint had been generated by extracting features from 20 Wi-Fi scans, which took approximately two minutes. The baseline system evaluation was conducted during the summer semester (May - July, 2010) with much more interference from other people and their electronic devices. Thus, the RSS data provided by users are more capable of describing the Wi-Fi characteristics of the current environment.

As mentioned earlier in Section 'Human-Centric collaborative feedback model', the parameters in the feedback model are used to adjust the rate of change of the α and β factors (i.e., the sensitivity of our user feedback model). In production environments, the sensitivity of the user feedback model will depend on the number of users and the degree of trust of those users. For the purpose of evaluation, we increased the sensitivity of the

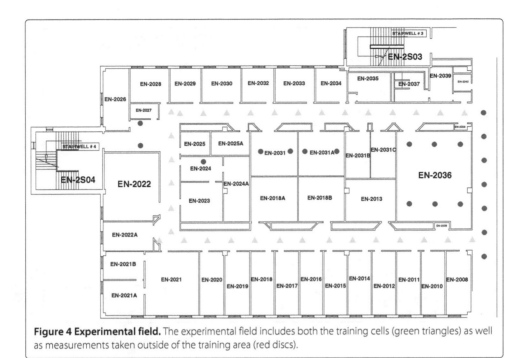

Figure 4 Experimental field. The experimental field includes both the training cells (green triangles) as well as measurements taken outside of the training area (red discs).

user feedback model in order to speed up the rate at which the system is able to learn from user feedback.

We set the value of parameter α to be 1, which means that the magnification factor of parameter α is 2. The value of parameter β was set to be 0.6. As such, according to the design of our user feedback, these parameter setting will weight the first four users much larger than subsequent users, which grants the system a fast learning ability.

Baseline system evaluation

Since the time that a user is willing to spend waiting for a positioning result influences the service quality, we have conducted an experiment to investigate the relationship between time (i.e., the number of Wi-Fi scans) and system performance. We use the baseline system to determine the smallest number of Wi-Fi scans (measured at one scan per second) needed for the system to produce a reasonably accurate result. At the same time, the performance of our baseline system can be evaluated with respect to other similar systems described in the literature.

In the training area, for each survey point, we have collected 20 scans of the Wi-Fi RSS, using these incrementally to query the positioning system. The average positioning error after each scan is plotted as the bottom curve in Figure 5. We can observe that for a small number of scans, the system has an error between 2 and 4m. As more scanned RSS data are used (i.e., greater than four), the accuracy stabilizes at around 2m.

The system precision, as another very important metric for system performance, is plotted in Figure 6. We selected the positioning precision for 9 out of the 20 scans, illustrating three phases of Wi-Fi sampling. The early phase consists scans 1, 2, and 3 (red curves). In this phase, due to insufficient Wi-Fi RSS data, the precision is low. The second phase includes scans 5, 10, and 15 (green curves), it is in the middle of the Wi-Fi sampling and has more Wi-Fi RSS data than the first phase. The last phase is at the end

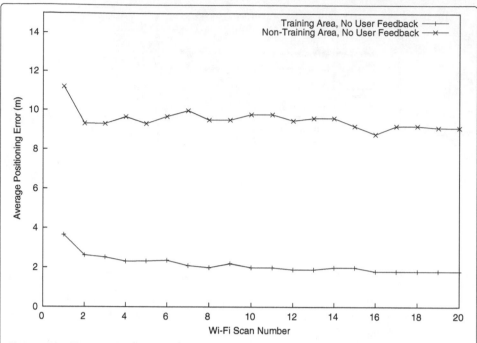

Figure 5 Baseline system accuracy, without user feedback. Using the baseline system, the positioning error becomes relatively stable using just four Wi-Fi scans. Note that the system is significantly more accurate within the training area.

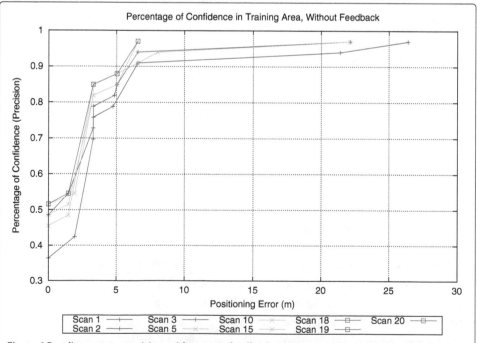

Figure 6 Baseline system precision, without user feedback, training area. The precision of first three scans (red curve) is much lower than later scans (green curves for scan 5,10, and 15 and blue curves for 18, 19, and 20). However, the blue and green curves are very close to each other, indicating the precision after four scans is not improved significantly.

of Wi-Fi sampling (scans 18, 19, and 20), which includes all RSS vectors (blue curves). From Figure 6, we can see that the green and blue curves are very close to each other, which means that a scan number greater than four will not generate significant precision improvement. However, if the Wi-Fi scan number is small (i.e., less than four), the probability of generating outliers is considerably high.

Similarly, in the non-training area, we also collected 20 scans for each position. We plotted the positioning accuracy for the number of scans as the top curve in Figure 5 and positioning precision in Figure 7. In this case, the system performance is significantly lower than in the training area due to the lack of system anchors. However, in both the training area and non-training area, four scans provide a reasonable trade-off between performance and positioning time. Therefore, we use this as the number of scans in the remainder of our experiments.

According to the analysis of our baseline system, the average positioning error is between 2m and 4m, respectively, depending on the Wi-Fi sampling time. It is in fact only marginally worse than the 0.7m to 4m average positioning error yielded by the best-performing but intensively trained Horus system (using 100 Wi-Fi scans and much smaller grid space of 1.52 m and 2.13 m) [16]. Thus, we believe this baseline system is qualified to evaluate the value of the proposed human-centric collaborative feedback model.

Collaborative feedback model evaluation

In order to evaluate the benefits of the collaborative feedback model, we have defined a number of different scenarios that represent specific types of behaviours of users. While we do not claim that any of these evaluations represents what would occur in real world

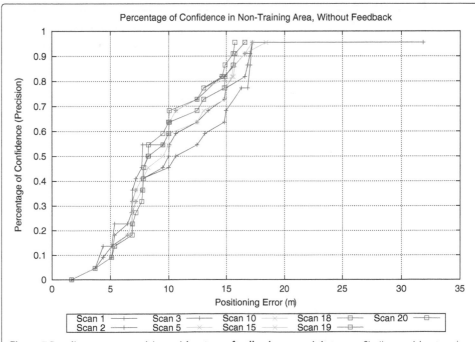

Figure 7 Baseline system precision, without user feedback, non-training area. Similar precision trend can be found in non-training area, blue curves and green curves are similar but both apart from red curves.

use, they allow us to examine how the system will react to different types of feedback. Our future plans for real-world field trials are discussed in Section 'Conclusions and future work.'

Knowledgable and helpful feedback

Next, we investigate how the user feedback model improves the system performance. In this scenario, whenever the system returns a position that does not match the true position of the user, feedback was provided. We modelled the user as being knowledgable and helpful; whenever the position was inaccurate, the user suggested positive feedback 80% of the time, and negative feedback 20% of the time. We believe it is a reasonable choice for situations where users are highly motivated to provide accurate and positive feedback. In fact, there may be many other users who are providing null feedback (i.e., using the system and trusting the results). However, since such types of users do not affect the evolution of the model, they are not discussed here.

Within the training area, we define a *round* as a traversal of all grid cells. In a round, the user stops at each survey position to scan the RSS for nearby APs (using four scans). If the result is correct, the user moves to the next position. Otherwise, the user provides feedback before moving on. The average positioning accuracy after nine such rounds of visiting and testing each position is plotted in Figure 8. In the course of providing this user feedback, the positioning error within the training area improved from approximately 2.5m to 1.5m after just four rounds. From there, little change was observed. Note that the baseline system accuracy ranged from 4m to 2m without feedback. At this point, with the integration of human-centric collaborative feedback, the system performance is further improved even in the well trained area.

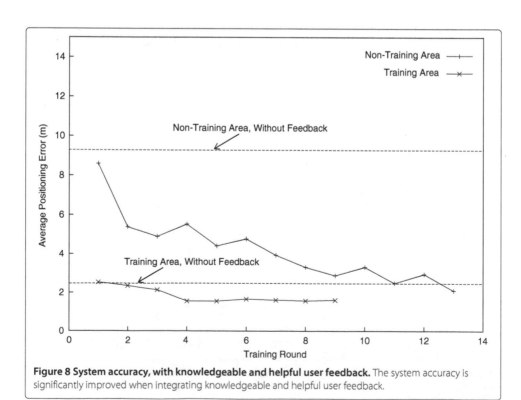

Figure 8 System accuracy, with knowledgeable and helpful user feedback. The system accuracy is significantly improved when integrating knowledgeable and helpful user feedback.

The precision is also improved after four rounds of user-involved positioning within the training area, as we can see in the green and blue curves which are closer to the y axis than red curves shown in Figure 9. Furthermore, green and blue curves are close to each other, which indicates that the model reaches its optimal performance after approximately four rounds of knowledgeable and helpful feedback.

Within the non-training area, the experiment followed the same procedure as in the training area, producing the data plotted in Figure 8. Because there was no training data in these regions, the initial positioning error was rather large. However, after 13 rounds of collecting user feedback, the error decreased from 9m to 2m. The precision is also significantly increased as plotted in Figure 10. As a result, the system performance in an area that had not been previously trained became comparable to the training area.

The reliable user feedback contains information (user fingerprint) that best characterizes the current Wi-Fi RSS features. Such helpful information can help the system to improve the performance. At the beginning of the test within the non-training area, the model contained only system anchors, and therefore could only return the position of a system anchor (i.e., within the training area) to the user. These positions were often far from the true position of the user. As a result of the positive feedback, user anchors were added and the relative weight of these anchors were enhanced by the α factor. Similarly, with the negative feedback, the weight of the system anchors were reduced by the β factor. As a result, the positioning accuracy increased as more user anchors become valid candidate positions.

What this means for indoor positioning systems is that the system training and maintenance costs can be reduced significantly by relying on knowledgable and helpful end users

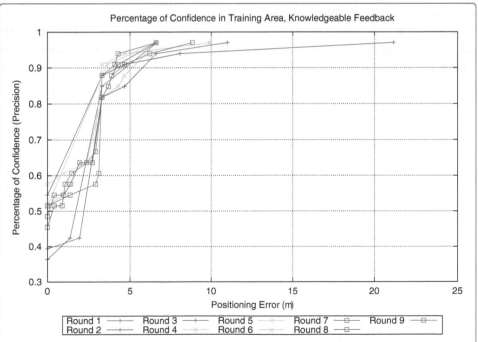

Figure 9 System precision, with knowledgeable and helpful user feedback, training area. In training area, the precision is improved via integrating knowledgeable user feedback. The green curves and blue curves are close, which indicates that the model is optimally trained after four rounds.

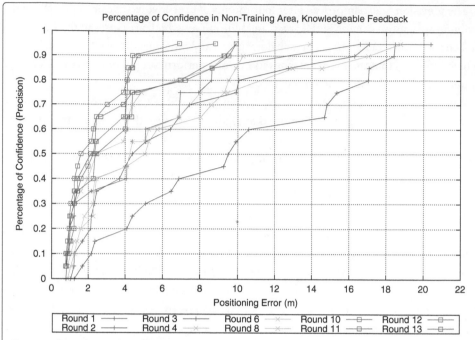

Figure 10 System precision, with knowledgeable and helpful user feedback, non-training area. In non-training area, the system precision is significantly increased as more and more knowledgeable user feedback is integrated.

working on a partially trained system, eventually achieving the same level of accuracy as a fully trained system. Also, the resolution of the positioning system is improved because many reliable user anchors fill the gap between system anchors, thus reducing the grid space or increasing the grid resolution.

At this point, the optimal combination of different types of user feedback is not considered. To conduct experiments testing each possible combination is impractical within a limited time period. In fact, this problem can be explored if we could use a simulation testbed. We can collect a large amount of real Wi-Fi RSS data to simulate the Wi-Fi scans. When the simulated positioning process is finished, virtual user positive or negative feedback can be generated to the evolve the model. As such, the system performance with an arbitrary combination of positive and negative feedback could be estimated.

Mixed feedback

In a real environment, user feedback can be either helpful or malicious. At this point, we assume that the accuracy of user feedback follows the normal distribution. Thus, the feedback from malicious users should exist as outliers. We could employ some supervised classification algorithms such as logistic regression or SVM to classify the malicious users. However, the Wi-Fi RSS fingerprinting based positioning is essentially an unsupervised or instances-based approach (similar to KNN). For instance-based learning, we can cluster different user feedback based on their RSS features and locations, which avoids labeling whether the user is benign or malicious. As described in the previous section, we take the grid-based clustering approach with predefined centres. The reliability of each cluster is compensated by our user feedback model. Furthermore, the performance of instance-based approaches is in fact highly dependent on whether we will have a large dataset or the noise level in training dataset. Thus, if the noise level is very high (e.g., all user feedback are from malicious users), the performance of the system will not be acceptable.

In this experiment, we test the model to determine its ability to recover from incorrect feedback. In particular, we model the user feedback as completely malicious at the beginning and as completely informative thereafter. Such a behaviour is not typical but it provides a "worst case scenario" study of the system, followed by its ability to recover from incorrect or malicious feedback.

Our focus here is on the training area only. As seen in the previous experiments, the non-training area can become nearly as good as the training area with sufficient user feedback. As such, we expect similar results within the non-training area as the training area with respect to mixed feedback.

During the initial phase of this experiment, whenever the system returns a correct position estimation, the malicious user has a 50% chance of either providing negative feedback of suggesting a random false position. When the system is incorrect, the malicious user provides null feedback. Following a similar methodology as the previous experiments, such malicious feedback was provided for four rounds. Another eight rounds of feedback from a knowledgeable and helpful user was then collected.

The position errors for this experiment are plotted in Figure 11. We observe that the system error starts out with around 4m and quickly increases to 14m as a result of the malicious feedback. At the same time, the system precision is also reduced to an unacceptable level, shown as the red curves in Figure 12. With an error of 14m and extremely low precision, the system is considered to be fairly disturbed by the malicious users. At

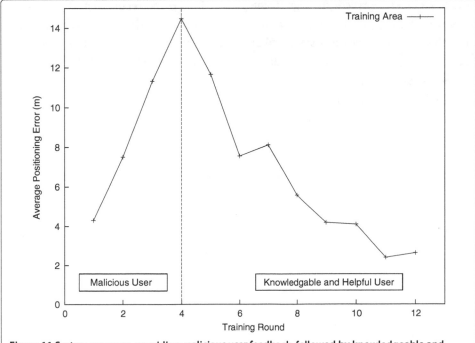

Figure 11 System accuracy, providing malicious user feedback, followed by knowledgeable and helpful user feedback. Providing malicious user feedback, followed by knowledgeable and helpful user feedback illustrates the ability of the model to self-recover.

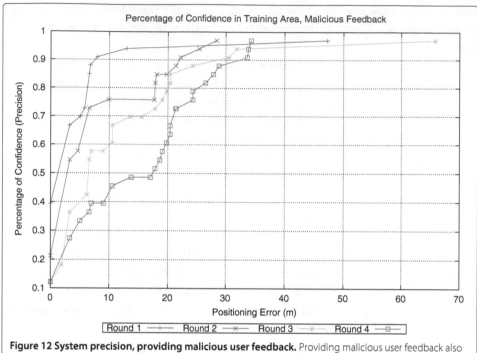

Figure 12 System precision, providing malicious user feedback. Providing malicious user feedback also reduces the system precision significantly.

this point, we turn the user into knowledgable and helpful to provide positive feedback whenever the system is incorrect.

The user behaviour in this case is the same as in the previous subsection. The helpful feedback quickly corrects the significant positioning errors, recovering to the starting accuracy after five rounds of feedback, and below 3m after eight rounds. At the same time, the system precision is stabilized as indicated by the blue curves in Figure 13. As a result, our system has recovered from the low accurate state by integrating helpful and knowledgeable feedback.

In real life, helpful and malicious feedback are often mixed together to feed the model. As such, the phenomena described in this experiment might be rarely observed. However, it in fact provides the "worst-case". If the model can eliminate the negative effect introduced by continuous malicious or unreliable user feedback, then it is reasonable to deduce that it is robust to malicious user feedback in more moderate or general cases.

Conclusions and future work

In this article, the primary contribution is the presentation and evaluation of a user feedback model which receives and processes human-centric collaborative feedback. The proposed user feedback model adjusts the positioning results via placing a compensation mask over the likelihood vector (distribution) generated in the positioning phase. The history of both positive feedback and negative feedback will affect the compensation ability of such a mask. In general, positive feedback generates user anchors and enhances their reliability. On the other hand, negative feedback reduces the trustworthiness of an anchor. All user feedback will be assigned low compensation power when first created and can be enhanced with multiple similar feedback events. As such, this user feedback model

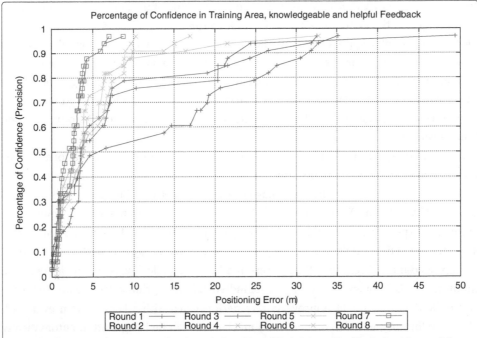

Figure 13 System precision, providing knowledgeable and helpful user feedback. Providing malicious user feedback, followed by knowledgeable and helpful user feedback also recovers the system precision to a normal level.

should be able to gradually update the system's knowledge and guide the system to learn the changes in the Wi-Fi indoor environments. Based on these principles, we have built a prototype and conducted experiments to evaluate it. Experimental results show the ability of the model to improve upon the positioning accuracy and precision in both regions that have been trained, as well as in nearby regions that do not include sufficient anchors. The model is also shown to be robust with respect to malicious feedback, quickly recovering based on helpful user feedback.

In general, storing arbitrary user feedback could require very large storage space and the computational cost of typical clustering algorithms (such as k-means) is high. However, the anchor merge mechanism proposed in our user feedback model merges all similar user anchors which avoids the need to store every user anchor. Furthermore, the grid-based clustering in the user feedback model only needs to cluster each user anchor within the same grid-cell, which significantly reduces the calculation time. As a result, even with the addition of the user feedback mechanisms to the positioning system, the resulting approach remains efficient.

Such a feedback model can be further refined and enhanced in a number of interesting ways. The first refinement is to use the temporal aspect of user feedback, such that different times (morning, noon, and night) of a day or different dates (weekdays, weekends, and holidays) is used to generate different RSS data patterns. For example, in a university cafeteria, due to the interference from human bodies and electronic devices, the RSS measurement generated during lunch time could be very different from that in the early morning. As such, the user feedback generated during lunch time may mislead the positioning activities at other times of the day. In order to solve this problem, the model should take advantage of the timestamp within the RSS fingerprint, limiting the candidate anchors to those that were created at about the same time of the day. This could increase the accuracy of the system in environments with time-related changes in human activities. More complex approaches could be developed that dynamically learn the features of when the RSS measurements are changing, using this to partition the data to generate different models for different times of the day. Also, we can introduce a forgetting mechanism which could remove user feedback from the system. It could be used to address situations where malicious feedback has been received but subsequent helpful feedback is not available.

The second aspect for refinement of this approach is to perform cross platform validation. In real indoor environments, users could carry different types of mobile devices. Due to the diversity of manufacture technologies in wireless network interface cards, the RSS generated by different Wi-Fi chips could also be different. However, our entire implementation and experiments are conducted on Apple iPhone and iPod Touch, which indicates its limitation in field validation. At this point, we argue that the system performance could be improved if the diversity of Wi-Fi chips in different mobile devices is considered. The simplest but efficient approach is to create individual fingerprints database for each type of mobile device. It might improve system performance with a large system overhead. More intelligently, an RSS compensation mechanism can be integrated to automatically adjust RSS patterns among different mobile devices.

The evaluations of the proposed approach have allowed us to validate the ability of the system to learn useful information from the collaborative feedback provided by the users. However, the specific scenarios were somewhat contrived and do not represent realistic user behaviour. As such, field trials within a real-world positioning domain (e.g., new students using the system to find their way around a university campus) are currently in the planning phases.

Competing interests
The authors declare that they have no competing interests.

Authors' contributions
All authors contributed equally to this work. YL designed and implemented the proposed prototype, and prepared the manuscript; OH analyzed and described the theoretic human-centric feedback model, supervised its analysis and edited the manuscript; YC defined the problem domain and refined the system, designed and developed the system evaluation process, supervised its analysis and edited the manuscript. All authors read and approved the final manuscript.

Acknowledgements
This work was funded by scholarships provided by the School of Graduate Studies at Memorial University to the first author, as well as NSERC Discovery Grants held by the second and third authors.

Author details
[1] Department of Computer Science, The University of Western Ontario, London, ON, Canada. [2] Department of Computer Science, Memorial University of Newfoundland, St.John's, NL, Canada. [3] Department of Computer Science, The University of Regina, Regina, SK, Canada.

References
1. Ladd AM, Bekris KE, Rudys AP, Wallach DS, Kavraki LE (2006) On the feasibility of using wireless ethernet for indoor localization. IEEE Trans Wireless Commun 5(8): 555–559
2. Harter A, Hopper A, Steggles P, Ward A, Webster P (2002) The anatomy of a context-aware application. Wirel Netw 8(2): 187–197
3. Bahl P, Padmanabhan VN (2000) RADAR: an in-building RF-based user location and tracking system. In: Proceedings of 19th IEEE international conference on computer communications. pp 775–784
4. Kaemarungsi K, Krishnamurthy P (2004) Properties of indoor received signal strength for WLAN location fingerprinting. In: Proceedings of international conference on mobile and ubiquitous systems: networking and services. pp 14–23

5. Kaemarungsi K, Krishnamurthy P (2004) Modeling of indoor positioning systems based on location fingerprinting. In: Proceedings of 23rd IEEE international conference on computer communications. pp 1012–1022
6. Bhasker ES, Brown SW, Griswold WG (2004) Employing user feedback for fast, accurate, low-naintenance geolocationing. In: Proceedings of the Second IEEE annual conference on pervasive computing and communications. pp 111–120
7. Bolliger P (2008) Redpin-adaptive, zero-configuration indoor localization through user collaboration. In: Proceedings of the first ACM international workshop on mobile entity localization and tracking in GPS-less environments. pp 55–60
8. Gallagher T, Li B, Dempster AG, Rizos C (2010) Database updating through user feedback in fingerprint-based Wi-Fi location systems. In: Proceedings of ubiquitous positioning indoor navigation and location based service. pp 1–8
9. Park J, Charrow B, Curtis D, Battat J, Minkov E, Hicks J, Teller S, Ledlie J (2010) Growing an organic indoor location system. In: Proceedings of the 8th international conference on mobile systems, applications, and services. pp 271–284
10. Hossain AM, Van HN, Soh WS (2010) Utilization of user feedback in indoor positioning system. Pervasive and Mob Compu 6(4): 467–481
11. Kushki A, Plataniotis KN, Venetsanopoulos AN (2007) Kernel-based positioning in wireless local area networks. IEEE Trans Mob Compu 6(6): 689–705
12. Schölkopf B, Smola AJ (2002) Learning with kernels. MIT Press, Cambridge
13. Haeberlen A, Flannery E, Ladd AM, Rudys A, Wallach DS, Kavraki LE (2004) Practical robust localization over large-scale 802.11 wireless networks. In: Proceedings of the 10th annual international conference on mobile computing and networking. pp 70–84
14. Vossiek M, Wiebking L, Gulden P, Wiehardt J, Hoffmann C, Heide P (2003) Wireless local positioning. IEEE Microw Mag 4(4): 77–86
15. Kariv O, Hakimi SL (1979) An algorithmic approach to network location problems. I: The p-centers. SIAM J Appl Math 37(3): 513–538
16. Youssef M, Agrawala A (2005) The horus WLAN location determination system. In: Proceedings of the 3rd international conference on mobile systems, applications, and services. pp 205–218

A low computational complexity V-BLAST/STBC detection mechanism in MIMO system

Jin Hui Chong[1], Chee Kyun Ng[2,3*], Nor Kamariah Noordin[3] and Borhanuddin Mohd Ali[3]

* Correspondence:
mpnck@upm.edu.my
[2]Institute of Gerontology, University Putra Malaysia, UPM Serdang 43400 Selangor, Malaysia
[3]Department of Computer and Communication Systems Engineering, Faculty of Engineering, University Putra Malaysia, UPM Serdang 43400 Selangor, Malaysia
Full list of author information is available at the end of the article

Abstract

The idea of multiple antenna arrays has evolved into multiple-input multiple-output (MIMO) system, which provides transmit and receive diversities. It increases robustness of the effect of multipath fading in wireless channels, besides yielding higher capacity, spectral efficiency and better bit error rate (BER) performance. The spatial diversity gain is obtained by transmitting or receiving multiple copies of a signal through different antennas to combat fading and improves the system BER performance. However, the computational complexity of MIMO system is inevitably increased. Space-time coding (STC) technique such as Alamouti's space-time block code (STBC) that combines coding, modulation and signal processing has been used to achieve spatial diversity. Vertical Bell Laboratories Layered Space-Time (V-BLAST) uses antenna arrays at both the transmitter and receiver to achieve spatial multiplexing gain. Independent data streams that share both frequency bands and time slots are transmitted from multiple antennas and jointly detected at the receiver. The theoretical capacity of V-BLAST increases linearly with the number of antennas in rich scattering environments. It's well-known that maximization of spatial diversity gain leads to degradation of spatial multiplexing gain or vice versa. In order to achieve spatial multiplexing and diversity gains simultaneously, the V-BLAST/STBC scheme has been introduced. This hybrid scheme increases MIMO system capacity and maintains reliable BER performance at the same time. However, both V-BLAST and STBC layers, in this hybrid scheme, assume each other as an interferer. Thus, the symbols must be decoded with a suitable detection mechanism. In this paper, a new low complexity detection mechanism for V-BLAST/STBC scheme based on QR decomposition, denoted as low complexity QR (LC-QR) decomposition, is presented. The performance of the proposed LC-QR decomposition detection mechanism in V-BLAST/STBC transceiver scheme is compared with other detection mechanisms such as ZF, MMSE and QR decomposition. It is shown that the BER performance in V-BLAST/STBC scheme is better than V-BLAST scheme while its system capacity is higher than orthogonal STBC scheme when the LC-QR decomposition detection mechanism is exploited. Moreover, the computational complexity of proposed LC-QR decomposition mechanism is significantly lower than other abovementioned detection mechanisms.

Keywords: MIMO; V-BLAST; STBC; MMSE; ZF; QR decomposition; Spatial diversity gain; Spatial multiplexing gain

Introduction

Conventional single-input single-output (SISO) system, which is a wireless communication system with a single antenna at the transmitter and receiver, is vulnerable to multipath fading effect. Multipath is the arrival of the multiple copies of transmitting signal at the receiver through different angles, time delay or differing frequency (Doppler) shifts due to the scattering of electromagnetic waves. Each copy of the transmitted signal will experience differences in attenuation, delay and phase shift while travelling from the transmitter to the receiver. As a result, constructive or destructive interference is experienced at the receiver. The random fluctuation in signal level, known as fading [1,2], can severely affect the quality and reliability of wireless communication. Strong destructive interference will cause a deep fade and temporary failure of communication due to severe signal power attenuation. Moreover, the constraints posed by limited power, capacity and scarce spectrum make the design of SISO with high data rate and reliability extremely challenging.

The use of multiple antennas at the receiver and transmitter in a wireless network is rapidly superseding SISO to provide higher data rates at longer ranges especially for Long Term Evolution (LTE) systems [3] without consuming extra bandwidth or power. It is also a solution to the capacity limitation of the current wireless systems. The idea of multiple antennas has evolved into multiple-input multiple-output (MIMO) system, which provides transmit and receive diversities. It increases robustness of the effect of multi-path fading in wireless channels, besides yielding higher capacity, spectral efficiency and better bit error rate (BER) performance over conventional SISO systems in multipath fading environments [1,4]. However, the revolution of SISO to MIMO causes the computation complexity to be increased.

Vertical Bell Laboratories Layered Space-Time (V-BLAST) uses antenna arrays at both the transmitter and receiver to achieve spatial multiplexing gain. Independent data streams that share both frequency bands and time slots are transmitted from multiple antennas and jointly detected at the receiver. The theoretical capacity of V-BLAST increases linearly with the number of antennas in rich scattering environments [5]. The spatial diversity gain is obtained by transmitting or receiving multiple copies of a signal through different antennas. This scheme is designed to combat fading and improves the system BER performance. Space-time coding (STC) technique such as space-time trellis code (STTC) that combines coding, modulation and signal processing has been used to achieve spatial diversity [6]. It achieves maximum diversity and coding gain but the system computational complexity increases exponentially with transmission rate. Alamouti's space-time block code (STBC) [7] is another technique used to reduce the computational complexity in STTC. It supports linear decoding complexity for maximum-likelihood (ML) decoding. Orthogonal space-time block code (O-STBC), which is a generalization of the Alamouti's scheme to an arbitrary number of transmit antennas, was introduced in [8].

However, it was shown in [9] that there is a trade-off between spatial diversity gain and spatial multiplexing gain of MIMO systems. For instance, while the V-BLAST scheme increases spatial multiplexing gain, but it does not provide any spatial diversity gain. The V-BLAST scheme is more susceptible to multipath fading and noise compared to Alamouti's STBC scheme as there is no redundant information. Besides, the error propagation in V-BLAST detection causes BER performance degradation and limits the potential capacity of the V-BLAST scheme [10]. Although Alamouti's STBC provides full transmit and receive antenna diversity, the maximum code rate of one can be achieved for two transmit antennas only. For more than two antennas, the maximum possible code rate is 3/4 [11], thus Alamouti's STBC could not satisfy the demand of the desired high system capacity in real time system with good quality of service (QoS) [12,13]. Therefore, in order to achieve spatial multiplexing and diversity gains simultaneously, the hybrid MIMO system has been introduced [14-16]. One of the hybrid MIMO systems is V-BLAST/STBC scheme. However, this hybrid scheme will further induce inevitably higher computational complexity in designing the system.

The V-BLAST/STBC scheme, which was introduced in [14] is a combination of the Alamouti's STBC and V-BLAST schemes. A number of research efforts on V-BLAST/STBC scheme have been carried for MIMO system with the goal of maximizing the system capacity and reducing its computational complexity. The V-BLAST/STBC scheme improves the performance of MIMO by combining spatial multiplexing and diversity techniques together [17]. However, the spatially-multiplexed V-BLAST and STBC layers in the V-BLAST/STBC scheme assume each other as an interferer. Therefore, the transmitted symbols must be decoded with well-known detection mechanisms such as zero-forcing (ZF), minimum mean-squared error (MMSE) and QR decomposition which are employed in V-BLAST scheme [18]. Thus, the lowest computation complexity detection mechanism will be preferred. In this paper, a new detection mechanism based on QR decomposition, denoted as low complexity QR (LC-QR) decomposition, is presented. The QR decomposition of $A \times B$ channel matrix H is a factorization H = QR, where Q is $A \times B$ unitary matrix and R is $B \times B$ upper triangular matrix. The computational implementation of QR decomposition is less than ZF and MMSE [19], thus the computational complexity of V-BLAST/STBC scheme can be further reduced by using the proposed LC-QR decomposition detection mechanism.

The performance of V-BLAST/STBC transceiver scheme with proposed LC-QR decomposition mechanism is compared with V-BLAST and Alamouti's STBC schemes. It is shown that the BER performance of V-BLAST/STBC scheme is better than V-BLAST scheme while the system capacity of V-BLAST/STBC scheme is higher than STBC scheme when the LC-QR decomposition mechanism is exploited. Moreover, the computational complexity of proposed LC-QR decomposition mechanism is significantly lower than traditional ZF, MMSE and QR decomposition detection mechanisms. Since MIMO scheme is considered as the latest multiple access technique for the next generation human computer interaction (HCI) [20] or mobile computing devices, especially in LTE-Advanced system, higher computational complexity inherited with it is inevitable. Any computational complexity reduction mechanism can further reduce the computational cost and power consumption. Therefore, by using the proposed LC-QR decomposition detection mechanism in V-BLAST/STBC MIMO scheme the system performance is not only significantly improved but the computational complexity of the overall system is also significantly reduced.

The rest of the paper is organized as follows. In Section System models, an overview of the hybrid V-BLAST/STBC system model is presented with its traditional ZF, MMSE and QR decomposition decoder mechanisms in the sub-sections. Then, the proposed new LC-QR decomposition detection mechanism is introduced in Section LC-QR

Decomposition Mechanism. In Section The Computational Complexity of LC-QR Decomposition Compared with ZF, MMSE and QR Decomposition Detection Mechanisms, the computational complexity comparison of LC-QR decomposition with other detection mechanisms is discussed. The system capacity and probability of error in V-BLAST/STBC scheme with LC-QR decomposition are examined in Sections System Capacity of V-BLAST/STBC Scheme with LC-QR Decomposition and Probability of Error in V-BLAST/STBC Scheme with LC-QR Decomposition respectively. Section Performance Evaluation of LC-QR Decomposition in V-BLAST/STBC Scheme illustrates the system performance of proposed LC-QR decomposition in V-BLAST/STBC scheme. Finally, this paper concludes in Section Conclusions.

System models

The V-BLAST/STBC scheme, which was introduced in [14,17], is a combination of the Alamouti's STBC and V-BLAST schemes. It provides spatial diversity gain for high priority data and spatial multiplexing gain for low priority data simultaneously by partitioning a single data stream into two parallel sub-streams according to the data priority. The high priority data (e.g. frame header, I-frame, P-frame) is assigned to the STBC layer for extra protection while low priority data (e.g. B-frame, best-effort data) is sent to V-BLAST layer with higher capacity. Since high priority data is more important than low priority data, the corruption of high priority data will severely affect the real time service quality. For instance, error of any missing data in the first enhancement of P-frame layer is propagated to the subsequent P-frames, and it significantly degrades the perceived MPEG video quality. In contrast, any data loss in the B-frame layer affects only the corresponding frame, as it is not referred by other frames for decoding.

The block diagram of a V-BLAST/STBC transceiver model with M ($M \geq 3$) transmit and N ($N \geq M - 1$) receive antennas is shown in Figure 1. A single main data stream is de-multiplexed into two sub-data streams according to the data priority. The high priority data is assigned to the STBC layer for extra gain while low priority data is sent to V-BLAST layer with higher capacity. As the Alamouti's STBC layer spans two

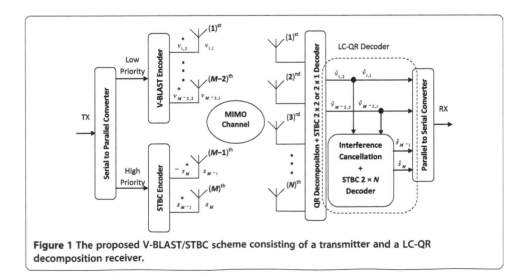

Figure 1 The proposed V-BLAST/STBC scheme consisting of a transmitter and a LC-QR decomposition receiver.

symbol intervals, the V-BLAST/STBC scheme transmission matrix over two consecutive symbol periods is given as

$$
\mathbf{x} = \begin{bmatrix} v_{1,1} & v_{1,2}^* \\ \vdots & \vdots \\ v_{M-2,1} & v_{M-2,2}^* \\ s_{M-1} & -s_M^* \\ s_M & s_{M-1}^* \end{bmatrix} \cdot \left. \begin{array}{c} \\ \\ \end{array} \right\} \begin{array}{l} \text{V-BLAST} \\ \text{Layer} \end{array} \\ \left. \begin{array}{c} \\ \\ \end{array} \right\} \begin{array}{l} \text{STBC} \\ \text{Layer} \end{array} \tag{1}
$$

where * denotes the complex conjugate operation. The transmitted symbols are assumed to go through a Naftali channel coefficient matrix H where H is the $N \times M$ matrix as

$$
\mathbf{H} = \begin{bmatrix} h_{1,1} & \cdots & h_{1,M-1} & h_{1,M} \\ h_{2,1} & \cdots & h_{2,M-1} & h_{2,M} \\ \vdots & \vdots & \vdots & \vdots \\ h_{N,1} & \cdots & h_{N,M-1} & h_{N,M} \end{bmatrix} \tag{2}
$$

The complex channel coefficient of the Naftali channel model using random uniformly distributed phase and Rayleigh distributed magnitude can be described as

$$
h_k = N\left(0, \frac{\sigma_k^2}{2}\right) + jN\left(0, \frac{\sigma_k^2}{2}\right) \tag{3}
$$

where $\sigma_k^2 = \sigma_0^2 \exp(-kT_s/T_{rms})$, $\sigma_0^2 = 1 - \exp(-T_s/T_{rms})$, and $N\left(0, \frac{\sigma_k^2}{2}\right)$ is a zero mean Gaussian random variable with variance $\frac{\sigma_k^2}{2}$ produced by generating an $N(0,1)$ Gaussian random number and multiplying it by $\frac{\sigma_k}{\sqrt{2}}$. The $\sigma_0^2 = 1 - \exp(-T_s/T_{rms})$ is chosen so that the condition $\sum_{k=0}^{k\max} \sigma_k^2 = 1$ is satisfied to ensure the same average received power. The parameters T_s and T_{rms} represent sampling period and delay spread of the channel respectively. The number of samples to be taken in the impulse response should ensure sufficient decay of the impulse response to avoid inter symbol interference.

At the receiver, the received matrix over two consecutive symbol periods can be expressed as y = Hx + z or

$$
\begin{bmatrix} y_{1,1} & y_{1,2} \\ y_{2,1} & y_{2,2} \\ \vdots & \vdots \\ y_{N,1} & y_{N,2} \end{bmatrix} = \begin{bmatrix} h_{1,1} & \cdots & h_{1,M-1} & h_{1,M} \\ h_{2,1} & \cdots & h_{2,M-1} & h_{2,M} \\ \vdots & \vdots & \vdots & \vdots \\ h_{N,1} & \cdots & h_{N,M-1} & h_{N,M} \end{bmatrix} \begin{bmatrix} v_{1,1} & v_{1,2}^* \\ \vdots & \vdots \\ v_{M-2,1} & v_{M-2,2}^* \\ s_{M-1} & -s_M^* \\ s_M & s_{M-1}^* \end{bmatrix} + \begin{bmatrix} z_{1,1} & z_{1,2} \\ z_{2,1} & z_{2,2} \\ \vdots & \vdots \\ z_{N,1} & z_{N,2} \end{bmatrix} \tag{4}
$$

where y is the $N \times 2$ received signal matrix and x is the V-BLAST/STBC $M \times 2$ transmission matrix. z is the additive white Gaussian noise (AWGN) $N \times 2$ complex matrix with unit variance σ^2 and zero mean. For simplicity, it is assumed that the Naftali channel is constant across two consecutive symbol transmission periods, and hence the entries of H are average Naftali channel coefficients. The received matrix over two time intervals in (4) is re-arranged into a single vector to facilitate formulating the detection mechanism resulting as $V = \vec{H} S + N$ or

$$
\begin{bmatrix} y_{1,1} \\ y_{2,1} \\ \vdots \\ y_{N,1} \\ y_{1,2}^* \\ y_{2,2}^* \\ \vdots \\ y_{N,2}^* \end{bmatrix} = \begin{bmatrix} h_{1,1} & \cdots & h_{1,M-2} & 0 & \cdots & 0 & h_{1,M-1} & h_{1,M} \\ h_{2,1} & \cdots & h_{2,M-2} & 0 & \cdots & 0 & h_{2,M-1} & h_{2,M} \\ \vdots & \cdots & \vdots & \vdots & \cdots & \vdots & \vdots & \vdots \\ h_{N,1} & \cdots & h_{N,M-2} & 0 & \cdots & 0 & h_{N,M-1} & h_{N,M} \\ 0 & \cdots & 0 & h_{1,1}^* & \cdots & h_{1,M-2}^* & h_{1,M}^* & -h_{1,M-1}^* \\ 0 & \cdots & 0 & h_{2,1}^* & \cdots & h_{2,M-2}^* & h_{2,M}^* & -h_{2,M-1}^* \\ \vdots & \cdots & \vdots & \vdots & \cdots & \vdots & \vdots & \vdots \\ 0 & \cdots & 0 & h_{N,1}^* & \cdots & h_{N,M-2}^* & h_{N,M}^* & -h_{N,M-1}^* \end{bmatrix} \begin{bmatrix} v_{1,1} \\ \vdots \\ v_{M-2,1} \\ v_{1,2} \\ \vdots \\ v_{M-2,2} \\ s_{M-1} \\ s_M \end{bmatrix} + \begin{bmatrix} z_{1,1} \\ z_{2,1} \\ \vdots \\ z_{N,1} \\ z_{1,2}^* \\ z_{2,2}^* \\ \vdots \\ z_{N,2}^* \end{bmatrix}
$$

$$(5)$$

From (5), it can be easily seen that the obtained system is equivalent to a spatial multiplexing scheme. The spatially multiplexed V-BLAST and STBC layers in the V-BLAST/ STBC scheme assume each other as interferer. Therefore, the transmitted symbols can be decoded with well-known detection techniques such as ZF, MMSE and QR decomposition which are employed in V-BLAST scheme [18]. The ZF and MMSE techniques involve the computation of Moore-Penrose pseudo-inverse of a matrix with cubic computational complexity. Beside MMSE and ZF, QR decomposition is also a common signal processing technique for MIMO detection [21]. The QR decomposition of $A \times B$ channel matrix H is a factorization H = QR, where Q is $A \times B$ unitary matrix and R is $B \times B$ upper triangular matrix. The computational implementation of QR decomposition is less than ZF and MMSE [19], thus the computational complexity of V-BLAST/STBC scheme can be reduced using QR decomposition. The brief overview of ZF, MMSE and QR decomposition decoder are presented in following sub-sections.

Zero-forcing (ZF) decoder

A ZF V-BLAST/STBC receiver architecture is given in [18,22] where all the undesired sub-data streams are nulled by linear weighting receive vector V at each detecting step. The ZF decoded symbol $\hat{S}_i^{ZF}$ of the i-th sub-stream is calculated by multiplying the i-th row of the equalizer filter matrix W with the receive vector, and $\hat{S}_i^{ZF}$ is given by

$$\hat{S}_i^{ZF} = (W)_i V \tag{6}$$

where $(W)_i$ represents the i-th row of matrix W corresponds the criterion in use. The equalizer filter matrix W is then given by

$$W = \left(\vec{H}^H \vec{H} \right)^{-1} \vec{H}^H \tag{7}$$

In an orthogonal channel matrix, ZF is identical to ML. However, in general ZF leads to noise amplification, which is especially observed in systems with the same number of transmit and receive antennas.

Minimum mean squared error (MMSE) decoder

In a MMSE decoder, each received sub-data stream is the superposition of the desired signal [22]. The undesired sub-data streams are considered as interference. At each decoding step, all undesired sub-streams are nulled by linear weighting receive vector V. The MMSE decoded symbol $\hat{S}_i^{MMSE}$ of the i-th sub-stream is calculated by multiplying the

i-th row of the equalizer filter matrix D with the receive vector. Hence, $\hat{S}_i^{\mathrm{MMSE}}$ for MMSE criterion is given as

$$\hat{S}_i^{\mathrm{MMSE}} = (D)_i V \tag{8}$$

where $(D)_i$ represents the i-th row of matrix D corresponding to the criterion in use. The equalizer filter matrix D is then given by

$$D = \left(\vec{H}^H \vec{H} + \sigma^2 I_{2(M-1)} \right)^{-1} \vec{H}^H \tag{9}$$

where $I_{2(M-1)}$ is the $2(M-1) \times 2(M-1)$ identity matrix. The MMSE detector takes the noise term into account and leads to performance enhancement compared to ZF consequently.

QR decomposition decoder

The QR decomposition decoder is applied to the equivalent channel matrix $\vec{H}$ to start the V-BLAST/STBC detection mechanism. QR decomposition is performed with $\vec{H} = \vec{Q} \vec{R}$ which is given as

$$\vec{H} = \underbrace{\begin{bmatrix} q_{1,1} & \cdots & q_{1,2M-2} \\ q_{2,1} & \cdots & q_{2,2M-2} \\ \vdots & \cdots & \vdots \\ q_{2N-1,1} & \cdots & q_{2N-1,2M-2} \\ q_{2N,1} & \cdots & q_{2N,2M-2} \end{bmatrix}}_{\vec{Q}} \underbrace{\begin{bmatrix} r_{1,1} & r_{1,2} & \cdots & \cdots & r_{1,2M-3} & r_{1,2M-2} \\ 0 & r_{2,2} & \cdots & \cdots & r_{2,2M-3} & r_{2,2M-2} \\ 0 & 0 & \vdots & \vdots & \vdots & \vdots \\ 0 & 0 & \vdots & \vdots & \vdots & \vdots \\ 0 & 0 & \cdots & \cdots & r_{2M-3,2M-3} & r_{2M-3,2M-2} \\ 0 & 0 & \cdots & \cdots & 0 & r_{2M-2,2M-2} \end{bmatrix}}_{\vec{R}} \tag{10}$$

where $\vec{Q}$ is a unit norm orthogonal columns $2N \times 2(M-1)$ matrix and $\vec{R}$ is a $2(M-1) \times 2(M-1)$ upper triangular square matrix. The QR factorization can be calculated with the Householder reflection [23]. Left-multiplying (5) by $\vec{Q}H$ results $\vec{V} = \vec{R} S + \vec{N}$ or

$$\begin{bmatrix} \vec{y}_{1,1} \\ \vec{y}_{2,1} \\ \vec{y}_{3,1} \\ \vec{y}_{4,1} \\ \vec{y}_{5,1} \\ \vec{y}_{6,1} \end{bmatrix} = \begin{bmatrix} r_{1,1} & r_{1,2} & \cdots & \cdots & r_{1,2M-3} & r_{1,2M-2} \\ 0 & r_{2,2} & \cdots & \cdots & r_{2,2M-3} & r_{2,2M-2} \\ 0 & 0 & \vdots & \vdots & \vdots & \vdots \\ 0 & 0 & \vdots & \vdots & \vdots & \vdots \\ 0 & 0 & \cdots & \cdots & r_{2M-3,2M-3} & r_{2M-3,2M-2} \\ 0 & 0 & \cdots & \cdots & 0 & r_{2M-2,2M-2} \end{bmatrix} \begin{bmatrix} v_{1,1} \\ \vdots \\ v_{M-2,1} \\ v_{1,2} \\ \vdots \\ v_{M-2,2} \\ s_{M-1} \\ s_M \end{bmatrix} + \begin{bmatrix} \vec{z}_{1,1} \\ \vec{z}_{2,1} \\ \vec{z}_{3,1} \\ \vec{z}_{4,1} \\ \vec{z}_{5,1} \\ \vec{z}_{6,1} \end{bmatrix} \tag{11}$$

where $\vec{V} = \vec{Q}HV$ and $\vec{N} = \vec{Q}HN$. From (11), s_M is decoded first, followed by $s_{M-1},...,$ and finally $v_{1,1}$.

LC-QR decomposition mechanism

The computational complexity of ZF, MMSE and QR decomposition with $\vec{H}$, which have been discussed in the previous section, is high because of the equivalent channel matrix $\vec{H}$ with dimension $2N \times 2(M-1)$ in (5). Therefore, a low complexity V-BLAST/

STBC detection mechanism with QR decomposition, denoted as LC-QR decomposition, is proposed. Instead of decoding the transmitted symbols with the equivalent channel matrix $\vec{H}$ with dimension $2N \times 2(M-1)$, the original channel matrix H in (2) with dimension $N \times M$ is utilized. If $N < M - 1$, the LC-QR decomposition mechanism is invalid and not applicable. The flow chart of LC-QR decomposition mechanism is shown in Figure 2.

Case A: *N* receive antenna is greater than or equal to *M* transmit antenna ($N \geq M$)
The five steps of the LC-QR decomposition mechanism for case A ($N \geq M$) are described as follows.

Step 1: Application of QR decomposition to the channel matrix H

The QR decomposition is applied to the channel matrix H with dimension $N \times M$ to start the V-BLAST/STBC detection mechanism. The QR decomposition is performed with H = QR by

$$
\mathbf{H} = \underbrace{\begin{bmatrix} Q_{1,1} & Q_{1,2} & \cdots & Q_{1,M} \\ Q_{2,1} & Q_{2,2} & \cdots & Q_{2,M} \\ \vdots & \vdots & \vdots & \vdots \\ Q_{N,1} & Q_{N,2} & \cdots & Q_{N,M} \end{bmatrix}}_{Q} \underbrace{\begin{bmatrix} R_{1,1} & R_{1,2} & \cdots & R_{1,M} \\ 0 & R_{2,2} & \cdots & R_{2,M} \\ 0 & 0 & \cdots & \vdots \\ 0 & 0 & 0 & R_{M,M} \end{bmatrix}}_{R} \tag{12}
$$

where Q is a unit norm orthogonal columns $N \times M$ matrix and R is a $M \times M$ upper triangular square matrix.

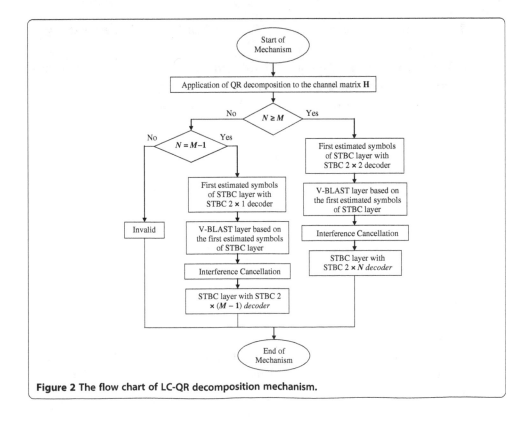

Figure 2 The flow chart of LC-QR decomposition mechanism.

Left-multiplying (4) by Q^H, we get $\tilde{y} = \mathbf{R}x + \tilde{z}$ or

$$
\begin{bmatrix} \tilde{y}_{1,1} & \tilde{y}_{1,2} \\ \tilde{y}_{2,1} & \tilde{y}_{2,2} \\ \vdots & \vdots \\ \tilde{y}_{M,1} & \tilde{y}_{M,2} \end{bmatrix} = \begin{bmatrix} R_{1,1} & R_{1,2} & \cdots & R_{1,M} \\ 0 & R_{2,2} & \cdots & R_{2,M} \\ 0 & 0 & \cdots & \vdots \\ 0 & 0 & 0 & R_{M,M} \end{bmatrix} \begin{bmatrix} v_{1,1} & v_{1,2}^* \\ \vdots & \vdots \\ v_{M-2,1} & v_{M-2,2}^* \\ s_{M-1} & -s_M^* \\ s_M & s_{M-1}^* \end{bmatrix} + \begin{bmatrix} \tilde{z}_{1,1} & \tilde{z}_{1,2} \\ \tilde{z}_{2,1} & \tilde{z}_{2,2} \\ \vdots & \vdots \\ \tilde{z}_{M,1} & \tilde{z}_{M,2} \end{bmatrix}
$$

(13)

where $\tilde{y} = Q^H y$ and $\tilde{z} = Q^H z$.

Step 2: Calculate the first estimated symbols of STBC layer with STBC 2×2 decoder

In QR decomposition, the triangular properties of R allow the sequence of transmitted symbols to be recovered by simple backward substitution with cancellation. If decision error exists in the first detected sub-data streams, the decision feedbacks will significantly increase the probability of error in decoding the subsequent sub-data streams. Therefore, the first decoding decision is made based on STBC layer first so as to decrease the probability of error in decoding the V-BLAST layer. In step 2, $R_{M-1,M-1}$, $R_{M-1,M}$ and $R_{M,M}$ of upper triangular square matrix R are utilized to calculate the first estimated symbols of the STBC layer with STBC 2×2 decoder. These parameters are derived as

$$
\tilde{s}_{M-1} = Q\left(R_{M-1,M-1}^* \tilde{y}_{M-1,1} + R_{M-1,M}\tilde{y}_{M-1,2}^* + R_{M,M}\tilde{y}_{M,2}^* \right)
$$

(14)

$$
\tilde{s}_M = Q\left(R_{M-1,M}^* \tilde{y}_{M-1,1} - R_{M-1,M-1}\tilde{y}_{M-1,2}^* + R_{M,M}^* \tilde{y}_{M,1} \right)
$$

(15)

where $Q(\cdot)$ denotes the quantization (slicing) operation appropriate to the constellation in use.

Step 3: Decode the data symbols of V-BLAST layer based on the first estimated symbols of STBC layer

The V-BLAST layer data symbols are decoded with the properties of upper triangular square matrix R in (13) and first estimated symbols of STBC layer. These layer symbols in the first and second time slot are then derived in a successive way as

$$
\hat{v}_{i,1} = Q\left(\frac{\tilde{y}_{i,1} - \left(\sum_{j=i+1}^{M-2} R_{i,j}\hat{v}_{j,1} + R_{i,M-1}\tilde{s}_{M-1} + R_{i,M}\tilde{s}_M \right)}{R_{i,i}} \right)
$$

(16)

$$
\hat{v}_{i,2} = Q\left(\left(\frac{\tilde{y}_{i,2} - \left(\sum_{j=i+1}^{M-2} R_{i,j}\hat{v}_{j,2} + R_{i,M-1}\left(-\tilde{s}_M^*\right) + R_{i,M}\left(\tilde{s}_{M-1}^*\right) \right)}{R_{i,i}} \right)^* \right)
$$

(17)

Step 4: Interference cancellation

A new modified received $N \times 2$ matrix, s is created by subtracting the data symbols of V-BLAST layer from the original received matrix y in this step, which results in the following matrix

$$\begin{bmatrix} s_{1,1} & s_{1,2} \\ s_{2,1} & s_{2,2} \\ \vdots & \vdots \\ s_{N,1} & s_{N,2} \end{bmatrix} = \begin{bmatrix} y_{1,1} & y_{1,2} \\ y_{2,1} & y_{2,2} \\ \vdots & \vdots \\ y_{N,1} & y_{N,2} \end{bmatrix} - \begin{bmatrix} h_{1,1} & \cdots & h_{1,M-2} \\ h_{2,1} & \cdots & h_{2,M-2} \\ \vdots & \vdots & \vdots \\ h_{N,1} & \cdots & h_{N,M-2} \end{bmatrix} \begin{bmatrix} \hat{v}_{1,1} & \hat{v}_{1,2}^* \\ \vdots & \vdots \\ \hat{v}_{M-2,1} & \hat{v}_{M-2,2}^* \end{bmatrix} \tag{18}$$

Step 5: Decode the data symbols of STBC layer from the new modified received matrix with STBC $2 \times N$ decoder

The data symbols of STBC layer are decoded from the new modified received matrix s with STBC $2 \times N$ decoder and are given by

$$\hat{s}_{M-1} = Q\left(\sum_{k=1}^{N} \left(h_{k,M-1}^* s_{k,1} + h_{k,M} s_{k,2}^* \right) \right) \tag{19}$$

$$\hat{s}_M = Q\left(\sum_{k=1}^{N} \left(h_{k,M}^* s_{k,1} - h_{k,M-1} s_{k,2}^* \right) \right) \tag{20}$$

Case B: N receive antenna is less than M transmit antenna by 1 ($N = M - 1$)

The five steps of the LC-QR mechanism for case B ($N = M - 1$) are described as follows.

Step 1: Application of QR decomposition to the channel matrix H

The QR decomposition is applied to the channel matrix H with dimension $(M - 1) \times M$ to start the V-BLAST/STBC detection mechanism. The QR decomposition is performed with H = QR by

$$\mathbf{H} = \underbrace{\begin{bmatrix} Q_{1,1} & Q_{1,2} & \cdots & Q_{1,M-1} \\ Q_{2,1} & Q_{2,2} & \cdots & Q_{2,M-1} \\ \vdots & \vdots & \vdots & \vdots \\ Q_{M-1,1} & Q_{M-1,2} & \cdots & Q_{M-1,M-1} \end{bmatrix}}_{Q} \underbrace{\begin{bmatrix} R_{1,1} & R_{1,2} & \cdots & R_{1,M-1} & R_{1,M} \\ 0 & R_{2,2} & \cdots & R_{2,M-1} & R_{2,M} \\ 0 & 0 & \cdots & \vdots & \vdots \\ 0 & 0 & 0 & R_{M-1,M-1} & R_{M-1,M} \end{bmatrix}}_{R} \tag{21}$$

where Q is a unit norm orthogonal columns $(M - 1) \times (M - 1)$ matrix and R is a $(M - 1) \times M$ upper triangular square matrix. Left-multiplying (4) by Q^H, we get $\tilde{y} = Rx + \tilde{z}$ or

$$\begin{bmatrix} \tilde{y}_{1,1} & \tilde{y}_{1,2} \\ \tilde{y}_{2,1} & \tilde{y}_{2,2} \\ \vdots & \vdots \\ \tilde{y}_{M-1,1} & \tilde{y}_{M-1,2} \end{bmatrix} = \begin{bmatrix} R_{1,1} & R_{1,2} & \cdots & R_{1,M-1} & R_{1,M} \\ 0 & R_{2,2} & \cdots & R_{2,M-1} & R_{2,M} \\ 0 & 0 & \cdots & \vdots & \vdots \\ 0 & 0 & 0 & R_{M-1,M-1} & R_{M-1,M} \end{bmatrix} \begin{bmatrix} v_{1,1} & v_{1,2}^* \\ \vdots & \vdots \\ v_{M-2,1} & v_{M-2,2}^* \\ s_{M-1} & -s_M^* \\ s_M & s_{M-1}^* \end{bmatrix}$$
$$+ \begin{bmatrix} \tilde{z}_{1,1} & \tilde{z}_{1,2} \\ \tilde{z}_{2,1} & \tilde{z}_{2,2} \\ \vdots & \vdots \\ \tilde{z}_{M-1,1} & \tilde{z}_{M-1,2} \end{bmatrix} \tag{22}$$

where $\tilde{y} = Q^H y$ and $\tilde{z} = Q^H z$.

Step 2: Calculate the first estimated symbols of the STBC layer with STBC 2×1 decoder

In QR decomposition, the triangular properties of R allow the sequence of transmitted symbols to be recovered by simple backward substitution with cancellation. If decision error exists in the first detected sub-data streams, the decision feedbacks will significantly increase the probability of error in decoding the subsequent sub-data streams. Therefore, the first decoding decision is made based on STBC layer first so as to decrease the probability of error in decoding the V-BLAST layer. In step 2, $R_{M-1,M-1}$ and $R_{M-1,M}$ of upper triangular square matrix R are utilized to calculate the first estimated symbols of the STBC layer with STBC 2×1 decoder. These parameters are derived as

$$\tilde{s}_{M-1} = Q\left(R^*_{M-1,M-1}\tilde{y}_{M-1,1} + R_{M-1,M}\tilde{y}^*_{M-1,2}\right) \tag{23}$$

$$\tilde{s}_M = Q\left(R^*_{M-1,M}\tilde{y}_{M-1,1} - R_{M-1,M-1}\tilde{y}^*_{M-1,2}\right) \tag{24}$$

where $Q(\cdot)$ denotes the quantization (slicing) operation appropriate to the constellation in use.

Step 3: Decode the data symbols of V-BLAST layer based on the first estimated symbols of STBC layer

The V-BLAST layer data symbols are decoded with the properties of upper triangular square matrix R in (22) and first estimated symbols of STBC layer. These layer symbols in the first and second time slot are then derived in a successive way as

$$\hat{v}_{i,1} = Q\left(\frac{\tilde{y}_{i,1} - \left(\displaystyle\sum_{j=i+1}^{M-2} R_{i,j}\hat{v}_{j,1} + R_{i,M-1}\tilde{s}_{M-1} + R_{i,M}\tilde{s}_M\right)}{R_{i,i}}\right) \tag{25}$$

$$\hat{v}_{i,2} = Q\left(\left(\frac{\tilde{y}_{i,2} - \left(\displaystyle\sum_{j=i+1}^{M-2} R_{i,j}\hat{v}_{j,2} + R_{i,M-1}\left(-\tilde{s}^*_M\right) + R_{i,M}\left(\tilde{s}^*_{M-1}\right)\right)}{R_{i,i}}\right)^*\right) \tag{26}$$

Step 4: Interference Cancellation

A new modified received $(M-1) \times 2$ matrix, s is created by subtracting the data symbols of V-BLAST layer from the original received matrix y in this step, which results in the following matrix

$$\begin{bmatrix} s_{1,1} & s_{1,2} \\ s_{2,1} & s_{2,2} \\ \vdots & \vdots \\ s_{M-1,1} & s_{M-1,2} \end{bmatrix} = \begin{bmatrix} y_{1,1} & y_{1,2} \\ y_{2,1} & y_{2,2} \\ \vdots & \vdots \\ y_{M-1,1} & y_{M-1,2} \end{bmatrix} - \begin{bmatrix} h_{1,1} & \cdots & h_{1,M-2} \\ h_{2,1} & \cdots & h_{2,M-2} \\ \vdots & \vdots & \vdots \\ h_{M-1,1} & \cdots & h_{M-1,M-2} \end{bmatrix} \begin{bmatrix} \hat{v}_{1,1} & \hat{v}^*_{1,2} \\ \vdots & \vdots \\ \hat{v}_{M-2,1} & \hat{v}^*_{M-2,2} \end{bmatrix} \tag{27}$$

Step 5: Decode the data symbols of STBC layer from the new modified received matrix with STBC $2 \times (M-1)$ decoder

The data symbols of STBC layer are decoded from the new modified received matrix s with STBC $2 \times (M - 1)$ decoder and are given by

$$\hat{s}_{M-1} = Q\left(\sum_{k=1}^{M-1}\left(h_{k,M-1}^* s_{k,1} + h_{k,M} s_{k,2}^*\right)\right) \tag{28}$$

$$\hat{s}_M = Q\left(\sum_{k=1}^{M-1}\left(h_{k,M}^* s_{k,1} - h_{k,M-1} s_{k,2}^*\right)\right) \tag{29}$$

The computational complexity of LC-QR decomposition compared with ZF, MMSE and QR decomposition detection mechanisms

The channel matrix H with dimension $N \times M$ is used to analyze the computational complexity of the LC-QR decomposition. The equivalent channel matrix $\vec{H}$ with dimension $2N \times 2(M - 1)$ is used to analyze the computational complexity of ZF, MMSE and QR decomposition. It is observed that there are zeros in channel matrix $\vec{H}$, therefore the multiplication and addition with zero are not taken into account in ZF and MMSE complexity calculation. The detail of computational complexity of each mechanism is presented in the following sub-sections.

Zero-Forcing (ZF) with $\vec{H}$

From (7), the process to calculate the ZF equalizer filter matrix W is divided into four steps.

Step 1 involves multiplication of $\vec{H}^H$ with $\vec{H}$, it requires $8N(M - 1)^2$ multiplications and $4(2N - 1)(M - 1)^2$ additions, so the number of complex arithmetic operations in step 1 is $4(4N - 1)(M - 1)^2$.

Step 2 involves Gaussian elimination matrix inversion of $\vec{H}^H\vec{H}$. According to [23], the computational complexity of Gaussian elimination matrix inversion with dimension $a \times b$ matrix is $O(ab^2)$. Since the dimension of matrix $\vec{H}^H\vec{H}$ is $2(M - 1) \times 2(M - 1)$, thus the number of complex arithmetic operations in step 2 is $8(M - 1)^3$.

Step 3 performs multiplication of $\left(\vec{H}^H\vec{H}\right)^{-1}$ with $\vec{H}^H$, it requires $8N(M - 1)^2$ multiplications and $8N(M - 1)^2 - 4N(M - 1)$ additions, then the number of complex arithmetic operations in step 3 is $16N(M - 1)^2 - 4N(M - 1)$.

In step 4, the decoded symbols with ZF mechanism are calculated by multiplying equalizer filter matrix W with the receive vector V and it needs $4N(M - 1)$ multiplications and $2(2N - 1)(M - 1)$ additions. So, the number of complex arithmetic operations in step 4 is $2(4N - 1)(M - 1)$.

Finally, the total complex arithmetic operation of ZF V-BLAST/STBC is $8(M - 1)^3 + 4(8N - 1)(M - 1)^2 + 2(2N - 1)(M - 1)$.

Minimum mean-squared error (MMSE) with $\vec{H}$

From (9), the process to calculate the MMSE equalizer filter matrix D is divided into five steps.

Step 1 involves multiplication of $\vec{H}^H$ with $\vec{H}$, it requires $8\,N(M-1)^2$ multiplications and $4(2\,N-1)(M-1)^2$ additions, so the number of complex arithmetic operations in step 1 is $4(4\,N-1)(M-1)^2$.

Step 2 performs the addition of $\vec{H}^H\,\vec{H}$. with $\sigma^2 I_{2(M-1)}$, it requires $I_{2(M-1)}$ additions, and then the number of complex arithmetic operations in step 2 is $I_{2(M-1)}$.

Step 3 involves Gaussian elimination matrix inversion of $\left(\vec{H}^H\,\vec{H}+\sigma^2 I_{2(M-1)}\right)$. Since the dimension of matrix $\left(\vec{H}^H\,\vec{H}+\sigma^2 I_{2(M-1)}\right)$ is $2(M-1)\times 2(M-1)$, thus the number of complex arithmetic operations in step 3 is $8(M-1)^3$ [23].

Step 4 performs multiplication of $\left(\vec{H}^H\,\vec{H}+\sigma^2 I_{2(M-1)}\right)^{-1}$ with $\vec{H}^H$, it requires $8\,N(M-1)^2$ multiplications and $8\,N(M-1)^2-4\,N(M-1)$ additions, then the number of complex arithmetic operations in step 4 is $16\,N(M-1)^2-4\,N(M-1)$.

In step 5, the decoded symbols with MMSE mechanism are calculated by multiplying equalizer filter matrix D with the receive vector V and it needs $4\,N(M-1)$ multiplications and $2(2\,N-1)(M-1)$ additions. So, the number of complex arithmetic operations in step 5 is $2\,(4\,N-1)\,(M-1)$.

Finally, the total complex arithmetic operation of MMSE V-BLAST/STBC is $8(M-1)^3+4(8\,N-1)(M-1)^2+4\,N(M-1)$.

Conventional QR decomposition with $\vec{H}$

Step 1 involves application of QR decomposition to the channel matrix $\vec{H}$ and multiplication of $\vec{Q}\,H$ with V. According to [23], the computational complexity of QR decomposition by Householder reflection with size a × b matrix is $O(ab^2-b^3/3)$. Since the dimension of channel matrix $\vec{H}$ is $2\,N\times 2(M-1)$, thus the number of complex arithmetic operations for the QR decomposition of $\vec{H}$ being $8\,N(M-1)^2-(8/3)(M-1)^3$. Besides, for the multiplication of $\vec{Q}\,H$ with V, it needs $2\,N\times 2\,(M-1)$ multiplications and $(2\,N-1)\times 2(M-1)$ additions. Therefore, the number of complex arithmetic operations in step 1 is $8\,N\,(M-1)^2-(8/3)(M-1)^3+2(4\,N-1)\times(M-1)$.

Step 2 decodes the transmitted symbols with backward substitution with cancellation; it requires $(M-2)\times(2\,M-3)$ additions, $2(M-1)-1$ subtractions, $(2\,M-3)\times(M-1)$ multiplications and $2(M-1)$ divisions.

Finally, the total complex arithmetic operation of conventional QR decomposition is $8\,N(M-1)^2-(8/3)(M-1)^3+(2\,M-3)^2+2(M-1)(4\,N+1)-1$.

LC-QR decomposition with H

Step 1 of LC-QR decomposition involves application of QR decomposition to the channel matrix H and multiplication of Q^H with y. Since the dimension of channel matrix H is $N\times M$, thus the number of complex arithmetic operations for the QR decomposition of H is $NM^2-M^3/3$. Besides, for the multiplication of Q^H with you, it needs $N\times M$ multiplications and $(N-1)\times M$ additions. Therefore, the number of complex arithmetic operations in step 1 is $NM^2-M^3/3+M(2\,N-1)$.

Step 2 of LC-QR decomposition calculates the first estimate symbols of the STBC layer with STBC 2×2 decoder. It needs six multiplications, three additions and one subtraction. So, the number of complex arithmetic operations in step 2 is ten.

Step 3 of the LC-QR decomposition decodes the data symbols of V-BLAST layer based on the first estimate symbols of STBC layer, so it requires $(M-2)(M-1)$ additions, $2(M-2)$ subtractions, $(M-2)(M+1)$ multiplications and $2(M-2)$ divisions. Therefore, the number of complex arithmetic operations in step 3 is $2(M-2)(M+2)$.

Step 4 of LC-QR decomposition involves interference cancellation, thus it requires $2N(M-2)$ multiplications, $2N(M-3)$ additions and $2N$ subtractions. Therefore, the number of complex arithmetic operations in step 4 is $4N(M-2)$.

In Step 5, it decodes the data symbols of the STBC layer from the new modified received matrix s with STBC $2 \times N$ decoder, it requires $4N$ multiplications, $N + 2(N-1)$ additions and N subtractions. Therefore, the number of complex arithmetic operations in step 5 is $2(4N-1)$.

Finally, the total complex arithmetic operation of LC-QR is $NM^2 - M^3/3 + (M+2)(2N-1) + 2(M-2)(M+2) + 4N(M-1) + 10$.

The comparison of number of complex arithmetic operations and reduction of computational complexity for ZF, MMSE, QR decomposition with $\vec{H}$ and LC-QR decomposition detection mechanism with H is shown in Tables 1 and 2 respectively. From Table 2, it can be observed that the proposed LC-QR decomposition detection mechanism significantly reduces the arithmetic complexity compared to ZF, MMSE and QR decomposition mechanisms.

System capacity of V-BLAST/STBC scheme with LC-QR decomposition

The instantaneous capacity of an orthogonal STBC of rate r_c and M transmit antennas, denoted as C_{STBC}, is given by [24]

$$C_{STBC} = r_c \log_2 \left(1 + \frac{\rho}{M} \|\mathbf{H}\|^2\right) \tag{30}$$

where ρ is the signal-to-noise ratio (SNR) per receive antenna. According to (14) and (15), only $R_{M-1,M-1}$, $R_{M-1,M}$ and $R_{M,M}$ of upper triangular square matrix R are required to decode the STBC layer, thus the instantaneous system capacity of the STBC layer of the LC-QR with $r_c = 1$ and $M = 4$, denoted as C_{P_STBC}, is [25]:

$$C_{P\_STBC} = \log_2 \left(1 + \frac{\rho}{4} \left(\left|R_{M-1,M-1}\right|^2 + \left|R_{M-1,M}\right|^2 + \left|R_{M,M}\right|^2\right)\right) \tag{31}$$

From the procedure of decoding V-BLAST layer symbols in (16) and (17), the SNR of every V-BLAST channel can be determined. The received sub-data streams of V-BLAST layer in the first time slot are given by

$$\tilde{y}_{i,1} = R_{i,i} v_{i,1} + \sum_{j=i+1}^{M-2} R_{i,j} \hat{v}_{j,1} + \left(R_{i,M-1} \tilde{s}_{M-1} + R_{i,M} \tilde{s}_M\right) + \tilde{z}_{i,1} \tag{32}$$

while the received sub-data streams of V-BLAST layer in the second time slot are given by

Table 1 Comparison of number of complex arithmetic operations for ZF, MMSE, QR decomposition and LC-QR decomposition detection mechanisms

Complex arithmetic operation	ZF with $\hat{H}$	MMSE with $\hat{H}$	QR decomposition with $\hat{H}$	LC-QR with H
Addition	$4(4N-1)\times(M-1)^2-2(M-1)$	$4(4N-1)\times(M-1)^2$	$2(2N-1)\times(M-1)+(M-2)\times(2M-3)$	$N(3M-2)+(M-3)\times(M-1)$
Subtraction	-	-	$2M-3$	$2(M-2)+2N+1$
Multiplication	$4N(M-1)\times(4M-3)$	$4N(M-1)\times(4M-3)$	$(M-1)\times(4N+2M-3)$	$M^2+3MN-M+4$
Division	-	-	$2(M-1)$	$2(M-2)$
Householder reflection	-	-	$8N(M-1)^2-(8/3)(M-1)^3$	$NM^2-M^3/3$
Gaussian elimination	$8(M-1)^3$	$8(M-1)^3$	-	-
Total	$8(M-1)^3+4(8N-1)(M-1)^2+$ $2(2N-1)(M-1)$	$8(M-1)^3+4(8N-1)(M-1)^2+$ $4N(M-1)$	$8N(M-1)^2-(8/3)(M-1)^3+(2M-3)^2+$ $2(M-1)(4N+1)-1$	$NM^2-M^3/3+(M+2)(2N-1)+2(M-2)(M+2)+$ $4N(M-1)+10$

Table 2 Reduction of computational complexity for ZF, MMSE and QR decomposition compared to LC-QR decomposition detection mechanisms

Complex arithmetic operation	Reduction of computational complexity compared to ZF and MMSE with H (%)				Reduction of computational complexity compared to QR decomposition with H (%)			
	$M=4$		$M=5$		$M=4$		$M=5$	
	$N=4$	$N=5$	$N=5$	$N=6$	$N=4$	$N=5$	$N=5$	$N=6$
Addition	93.2	92.2	94.0	94.1	17.3	17.2	21.5	21.1
Subtraction	-	-	-	-	-	-	-	-
Multiplication	89.7	90.3	92.7	93.0	-	-	8.3	8.1
Division	-	-	-	-	33.3	33.3	25.0	25.0
Householder reflection	-	-	-	-	80.6	79.9	82.1	81.8
Gaussian elimination	-	-	-	-	-	-	-	-
Total	87.9	87.7	90.9	90.7	51.5	53.0	59.3	60.5

$$\tilde{y}_{i,2} = R_{i,i}v_{i,2}^* + \sum_{j=i+1}^{M-2} R_{i,j}\hat{v}_{j,2}^* + \left(R_{i,M-1}\left(-\tilde{s}_M^*\right) + R_{i,M}\left(\tilde{s}_{M-1}^*\right) \right) + \tilde{z}_{i,2} \tag{33}$$

where $i = 1, ..., M - 2$. Here, it is assumed that when the V-BLAST layer symbols are decoded, the previously decoded first estimated symbols of STBC layer have been cancelled properly. Hence, decoding of $\hat{v}_{i,1}$ and $\hat{v}_{i,2}$ become

$$\hat{v}_{i,1} = v_{i,1} + \frac{\tilde{z}_{i,1}}{R_{i,i}} \tag{34}$$

$$\hat{v}_{i,2} = \left(v_{i,2}^* + \frac{\tilde{z}_{i,2}}{R_{i,i}} \right)^* \tag{35}$$

It can be observed from (25) and (26) that the SNR of i-th detected sub-data stream of V-BLAST layer over two time slots is determined by the diagonal element $|R_{i,i}|^2$ of R where $i = 1, 2$. So, the SNR of i-th detected sub-data stream, denoted as ρ_i, becomes

$$\rho_i = \frac{\rho \, |R_{i,i}|^2}{M} \tag{36}$$

Since the V-BLAST layer of V-BLAST/STBC scheme transmits four data symbols over two consecutive symbol transmission periods, the instantaneous system capacity of the V-BLAST layer of LC-QR decomposition, denoted as $C_{P\_V-BLAST}$, is [26]

$$C_{P\_V-BLAST} = \frac{4 \log_2 \left(1 + \min_{i \in \{1,...,M-2\}} \rho_i \right)}{2} = 2 \log_2 \left(1 + \min_{k \in \{1,...,M-2\}} \frac{\rho \, |R_{i,i}|^2}{4} \right) \tag{37}$$

Therefore, the total capacity of V-BLAST/STBC Scheme with LC-QR decomposition, denoted as $C_{P\_LC\text{-}QR}$, is the summation of C_{P_STBC} and $C_{P\_V\text{-}BLAST}$ as

$$C_{P\_LC\text{-}QR} = C_{P\_STBC} + C_{P\_V\text{-}BLAST} = \log_2\left(1 + \frac{\rho}{4}\left(\left|R_{M-1,M-1}\right|^2 + \left|R_{M-1,M}\right|^2 + \left|R_{M,M}\right|^2\right)\right)$$
$$+ 2\log_2\left(1 + \min_{k\in\{1,\ldots,M-2\}} \frac{\rho\left|R_{i,i}\right|^2}{4}\right)$$

(38)

Probability of error in V-BLAST/STBC scheme with LC-QR decomposition

A MIMO communication system with M transmit and N receive antennas is considered in a Rayleigh frequency flat-fading channel. The received signal is given by

$$y = Hx + z \tag{39}$$

where y is the $N \times 2$ received signal matrix and H is the $N \times M$ Rayleigh flat fading channel matrix. z is the AWGN $N \times 2$ complex matrix with unit variance σ_z^2 and zero mean. It is assumed that the entries of H are circularly symmetric, independent and identically distributed (i.i.d.) with zero-mean and unit variance σ_h^2. It is also assumed that the transmission matrix and with uniform power is independent. The covariance matrix of x is $E\left[\mathbf{xx}^*\right] = \sigma_x^2 I$, where $E\left[\bullet\right]$ denotes the expected value and $(\bullet)^*$ is the conjugate transpose. The SNR, denoted as γ, is defined as below

$$\gamma = \frac{\sigma_x^2}{\sigma_z^2} \tag{40}$$

Analytical model of V-BLAST layer

Denote the QR decomposition of H as H = QR. The matrix R is upper triangular matrix with diagonal real number elements. The entries of R are independent of each other. The off diagonal elements $R_{i\,j}$, for $1 \leq i < j \leq M$, are zero-mean complex Gaussian with unit variance. The square of the i-th diagonal element of R, denoted as $R_{i\,i}^2$, is a chi-square distribution with the $2k$ degrees of freedom, where k is determined by the diversity gain of V-BLAST scheme. Therefore, the probability density function (PDF) of post-detection SNR of V-BLAST scheme with chi-square distribution and $2k$ degrees of freedom, denoted as $f_V(x, 2k)$, is given by [27]

$$f_V(x, 2k) = \frac{1}{\sigma^{2k}2^k\,\Gamma(k)}x^{k-1}e^{(-x/2\sigma^2)} \tag{41}$$

where $\Gamma(k)$ is the gamma function given by

$$\Gamma(k) = \int_0^\infty t^{k-1}e^{-t}dt, \quad k > 0$$

If k is a positive integer, then $\Gamma(k) = (k-1)!$. The received V-BLAST/STBC matrix is given by $\tilde{y} = \mathbf{R}x + \tilde{z}$ as in (13). Hence, the received sub-data streams of V-BLAST layer in the first and second time slot are given by

$$\tilde{y}_{i,1} = R_{i,i}v_{i,1} + \sum_{j=i+1}^{M-2} R_{i,j}\hat{v}_{j,1} + \left(R_{i,M-1}\tilde{s}_{M-1} + R_{i,M}\tilde{s}_M\right) + \tilde{z}_{i,1} \tag{42}$$

$$\tilde{y}_{i,1} = R_{i,i}v_{i,1} + \sum_{j=i+1}^{M-2} R_{i,j}\hat{v}_{j,1} + \left(R_{i,M-1}\tilde{s}_{M-1} + R_{i,M}\tilde{s}_M\right) + \tilde{z}_{i,1} \tag{43}$$

where $i = 1, ..., M - 2$. It is assumed that the propagation error effect is cancelled properly, then (42) and (43) are simplified to

$$\tilde{y}_{i,1} = R_{i,i}v_{i,1} + \tilde{z}_{i,1} \tag{44}$$

$$\tilde{y}_{i,2} = R_{i,i}v_{i,2}^* + \tilde{z}_{i,2} \tag{45}$$

The instantaneous post-detection SNR is determined by the $R_{i,i}^2$. It is shown in [28] that the diversity gain of i-th detected sub-data stream layer of V-BLAST scheme is $(N - i + 1)$. Thus, $R_{i,i}^2$ is a chi-square distribution with the degree of freedom 2 $(N - i + 1)$, which is denoted as $\chi_{2(N-i+1)}^2$. It can be observed that the when the i is larger, the diversity gain of the i-th layer becomes smaller. Consequently, the largest or M-th layer limits the overall performance of V-BLAST scheme at high SNR. Therefore, the overall diversity gain of V-BLAST scheme is $N - M + 1$ [29].

After that, M_V is defined as the number of transmit antenna of V-BLAST layer in V-BLAST/STBC scheme. Then, the effective diversity gain of V-BLAST layer in V-BLAST/STBC scheme becomes $N - M_V + 1$. Thus, substituting $k = N - M_V + 1$ into (41), the PDF of instantaneous post-detection SNR of V-BLAST layer in V-BLAST/ STBC scheme with chi-square distribution and $2(N - M_V + 1)$ degrees of freedom, denoted as $f_{VS}^V(x, 2(N - M_V + 1))$, is given by

$$f_{VS}^V(x, 2(N-M_V + 1)) = \frac{1}{\sigma^{2(N-M_V+1)}2^{(N-M_V+1)}\,\Gamma(N-M_V + 1)}x^{N-M_V}e^{(-x/2\sigma^2)} \tag{46}$$

It is shown in [30] that BER of M-ary quadrature amplitude modulation (M-QAM) over AWGN noise is given by

$$P_{e,\text{M-QAM}}(\gamma) = \frac{4}{\log_2 M}\left(1 - \frac{1}{\sqrt{M}}\right) \times \sum_{i=1}^{\sqrt{M}/2} Q\left((2i-1)\sqrt{\frac{3\gamma \log_2 M}{(M-1)}}\right) \tag{47}$$

where $Q(\bullet)$ is Gaussian Q-Function given by

$$Q(x) = \frac{1}{2}\left(1 - erf\left(\frac{x}{\sqrt{2}}\right)\right) \tag{48}$$

and the error function $erf(\bullet)$ is defined as

$$erf(x) = \frac{2}{\sqrt{\pi}}\int_0^x e^{-t^2}\,dt \tag{49}$$

It is shown in [31] that the average error probability can be obtained by averaging the conditional error probability of modulation scheme over the PDF of instantaneous post-detection SNR of MIMO scheme. Therefore, the BER performance of V-BLAST layer in V-BLAST/STBC scheme with M-QAM modulation, M_V and N, denoted as $P_{e,\text{M-QAM},VS}^V(M_V, N, \gamma)$, can be computed by integrating (46) and (47) to become

$$
\begin{aligned}
P_{e,\text{M-QAM},VS}^V(M_V, N, \gamma) &= \int_0^\infty P_{e,\text{M-QAM}}(\gamma) f_{VS}^V(x, 2(N{-}M_V + 1))\, dx \\
&= \int_0^\infty \frac{4}{\log_2 M}\left(1 - \frac{1}{\sqrt{M}}\right) \times \sum_{i=1}^{\sqrt{M}/2} Q\left((2i{-}1)\sqrt{\frac{3\,\log_2 M\,\gamma\,x}{(M{-}1)}}\right) \\
&\quad \times \frac{1}{\sigma^{2(N-M_V+1)} 2^{(N-M_V+1)}\,\Gamma(N{-}M_V + 1)} x^{N-M_V} e^{(-x/2\sigma^2)}\, dx
\end{aligned}
$$

$$(50)$$

Analytical model of STBC layer

From (18), interference cancellation is performed by subtracting the data symbols of V-BLAST layer. Before interference cancellation, the received i-th sub-data stream in l-th time slot is given by

$$
y_{i,l} = \underbrace{h_{i,M-1} s_{M-1} + h_{i,M} s_M}_{\substack{\text{STBC layer} \\ \text{symbols}}} + \underbrace{\sum_{j=i}^{M-2} h_{i,j} v_{j,l} + z_{i,l}}_{\substack{\text{Interference} \\ \text{AWGN noise}}}
$$

$$(51)$$

It can be seen from (51) that the received i-th sub-data stream is composed of STBC layer symbols, AWGN noise and the potential propagation error from V-BLAST layer. The equivalent noise is the combination of the last two parts.

In the ideal case where there is no propagation error from V-BLAST layer, the BER analysis of STBC layer is the same as BER analysis of the Alamouti's STBC scheme with two transmit and N receive antennas. The instantaneous post-detection SNR of Alamouti's STBC scheme with two transmit and N receive antennas, denoted as γ_S, is given by

$$
\gamma_S = \gamma \sum_{i=1}^N \left(|h_{i,1}|^2 + |h_{i,2}|^2\right)
$$

$$(52)$$

Since $h_{i,1}$ and $h_{i,2}$ are circularly symmetric, i.i.d. Gaussian random variables with zero-mean and unit variance, the γ_S has a chi-square distribution with $2 \times 2 \times N$ degrees of freedom.

The diversity gain of O-STBC scheme is given by $M \times N$ [32]. So, the PDF of instantaneous post-detection SNR of O-STBC scheme with chi-square distribution and $2 \times M \times N$ degrees of freedom, denoted as $f_S(x, 2MN)$, is given by

$$
f_S(x, 2MN) = \frac{1}{\sigma^{2MN} 2^{MN}\,\Gamma(MN)} x^{MN-1} e^{(-x/2\sigma^2)}
$$

$$(53)$$

The BER of O-STBC scheme with M transmit and N receive antennas and M-QAM modulation, denoted as $P_{e,\text{M-QAM}}^S(M, N, \gamma)$, can be calculated by integrating (47) and (53) as follows

$$P_{e,\text{M-QAM}}^{S}(M,N,\gamma) = \int_{0}^{\infty} P_{e,\text{M-QAM}}(\gamma) f_S(x,2MN)\ dx$$

$$= \int_{0}^{\infty} \frac{4}{\log_2 \text{M}} \left(1 - \frac{1}{\sqrt{\text{M}}}\right) \times \sum_{i=1}^{\sqrt{\text{M}}/2} Q\left((2i-1)\sqrt{\frac{3\ \log_2\text{M}\ \gamma\ x}{(\text{M}-1)}}\right)$$

$$\times \frac{1}{\sigma^{2MN} 2^{MN}\ \Gamma(MN)} x^{MN-1} e^{(-x/2\sigma^2)}\ dx$$

(54)

From (19) and (20), the STBC layer of V-BLAST/STBC scheme is decoded with STBC $2 \times N$ decoder after the V-BLAST layer is decoded. Therefore, the BER performance of V-BLAST layer dominates the BER performance of STBC layer. The statistical properties of BER performance of STBC layer are said to be conditional.

M_S is defined as the number of transmit antenna of Alamouti's STBC layer in V-BLAST/STBC scheme, where $M_S = 2$. On the other hand, an event with k symbol errors detection in V-BLAST layer, denoted as A_k, is defined where $k \le 2M_V$. Then, $\left(P_{e,\text{M-QAM}}^{S}(M_S,N,\gamma) \mid A_k\right)$ is defined as the $P_{e,\text{M-QAM}}^{S}(M_S,N,\gamma)$ after the event A_k happens. On the other hand, the symbol error rate (SER) of V-BLAST layer with M_V transmit, N receive antennas and M-QAM modulation over AWGN noise, denoted as $P_{SER,\text{M-QAM}}^{V}(M_V,N,\gamma)$, can be expressed as [33]

$$P_{SER,\text{M-QAM}}^{V}(M_V,N,\gamma) = 2\left(1 - \frac{1}{\sqrt{\text{M}}}\right) erfc\left(\sqrt{\frac{3\gamma}{2(\text{M}-1)}}\right)$$

(55)

where $erfc(x) = 1 - erf(x)$.

Since there is no symbol errors detection in V-BLAST layer, the A_k becomes A_0. Hence, the BER performance of STBC layer in V-BLAST/STBC scheme in ideal case is the same as the BER performance of Alamouti's STBC scheme. Therefore, the BER performance of STBC layer in V-BLAST/STBC scheme in the ideal case with M-QAM modulation, M_S and N, denoted as $P_{e,\text{M-QAM},VS}^{ideal}(M_S,N,\gamma)$, can be computed as

$$P_{e,\text{M-QAM},VS}^{ideal}(M_S,N,\gamma) = \left(P_{e,\text{M-QAM}}^{S}(M_S,N,\gamma)\mid A_0\right) \times \left(1 - \left(P_{SER,\text{M-QAM}}^{V}(M_V,N,\gamma)\right)\right)$$

(56)

where $\left(P_{e,\text{M-QAM}}^{S}(M_S,N,\gamma)\mid A_0\right) = P_{e,\text{M-QAM}}^{S}(M_S,N,\gamma)$.

In the non-ideal case, there is a propagation error from V-BLAST layer as more than or equal to one symbols of V-BLAST layer are decoded wrongly. The σ_V^2 and σ_S^2 are defined as unit variance of V-BLAST and STBC layer respectively, where $\sigma_V^2 = \sigma_S^2 = \sigma_x^2$. From (51), the combination of interference and AWGN noise with k V-BLAST symbol errors detection can be written as $\sigma_z^2 + k\ \sigma_V^2$. Then, the effective SNR for STBC layer with k V-BLAST symbol errors detection, denoted as $\tilde{\gamma}_{(k)}$, can be written as

$$\tilde{\gamma}_{(k)} = \frac{\sigma_S^2}{\sigma_z^2 + k\ \sigma_V^2}$$

(57)

where $\sigma_z^2 \neq 0$. Dividing (57) by σ_z^2, will get

$$\tilde{\gamma}_{(k)} = \frac{\gamma_S}{1 + k\ \gamma_V}$$

(58)

where $\gamma_V = \gamma_S = \gamma$. Figure 3 shows the block diagram of analytical model of STBC layer in V-BLAST/STBC scheme.

The BER performance of STBC layer in V-BLAST/STBC scheme in non-ideal case with k-th detection V-BLAST symbol errors, M-QAM modulation, M_S and N, denoted as $P^{non-ideal}_{e,\text{M-QAM},VS}\left(M_S, N, \tilde{\gamma}_{(k)}\right)$, can be computed as

$$
\begin{aligned}
P^{non-ideal}_{e,\text{M-QAM},VS}\left(M_S, N, \tilde{\gamma}_{(k)}\right) &= \left(P^S_{e,\text{M-QAM}}\left(M_S, N, \tilde{\gamma}_{(k)}\right) \mid A_k\right) \times \left(P^V_{SER,\text{M-QAM}}(M_V, N, \gamma)\right)^k \\
&= \sum_{k=1}^{2M_V} P^S_{e,\text{M-QAM}}\left(M_S, N, \tilde{\gamma}_{(k)}\right) \times \binom{2M_V}{k} \times \left(P^V_{SER,\text{M-QAM}}(M_V, N, \gamma)\right)^k \\
&\quad \times \left(1 - P^V_{SER,\text{M-QAM}}(M_V, N, \gamma)\right)^{2M_V - k}
\end{aligned}
$$

$$(59)$$

where

$$
\binom{2M_V}{k} = \frac{(2M_V)!}{k!(2M_V - k)!}
$$

$$(60)$$

which is the number of k permutations of an $2M_V$-element set. Meanwhile, $\left(P^V_{SER,\text{M-QAM}}(M_V, N, \gamma)\right)^k \times \left(1 - P^V_{SER,\text{M-QAM}}(M_V, N, \gamma)\right)^{2M_V - k}$ denotes the probability of error of V-BLAST layer with event A_k.

It is known that $P^V_{SER,\text{M-QAM}}(M_V, N, \gamma) \neq 0$ for all SNR when $\sigma_z^2 \neq 0$. As long as $P^V_{SER,\text{M-QAM}}(M_V, N, \gamma) \neq 0$, k exists for $1, \ldots, 2M_V$. So, it can deduced that σ_z^2 is uncorrelated with k when $\sigma_z^2 \neq 0$. Finally, the BER performance of STBC layer in V-BLAST/STBC scheme with M-QAM modulation, M_V and N, denoted as $P^S_{e,\text{M-QAM},VS}(M_V, N, \gamma)$, can be computed as

$$
P^S_{e,\text{M-QAM},VS}(M_V, N, \gamma) = P^{ideal}_{e,\text{M-QAM},VS}(M_S, N, \gamma) + P^{non-ideal}_{e,\text{M-QAM},VS}\left(M_S, N, \tilde{\gamma}_{(k)}\right) \quad (61)
$$

Analytical model of V-BLAST/STBC scheme

By combining (50) and (61), the final overall BER performance $P^O_{e,\text{M-QAM},VS}(M, N)$ for V-BLAST/STBC scheme with M-QAM modulation, M transmit and N receive antennas can be computed as

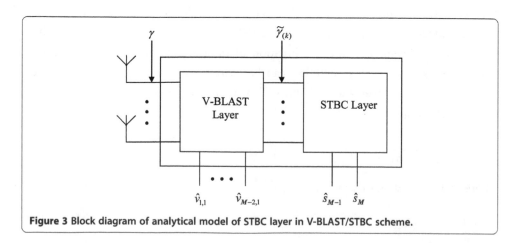

Figure 3 Block diagram of analytical model of STBC layer in V-BLAST/STBC scheme.

$$P^O_{e,\text{M-QAM},VS}(M,N) = \frac{\text{m} \times P^V_{e,\text{M-QAM},VS}(M_V,N,\gamma) + \text{n} \times P^S_{e,\text{M-QAM},VS}(M_V,N,\gamma)}{\text{m} + \text{n}}$$

(62)

where $M_S = 2$ and $M_S + M_V = M$. The m and n are the symbol transmission rates of V-BLAST and STBC layer respectively.

Performance evaluation of LC-QR decomposition in V-BLAST/STBC scheme

The simulations have been performed on the MIMO system using MATLAB to evaluate the performance of the V-BLAST/STBC scheme with ZF, MMSE and QR decomposition with $\vec{H}$ and LC-QR decomposition with H. The 4-ary quadrature amplitude modulation (4-QAM) constellation is used in these simulations with Rayleigh flat-fading channel as well as Naftali channel. The entries of Rayleigh flat-fading channel matrix are circularly symmetric, i.i.d. Gaussian random variables with zero-mean and unit variance. The symbol rate of ZF V-BLAST 4×4, O-STBC 4×4 and V-BLAST/STBC 4×4 is shown in Table 3.

Figure 4 depicts the 10% and 1% outage capacity for MIMO (theoretical limit), ZF V-BLAST, O-STBC and V-BLAST/STBC with LC-QR decomposition in 4×4 system. The spectral efficiency of ZF V-BLAST changes a lot with different outage probability. For instance, ZF V-BLAST requires 8 dB to maintain the capacity of 15 bps/Hz when it proceeds from 10% to 1% outage probability. This is caused by lack of diversity of ZF V-BLAST. In contrast, the V-BLAST/STBC with LC-QR decomposition just requires 3 dB to maintain at the capacity of 15 bps/Hz. Last but not least, the O-STBC is the most stable one, as the curve of 10% outage capacity is very close to the curve of 1% outage capacity. Besides, it can be observed that the capacity of ZF V-BLAST with 10% outage probability is the highest among the considered schemes for SNR higher than 37 dB. Meanwhile, the capacity of V-BLAST/STBC with 10% outage probability is close to MIMO capacity at low SNR.

Figure 5 shows the BER performance comparison of ZF V-BLAST 4×4, O-STBC 4×4 with rate ¾ and V-BLAST/STBC 4×4 with LC-QR decomposition in Rayleigh flat-fading channel environment, which is constant across four consecutive symbol transmission periods. It could be seen that the BER performance of O-STBC 4×4 with symbol rate ¾ is the best among the considered schemes as it is a pure spatial diversity scheme with full diversity gain. Moreover, O-STBC does not suffer from inter-symbol interference (ISI) as the transmitted symbols are orthogonal to one another. In contrast, ZF V-BLAST 4×4 with symbol rate four is the worst among the schemes because it is a pure spatial multiplexing scheme which suffers from poor diversity gain. Besides, interference between transmitted symbols in ZF V-BLAST scheme greatly reduces the BER performance. It could be seen that the V-BLAST/STBC 4×4 with symbol rate three shows a compromise of BER performance with respect to pure spatial multiplexing or diversity scheme.

Table 3 Symbol rate of various 4×4 MIMO schemes

MIMO scheme	Symbol rate (symbol/symbol transmission period)
ZF V-BLAST 4×4	4
O-STBC 4×4	3/4
V-BLAST/STBC 4×4	3

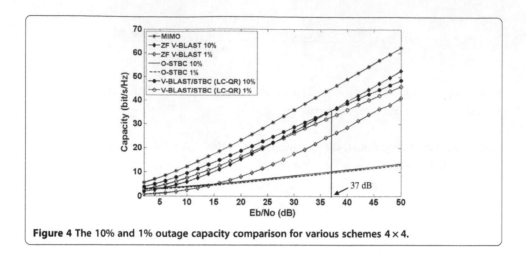

Figure 4 The 10% and 1% outage capacity comparison for various schemes 4 × 4.

It can be concluded that Figures 4 and 5 present the tradeoffs among ZF V-BLAST, O-STBC and V-BLAST/STBC with LC-QR decomposition in 4 × 4 MIMO system. The O-STBC achieves the best BER performance, but the system capacity is the lowest among the considered schemes. Meanwhile, the system capacity of ZF V-BLAST with 10% outage capacity is the highest for SNR above 37 dB, but the BER performance is the worst among the considered schemes. On the other hand, the system capacity of V-BLAST/STBC with LC-QR decomposition is close to MIMO and better than ZF V-BLAST for SNR below 37 dB. Moreover, the BER performance of V-BLAST/ STBC with LC-QR decomposition is significantly better than ZF V-BLAST as V-BLAST/ STBC achieves spatial multiplexing and diversity gain simultaneously.

Figure 6 shows the BER performance of various mechanisms in V-BLAST/STBC scheme with Rayleigh flat-fading channel model, which is constant across two consecutive symbol transmission periods. The LC-QR decomposition 3 × 2 with H outperforms ZF 3 × 2 and MMSE 3 × 2 with $\vec{H}$ by more than 2 dB gain at BER of 10^{-3}. At the same time, the LC-QR decomposition 3 × 2 with H outperforms QR 3 × 2 with $\vec{H}$ by approximately 1.5 dB gain at BER of 10^{-3}. This is because the estimated candidate of STBC layer, which is more robust than V-BLAST layer, is decoded first. After decoding the

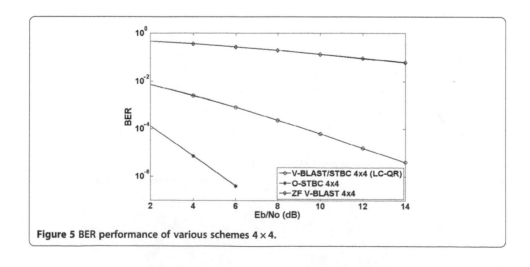

Figure 5 BER performance of various schemes 4 × 4.

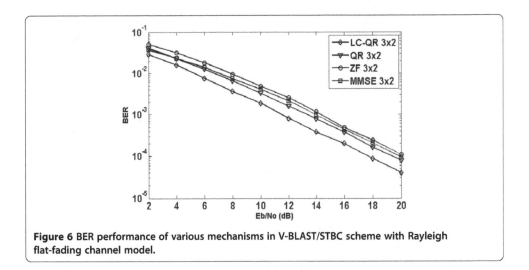

Figure 6 BER performance of various mechanisms in V-BLAST/STBC scheme with Rayleigh flat-fading channel model.

estimated candidate of STBC layer, interference cancellation activity is performed to produce a new modified received signal matrix s with less interference. For ZF and MMSE mechanisms, there is no interference cancellation activity.

It is clear that V-BLAST layer performance dominates over final decisions of STBC layer in (25) and (26). With increasing SNR, the probability of error in decoding the V-BLAST layer is reduced, the probability of correct decoding is increased at the STBC layer. As the V-BLAST layer transmits four data symbols while STBC layer transmits two data symbols over two consecutive symbol transmission periods, thus a better BER performance of V-BLAST layer with LC-QR decomposition leads to overall V-BLAST/STBC system performance improvement.

Figure 7 illustrates the BER performance comparison of various mechanisms in V-BLAST/STBC scheme with a Naftali channel model under different maximum delay spread environment. The LC-QR decomposition 4×4 outperforms ZF 4×4 and MMSE 4×4 by approximately 2 dB gain at BER of 10^{-3} for both indoor (200 ns) and outdoor (1.6 μs) environment. At the same time, the LC-QR decomposition 4×4 outperforms QR decomposition 4×4 by approximately 1 dB gain at BER of 10^{-3} for both indoor

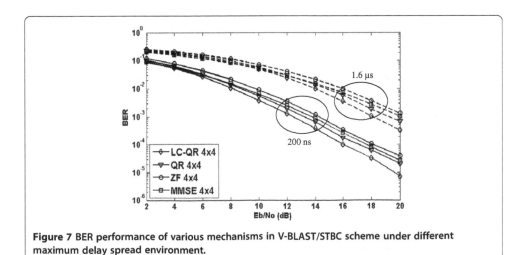

Figure 7 BER performance of various mechanisms in V-BLAST/STBC scheme under different maximum delay spread environment.

and outdoor environment. In order to maintain the BER of 10^{-3}, the LC-QR decomposition with a maximum delay spread = 1.6 μs requires 6 dB gain compared to indoor environment with a maximum delay spread = 200 ns.

Figure 8 depicts BER performance of various mechanisms in V-BLAST/STBC scheme under different maximum delay spread environment at 16 dB. From Figures 7 and 8, it can be observed that performance BER of all considered mechanism degrades when the maximum delay spread is increasing because the delayed signal from multi-path overlaps the direct signal for the next symbol, thus ISI occurs. Moreover, it is well known that the delay spread causes frequency selective fading in the channel, which acts like a finite impulse response (FIR) filter. If the delay spread is comparable or larger than the symbol duration, the frequency-selective channel will distort the signal and not all frequency components fade simultaneously. As a result, the orthogonality of V-BLAST/STBC data symbols could not be maintained, thus the BER performance declines.

Figure 9 plots the BER performance of LC-QR decomposition with different standard deviations of channel estimation error σ_E and delay spread = 200 ns. On the other hand, Figure 10 shows the BER performance of various mechanisms in V-BLAST/STBC scheme with channel estimation error and delay spread = 200 ns at 16 dB. It can be observed that the increase of standard deviation of channel estimation error decreases the BER of all considered mechanisms as channel estimation error is considered as an additional noise in the receiver. Consequently, irreducible error floor occurs when SNR increases in Figure 9. According to Figure 10, it can be deduced that all the considered mechanisms suffer from the same amount of noise variance from channel estimation error, because the equivalent channel matrix for ZF, MMSE and QR decomposition does not reduce the effect of channel estimation error.

Figure 11 illustrates the percentage of computational complexity reduction of the LC-QR decomposition with H compared to ZF, MMSE and QR decomposition with $\vec{H}$ for $N \geq M$. It can be observed that the LC-QR decomposition reduces the arithmetic operation complexity by at least 80% compared to ZF and MMSE with $\vec{H}$ as well as 35% compared to QR decomposition with $\vec{H}$. Thus, the LC-QR decomposition shows significant computational complexity improvement. The main reason is that the LC-QR decomposition utilizes channel matrix H with smaller dimension instead of an

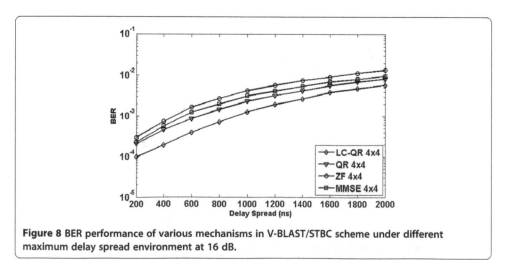

Figure 8 BER performance of various mechanisms in V-BLAST/STBC scheme under different maximum delay spread environment at 16 dB.

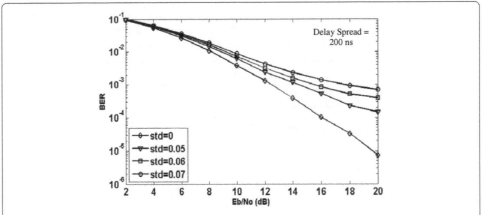

Figure 9 BER performance of LC-QR 4×4 with different standard deviations of channel estimation error σ_E and delay spread = 200 ns.

equivalent channel matrix $\vec{H}$. It also can be seen that the percentage of computational complexity reduction of the LC-QR decomposition greatly increases when M is increasing and N is constant. This is due to the calculation of Gaussian elimination matrix inversion of $\vec{H}^H \vec{H}$ and $\left(\vec{H}^H \vec{H} + \sigma^2 I_{2(M-1)} \right)$, which requires $8(M-1)^3$ complex arithmetic operation, for ZF and MMSE with $\vec{H}$ respectively. Note that the calculation of Gaussian elimination matrix inversion of $\vec{H}^H \vec{H}$ and $\left(\vec{H}^H \vec{H} + \sigma^2 I_{2(M-1)} \right)$ does not need the information of N and it increases significantly when M becomes bigger. On the other hand, the calculation of QR decomposition with Householder reflection for $\vec{H}$ is $8 N(M-1)^2 - (8/3)(M-1)^3$. Since N is equal to or greater than M, the arithmetic operation of $8 N(M-1)^2 - (8/3)(M-1)^3$ becomes significant when M is increasing. The performance evaluations from these figures show that by using the proposed LC-QR decomposition detection mechanism in V-BLAST/STBC MIMO scheme the system performance is not only significantly improved but the computational complexity of the overall system is also significantly reduced. Hence, the computational cost and

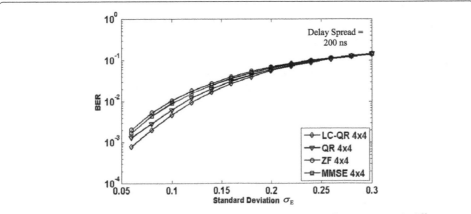

Figure 10 BER performance of various mechanisms in V-BLAST/STBC scheme 4×4 with different standard deviations of channel estimation error σ_E and delay spread = 200 ms at 16 dB.

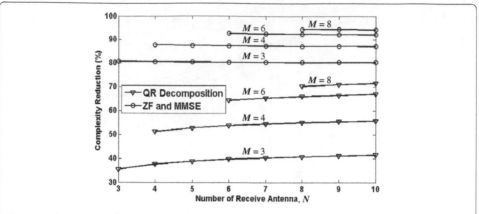

Figure 11 Percentage of computational complexity reduction of LC-QR decomposition compared to ZF, MMSE and QR decomposition with different M and N for $N \geq M$.

power consumption will be reduced for the next generation MIMO mobile computing devices can be reduced significantly from the reduction of computational complexity.

Conclusions

In this paper, it is illustrated that V-BLAST/STBC scheme, which achieves spatial multiplexing and diversity gains simultaneously, increases system capacity and maintains reliable BER performance to accommodate the ever growing demand for real time system with tolerably lower QoS. It is also shown that the system capacity of LC-QR decomposition V-BLAST/STBC scheme is close to the ideal MIMO system and better than ZF V-BLAST for SNR below 37 dB. Moreover, the BER performance of LC-QR decomposition V-BLAST/STBC is significantly better than ZF-VBLAST. The LC-QR decomposition mechanism has also significantly reduced the arithmetic operation complexity and remains a satisfactory BER performance compared to ZF, MMSE and QR decomposition mechanisms. The reduction of computational complexity in V-BLAST/STBC MIMO scheme will see a significant reduction in computational cost and power consumption for next generation MIMO mobile computing devices.

Competing interests
The authors declare that they have no competing interests.

Authors' contributions
JHC and CKN carried out the conceptualization, background study, simulated the concept, jointly drafted the manuscript and reviewed the manuscript. NKN and BMA carried out the conceptualization, jointly drafted the manuscript and reviewed the manuscript. All authors read and approved the final manuscript.

Author details
[1]Department of Computer Science and Mathematics, Faculty of Applied Sciences and Computing, Tunku Abdul Rahman University College, Jalan Genting Kelang, Setapak 53300 Kuala Lumpur, Malaysia. [2]Institute of Gerontology, University Putra Malaysia, UPM Serdang 43400 Selangor, Malaysia. [3]Department of Computer and Communication Systems Engineering, Faculty of Engineering, University Putra Malaysia, UPM Serdang 43400 Selangor, Malaysia.

References
1. Foschini GJ, Gans MJ (1998) On Limits of Wireless Communications in A Fading Environment When Using Multiple Antennas. Wirel Pers Commun 6:311–335
2. Mohamad R, Salleh WMHWM, Anas NM (2012) Multiband OFDM and OFDM Simulation Software using MATLAB® Graphical User Interface. J Convergence 3(1):1–4
3. Shbat MS, Tuzlukov V (2011) Dynamic Frequency Reuse Factor Choosing Method for Self Organizing LTE Networks. J Convergence 2(2):13–18

4. Telatar E (1999) Capacity of Multi-Antenna Gaussian Channels. Eur Trans Telecommun 10(6):585–595
5. Golden GD, Foschini CJ, Valenzuela AR, Wolniansky PW (1999) Detection Mechanism and Initial Laboratory Results Using V-BLAST Space-Time Communication Architecture. Electron Lett 35(1):14–16
6. Tarokh V, Seshadri N, Calderbank AR (1998) Space-Time Codes for High Data Rate Wireless Communications: Performance Criterion and Code Construction. IEEE Trans Inf Theory 44(2):744–765
7. Alamouti SM (1998) A Simple Transmit Diversity Technique for Wireless Communications. IEEE J Sel Areas Commun 16(8):1451–1458
8. Tarokh V, Jafarkhani H, Calderbank AR (1999) Space-Time Block Codes from Orthogonal Designs. IEEE Trans Inf Theory 45(5):1456–1467
9. Zheng L, Tse DNC (2003) Diversity and Multiplexing: A Fundamental Tradeoff in Multiple Antenna Channels. IEEE Trans Inf Theory 49(5):1073–1096
10. Jafarkhani H (2005) Space Time Coding: Theory and Practice. Cambridge University Press, The Pitt Building, Trumpington Street, Cambridge, CB2 1RP United Kingdom
11. Wang H, Xia XG (2003) Upper Bounds of Rates of Complex Orthogonal Space-Time Block Codes. IEEE Trans Inf Theory 49(10):2788–2796
12. Luo H, Shyu ML (2011) Quality of Service Provision in Mobile Multimedia - A Survey. Human-centric Computing Information Sci 1(5):1–15
13. Bhattacharya A, Wu W, Yang Z (2012) Quality of Experience Evaluation of Voice Communication: An Affect-Based Approach. Human-centric Computing and Information Sci 2(7):1–18
14. Mao T, Motani M (2005) STBC-VBLAST for MIMO Wireless Communication Systems. Proc IEEE ICC (ICC 2005) 4:2266–2270
15. Meng C, Tuqan J (2007) Precoded STBC-VBLAST for MIMO Wireless Communication Systems. Proc IEEE Int Conf Acoust Spee (ICASSP 2007) 3:337–340
16. Thompson JS, Tan HS, Sun Y (2004) Investigation of Hybrid MIMO Techniques. In: Proceedings of 5th IEE International Conference on 3G Mobile Communication Technologies (3G 2004) 1-5
17. Longoria-Gandara O, Sanchez-Hernandez A, Cortez J, Bazdresch M, Parra-Michel R (2007) Linear Dispersion Codes Generation from Hybrid STBC-VBLAST Architectures. In: Proceedings of 4th International Conference Electrical and Electronics Engineering (ICEEE 2007) 142-145
18. Sandeep G, Ravi-Teja C, Kalyana-Krishnan G, Reddy VU (2007) Low Complexity Decoders for Combined Space Time Block Coding and V-BLAST. In: Proceedings of IEEE Wireless Communications and Networking Conference (WCNC 2007) 582-587
19. Wai WK, Tsui CY, Cheng RS (2000) A Low Complexity Architecture of the V-BLAST System. Proc IEEE WCNC (WCNC 2000) 1:310–314
20. Karray F, Alemzadeh M, Saleh JA, Arab MN (2008) Human-Computer Interaction: Overview on State of the Art. Int J Smart Sensing Intelligent Syst 1(1):137–159
21. Verdú S (1998) Multiuser Detection. Cambridge University Press, The Pitt Building, Trumpington Street, Cambridge, CB2 1RP United Kingdom
22. LiuLiu, Wang Y (2008) Spatially Selective STBC-VBLAST in MIMO Communication System. In: Proceedings of International Conference on Communications, Circuits and Systems (ICCCAS 2008) 195-199, 25-27 May 2008
23. Karniadakis GE, Kirby RM II (2003) Parallel Scientific Computing in C++ and MPI. Cambridge University Press, The Pitt Building, Trumpington Street, Cambridge, CB2 1RP United Kingdom
24. Sandhu S, Paulraj A (2000) Space-Time Block Codes: A Capacity Perspective. IEEE Commun Lett 4(12):384–386
25. Papadias CB, Foschini GJ (2002) On the Capacity of Certain Space-Time Coding Schemes. EURASIP J Appl Sig Process 2002(1):447–458
26. Gorokhov A, Gore DA, Paulraj AJ (2003) Receive Antenna Selection for MIMO Spatial Multiplexing: Theory and Mechanisms. IEEE Trans Signal Process 51(11):2796–2807
27. Ziemer RE, Tranter WH (2002) Principles of Communication: Systems, Modulation and Noise, 5th Edition. John Wiley & Sons, New York, United States of America
28. Tse D, Viswanath P (2005) Fundamentals of Wireless Communication. Cambridge University Press, New York, United States of America
29. Paulraj A, Nabar R, Gore D (2003) Introduction to Space-Time Wireless Communications. Cambridge University Press, The Pitt Building, Trumpington Street, Cambridge, CB2 1RP United Kingdom
30. Lu J, Letaief KB, Chuang JCI, Liou ML (1999) M-PSK and M-QAM BER Computation Using Signal-Space Concepts. IEEE Trans Commun 47(2):181–184
31. Proakis JG (2001) Digital Communications, 4th edn. McGraw-Hill, New York, United States of America
32. Yang L (2008) Outage Performance of OSTBC in Double Scattering MIMO Channels. Wirel Pers Commun 45(2):225–230
33. Kiessling M, Speidel J (2003) Analytical Performance of MIMO Zero-Forcing Receivers in Correlated Rayleigh Fading Environments. In: Proceedings of 4th IEEE Workshop on Signal Processing Advances in Wireless Communications (SPAWC 2003) 383-387, 2003

3

SAR assessment on three layered spherical human head model irradiated by mobile phone antenna

Balamurugan Rajagopal and Lalithambika Rajasekaran[*]

* Correspondence:
srlalithambika@gmail.com
Anna University Regional Centre,
Coimbatore 641047 TN, India

Abstract

With the increasing application of wireless communication devices, mobile phone handsets are used by peoples of various age groups. This paper make an effort to asses the mobile phone radiation exposure effect on 4 years old, 8 years old children and an adult head model. Here, human head is modeled as a three layered sphere composed of skin, skull and brain. Hand held device model (with and without resistive sheet) having dipole antenna enclosed by plastic cover is used for human interaction. The software simulation performed by General Electro Magnetic Simulator, based on Finite Difference Time Domain technique yields Specific Absorption Rate and 3D-thermal distribution on spherical human head. Comparison of 1 g SAR, 10 g SAR values for adult and children head show that, children head absorbs more power than adult. Further, the application of resistive sheet on handset shows effective decrement in coupled power.

Keywords: Finite Difference Time Domain (FDTD); Specific Absorption Rate (SAR); Thermal effect; Electro Magnetic (EM) radiation

Introduction

With the rapid increase in technology, the world without communication is unimaginable. So, mobile phone handset devices act like another hand to human society. Every product has its own advantages as well as disadvantages. However, we never thought of biological ill effects due to mobile phones a wireless communication device used by various age groups [1]. The abundant usage of handsets has kindled some interest in few scientist and researchers regarding the ill effects due to Electro Magnetic radiation emitted by mobile phone antenna. Some research studies shows that, while placing mobile phone nearer to head, the emitted EM radiation gets coupled to human head tissues, which might alter the basic biological function of cells. Even, we can sense the temperature increment in outer case of handset as well as ear, where handsets are pressed while talking for longer hours.

The temperature increment in human tissue is due to power coupled and it may vary with interacting environment. However, the sensed heat gets eventually decreased to equilibrium due to blood circulation. The consequences of excessive heating in the body vary from temporary disturbances in cell functions to permanent destruction of tissues. Areas with less efficient cooling by the circulation, e.g. the lens of the eye, brain cells are more susceptible to electromagnetic radiation. Since, the usage of mobile phones is inevitable in this modern technological world, and the radiation exposure from mobile phone is non uniform, limits can be précised in terms of Specific Absorption Rate (SAR) with an averaging mass of 1 g and 10 g of tissue in the shape of cube. Further, heat induced in tissues signifies the well known adverse health effect at microwave frequencies [2,3]. The analysis of power absorbed by the human head and the antenna performance are necessary for the compliance testing of mobile phones performance. This coupled field can be efficiently calculated by numerical method based on finite difference time domain technique [4].

This paper endeavor to assess the health hazards, particularly the power absorbed by tissues and thermal effects due to exploitation of mobile phones. Further, a simple and comprehend method of SAR decrement due to usage of resistive sheet on user-front side of handset case is also introduced and performance is analyzed. The work includes evaluation of specific absorption rate for children and adult with same electromagnetic environment. Results might enlighten the mobile phone users regarding radiation exposure effect from mobile phones and, ultimately results in the minimization of an individual's risks.

Section Model development includes development of mobile phone antenna model, human head model and hand held device model. Section Measurement of power absorbed gives description about measurement of SAR and heat induced when mobile phone is in proximity with the human head model. Section Numerical results and discussions comprises of numerical results and discussions. Finally, section Conclusion covers the conclusion of the work.

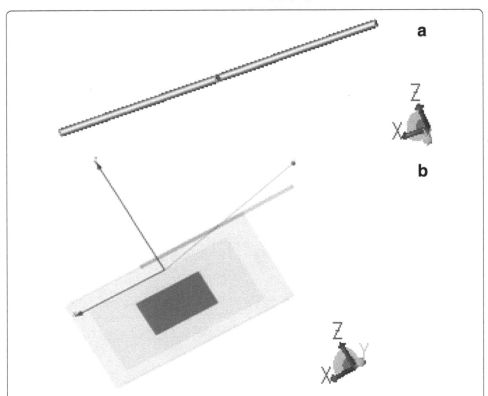

Figure 1 Half- Wave length dipole antenna is designed for 900MHz frequency and is embedded in Mobile phone casing for Near field interaction analysis. a Dipole Antenna [simulated dipole antenna with excitaion feed at the centre]. **b** Mobile Phone Model [mobile handset model with dipole antenna embedded].

Model development

Antenna model

In this work, ($\lambda/2$) dipole antenna (shown in Figure 1) with single excitation port is placed in free space [3]. The length of the half wavelength dipole is 147 mm for the operating frequency range of 0.9-1.5 GHz. The feed gap size is 1.8 mm, hence the length

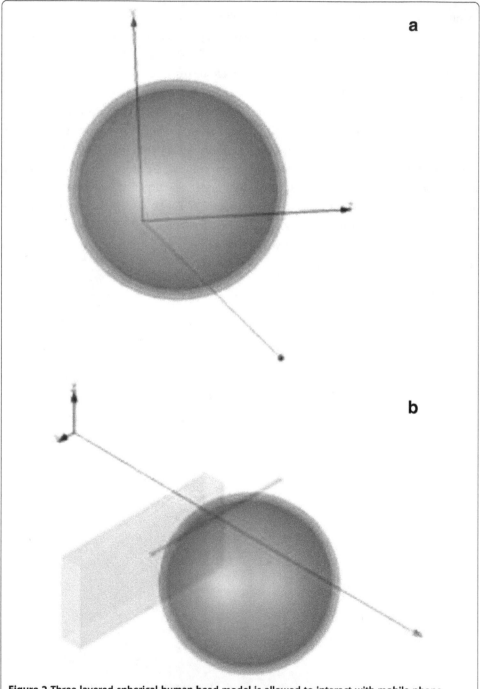

Figure 2 Three layered spherical human head model is allowed to interact with mobile phone antenna for analysis of SAR and Thermal distribution. a. Three layered Head model [simulated head model with skin, skull and brain layer]. **b** Mobile phone interaction with head [mobile phone handset interacted with three layered head model].

Table 1 Properties of tissues in human head

Tissue	Brain diameter (mm)	Skull thickness (mm)	Skin thickness (mm)
4 year child	136.1	3.1	3.6
8 year child	140.6	3.5	4
Adult	160.1	8.9	7.2
Permittivity	52.7	12.5	35.2
Conductivity (S/m)	0.94	0.14	0.60

of each arm of dipole is 73.5 mm and radius is 1.8 mm. The material of dipole arms are selected to be perfect electric conductor. The lumped port excitation with 50 ohm internal resistance is located in the feed gap. Maximum working frequency of 3 GHz is specified for excitation source. Antenna performance was analyzed in section Conclusion by considering the parameters such as, the current distribution in each arm of dipole antenna, S – parameter. Starting with these initial requirements, we optimized the design through simulations using commercial software package based on the Finite-Difference Time-Domain technique. For analyzing SAR and thermal distributions, the near field environment may include a human head and antenna enclosed by a plastic frame, which may influence on antenna performance.

User head model

The user's head (4 years child, 8 years child and an adult) was modeled as a sphere with three layers [5] such as skin, skull and brain as shown in Figure 2a, using GEMS [6].

Human body tissues have different values of dielectric properties that is, permittivity and conductivity and these properties are the functions of several variables such as frequency, geometry and size of tissue, and water contents [5]. Table 1 shows the model properties and dimensions used in used in simulation.

Hand held device model

A handheld device model (shown in Figure 1b) used for human interaction was modeled by GEMS. Figure 2b shows the interaction of handheld geometric model which has a maximum dimension of 167 mm × 23 mm × 83 mm with spherical human head. Components considered for simulation are feeding port (dipole antenna), plastic cover ($er = 4.4$) and plastic cover was modeled as dielectric materials [7].

Measurement of power absorbed

Specific absorption rate

Specific absorption rate [8] is defined as the rate at which RF power is absorbed per unit mass by any part of the body given by

$$SAR = (\sigma|E|^2)/(\rho) \qquad (1)$$

$$SAR = C(dT/dt) \qquad (2)$$

Where, E is the effective value of the electric field intensity (V/m), dT/dt is the time derivative of the temperature (K/s), σ is the electrical conductivity (S/m), ρ is the mass density (kg/m3) and c is the specific heat (J/kg K). The unit of SAR is W/kg. Due to evolution in wireless technologies, dosimetric evaluation of handheld device is highly

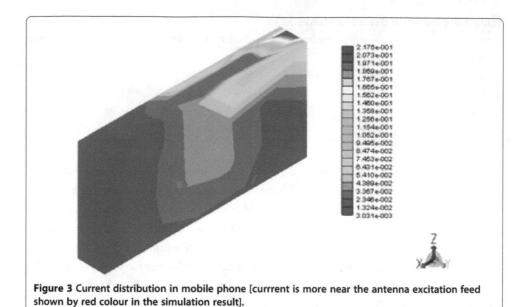

Figure 3 Current distribution in mobile phone [currrent is more near the antenna excitation feed shown by red colour in the simulation result].

desirable for safety environment [9]. For radio frequency signals, SAR value is calculated for either 1 g (Australia, United States) or 10 g (Europe, Japan) of simulated biological tissue in the shape of a cube. Partial (localized) non occupational exposure is limited to a spatial peak value not exceeding 1.6 W/kg (Australia, United States) and 2.0 W/kg (Japan). The partial exposure SAR limit recommended by the Council of the European Union and adopted by India is also 1.6 W/kg [3].

Tissues are made up of water, different salts and organic compounds and they can be considered as a mixture of insulators and conductors. Brain tissue is rich in water along with fat content and cerebrospinal fluid along the ventricles and extends to flow along spinal cord. When a portable cellular telephone is in the typical use position, the nearest brain tissue is in matter of relatively uniform dielectric characteristics with macroscopic values of dielectric constant and conductivity $\varepsilon_r = 52.7$ and $\sigma = 0.94$ S/m in the frequency band of interest.

Thermal effects

Thermal effects are due to rise in temperature produced by the energy absorbed from oscillating electric fields emitted by mobile phone antennas as shown in Figure 3. The dark red colour shows higher temperature near antenna feeding point and get varies along the length of the case. Similarly, the current generated in brain tissue as in

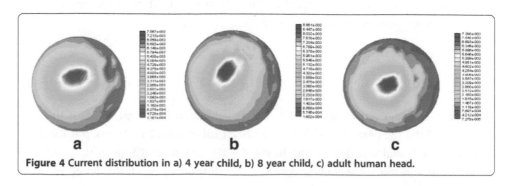

Figure 4 Current distribution in a) 4 year child, b) 8 year child, c) adult human head.

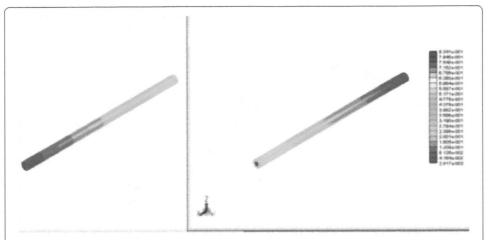

Figure 5 Current distribution of arm 1 and arm 2 in dipole antenna [current is higher near the feeding point and becomes zero and start its path as a electromagnetic wave for communication at rear end].

Figure 4 shows temperature variation. The power coupled causes the temperature to rise until, this induced heat reaches stable equilibrium value through blood circulation along the body which will take several minutes from the moment RF exposure occurs. Generally, thermal energy is dissipated from the body by sweating and increased peripheral circulation. The consequences of excessive heating in the body vary from temporary disturbances in cell functions to permanent destruction of tissues.

Studies [10] indicate that, the lens of eye may experience a temperature increase of 1°C at SAR level of 10 W/kg. At cell level the heating cause damage by disturbing the functioning of proteins. Cells begin to die when the temperature rises more than 5°C, but the tissues can endure momentary increases of tens of degrees.

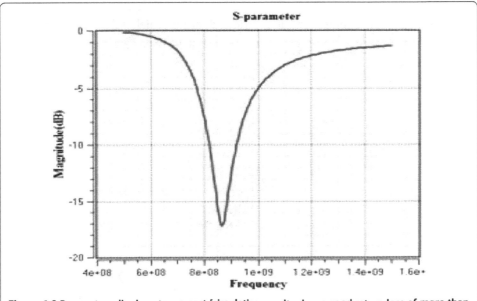

Figure 6 S-Parameters dipole antenna port [simulation results shows good return loss of more than 15 dB, suitable for mobile communication].

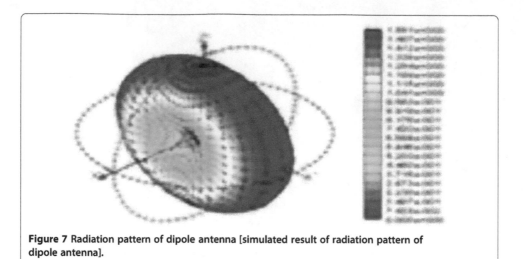

Figure 7 Radiation pattern of dipole antenna [simulated result of radiation pattern of dipole antenna].

Numerical results and discussions

FDTD simulations

Simulations using GEMS, a commercially available software package have been carried out in this paper. Finite Difference Time Domain is the popular computational technique, used for the computation of electromagnetic field and also its interaction with other materials. Here, computational space is divided into a Cartesian coordinate grid of voxels and then allocates the components of the electric and magnetic fields to specified locations on each voxel. This scheme is known as Yee lattice and the components are distributed in such a way that, every H-field component is surrounded by E-field components and vice versa. In addition to discretizing E and H in the space, the temporal changes in the fields are computed at discrete time intervals. For spatial grid separations of Δt, the fields may be written as

$$F(x, y, z, t) = F(i\Delta x, j\Delta y, k\Delta z, n\Delta t) \tag{3}$$

From this the x, y, z component of electric and magnetic field values are calculated at each time by updating the values from the previous time step by the curl of the

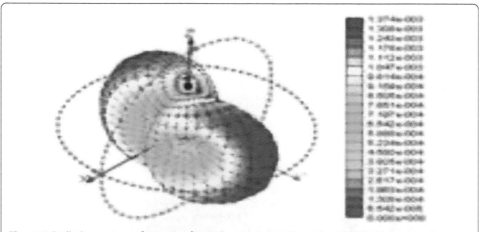

Figure 8 Radiation pattern of antenna due to human interaction. [altered radiation pattern from the original pattern due to human interaction].

Table 2 SAR averaged over 1 g and 10 g tissue when phone (without resistive sheet) placed near head

Model	4-year child	8-year child	Adult
1-g SAR (W/Kg)	20.47	14.27	4.27
10-g SAR (W/Kg)	8.13	6.92	2.78
Max SAR (W/Kg)	149.9	73.10	11.15
Average SAR (W/Kg)	0.52	0.48	0.168

complementary field. The computational starting point is defined by the initial condition, achieved by applying a sinusoidal or impulsive propagating wave beginning at n = 0. At each increment of n, the solution for E and H evolve as wave propagates [3,11]. In this section, first the performance evaluation of antenna in free space is considered. Further, the interaction of six layered spherical human head with mobile phone is evaluated for measurement of SAR and heat induced.

Evaluation of antenna in free space
Current distribution and S- parameters
General Electro Magnetic Simulator was used to generate animations of the electric surface currents with feeding port excited. Current distribution along the arms of dipole antenna is shown in Figure 5. The excitation of the port induces high-magnitude surface currents in the proximity of each feed, but a null-current area is clearly shown to exist at the open circuit end. The simulated S-parameter of the λ /2 dipole antenna is shown in Figure 6.

The results indicate that, for frequency band of interest (0.9–1.5 GHz), feeding port provides a better return loss of 15 dB, suitable for wireless communication applications [12,13].

Radiation pattern and efficiency
Figure 7 illustrates the simulated 3-D gain patterns for (λ/2) dipole antenna, for the operating frequency of 0.9 GHz. The total efficiency of an antenna is defined as the ratio of total radiated power to the incident power at the feed. Forward efficiency of antenna in free space is found to be 95% at 0.9 GHz. From Figure 8, it is also seen that, the original radiation pattern of dipole antenna get altered due human head interaction [14].

Mobile phone interaction with head model
SAR analysis
The spherical human head composed of three inner layers (as in Table 1) is simulated and is allowed to interact with the mobile phone placed very near to ear (pressing the ear).

Table 3 SAR values averaged over tissues when phone with resistive sheet placed near user head model

Model	4-year child	% decrement	8-year child	% decrement	Adult	% decrement
1-g SAR (W/Kg)	9.709	52.5	5.825	59.2	2.13	50.1
10-g SAR (W/Kg)	4.43	45.5	3.24	53.1	1.35	51.4
Max SAR (W/Kg)	65.77	55.5	23.90	67.3	6.36	42.9
Average SAR (W/Kg)	0.32	38.9	0.243	49.3	0.095	43.15

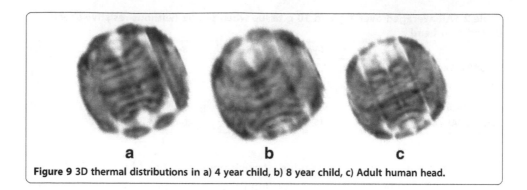

Figure 9 3D thermal distributions in a) 4 year child, b) 8 year child, c) Adult human head.

The values of maximum SAR, average SAR and SAR averaged over 1 and 10 g of human tissue have been computed, when mobile phone placed near human head and are listed in Tables 2 and 3. The power absorption level of each layer differs due to its thickness, conductivity and permittivity [15]. Current distribution and 3D thermal distribution in head is shown in Figures 4 and 9. From the results obtained (shown in Figures 10 and 11), the SAR values are higher for children.

In this work, application of resistive sheet of 50 ohm is placed on the user front side of mobile phone handset case. And the comparative result shows, considerable decrement in power coupled. This introduced method shows maximum of 50% decrement in power coupled.

Conclusion

From the studies and above simulation results, it is concluded that, the power absorbed by children head is higher than adult. It might be due to variation in the head tissue layer thickness, which is lower in case of children. Since, the skull bone of adult is very thick comparatively; the intensity of power coupled to the brain is lesser. Further, the inclusion of 50 ohm resistive sheet in handset decreases the power coupled with the human head.

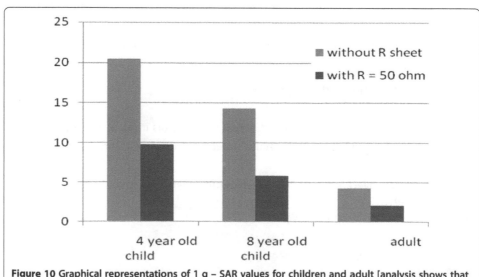

Figure 10 Graphical representations of 1 g – SAR values for children and adult [analysis shows that child head absorbs more radiation than adult].

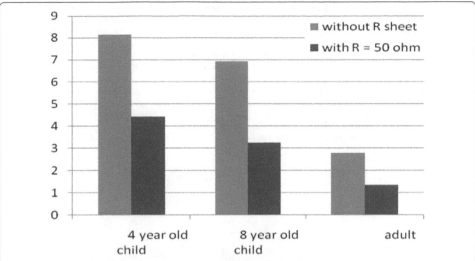

Figure 11 Graphical representations of 10 g – SAR values for children and adult [analysis indicates that resistive sheet in mobile phone handset considerably reduces the power coupled to human head].

Competing interests
The authors declare that they have no competing interest.

Authors' contributions
BR has published papers in the area of intellectual property rights and had been member of various technical societies. In this work, BR contributed the whole research idea and extended his help through out the work like documentation to final verification. LR done simulation and documentation work. Both the author has read the final manuscript. Both authors read and approved the final manuscript.

Authors' information
Balamurugan Rajagopal was born in Tamil Nadu, India in 1981. He received the Bachelor's degree in EIE from NIT Jalandar, Punjab, India and Master's in Electrical Engineering from Anna University, TN, India. Since 2007, he is working as an Assistant Professor in Department of Electrical Engineering in Anna University Regional Centre, Coimbatore, TN, India. He's been granted for staff mobility program through Heritage program and India for you. His research interest includes Intellectual Property Rights, Power electronic converters for renewable energy systems, Bio-electromagnetics. Lalithambika Rajasekaran was born in Tamil Nadu, India in 1987. She received the Bachelor degree in Electronics and Communication Engineering and Master's in Electrical Engineering in 2009 and 2013 respectively from Anna University, Tamil Nadu, India. She was awarded with Gold medal in her Masters degree. Her research interest includes Bio- Electromagnetics, power electronic converters for renewable energy systems.

Acknowledgment
I wish to thank Doctors of various hospitals by giving their valuable explanations regarding Human anatomy and the difference between adult and child head.

References
1. Abdelhamid H, Emmanuelle C, Azeddine G, Man-Fa"I W, Joe W (2010) 'Analysis of power absorbed by children's head as a result of new usages of mobile phone'. IEEE Trans Electromagn Compat 52:4
2. Rowley JT, Waterhouse RB (1999) 'Performance of shorted microstrip patch antennas for mobile communications handsets at 1800 MHz'. IEEE Trans Antennas Propag 47:5
3. Kraus JD, Fleich DA (1999) "Electromagnetics with applications', Fifthth edn. New York: Mc-Graw-Hill
4. Carr JJ (2001) 'Practical antenna handbook', Fourthth edn. New York: Mc Graw-Hill, ISBN-10: 0071374353
5. Anderson V (2003) 'Comparisons of peak SAR levels in concentric sphere head models of children and adults for irradiation by a dipole at 900 MHz' Institute of Physics Publishing Physics in Medicine and Biology. Phys Med Biol 48:3263–3327
6. Simulation tool, 'General Electromagnetic Simulator', http://www.2comu.com
7. Rao Q, Wang D (2010) 'A compact dual port diversity antenna for long-term evolution handheld devices'. IEEE Trans VehTech 59:59
8. Kivekas O, Ollikainen J, Lehtiniemi T, Vainikainen P (2004) 'Bandwidth, SAR and efficiency of internal mobile phone antennas'. IEEE Trans Electromagn Compat, 46(1):71–86

9.   Jensen MA, Rahmat-Samii Y (1994) 'Performance analysis of antennas for hand-held transceivers using FDTD'. IEEE Trans Antennas Propag 42(8):1106–1113

10. Environmental Working Group (2009) 'Cell Phone Radiation, Science Review on Cancer Risk and Children Health'. http://www.ewg.org/cellphoneradiation/fullreport

11. Bansal R (ed) (2004) 'Handbook of engineering electromagnetics'. Marcel Dekker, USA

12. Rao Q, Wilson K (2011) 'Design, modeling, and evaluation of a multiband MIMO/Diversity Antenna System for small wireless mobile terminals'. IEEE Trans Comp Packag Manufact Technol 01:03

13. Vaughan RG, Anderson JB (1987) 'Antenna diversity in mobile communications'. IEEE Trans Veh Technol Vt-36 (4):149–172

14. Tang CK, Fung LC, Leung SW (2007) 'Electromagnetic field radiation of mobile phone inside metallic enclosure'. IEEE International Symposium on Electromagnetic Compatibility, 2007 1–6

15. Ilvonen S, Sarvas J (2007) 'Magnetic-field-induced elf currents in a human body by the use of a GSM phone'. IEEE Trans Electromagn Compat 49:2

4

A subjective job scheduler based on a backpropagation neural network

Anilkumar Kothalil Gopalakrishnan

Correspondence:
anil@scitech.au.edu
Distributed and Parallel Computing
Research Laboratory, Department of
Computer Science, Faculty of
Science and Technology,
Assumption University, Soi 24,
Ramkhamheang Road, Hua Mak,
Bang Kapi, Bangkok 10240, Thailand

Abstract

This paper aims to present and discuss the concept of a subjective job scheduler based on a Backpropagation Neural Network (BPNN) and a greedy job alignment procedure. The subjective criteria of the scheduler depend on the solution plan for a given job scheduling problem. When the scheduler is provided with desired job selection criteria for the problem, it generates user satisfying solution from a set of valid jobs. The job validation procedure is based on the similarity measure of the jobs with the seen dataset of the scheduler. The seen dataset is based on the subjective criteria of the scheduler. The prioritized and valid jobs are allowed to execute concurrently on the given identical machines. The satisfying criterion of the scheduler indicates the user satisfaction of the scheduler and is based on three measures: convergence test of the BPNN, job validity test and cost evaluation. The simulations presented in this paper indicate that the proposed scheduler approach is one of the most effective strategies of structuring a subjective job scheduler.

Keywords: Backpropagation neural network; Greedy task alignment procedure; Seen data; Unseen data; Subjective criteria; Satisfying criterion; Convergence test; Job validity test; Cost evaluation

Introduction

Job scheduling problems fall into a class of intractable numerical problems that are complex in nature and may not provide subjective satisfying solutions. For instance, in traditional job scheduling each job consists of m sub-jobs called *subtasks* or *tasks*, with one machine for each task. As shown in [1,2], if there are n jobs with each machine, then $(n!)^m$ solution patterns are possible. The subjective job scheduler with a satisfying criterion based on a backpropagation neural network (BPNN) [3-5] simplifies the solution complexities in job scheduling. In this context, the utilization of the parallel processing ability of the BPNN and the significance of the greedy algorithm [6,7] allow the formulation of a job scheduler which is suitable for generating user satisfying solutions. That is, the proposed scheduler has an ability to yield user satisfying solutions, especially for a problem with n independent jobs on m identical machines.

Details of the problem

In this research, a combination of a 3-layer BPNN and a greedy job alignment procedure are used to generate a "best" job scheduling result that satisfies a user for the job scheduling problem with n independent jobs on m identical machines.

It is assumed that all the jobs in a selected problem have different priorities as per the user and select the "best" possible jobs from the job queue based on the predefined job selection criteria, called *subjective criteria*. That is, prior to a scheduling process, the scheduler detects the user feasible jobs from the job queue which are supposed to be the in the valid form of the subjective criteria of the scheduler called *valid jobs* (if any). After a set of valid jobs is recognized, the scheduler allocates those jobs into the given identical machines in a concurrent manner without missing the essentiality of the top priority jobs. In this way, the scheduler maximizes the utilization of the machines to avoid any 'idle' machine states during its action. Moreover, it is assumed that all machines are operating in parallel and jobs are allowed to migrate to any available machines without violating their priority order. The greedy task alignment procedure always determines the reasonable finishing time schedule from a given scheduling problem.

The initial dataset which is generated based on the user's subjective criteria for the initial training of the BPNN called the *seen data*. These seen data and the job alignment procedure are meant to carry the details of how the job selection process happens and how the jobs are to be aligned on the machines. In this case, the user is replaced by the scheduler permanently. That is why this scheduler is named as a *subjective job scheduler*. Furthermore, this job scheduler employs the greedy algorithms which are, by their characteristics, quicker and they do not need to consider the details of all solution alternatives of the job scheduling problem.

Problem statement

In real life situations, people seek things that give them or provide optimum sense of satisfaction; therefore, all the endeavors of man are geared to finding it at all costs. On the other hand, the productions and service industry are working hard to develop goods and services that meet optimal satisfaction. In the current applications of technology, there is a need of having job schedulers that do not only schedule jobs but also provide the much needed satisfaction. Work procedures such as order of priority, time, due date and others have occupied a substantial search space unnecessarily making it almost impossible to determine whether the results are satisfactory or not [8]. Whenever a user is faced with many jobs at a time, as a human being, the user will select a set of feasible jobs subjectively and will be persuaded to complete them together without incurring any overhead. The proposed scheduler shows how a job scheduling agent would handle the above mentioned situation in an effective way.

Description of the problem and the structure of the scheduler

The proposed job scheduler is meant to solve job scheduling problems such as n independent jobs on m machines. The scheduling problem can be described as follows: denote $J = \{1, .. , j\}$ and $M = \{1,..., m\}$ as the job set and the machine set, where J and M are the number of independent jobs and identical machines, respectively. The scheduler always starts with a set of input jobs (input jobs are *unseen jobs*) which are available in the queue, also called a *job queue*. Each job in the job queue is represented by a set of parameters referred to as *job attributes*. Let's say a job, J_1 can be represented as $\{a_{11} \wedge a_{12} \wedge .... \wedge a_{1n}\}$, where $a_{11}, a_{12},..$, etc., are the conjunctions of the attributes of the job J_1. In this paper, a job has four attributes provided in order to estimate its *priority*,

P. It is assumed that these four parameters of a job are known in advance and are defined as follows:

- *R,* job *release-event,* is the estimated triggering time of the job execution request [9].
- *K,* job *computation time,* is the time to complete the execution of the task.
- *D,* job relative *deadline,* is the maximum acceptable delay for its processing [9].
- *L,* job *critical type,* indicates whether the job is critically needed.

The subjective criteria for determining the priority of a job and also the subjective criteria used to identify valid jobs out of a set of input jobs depend on the nature and the definition of these four attributes. The job attributes of the scheduler may vary with the nature of the scheduling problems and users' preferences. Here the scheduler detects the *execution concurrency* of a set of valid jobs based on the job priorities and the priorities of the jobs depend on the subjective criteria of the scheduler as specified by the user. At this point, the priority definition of a job is informal. That means that the priority of a job cannot be described formally and it can only be detected through the subjective criteria of the scheduler. Subjective criteria for generating seen data for the scheduler for assigning priority to each valid job are described in Section Subjective criteria. Though the *deadline* attribute of a job is an important one for detecting its priority, it is considered that jobs are soft in nature such that a deadline is never missed to jeopardize the performance of the scheduler. Figure 1 shows the structure of the scheduler with a BPNN (3-layered BPNN with a network topology of four input neuron, thirty hidden neurons and one output neuron), a *job queue,* a *priority queue,* BPNN convergence test, job validation test, cost evaluation, greedy job alignment procedure and machine set. The scheduler is formulated in such a way that it works with a set of jobs simultaneously at a time.

The selected 3-layer BPNN is trained with a backpropagation algorithm with the seen data until its Mean Squared Error (MSE) is reduced to a value less than 0.001. Section Subjective criteria shows the details of generating the seen data for the BPNN.

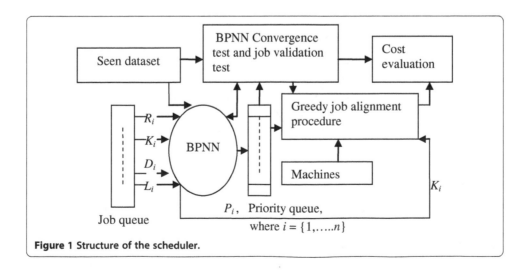

Figure 1 Structure of the scheduler.

Description of backpropagation neural networks

The neurons are connected by links and each link has a numerical weight associated with it. Weights are the basic means of long-term memory in neural networks [4]. They express the strength, or in other words, importance of each neuron input. A neural network 'learns' through repeated adjustments of these weights. The neurons are connected to the external environment through the input and output layers. The weights are modified to bring the network input/output behavior in line with that of the environment. Figure 2 shows the structure of a typical neuron.

Each neuron in the neural network is an elementary information-processing unit. It has the means of computing its *activation level* given the inputs and numerical weights. To build an artificial neural network, first it is to be decided how many neurons are to be used and how the neurons are to be connected to form a network. Then the learning algorithm to be used is selected. Finally, the neural network is trained with the selected supervised training algorithm. Training of the neural network means that the learning algorithm initializes the weights of the network and updates the weights from a set of training examples (seen data). In this paper, the backpropagation algorithm is used to train the 3-layer neural network (hence it is called a *backpropagation neural network*). Typically, a backpropagation neural network (BPNN) is a multilayer neural network that has three or four layers. The layers are fully connected, that is, every neuron in each layer is connected to every other neuron in the adjacent forward layer. A neuron determines its output by computing its net weight input as [4]:

$$X = \sum_{i=1}^{n} x_i w_i - \theta \qquad (1)$$

where the variable, X, is the net weighted input to the neuron, x_i is the value of input i, w_i is the weight of input i, n is the number of neuron inputs, and θ is the threshold applied to the neuron. The *sigmoid activation* function guarantees that the neuron output is bounded between 0 and 1. The neuron in this

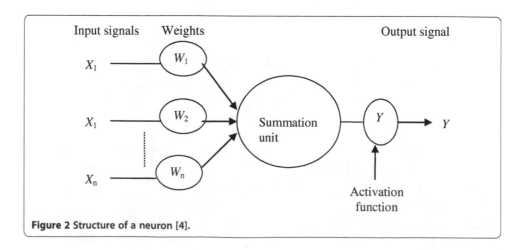

Figure 2 Structure of a neuron [4].

backpropagation network uses a sigmoid activation function. Hence the output $Y^{sigmoid}$ of the neuron is given as [4]:

$$Y^{sigmoid} = 1/\left(1 + e^{-X}\right). \tag{2}$$

The BPNN with four input variables and one output variable used in this paper is shown in Figure 3, where R, K, D, L and P are the *release-event, computation time, relative deadline, critical type* and *priority* of the given job. In a typical 3-layer BPNN, the computation time will be asymptotically Θ ($ih + ho$), where i, h, and o are the number of input neurons, hidden neurons and output neurons, respectively. Again, the main function of the BPNN is to assign priorities to the jobs based on the given subjective criteria.

Subjective criteria

In order to generate a seen dataset for the initial training of the BPNN of the scheduler, there are five numerical values with their proper linguistic terms applied along with the parameters of each job. The four parameters of a job with their numerical values and linguistic terms are as follows:

I. R_i is the *release-event* of job i with values: [0.1 (*very small*), 0.3 (*small*), 0.5 (*not small*), 0.7 (*long*), 0.9 (*very long*)].
II. K_i is the *computation time* of job i with values: [0.1 (*very low*), 0.3 (*low*), 0.5 (*not low*), 0.7 (*high*), 0.9 (*very high*)].
III. D_i is the *deadline* of job i with values: [0.1 (*very near*), 0.3 (*near*), 0.5 (*not near*), 0.7 (*far*), 0.9 (*very far*)].
IV. L_i is the *critical type* of job i with values: [0.1 (*very low*), 0.3 (*low*), 0.5 (*not low*), 0.7 (*high*), 0.9 (*very high*)].

The output of the BPNN, P_i, is the *priority* of job i ranging from 0.01 (*very low* priority) to 0.99 (*very high* priority).Based on the numerical values and linguistic terms of the

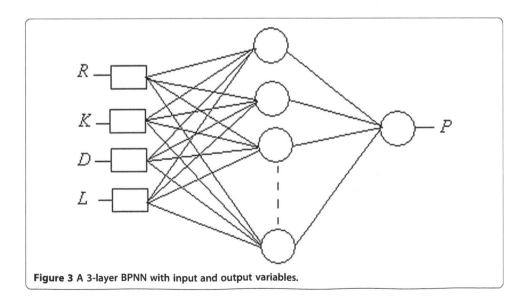

Figure 3 A 3-layer BPNN with input and output variables.

attributes of a job, the criteria for generating the seen data (including both input and output data patterns) for finding job priority are as listed below:

(a) A valid job with a *very high / high* computation time never holds a *very near / near* deadline (deadline must be greater than or equal to computation time).

(b) A valid job with a *very long / long* release-event never holds a *very near / near* deadline.

(c) A *very high* critical job should hold a *very near* deadline.

(d) A *very high* critical job never holds a *very far* deadline.

(e) A *very high / high* critical job never holds a *very high / high* computation time.

(f) A valid job with a *very small / small* release-event, a *very low / low* computation time, a *very near/ near* deadline and a *very high / high* critical type holds a *very high / high* priority.

(g) A valid job with a *not small / long / very long* release event, a *not near / far / very far* deadline, a *not low / high / very high* computation time and a *very low / low / not low* critical type can achieve only a priority value which is proportional to its critical type value.

(h) A valid job with a *very long / long* release-event, a *very high / high* computation time, a *very far / far* deadline and a *very low / low* critical type holds a *very low / low* priority.

(i) A valid job with a *not small / long* release-event, a *not near / far* deadline and a *not low* critical type will get a priority value which is proportional to its critical type.

(j) A valid job with a *very small / small* release-event, a *very high / high* computation time, a *not near* deadline and a *not low* critical type will hold a priority value which is proportional to its deadline.

(k) A valid job with a *very long / long* release-event, a *very high / high* computation time, a *very far / far* deadline and a *very low / low* critical type has a priority which is proportional to its critical type.

A sample seen dataset with input variables and their respective output data patterns based on the above subjective criteria is shown in Additional file 1: Table S1.

Greedy job alignment procedure

The greedy job alignment procedure helps to generate possible alignment patterns of valid jobs on their respective machines based on their priority values. The jobs are sorted in descending order of their priorities to allocate them on the given identical machines. The greedy procedure of the scheduler reduces the finishing time of the jobs on the machines by allowing similar priority jobs to execute concurrently on the given identical machines [10]. Assume that the job *priority queue*, q has n indices and can be represented as $q[0],..., q[n\text{-}1]$ and it holds J valid jobs $\{J_1,..., J_n\}$ at a time. Let there are M identical machines in the scheduler and are represented as the set $\{M_1,..., M_m\}$. The relationship between machines and jobs of the scheduler is $J > M$. Based on their priorities, the valid jobs are concurrently executed by the given machines as shown below:

$$\{(M_1 : q[0], q[n\text{-}2], ...)\}$$
$$\{(M_2 : q[1], q[n\text{-}3], ...)\}$$
$$\{(M_m : q[n\text{-}1], q[n\text{-}1]), ..\}.$$

The greedy procedure sorts the computation times of each machine to find the finishing time, *FT*, of the schedule. The maximum value of the finishing time is considered as the feasible solution for the schedule (Section Cost evaluation shows the details of the finishing time calculation).

Convergence test of the BPNN

There is a convergence test added along with the traditional backpropagation algorithm to verify the initial training process of the BPNN. The initial training of the BPNN depends on the size of the seen data and the topology of the network. Once the BPNN is trained with the seen dataset until its MSE is 0.001, it is essential to ensure that the BPNN is free from problems such as 'over-fitting' and local maxima during its initial training process. The details of the convergence test of the BPNN are given here:

(i) Train the BPNN with the seen dataset by proper training parameters such as *learning rate* (α) and *momentum term* (β) until its MSE is reduced to a value less than 0.001.

(ii) Select the input data pattern from the seen dataset after its training.

(iii) Select the output data from the seen data after its training (say, *Q*) similarly to step (ii),.

(iv) Input the selected data pattern (from step ii) to the BPNN and find its output by the BPNN (say, *Q'*).

A *similarity measure* of *Q* and *Q'*, *S* (*Q, Q'*) is the convergence test of the BPNN and can be interpreted as follows: if *S* (*Q, Q'*) is above or equal to +0.99, then the selected BPNN is an acceptable one and is considered as *true*. Otherwise, the BPNN is considered as unacceptable (*false*) and allow the BPNN to repeat its training with different parameters and topologies until an acceptable net topology is seen.

A correlation coefficient statistics [11] was used to measure the similarity between two datasets of equal size and the results showed values between −1 and +1 on the basis of the datasets. The mathematical formulae of the correlation coefficients are included below. Let S_{bj} be the normalized similarity between two sets of attribute values X_i and X_j of datasets *i* and *j*. The analytical expression of S_{bj} is;

$$S_{i,j} = \left(\sum_{k=1}^{n}(X_{i,k} = \overline{X}i) \times (X_{j,k} - \overline{X_j}) \right) \bigg/ \sum_{k=1}^{n}(X_{i,k} - \overline{X_i})^2 \times \sum_{k=1}^{n}(X_{j,k} - \overline{X_j})^2]^{1/2}, \qquad (3)$$

where

$$\overline{X}_i = 1 \bigg/ n \times \left(\sum_{k=1}^{n} X_{i,k} \right) \qquad (4)$$

and

$$\overline{X}j = 1 \bigg/ n \times \left(\sum_{k=1}^{n} X_{j,k} \right). \qquad (5)$$

Like with the BPNN convergence test procedure, there is a job validity test procedure of the scheduler as described in the following section.

Job validity test

The job validity test, V, of the scheduler provides a degree of measure of the *unseen data* (input jobs) of the scheduler with respect to its seen dataset. The job validity test depends on the similarity measure of the unseen data (input jobs) and seen dataset of the scheduler for a given problem. For instance, consider each job in a problem that has a set of four attributes. Hence a set of n jobs has a size of $n \times 4$ (i.e., n rows and 4 columns) for the unseen data values. The similarity measure of an input job (unseen) is calculated with each seen data value (except its seen priority value) of the scheduler. The resulted similarities (called *correlation values*) are stored in a buffer and then the maximum value is selected as the job's correlation value. The job is valid only when its correlation value is greater than zero. Similarly, the scheduler finds the correlation values of all input jobs in the job queue. The scheduler selects only valid jobs for their priority estimation.

Let the seen data be given index i and the unseen data be given index j and $X_i, X_{i+1},...,$ X_{i+n}, are the n parameters of set i and $X_j, X_{j+1},..., X_{j+n}$, are the n parameters of set j (assuming that the sizes of sets i and j are the same). Then the validity of sets i and j, $V_{i,j}$, based on Equation (3) can be given as:

$$V_{i,j} = \left(\sum_{k=1}^{n} (\overline{X_{i,k}} - \overline{Y_i}) \times (\overline{X_{j,k}} - \overline{Y_j}) \right) \Big/ \left[\sum_{k=1}^{n} (\overline{X_{i,k}} - \overline{Y_i})^2 \times \sum_{k=1}^{n} (\overline{X_{j,k}} - \overline{Y_j})^2 \right]^{1/2},$$

$$(6)$$

where

$$\overline{X_{i,k}} = 1 \Big/ n \times \left(\sum_{i=1}^{n} X_{i,k} \right), \tag{7}$$

$$\overline{X_{j,k}} = 1 \Big/ n \times \left(\sum_{j=1}^{n} X_{j,k} \right), \tag{8}$$

$$\overline{Y_i} = 1 \Big/ n \times \left(\sum_{k=1}^{n} \overline{X_{i,k}} \right) \tag{9}$$

and

$$\overline{Y_j} = 1 \Big/ n \times \left(\sum_{k=1}^{n} \overline{X_{j,k}} \right). \tag{10}$$

Based on Equation (6), the correlation value of unseen job i, can be given as:

$$V_i = \max(V_{i,1}, V_{i,2}, V_{i,3}, ... V_{i,j}), \tag{11}$$

where $V_{i,1}, V_{i,2}, V_{i,3},..., V_{i,j}$ are the correlation values of job i with *seen_ job_ data*$_1$, *seen_ job_data*$_2$,.... , etc. *If $V_i > 0$, then it is assumed that the unseen job i, is based on the scheduler's subjective criteria and is valid.* The job validity test V, is *true* only when the size of valid jobs is greater than the size of machines for a given problem.

Cost evaluation

The cost evaluation of the scheduler depends on its *cost value*, *C*, and is based on its finishing time. The cost evaluation of a multi-machine job scheduler can be expressed by the following theorem [7]:

Every feasible schedule has a finishing time which is not earlier than the time

$$T = \left(\sum_{i=1}^{n} K_i \right) / m, \tag{12}$$

where K_i $\{i = 1,..., n\}$ is the computation time of i jobs and m is the number of machines. It is assumed that all machines are operating in parallel and each machine has an initialization time, w_{ti} $\{i = 1,..., n\}$, in order to prepare for a job processing. Let T_{m1} is the total computation time taken by machine m_1 and is given as:

$$T_{m1} = w_{t1*} \sum_{i=1}^{n} K_{1i}, \tag{13}$$

where K_{1i} $\{i = 1,..., n\}$ is the computation time of i jobs on machine m_1. Similarly, T_{mn} is the total computation by n^{th} machine, m_n of the scheduler and is given as:

$$T_{mn} = w_{t,mn*} \sum_{i=1}^{n} K_{ni} \tag{14}$$

For simplicity, it is assumed that w_{ti} is 1. Hence the finishing time, *FT*, of a complete schedule with n machines can be estimated as

$$FT = \max\{T_{m1}, T_{m2}, ..., T_{mn}\}. \tag{15}$$

During a scheduling result with a finishing time, *FT*, the m machines of the scheduler can use a total of at most ($m \times FT$) time units [7]. At this time, for executing all valid jobs requires $\sum_{i=1}^{n} K_i$ time units. Hence the cost value, *C*, of the scheduler can be derived from Equations (12) and (15) as follows:

$$C = [FT - T], \tag{16}$$

where T is the average execution time of n jobs on m machines (see Equation (12)).

Based on Equation (16), the cost term can be interpreted, as follows:

- If C is equal to 0, then it is a *'good enough'* schedule and C is *true*.
- If $C > 0$, then it is a *'reasonable'* schedule and C is *true*.

For both cases, it can be noticed that C is *true*. The reason is that the scheduler never generates a *non-reasonable* schedule due to the application of the greedy alignment procedure. Furthermore, due to the application of Equation (16), the cost, *C*, of a feasible schedule will never reach a value greater than or equal to 1.

Definition of satisfying criterion

The satisfying criterion, *Sat*, of the scheduler is a binary term which indicates the satisfaction of the scheduler for a given problem. The *Sat* of the scheduler can be defined in terms of three binary measures: (i) *S*; (ii) *V*; and (iii) *C*, where *S*, *V* and *C* are the binary results of convergence test, job validity test and cost evaluation of the scheduler, respectively. The propositional logic representation of *Sat* with respect to the atomic variables *S*, *V* and *C* can be expressed as [8]:

$$((S \wedge V \wedge C) \rightarrow Sat). \tag{17}$$

The interpretation of Equation (17) is that if *S*, *V* and *C* are *true*, then it is possible to say that *Sat* is *true*. Otherwise, it is not possible to claim that *Sat* is *true*. Because of the application of BPNN convergence test, job validity test and cost evaluation, the proposed scheduler always generates user-satisfactory schedules. Whenever all the jobs in the job queue are invalid, then the scheduler will indicate an unsatisfying situation. The same situation will happen when the number of valid jobs is less than the number of given machines for a problem.

Procedure of the scheduler

The implementation of the proposed procedure includes the following distinct steps:

(i) Generate jobs and machines randomly.
(ii) *Declarations:* Let *M* be the set of *m* identical machines, where $\forall M = 0$ (initialize all machines). The selection criteria of both job and machine can be given as *J* > *M*, where *J* is the total number of jobs in the job queue.
(iii) *Job validation test:* Checks whether any invalid job(s) available in the job queue. If so, such jobs will be exempted from the job queue.
(iv) *Backpropagation algorithm:* The backpropagation algorithm trains the BPNN for assigning priorities to each valid job. Let *P* is a set of priorities of *n* jobs and *P* can be denoted as $\{P_1, P_2, ..., P_n\}$. The convergence test measures the acceptability of the BPNN before its selection.

Table 1 Unseen dataset of twelve jobs with their respective correlation values

Job	R	K	D	L	Correlation
J_1	0.32	0.65	0.10	0.54	−0.34015
J_2	0.76	0.54	0.65	0.76	−0.31479
J_3	0.98	0.76	0.54	0.54	−0.69395
J_4	0.32	0.21	0.87	0.32	0.50865
J_5	0.32	0.87	0.98	0.10	0.128618
J_6	0.65	0.54	0.65	0.32	−0.37259
J_7	0.32	0.98	0.98	0.54	0.28644
J_8	0.65	0.21	0.21	0.21	−0.83024
J_9	0.10	0.32	0.54	0.65	0.92431
J_{10}	0.21	0.54	0.98	0.10	0.33508
J_{11}	0.21	0.98	0.76	0.87	0.43142
J_{12}	0.76	0.32	0.76	0.54	−0.20152

Table 2 Order of valid jobs with their priority values by BPNN in twelve jobs on three machines problem

Valid job	P
J_9	0.488
J_{11}	0.265
J_4	0.237
J_7	0.119
J_{10}	0.029
J_5	0.007

(v) *Greedy job alignment procedure:* The job alignment procedure aligns valid jobs into a set of identical machines for their concurrent execution based on their priorities. The alignment procedure returns a best finishing time, *FT*, of the schedule which is either 'good enough' or a reasonable one.

(vi) *Cost evaluation:* The cost evaluation of the scheduler evaluates result of a schedule to either a *good enough* or a *reasonable* schedule on the basis of its finishing time, *FT*.

(vii) *Satisfying criterion:* Satisfying criterion defines the satisfying conditions of the scheduler. Whenever the number of valid jobs is zero and the number of valid jobs is less than the machines, then satisfying criterion of the scheduler fails.

(viii) Go to step (i).

Simulation results

The subjective scheduler is written in C++ and supportive simulations are made to show the satisfying nature of the scheduler for several given scheduling problems of different kinds. For the purposes of this study, three such kinds are shown: first, a problem with twelve jobs on three machines and second, a problem with sixteen jobs on four machines. Third, a problem with twenty one jobs on seven machines. In this section, the situations, such as the scheduler with only invalid jobs or when the size of the valid jobs is less than the size of the machines, are omitted. Details of the simulations carried out are given below.

Scheduling problem with twelve jobs on three machines

The unseen dataset of twelve jobs with their respective correlation values (as per Equation (6)) are shown in Table 1. As per Equation (3), the 3-layer BPNN is acceptable with a similarity value of +0.9978 (i.e., *S* is *true*). Table 1 shows that there are six valid jobs (J_4, J_5, J_7, J_9, J_{10} and J_{11}) in the job queue as per Equation (11) and the invalid jobs are

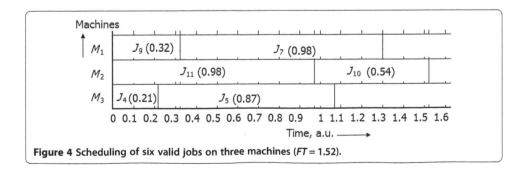

Figure 4 Scheduling of six valid jobs on three machines (*FT* = 1.52).

Table 3 Unseen dataset of sixteen jobs with their respective correlation values

Job	R	K	D	L	Correlation
J_1	0.32	0.43	0.65	0.54	0.93713
J_2	0.76	0.32	0.87	0.21	−0.11176
J_3	0.76	0.32	0.76	0.32	−0.21439
J_4	0.21	0.98	0.10	0.43	−0.01612
J_5	0.87	0.32	0.98	0.32	−0.11865
J_6	0.21	0.76	0.32	0.54	0.19192
J_7	0.98	0.21	0.32	0.76	−0.71251
J_8	0.98	0.87	0.21	0.10	−0.68731
J_9	0.65	0.21	0.21	0.43	−0.79364
J_{10}	0.98	0.21	0.87	0.10	−0.31559
J_{11}	0.21	0.32	0.76	0.10	0.50818
J_{12}	0.32	0.10	0.98	0.87	0.46068
J_{13}	0.65	0.65	0.10	0.98	−0.39876
J_{14}	0.21	0.98	0.87	0.76	0.63493
J_{15}	0.65	0.32	0.65	0.98	0.00138
J_{16}	0.43	0.10	0.54	0.87	0.17097

discarded. Validity, V, of the selected jobs is *true* because the size of the valid jobs is greater than the size of the identical machines (M_1, M_2 and M_3) for the problem. Priority order of the six valid jobs with their priority value, P, by the BPNN is shown in Table 2.

Figure 4 shows the scheduling of six valid jobs on three identical machines (M_1, M_2 and M_3). The computation time, K, of each job is shown in brackets. The greedy job alignment procedure allocates valid jobs on the given identical machines based on their order of the priority. The finishing time, FT, is 1.52 and cost value, C, is 0.22 and is *true* as per Equation (16) and the resulted schedule is a *reasonable* one. Because of the *true* values of S, V and C (as per Equation (17)), the schedule from scheduler for the given problem is a satisfying one.

Scheduling problem with sixteen jobs on four machines

A simulation of the scheduler with an unseen dataset of sixteen jobs on four identical machines (M_1, M_2, M_3 and M_4) is illustrated.

Table 3 shows an unseen dataset of sixteen jobs with their respective correlation values. From the Table 3, it can be noticed that there are seven valid jobs (J_1, J_6, J_{11}, J_{12},

Table 4 Order of valid jobs with their priority values by BPNN in sixteen jobs on three machines problem

Valid job	P
J_1	0.491
J_{16}	0.469
J_{15}	0.452
J_{14}	0.195
J_{12}	0.057
J_{11}	0.035
J_6	0.007

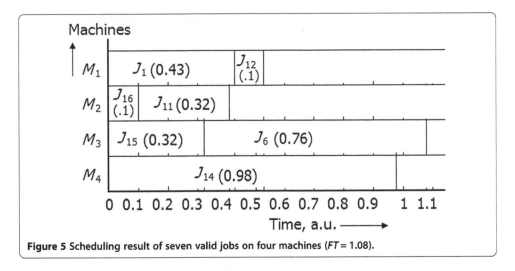

Figure 5 Scheduling result of seven valid jobs on four machines ($FT = 1.08$).

J_{14}, J_{15} and J_{16}) in the job queue. Validity, V, of the selected jobs is *true* because the size of the valid jobs is greater than the size of the identical machines (M_1, M_2, M_3 and M_4) for the problem. Priority order of the seven valid jobs with their priority values, P, by the BPNN is shown in Table 4.

Figure 5 shows the scheduling result of seven valid jobs on four identical machines (M_1, M_2, M_3 and M_4). The computation time, K, of each job is shown in brackets. The finishing time, FT, is 1.08 and cost value, C, is 0.33 and is *true* as per Equation (16). As

Table 5 Unseen dataset of twenty one jobs with their respective correlation values

Job	R	K	D	L	Correlation
J_1	0.76	0.10	0.54	0.10	−0.30535
J_2	0.76	0.65	0.87	0.65	0.01423
J_3	0.32	0.43	0.65	0.21	0.45152
J_4	0.43	0.54	0.43	0.65	0.19109
J_5	0.65	0.43	0.43	0.21	−0.48479
J_6	0.87	0.87	0.87	0.43	−0.16129
J_7	0.76	0.10	0.32	0.65	−0.47652
J_8	0.10	0.87	0.21	0.65	0.16139
J_9	0.21	0.65	0.21	0.87	0.12139
J_{10}	0.65	0.76	0.32	0.76	−0.35715
J_{11}	0.87	0.98	0.32	0.10	−0.54791
J_{12}	0.10	0.32	0.10	0.87	0.19261
J_{13}	0.65	0.43	0.54	0.87	−0.08543
J_{14}	0.43	0.76	0.87	0.87	0.55939
J_{15}	0.87	0.54	0.32	0.65	−0.64674
J_{16}	0.32	0.21	0.65	0.98	0.44291
J_{17}	0.98	0.32	0.76	0.1	−0.29859
J_{18}	0.32	0.43	0.87	0.21	0.48435
J_{19}	0.65	0.54	0.65	0.98	0.15131
J_{20}	0.43	0.32	0.32	0.65	−0.01266
J_{21}	0.76	0.32	0.98	0.65	0.10433

Table 6 Order of valid jobs with their priority values by BPNN in twenty one jobs on seven machines problem

Valid job	P
J_{19}	0.801
J_4	0.544
J_{12}	0.510
J_{16}	0.357
J_{14}	0.287
J_2	0.213
J_9	0.195
J_3	0.184
J_{21}	0.167
J_{18}	0.078
J_8	0.003

per the cost value, the resulted schedule is a *reasonable* one. As per Equation (17), the result from the scheduler for the given problem is a satisfying one.

Scheduling problem with twenty one jobs on seven machines

Similarly a simulation of the scheduler with an unseen dataset of twenty one jobs on seven identical machines (M_1, M_2, M_3, M_4, M_5, M_6 and M_7) is illustrated in this section. Table 5 shows an unseen dataset of twenty one jobs with their respective correlation values.

Table 5 shows that there are eleven valid jobs (J_2, J_3, J_4, J_8, J_9, J_{12}, J_{14}, J_{16}, J_{18}, J_{19} and J_{21}) in the job queue. The validity, V, of the selected jobs is *true*. Priority order of the eleven valid jobs with their priority values, P, by the BPNN is shown in Table 6.

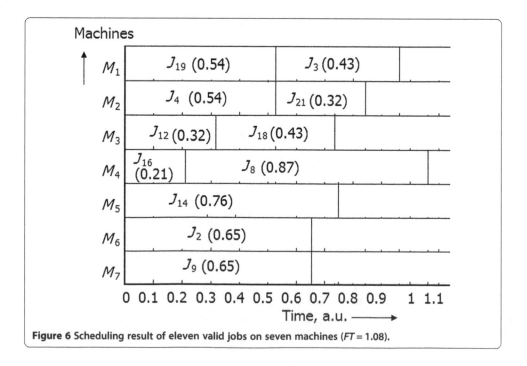

Figure 6 Scheduling result of eleven valid jobs on seven machines ($FT = 1.08$).

Figure 6 shows the scheduling of eleven valid jobs on seven identical machines (M_1, M_2, M_3, M_4, M_5, M_6 and M_7). The computation time, K, of each job is shown in brackets. The finishing time, FT, is 1.08 and cost value, C, is 0.263 and is *true* as per Equation (16). As per the cost value, the resulted schedule is a *reasonable* one and as per Equation (17), the result from the scheduler is a satisfying one.

Conclusions

The presented subjective job scheduler shows its ability in generating user satisfying schedules by establishing proper neural net training paradigm, exempting invalid jobs from the job queue and evaluating its results with a cost evaluation. The scheduler utilizes the customizable nature of the BPNN and the feature of the greedy algorithm.

The term 'job priority' of the scheduler cannot be described formally, that is, it is not possible to define the priority of a job in a normal way because that depends only on the given subjective influence. Therefore, the results of the scheduler are biased towards certain objective based on its subjective criteria.

The proposed scheduler is flexible enough to adopt views of various users for a given problem and it functions like an intelligent job scheduling agent for providing user satisfied results.

Additional file

Additional file 1: Table S1. sample seen dataset with four inputs and their respective output data patterns.

Competing interests
The author declares that he has no competing interests.

References
1. Cook SA (1971) The complexity of theorem proving procedures. Proceedings of the Third Annual ACM Symposium on the Theory of Computing 151:158
2. Garey MR, Johnson DS (1979) Computers and Intractability: A Guide to the Theory of NP-Completeness. Freeman and Co, New York
3. Rao VB, Rao HV (1996) Neural Networks & Fuzzy logic. BPB Publications, Delhi
4. Negnevitsky M (2005) Artificial Intelligence- A Guide to Intelligent Systems. Addison Wesley, Europe
5. Russell S, Norvig P (2004) Artificial Intelligence A Modern Approach. Pearson Education, New Jersey
6. Cormen TH, Leiserson CE, Rivest RL, Stein C (2001) Introduction to Algorithms. McGraw-Hill, Cambridge, Massachusetts London
7. Stinson S (1980) An Introduction to the Design and Analysis of Algorithms. Cambridge University Press, Cambridge
8. Anilkumar KG (2012) The Subjective Job Scheduler with a Satisfying Criterion Based a Backpropagation Neural Network. Network World, 2/2012, Technology Academy of Sciences of the Czech Republic (ASCR); Faculty of Transport, Czech Polytechnic University, Prague, 195–213
9. Cottet F, Delacroix J, Kaiser C, Mammeri Z (2002) Scheduling in Real-Time Systems. John Wiley & Sons Ltd, England
10. Anilkumar KG, Tanprasert T (2007) Generalized Job-shop Scheduler Using Feed Forward Neural Network and Greedy Alignment Procedure. In: Proc. IASTED Conference on Artificial Intelligence and Applications, IASTED (International Association of Science and Technology for Development). ACTA Press, Austria, pp 115–120
11. Johnson RA, Wichern DW (2002) Applied Multivariate Statistical Analysis. Prentice Hall, NJ

5

Development and testing of a visualization application software, implemented with wireless control system in smart home care

Jan Vanus[*], Pavel Kucera, Radek Martinek and Jiri Koziorek

* Correspondence: jan.vanus@vsb.cz
VSB TU Ostrava, Department of
Cybernetics and Biomedical
Engineering, Technical University of
Ostrava, 17. listopadu 15/2172, 708
33 Ostrava, Czech Republic

Abstract

This article describes the development of a visualization application software used to control operational and technical functions in the Smart Home system or Smart Home Care system via the wireless xComfort control system. Graphic visualization of a home electrical control system gives the user unprecedented comfort when controlling home systems. The user is able to obtain the information necessary to optimise the management of operational and technical functions in the building as well as information about energy consumption. Selected definitions of requirements for the visualization system, online access via the Internet, control via USB interface, and control requirements executed via mobile phone are the reasons why these technical elements were selected. This article describes their mutual relations, functions and connections within the system. At the end of this article we propose a method to test the reliability of the created software application as well as the wireless xComfort system under different conditions which stimulate different implementation methods applicable to a real building/ apartment unit. Measurement results can be used for the actual installation process and for optimal implementation of the active elements of the wireless system.

Keywords: Visualization; Wireless system; Smart home; Smart home care; Testing; Control

Introduction

Together with a growing standard of living in economically advanced countries, the human life is prolonged, which results in increased representation of elderly people in the society in Czech Republic (Figure 1). Their growth makes the society think about the specific needs of this age group [1]. With changes in life expectancy across the world, technologies enhancing well-being of individuals, specifically for older people, are subject to a new stream of research and development [2]. The nature of miniature wireless sensors and rapid developments in the wireless network technology have revolutionized home monitoring and surveillance systems. The new means and methods of collecting data efficiently and have led to novel applications for indoor wireless sensor networks [3]. Advances in computing, smart homes, and sensor technologies enable novel, longitudinal health monitoring applications in the home. Many home monitoring technologies have been proposed to detect health crises, support aging-in-place, and improve medical care [4]. To address the need for autonomous control of remote and distributed mobile

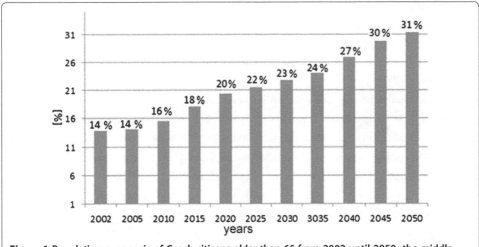

Figure 1 Population prognosis of Czech citizens older than 65 from 2002 until 2050 -the middle version (the Czech Statistical Office) [6].

systems, Machine-to-Machine (M2M) communications are rapidly gaining attention from both academia and industry. M2M communications have recently been deployed in smart grid, home networking, health care, and vehicular networking environments [5].

A considerable part of the behavior in smart environments relies on event-driven and rule specification. Rules are the mechanism most often used to enable user customization of the environment [7]. Some research workers propose socially acceptable physiological signal monitoring system consisting of a natural sensing interface and an intuitive information display [8]. Other studies in economic psychology have repeatedly revealed that energy consumption behavior in the household could be optimized through the provision of frequent and immediate feedback [9-11]. Another system is designed to make integration and interconnections of new metering devices and visualizations simple and constitutes a good basis for further research on awareness of energy usage in our (future) living environments [9]. Next was presented a fully distributed system and architecture based on a network of smart cameras to perform georeferenced tracking and activity recognition. Additionally an intuitive visualization was presented, where all information were integrated in one world model that is available ubiquitously [12]. A different paper proposes a new way of providing virtual smart home services using tangible mixed reality (MR), which provides more cost-effective and reliable visualization and simulation of the existing pervasive environment [13]. Other way of visualization is new HMI (Human-Machine Interface) system, which is based on statically positioned indicators for data output and a touch screen above them for data input. Indication elements consist of discrete light emitting diodes (LED), LED matrices, segment-type displays and small sized graphical visualization panels [14]. Some studies focuses on the application-layer simulation to propose a Visualization System of Context-aware Application Scenario Planning (VS-CaSP) for assisting non-technical developers and end-users in rapidly and easily designing the application scenario of smart buildings and in performing the accept-able and predictable simulation and evaluation [15]. The promising trend of visualization technology for textiles facilitates home consumers to approach and access both market information and application guidelines with easy means such as a remote controller, therefore, may help to promote the home textile consumptions significantly [16]. One of key components in the development of smart home technology is the detection and recognition of activities of daily life. Based on a self-adaptive neural network called Growing Self-Organizing Maps (GSOM), was presented a new computational approach to cluster analysis of human activities of daily living within smart home environment [17].

In connection with the dynamic progress of research and development of the above mentioned Tele Care, Health Care, Smart Home, Smart Home Care, Smart Grids, Smart Cities, Smart Metering technologies we would like to react to these trends by creating a platform for testing of new technologies. One of the segments of the built platform is the area of the support of elderly citizens living independently in their homes. There are efforts to use the above-mentioned current modern Smart Home Care technologies in terms of convenient controlling of home operational and technical functions by citizens over 65 years of age. Some companies in Czech market offer remote convenient controlling of Smart Home operational and technical functions using all available standard technologies such as mobile phones, tablets, iPods, iPads, iPhones and suchlike. However, in order to be connected to the supplied bus or wireless system, it is necessary to pay extra money for the license or the corresponding communication interface. The article focuses on the description of development and implementation of the visualization software of the application for controlling of home operational and technical functions within Smart Home Care using wireless xComfort system with subsequent testing in the environment of an apartment house.

Describe of the created visualization appliaction SmartHomeApp

In order to support the possibility of senior citizens living independently in their homes, we have created in our business a visualisation application called SmartHomeApp for intuitive, comfortable and remote controlling of home service systems within Smart Home Care (Figure 2).

In terms of the actual implementation of wiring, it is desirable to use technologies utilizing wireless technology (actuators and sensors) in houses with the already existing wiring. For control operational and technical functions in Smart Home and Smart Home Care, xComfort wireless technology is used. This technology uses 868.3 MHz radio frequency for communication. Transmission takes up a maximum of 1% of the entire time. Data are being confirmed during radio frequency communication between the actuator and the sensor. Data transfer may be protected by a password. Increase of the reach of RF signal between individual components is possible thanks to automatic signal transfer call Routing.

In terms of communication between the database and the visualization and active elements, a software driver was designed, which makes this communication possible. The developed visualization software SmartHomeApp was designed with regard to web interface requirements, ability to control the software via a mobile phone, via voice control and also with regard to easy expendability, scalability and modularity. The system consists of three logical parts (Figure 3):

user interface,
controlling computer,
USB interface/active elements.

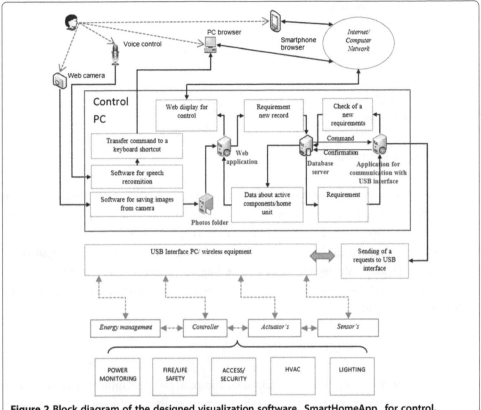

Figure 2 Block diagram of the designed visualization software SmartHomeApp for control, monitoring and visualization of operational and technical functions in Smart Home or Smart Home Care with xComfort wireless technology.

User interface acts as a layer between the user and the controlling computer. It displays system status information and provides inspection and control elements used to control active elements in the apartment.

The controlling computer secures interconnection between a device using USB interface and the user interface. It provides an environment for smooth operation of software elements used for active element control process. It accepts and registers whole system requests. It checks and sends changes, i.e. requests for system changes. It accepts change confirmations and forwards them to the system and to the user interface. It also stores information used later for optimization of system actuators installed in the housing unit. USB interface sends requests to active elements in the apartment and receives answer which is then forwarded to the control computer. By interconnecting these layers, it is possible to implement the created visualisation system for controlling of home operational and technical functions using wireless xComfort system. The process of model implementation of SmartHomeApp visualisation software:

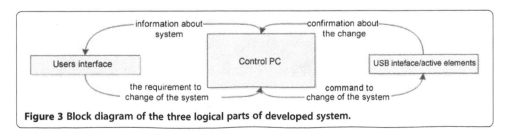

Figure 3 Block diagram of the three logical parts of developed system.

1. Creation of an apartment layout.
2. Specifications of used components.
3. Analysis of communication protocol and testing of packets.
4. Creation of visualisation application software (analysis, visualization implementation process).
5. Description of the use of other software applications.
6. Application testing.

1. Creation of apartment layout

The created visualisation of a model housing unit includes a hallway, bathroom, kitchen joined with the living room and a workroom joined with the sleeping room. The visualization is implemented as a clickable map (Figure 4). The floor layout of the apartment unit serves as the base for the clickable map. For the needs of the visualisation, the layout is divided into logical blocks according to rooms and the manner of their utilization. This division gives the user better view of rooms and simpler access to the desired active element.

2. Specifications of used components

Further it was necessary to specify individual components of xComfort wireless system with subsequent programming, the so-called setting of links between actuators using software tool EATON RF-System. The mutual cohesion of actuators and sensors may be monitored according to the lines on the computer screen (Figure 4).

3. Analysis of communication protocol and testing of packets

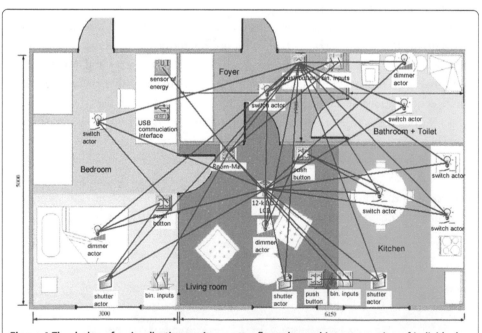

Figure 4 The design of a visualization environment   floor plan and interconnection of individual components in the wireless xComfort system of a Smart Home Care.

The communication protocol describes communication between individual components of xComfort wireless technology. The owner of this protocol is Eaton and its use and publishing is subject to contractual arrangement. The document describes in detail the communication in the Basic and the Comfort Mode. The following components were used for testing of the communication protocol:

switch actuator (CSAU-01/01),
blinds actuator (CSJA-01/02),
dimming actuator (CDAU-01/03),
binary input (CBEU-02/02),
push button (CTAA-02/01),
parameterization interface (CRSZ-00/01),
communication interface (CKOZ-00/14).

The shape of the packets sent to USB interface is defined in the communication protocol. The test was implemented on active connection elements of testing case using SimpleHIDWrite software. The following commands were used for controlling of the above mentioned actuators:

switch on,
switch off,
brighter
darker,
stop,
fully close,
fully open,
close one step,
open one step.

4. Description of the design of visualization and application software

It is a set of technical solutions covering various levels of controls, monitoring and visualization of statuses of controlled devices (xComfort wireless system actuators). One of the main parts of the system is an SQL server, where all system statuses and control instructions are saved. The control instructions are recorded. Each new record is recognized by the application and sent through control interface to the respective controlled elements. Then the controlled element sends information confirming whether the request was actually carried out. If the information specifying that the request was done is received, the status of the control device will change and the request is marked as completed. Here, the control unit represents visualization software, displays statuses of individual devices and options for their configurations. By using the database server it is possible to monitor the recorded instructions and processes, to evaluate results of individual instructions and thus find an optimal solution. The actual implementation of visualization was divided into multiple stages:

Analysis of SmartHomeApp web visualization,

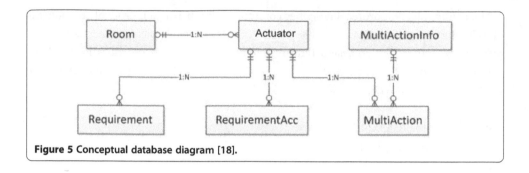

Figure 5 Conceptual database diagram [18].

Data analysis,
 USBinterfaceTransfer software analysis,
Visualization implementation process   client,
Visualization implementation process   server.
Analysis of SmartHomeApp web visualization

Web visualization SmartHomeApp is used by the user to control intelligent electrical system components. The key function is to control actuators through direct changes in the electrical system and collective/bulk modification of the electrical system [18].

Data analysis

Data analysis is described through a conceptual database diagram (Figure 5) and through a database scheme (Figure 6) with data dictionaries/terms used in Requirement , RequirementAcc , MultiActionInfo , MultiAction , Room and Actuator tables.

USBinterfaceTransfer software analysis

The USBinterfaceTransfer tool is used to send requests to USB interface. USB interface will send requests to active elements in the intelligent electrical system. The program repeatedly searches for incomplete/unexecuted records and then marks them as completed/done [18].

Visualization implementation process   client

Selection of technical elements necessary for the respective visualization is directly dependent on our efforts to make actuator controlling accessible via web browser and through a computer network or the Internet (Figure 7).

This part contains descriptions and sample uses of technical elements, which were used to create visualization environment for the client/at the clients facility. The client represents a web browser used by the user to access the application. If voice control system is used, it refers to an add-on program, which controls the web browser. Information provided to the user of the relevant web browser is dynamically loaded from the database, in this situation from MS SQL.

Transfer of information between the control computer and client is done via HTTP protocol. Document is structured using HTML and SCC. JavaScript is used as a higher form of a comfortable control system [19].

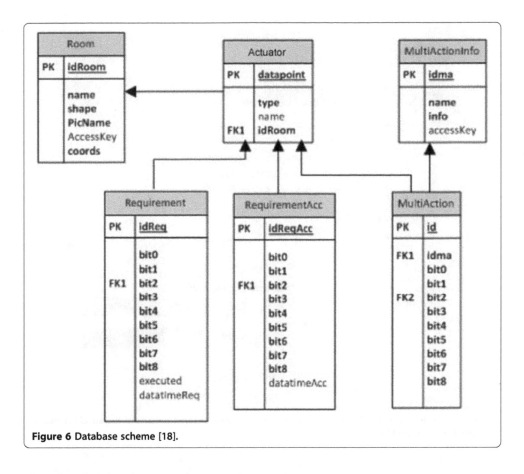

Figure 6 Database scheme [18].

Visualization implementation process   server

System elements in server are selected based on new trends, scalability and easy system expandability. The server side refers to all logical software products ensuring proper operation of applications used to control xComfort intelligent electrical installations. To achieve this, two programs are used: SmartHomeApp and USBinterfaceTransfer . The first program is created in ASP.NET environment, and the second one in .NET environment and both use C# language [19].

5. Software Tools Used in the Visualization Application

Software tools used in the application are described below:

Web Server
A computer program responsible for resolving http clients requests. For a web server, a web browser is considered to be the client. It is an essential part of web applications operation. The web server sends its response as a HTML document; it can be created dynamically, using, for example, PHP or ASP technology.

Database Server
The following section describes SmartHomeApp database structure, process of its creation and usage. The entire database is a subject of an analysis; just most important schemes will be described here.

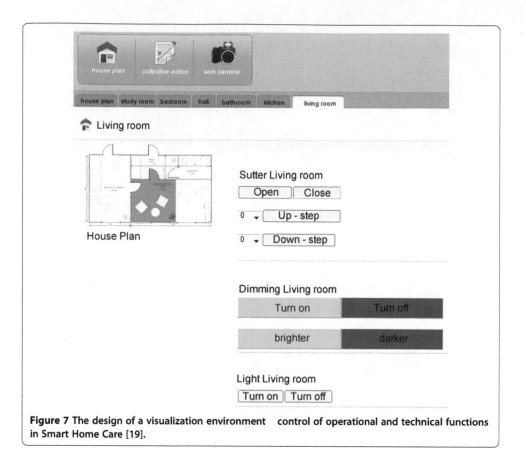

Figure 7 The design of a visualization environment   control of operational and technical functions in Smart Home Care [19].

Database creation:

CREATE DATABASE Smart Home COLLATE Czech CI AS; This command created the Smart Home database, and Collate command to set a character set was established. Czech character set was set by COLLATE Czech CI AS command which is case-insensitive (CI) and diacritics-sensitive.

Room table creation

Contains information about the room, vital to run the SmartHomeApp .

```
CREATE TABLE [dbo].[Room](
[idRoom] [int] PRIMARY KEY NOT NULL,
[name] [nvarchar](50) NULL,
[shape] [nvarchar](50) NULL,
[coords] [nvarchar](50) NULL,
[PicName] [nvarchar](50) NULL,
[accessKey] [nchar](1) NULL)
```

idRoom -It serves as a unique room identifier in the database.

Name -Room name to display in the system.

Shape -A basic shape to draw the room on the flat map.

Coords -Flat size coordinates.

PicName -An image file, showing room position drawn in.

accesKey -A selected shortcut key, necessary for simple, trouble free voice control.

PRIMARY KEY NOT NULL rule defines the column as a primary key, UNIQUE by default, but the UNIQUE clause can t be present.

Actuator table creation

Contains information about all actuators in the intelligent home system, which have to be controlled.

CREATE TABLE [dbo]. [actuator]

```
CREATE TABLE [dbo].[actor](
[datapoint] [bit] PRIMARY KEY NOT NULL,
[type] [bit] NULL,
[name] [nvarchar](50) NULL,
[idRoom] [int] NULL)
```

Datapoint Unique

actuator identifier in the system.

Type -Actuator type, blind or other.

Name -Name, actuator label in the system. It shows during the control process.

idRoom -Room identifier.

Requirement table creation

Contains commands for active elements of the flat. It contains both commands executed by saving a value in the executed column and commands waiting to be executed.

```
CREATE TABLE [dbo].[requirement](
[IdReq] [int] PRIMARY KEY NOT NULL,
[bit0] [bit] NULL,
[bit1] [bit] NULL,
[bit2] [bit] NULL,
[bit3] [bit] NULL,
[bit4] [bit] NULL,
[bit5] [bit] NULL,
[bit6] [bit] NULL,
[bit7] [bit] NULL,
[bit8] [bit] NULL,
[executed] [int] NULL)
```

idReq -Request number.

bit0   bit8 -A hexadecimal value, constituting the command packet.

executed -Information about request execution.

The above mentioned described the database core for active xComfort elements visualization.

By design, database engine usage doesn t matter. However, it is important to keep information about rooms and their attributes, and this goal is accomplished by the Room table. It is important keep a record which actuator belongs to a room, its type for different control and a number, under which it is registered in the active elements system, and, finally, saving requests for system changes. Command records enable to use the commands later during analyses. The database schema described above is not very suitable to analyze system behavior but it provides us with a core to run the system. To analyze operation and technology tools of the flat it is necessary to extend the system.

Web Application

SmartHomeApp web application is visualization software of the proposed system. It is a web application built on ASP.NET technology. One of the core requests to run a web application is a web server. To run an application for .NET, a framework is necessary. SmartHomeApp requires Framework 3.5. The best tool to meet requirements of a web application based on ASP.NET architecture is IIS (Internet information services). It is a set of Microsoft applications suited for Internet, including a web server. Thanks to its integration into the operating system it can cooperate with applications built on .NET very well and it can run web applications merged with other infrastructures [19].

USBinterfaceTransfer

USBinterfaceTrancfer helps to ensure communication between the database and USB communication interface. It is loosely based on the Generic HID open source library from EATON. The program is based on the .NET Framework 2.0 platform and written in C# language.

It is designed to keep detecting new records with new requests from the database. If a new request is found, the tool sends it to the USB communication interface.

MyVoice

The MyVoice software tool serves to recognize voice commands. To control Smart-HomeApp visualisation software by voice, a shortcut key control method was selected. It is necessary to keep perfect records about using defined keys for shortcuts. To fully control the system by voice, shortcuts have to be set for every feature, from menu keys to the room list to each function.

Generally, the browser prefers a HTML document shortcut key, but for MyVoice the situation is different. For voice control of technical functions is necessary solve problem with additive noise in speech signal [20].

Webcam

A webcam continually saves photos and then the images are displayed in a web browser. This principle is used by many computer programs. The Camera 2004 tool is used in the project. When designing the Smart Home Care with assistance service, the Distributed Direct Sensing system can be used. With regard to the senior citizens needs (respecting the privacy), it is necessary to activate the camera in dependence on evaluation of a predefined unexpected event (water overflow, detection of smoke, etc.). The citizen can decide when the camera should be activated. It is clear that modern technologies have only a supporting function in a comprehensive approach to the senior citizens needs [21].

6. Testing the Reliability of Wireless System for Operational and Technical Functions Control in Smart Home

Signal quality measuring method between the actuators (switching, dimming, window blinds) and the USB interface was selected to test the reliability of operational and technical functions which are controlled wirelessly in a Smart House using the proposed visualization application software (Figure 8).

In predetermined distances was placed a computer with visualization software

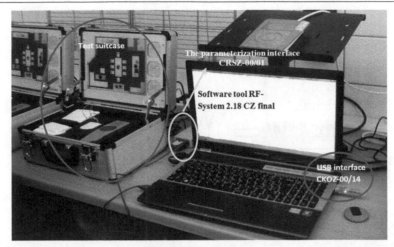

Figure 8 The laboratory workspace for design, programming, measurement, control and simulation of operational and technical functions in the Smart Home Care with using of the wireless xComfort system.

SmartHomeApp together with a connected USB interface CKOZ-00/14 and a testing briefcase containing a model of an apartment unit (Figure 9), (Figure 10), (Figure 11). Measurements were performed using parameterization interface CRSZ-00/01 and software tool Eaton RF-System 2.18 CZ Final. Then was measured of maximum communication distance between the actuator (switching, dimming, window blinds) and USB communication interface in all measured environments with using of the created visualization program SmartHomeApp .

The distance /[m] measurement -environment without any obstacles

An ideal status is if no solid obstacles stand in the way of the radio frequency signal travelling between the transmitter and receiver (Figure 9). Measurements showed huge differences in signal reception, mostly between window blinds and other actuators (Figure 12), (Table 1). Measurements also included testing of maximal signal reach for active switching element. Through additional testing was confirmed that USB interface using SmatHomeApp visualization operates reliably within a distance up to 150 meters.

During these measurements was established the optimal distance 20 m for switch actuator and dimming actuator and 10 m for shutter actuator (Table 1). The parameterization interface experiences serious problems trying to find active components in distances over 20 meters. This also limits the measurement of the signal quality.

The distance /[m] measurement -environment with one brick wall

Brick materials are the most common materials used to build houses and apartments. Brick wall testing represents a real life model and practical application (Figure 10). Signal loss due to a brick wall is directly connected to the thickness of the wall even though brick clay is a material with good properties when compared with other materials such as reinforced concrete structures or metal materials. There is possible observe and compare signal loss with a signal strength travelling through an environment without any obstacles (Figure 13), (Table 2). The maximum distance for control switching actuator using USB interface and SmartHomeApp visualization is 96 meters.

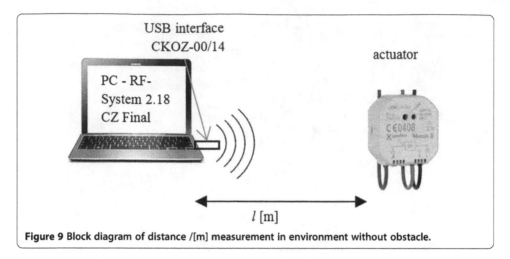

USB interface
CKOZ-00/14

actuator

PC - RF-
System 2.18
CZ Final

l [m]

Figure 9 Block diagram of distance /[m] measurement in environment without obstacle.

During these measurements was established the optimal distance 20 m for switch actuator and dimming actuator and 10 m for shutter actuator (Table 2). The parameterization interface experiences serious problems trying to find active components in distances over 20 meters. This also limits the measurement of the signal quality.

The distance /[m] measurement -environment with two brick walls

We have also simulated real-life conditions using an environment with two brick walls. This represents a situation when the signal needs to travel through one room for example, through a corridor between two rooms (Figure 11).

It is clear that in this scenario the signal strength travelling through two brick walls rapidly deteriorates (Figure 14), (Table 3).

In our simulated environment the first wall was placed directly behind the USB communication interface and the second wall was placed two meters from the first one. During these measurements was established the optimal distance 20 m for switch actuator and dimming actuator and 10 m for shutter actuator (Table 3). The parameterization interface experiences serious problems trying to find active components in distances over 20 meters. This also limits the measurement of the signal quality.

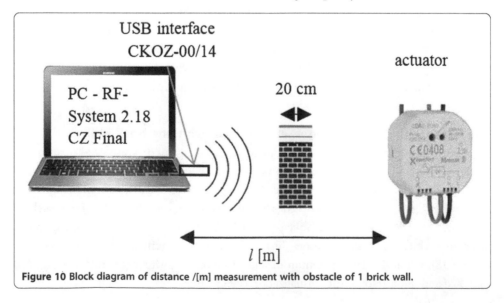

USB interface
CKOZ-00/14

actuator

PC - RF-
System 2.18
CZ Final

20 cm

l [m]

Figure 10 Block diagram of distance /[m] measurement with obstacle of 1 brick wall.

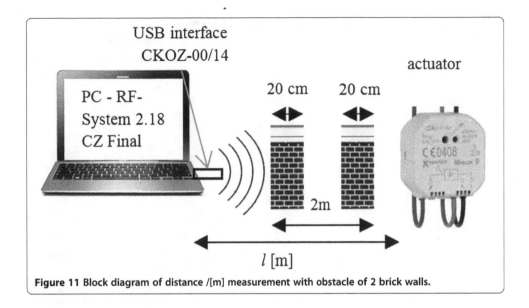

Figure 11 Block diagram of distance /[m] measurement with obstacle of 2 brick walls.

Discussion

The future development of visualization and intelligent houses.The rapid development of technologies available for houses today has created a situation where several electronic systems operate simultaneously in one house. Therefore, the integration of various installed technologies has become an important focus of many manufacturers producing these systems [22]. An automation control system which uses a wireless radio frequency may be integrated into these systems thanks to visualization tools. So this would enable us to have all technologies in one place and only distribute them around the house. One way to achieve this situation is to create a home multimedia center, where the functions of a multimedia server are handled by a small, low -power computer. Connecting to the Internet via a large number of computer peripherals allows us to connect many technologies that otherwise operate independently. As an example we can use integration of television, radio, and control of electrical systems and the Internet. Thanks to Wi-Fi [23], other devices at home may access the Internet as well. At the same time we can use a multimedia server to listen to Internet radios, or watch TV and store movies on a multimedia server, access the Internet and play computer games. Thanks to visualization,

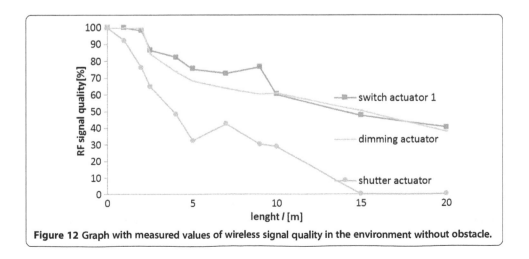

Figure 12 Graph with measured values of wireless signal quality in the environment without obstacle.

Table 1 The distance measurement in environment without any obstacle

Switch actuator		Shutter actuator		Dimming actuator	
Distance (from the source)	RF signal quality	Distance (from the source)	RF signal quality	Distance (from the source)	RF signal quality
/[m]	[%]	/[m]	[%]	/[m]	[%]
0	100	0	100	0	100
1	100	1	92.2	1	100
2	98.1	2	76	2	100
2.5	86.6	2.5	64.7	2.5	84.2
4	82.3	4	48.3	4	73.6
5	75.3	5	32.4	5	68.2
7	72.8	7	42.6	7	63.7
9	76.5	9	30.3	9	60.3
10	60.1	10	28.8	10	60.8
15	47.6	15	0	15	50.4
20	40.5	20	0	20	38

electrical wiring may also be easily controlled because the multimedia server can distribute the visualization system to other devices, such as smartphones, for example.

Integration of visualization

The designed visualization program is a software tool used to control the operational and technical functions of the relevant electrical system. Based on the process described in the analysis, this tool can be created using various programming languages/codes. The proposed solution for the integration of visualization was created with regard to ASP. NET technology and the C # language. The aim here is not the definition of an actual solution, but to demonstrate an alternative where this technology may take your house.

Raspberry Pi

Raspberry Pi is a computer the size of a credit card; it is small and energy-efficient, yet fully usable as a regular PC. Thanks to its small size and very low energy consumption, it is the

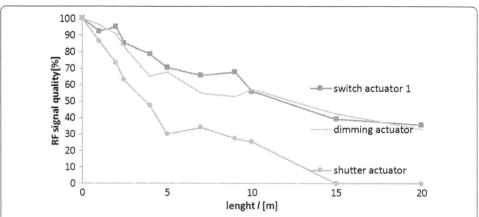

Figure 13 Graph with measured values of wireless signal quality in environment with obstacle of 1 brick wall.

Table 2 The distance measurement in environment with one obstacle

Switch actuator		Shutter actuator		Dimming actuator	
Distance (from the source)	RF signal quality	Distance (from the source)	RF signal quality	Distance (from the source)	RF signal quality
l[m]	[%]	l[m]	[%]	l[m]	[%]
0	100	0	100	0	100
1	92.4	1	86.2	1	96.4
2	95.1	2	73.5	2	90.6
2.5	85.3	2.5	63	2.5	83.1
4	78.8	4	47.2	4	65.3
5	70.6	5	29.9	5	67.8
7	65.8	7	34	7	54.8
9	67.7	9	27.3	9	53
10	56	10	25.2	10	57.3
15	39.5	15	0	15	42.6
20	35.9	20	0	20	33.1

ideal solution for continuously running applications. This makes it possible to use this device as a multimedia server, and in case of visualization also as a web server. The manufacturer offers an ARM operating system distributed as Linux versions Debian and Arch.

Database

A designed visualization program is a software product that utilizes many advanced features and large database machines. It is not necessary to use robust database servers such as MS SQL or Oracle. Compact and small databases may offer many benefits, in particular during distribution.

SQLite

The difference between a database built on a client server and SQLite is that the database server is not running as an independent process. SQLite is a small library that can be used simply by adding links or by adding a simple interface. Each SQLite database is stored in a .dbm file. The entire library is developed in C language and requires very low resources.

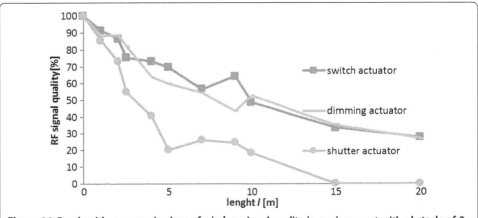

Figure 14 Graph with measured values of wireless signal quality in environment with obstacle of 2 brick walls.

Table 3 The distance measurement in environment with two obstacles

Switch actuator		Shutter actuator		Dimming actuator	
Distance (from the source)	RF signal quality	Distance (from the source)	RF signal quality	Distance (from the source)	RF signal quality
l[m]	[%]	l[m]	[%]	l[m]	[%]
0	100	0	100	0	100
1	91.4	1	85.5	1	88.3
2	86.6	2	73.2	2	88.8
2.5	75.5	2.5	54.8	2.5	82.5
4	73	4	40.4	4	64
5	69.7	5	20.1	5	60
7	56.5	7	26.2	7	54.4
9	64.5	9	24.6	9	43.6
10	48.7	10	18.5	10	52.7
15	33.6	15	0	15	35.1
20	28	20	0	20	27.3

The library itself uses only 25 kilobytes of memory. Thanks to these characteristics, it is the ideal candidate for microcomputers such as Raspberry Pi.

ASP.NET and C#

ASP.NET and C# are Microsoft technologies. However, if we are talking about Raspberry Pi and Linux distributions, such as the Debian system, there is no need to disregard these solutions.

Mono project

This is an open-source implementation of the NET Framework, according to official ECMA standards. With the real binary compatibility it is possible to put these files directly in Mono, even if they were created in the NET Framework.

Assessment of smart house development progress

The potential of the solution presented here is great. Thanks to the versatility of Raspberry Pi, really deep integration of electronic devices may be achieved. This is one of the ways visualization may eventually go and reach people interested in smart systems. It is a path that can bring a lot of benefits in terms of distributions, as it can deliver more variable solutions, and simplify implementation from the customers perspective, or from the point of view of the technician who is installing the system.

Conclusions

The first part of the article describes the development of the visualization application software SmartHomeApp and the structure with a wireless system xComfort for comfortable control of a building service system in the Smart Home or in the Smart Home Care. The visualization application program described above is designed as a web application using DBMS MS SQL to save operational data. In terms of communication between the database and the visualization and active elements, a software driver was designed, which makes this communication possible.

Visualization was designed with regard to web interface requirements, ability to control the software via a mobile phone and also with regard to easy expandability, scalability and modularity. Using modern technologies ASP.NET, MS SQL, NET C# allowed us to meet all these requirements. Availability of optimized web visualization application for various de-vices was achieved thanks to the use of HTML 5 and CSS 3 technologies. In addition to independent saving process of requirements affecting active system element behavior, data may also be used for presentation demonstrating the history of the system use. Data may also be presented in a certain way as to allow later optimization of the entire intelligent electrical installation. Further, an option to integrate web cameras and voice control into the system were also examined. The MyVoice software was used to control the visualization by voice and visualization requirements for integration between those two elements were also described. The second part of the article describes the testing method of the reliability of wireless control system for technical and operational functions control. Measured values correspond with tolerances shown in the USB communication device technical documentation. Even though the signal quality was rather low, there is possible active components control reliably and without any information loss. The quality of RF signal was measured with using parameterization interface. Measuring was done in a real apartment and not in a laboratory. Measuring of maximum communication distances between the actuator (switching, dimming, window blinds) and USB communication interface was done in all measured environments including. During these measurements was established the optimal distance 10 m for of the all wireless elements control.

Competing interests

The authors declare that they have no competing interests.

Authors contributions

All authors contributed to the content of this paper. All authors read and approved the final manuscript.

Acknowledgements

This paper has been elaborated in the framework of the project Opportunity for young researchers, reg. no. CZ.1.07/ 2.3.00/30.0016, supported by Operational Program Education for Competitiveness and co-financed by the European Social Fond and the state budget of the Czech Republic. This work was supported by project SP2014/156, Microprocessor based systems for control and measurement applications. of Student Grant System, VSB-TU Ostrava.

References

1. Vanus J, Koziorek J, Hercik R (2013) Design of a smart building control with view to the senior Citizens needs. Programmable Devices and Embedded Systems 12(1):422 427

2. Amirabdollahian F, Op den Akker R, Bedaf S, Bormann R, Draper H, Evers V, Gelderblom GJ, Ruiz CG, Hewson D, Hu N, Iacono I, Koay KL, Krose B, Marti P, Michel H, Prevot-Huille H, Reiser U, Saunders J, Sorell T, Dautenhahn K (2013) Accompany: Acceptable robotiCs COMPanions for AgeiNg Years - Multidimensional Aspects of Human-System Interactions, Human System Interaction (HSI). The 6th International Conference, Sopot, pp 570 577, Doi: 10.1109/HSI.2013.6577882

3. Basu D, Moretti G, Sen Gupta G, Marsland S (2013) Wireless Sensor Network Based Smart Home: Sensor Selection, Deployment and Monitoring, Sensors Applications Symposium (SAS). IEEE, Galveston, TX, pp 49 54, Doi: 10.1109/SAS.2013.6493555

4. Beaudin JS, Intille SS, Morris ME (2006) To track or not to track: user reactions to concepts in longitudinal health monitoring. J Med Internet Res 8(4):e29, http://www.jmir.org/2006/4/e29, Doi: 10.2196/jmir.8.4.e29

5. Booysen MJ, Gilmore JS, Zeadally S, Van Rooyen GJ (2012) Machine-to-Machine (M2M) Communications in Vehicular Networks. Ksii Transactions on Internet and Information Systems 6(2):529 546

6. Population prognosis Czech republic http://www.czso.cz/csu/2004ediciniplan.nsf/p/4025-04 [cit. 2014-3-11]

7. Catala A, Pons P, Jaen J, Mocholi JA, Navarro E (2013) A meta-model for dataflow-based rules in smart environments: evaluating user comprehension and performance. Sci Comput Program 78(10):19301950

8. Choi A, Woo W (2010) Daily physiological signal monitoring system for fostering social well-being in smart spaces. Cybern Syst 41(3):262 279

9. Fercher AJ, Hitz M, Leitner G (2009) Raising awareness of energy consumption in smart living environments. In: Callaghan V, Kameas A, Reyes A, Royo D, Weber M (eds) Conference: Intelligent Environments 2009 - Proceedings of the 5th International Conference on Intelligent Environments. Intelligent Environments, Barcelona, Spain, pp 91 98, Doi: 10.3233/978-1-60750-034-6-91

10. Ghidini G, Das SK, Gupta V, Ieee (2012) FuseViz: A Framework for Web-Based Data Fusion and Visualization in Smart Environments. 9th Ieee International Conference on Mobile Ad-Hoc and Sensor Systems, , pp 468 472

11. Giacomin J, Bertola D (2012) Human emotional response to energy visualisations. Int J Ind Ergon 42(6):542 552

12. Fleck S, Loy R, Vollrath C, Walter F, Strasser W (2007) Smartclassysurv - A Smart Camera Network for Distributed Tracking and Activity Recognition and Its Application to Assisted Living, ICDSC '07. First ACM/IEEE International Conference, 25-28 Sept. 2007. Distributed Smart Cameras, Vienna, p 211, Doi: 10.1109/ICDSC.2007.4357526

13. Lee JY, Seo D, Rhee GW, Hong SH, Nam JS (2008) Virtual and Pervasive Smart Home Services Using Tangible Mixed Reality, Parallel and Distributed Processing with Applications, 2008. ISPA '08. International Symposium, Sydney, NSW, pp 403 408, Doi: 10.1109/ISPA.2008.92

14. Pecka A, Osadcuks V (2010) Discrete Indicators and Touch-Panel Based Human-Machine Interface. Applied Information and Communication Technologies, Jelgava, Latvia, pp 295 300

15. Su J-M, Huang C-F (2014) An easy-to-use 3D visualization system for planning context-aware applications in smart buildings. Computer Standards & Interfaces 36(2):312 326

16. Su ZL, Wang RM, Wang Z, Xie HJ (2010) Channel Service for the Digital Home Oriented Textile Consumption. 3rd International Symposium of Textile Bioengineering and Informatics, Shanghai, Peoples R China, pp 154 158, Doi: 10.3993/tbis2010029

17. Zheng H, Wang H, Black N, Ieee (2008) Human activity detection in smart home environment with self-adaptive neural networks. Proceedings of 2008 Ieee International Conference on Networking, Sensing and Control 1 and 2:1505 1510

18. Vanus J, Kucera P, Koziorek J (2014) The software analysis used for visualization of technical functions control in smart home care, 3rd computer science on-line conference 2014 (CSOC 2014). Series: Advances in Intelligent Systems and Computing 285:549 558, doi:10.1007/978-3-319-06740-7_47

19. Vanus J, Kucera P, Koziorek J (2014) Visualization software designed to control operational and technical functions in smart homes, 3rd computer science on-line conference 2014 (CSOC 2014). Series: Advances in Intelligent Systems and Computing 285:559 569, doi:10.1007/978-3-319-06740-7_48

20. Martinek R, Al-Wohaishi M, Zidek J (2010) Software Based Flexible Measuring Systems for Analysis of Digitally Modulated Systems. In Roedunet International Conference (RoEduNet), 2010, 9th edn. IEEE, , pp 397 402

21. Chorianopoulos K (2013) Collective intelligence within web video. Human-centric Computing and Information Sciences 3:10, doi:10.1186/2192-1962-3-10

22. Augusto JC, Callaghan V, Cook D, Kameas A, Satoh I (2013) Intelligent Environments: a manifesto. Human-centric Computing and Information Sciences 3:12, doi:10.1186/2192-1962-3-12

23. Luo Y, Hoeber O, Chen Y (2013) Enhancing Wi-Fi fingerprinting for indoor positioning using human-centric collaborative feedback. Human-centric Computing and Information Sciences 3:2, doi:10.1186/2192-1962-3-2

6

Sensing spatial and temporal coordination in teams using the smartphone

Sebastian Feese[1*], Michael Joseph Burscher[2], Klaus Jonas[2] and Gerhard Tröster[1]

*Correspondence:
feese@ife.ee.ethz.ch
[1] Wearable Computing Laboratory,
ETH Zurich, Gloriastrasse 35, 8092
Zurich CH, Switzerland
Full list of author information is
available at the end of the article

Abstract

Teams are at the heart of today's organizations and their performance is crucial for organizational success. It is therefore important to understand and monitor team processes. Traditional approaches employ questionnaires, which have low temporal resolution or manual behavior observation, which is labor intensive and thus costly. In this work, we propose to apply mobile behavior sensing to capture team coordination processes in an automatic manner, thereby enabling cost-effective and real-time monitoring of teams. In particular, we use the built-in sensors of smartphones to sense interpersonal body movement alignment and to detect moving sub-groups. We aggregate the data on team level in form of networks that capture a) how long team members are together in a sub-group and b) how synchronized team members move. Density and centralization metrics extract team coordination indicators from the team networks. We demonstrate the validity of our approach in firefighting teams performing a realistic training scenario and investigate the link between the coordination indicators and team performance as well as experienced team coordination. Our method enables researchers and practitioners alike to capture temporal and spatial team coordination automatically and objectively in real-time.

Keywords: Wearable; Smartphone; Mobile behavior sensing; Network sensing; Team coordination; Team performance

Introduction

Teams and team work are essential in today's organizations [1]. To perform well as a team, members need to share information, coordinate their actions and support each other. These activities are commonly referred to as team processes, which convert inputs such as individual members' abilities into outcomes such as team performance [2].

In order to improve team performance, it is mandatory to monitor how team members work and interact with another. However, current approaches to monitor these team processes in situ and over time are limited. While questionnaires are ill-suited to capture the temporal sequence of interactions, manual behavioral observation that would be more suitable for that purpose is notably absent from group research [3]. One reason is that behavioral observation is time-consuming as the manual encoding of behavior usually takes many times longer than the actual interaction. As a result, most studies are limited to small samples and short observational periods. Consequently, researchers have called for new measurement systems capable of capturing the complexity of team processes [4].

In our view, ubiquitous computing can help to continuously monitor team processes in realistic environments and provide a new observational tool that can support team researchers and trainers with objective data on how team members interact and work with each other.

In this paper, we focus on team coordination, which is regarded a central teamwork process [5,6]. Team "coordination occurs when team members perform the same or compatible actions at the same time [7], p. 423". Following a mobile behavior sensing approach [8], we propose to automatically capture the temporal and spatial aspects of team coordination with the built-in sensors of smartphones. On the one hand, we capture the temporal aspect of coordination by continuously measuring and comparing motion activity levels of team members to quantify how well team members align their movement in time. On the other hand, we assess the spatial component of coordination by detecting moving sub-groups from radio-based proximity information. In particular, we make the following contribution:

1. We present an approach to use the smartphone as a sensing platform to capture individual and team behaviors. We record body movement of each team member and estimate proximity between team members.

2. From the sensor data, we extract sub-group and movement alignment networks that summarize a) how long team members are together in a sub-group and b) how synchronized team members move. Further, we propose to summarize the structures of the extracted team networks using density and centralization metrics as used in social network analysis.

3. We validate our approach in a study with professional firefighting teams performing high fidelity training missions in a firehouse and show how the proposed coordination indicators are correlated with objective and subjective coordination measures.

Related work

Team work

Team coordination in safety-critical environments has been assessed using different methodologies. A common approach includes behavioral observation. By observing recorded videos of the team interaction and encoding predefined behaviors, researchers can investigate temporal aspects of team processes such as patterns of interaction and changes over time [9-11]. Behavioral observation, however, is very resource-intensive and impractical for applied settings.

Another approach to team processes focuses on the structural characteristics of teamwork. Crawford et al. recently introduced a theoretical framework that considers structure [12]. By drawing on social network analysis (SNA), their theory proposes different types of networks to provide a more comprehensive explanation of the relationship between team processes and performance. SNA expresses the social environment as patterns or regularities in relationships among interaction units [13]. These relationships (i.e., ties) can be of different types. For example, a communication network could capture which members of a department communicate with each other on a regular basis. Such a network can reveal those members that are central to the dissemination of information within this department. The relationship data that makes up a social network can be represented and analyzed in different ways [14]. For a quantitative analysis, different relationship metrics can be derived from the data. These metrics can describe properties of individual members or of the whole team. The most common team-level metrics include density and centralization [15]. Network density is defined as the ratio between the actual number and the total number of ties in a network and is often used as an indicator of cohesion [13]. Centralization refers to the variance in ties per team member; low values indicate a structure in which each member has the same numbers of ties. Centralization reflects aspects of work organization and hierarchy.

Researchers have applied SNA to teams in organizations. For example, it has been suggested that centralization has a negative impact on team performance in complex tasks [16]. Zohar et al. showed that the density of a military teams communication network mediated the effects of transformational leadership on climate strength [17]. Likewise, a series of case studies with police and firefighting teams suggests that both teams have different network architectures (distributed vs. split) [18].

Despite the potential of SNA to uncover the underlying structure of team processes, the number of studies using SNA in team research is small [12,15]. We believe that part of this problem lies in the method itself as SNA, like behavioral observation, is very resource-intensive and often impractical for applied settings. One way to address this issue includes taking advantage of new developments from the field of mobile behavior sensing.

Mobile behavior sensing

Mobile Behavior Sensing aims at measuring and analysing human behavior from sensor data recorded with mobile devices [8,19,20]. Research in wearable and ubiquitous computing has shown how user context and behavior can be inferred from the smartphone's sensor data using signal processing and machine learning techniques. The integrated sensors capture device interaction, body movement, location and speech of the user as well as characteristics of the user's environment such as ambient light and sound. Characteristics features are then extracted from the sensor signals to make inferences about the context, state and behavior of a user.

Farrahi et al. used coarse location information from cell towers and clustered individual location traces to discover daily routines such as "going to work at 10am" or "leaving work at night" [21].

In order to give semantic meaning to recorded location information, features from ambient sound and video were fused to categorize location into place categories such as "college/education", "food/restaurant" or "home" [22,23].

The audio modality has been analyzed in the mobile setting to detect conversations, recognize speakers and estimate speaking duration [24-26], perceived basic emotions [27], perceived stress during a street promotion tasks [28] and to quantify sociability as one aspect of well-being [29].

On a macro level, Eagle et al. have first shown how mobile phones can be used to infer proximity networks of communities [20]. Relying on repeated Bluetooth scans, mobile phones were used to detect other nearby devices to estimate proximity between individuals. On the same dataset, topic models were later used to discover human interactions from the proximity data [30].

Before the smartphone was available, Choudhury et al. introduced the sociometer, a wearable device, to automatically sense body motion, communication and proximity networks [24]. Extending this line of research, Olguin et al. used a new version of the sociometer to collect behavioral data of nurses in a hospital. The results showed a positive relationship of group motion energy and speaking time with group productivity [31].

In previous work, we adopted the idea to use motion and speech activity to monitor teams. Our feasibility study showed that speech and motion activity are promising performance indicators in firefighting teams [32] which motivated us to design, build and distribute our mobile sensing app CoenoFire in a real fire brigade [33]. In this paper, we build on our approach to sense team proximity dynamics with the smartphone [34].

Sensing spatial and temporal coordination

From the review of related work, we conclude: Firstly, the smartphone can be used to capture the behavior of it's user and secondly, teams can be characterized by network metrics as commonly applied in social network analysis. Based on these findings, we propose to automatically sense spatial and temporal aspects of team coordination using the smartphone.

The spatial component of coordination is concerned with how team activities are distributed in space. For this reason, we detect moving sub-groups of team members. Team members within the same sub-group are in close proximity, whereas those of another sub-group are not. The temporal component of coordination is related to how team activities are aligned in time. Instead of detecting concrete activities (e.g. running), we measure the movement activity level that captures how long a team member was physically active during consecutive time intervals. By comparing the motion activity level signals of two team members, we measure how well they aligned their body movement in time. This is especially important for team members of first responder teams such as firefighters that move and work at least in pairs of two.

Approach

Our approach is schematically presented in Figure 1 and consists of the following steps:

1. Sensor data is recorded on the smartphones carried by each team member. The phone's sensors capture body motion by sensing acceleration, proximity to others by exchanging radio messages between nearby devices and height information by sensing atmospheric pressure.

2. Data of each team member is processed to derive the sub-group network which captures who was for how long in a sub-group with another team member, as well as the movement alignment network, which captures dependencies in activity levels between team members.

3. Network metrics as used in SNA are extracted from the team networks to capture the overall structure of the networks. Network density describes how well the nodes (team members) within the network are connected, whereas centralization measures how heterogeneously the nodes are connected to each other. Depending on the type of network (sub-group network or movement alignment network), connected therefore refers to how long team members were in the same sub-group or to how well they aligned their movement activity levels. We refer to density and centralization of the two team networks as team coordination indicators.

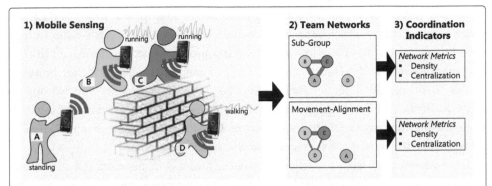

Figure 1 Schematic of our approach to sensing team coordination indicators. 1) The smartphone records body motion and proximity to others. 2) Pairwise movement alignment and sub-grouping are represented as networks. 3) Network metrics density and centralization extract team coordination indicators related to performance and perceived coordination.

In the example presented in Figure 1, person *A* is standing still while being in proximity with the running persons *B* and *C*. Person *D* on the other hand is walking behind a wall and is therefore not in any sub-group with another person. This leads to the presented sub-group network. As person *A* is in-sight with persons *B* and *C*, the sub-group graph shows them to be in one group, whereas person *D* is indicated to be alone. The movement alignment network shows person *B* and *C* to be best aligned because they are both running, whereas person *A* is worst aligned as she is the only person not moving. From the sub-group and movement alignment networks SNA metrics are derived to characterize overall network structures in order to capture team coordination indicators.

Smartphone sensing platform

Our data collection framework called CoenoFire is illustrated in Figure 2 and consists of two parts: the smartphone data recording app as the sensing front-end and a database and visualization server at the back-end. CoenoFire was developed to monitor firefighters during real-world incidents. Details on the system architecture were previously presented in [33].

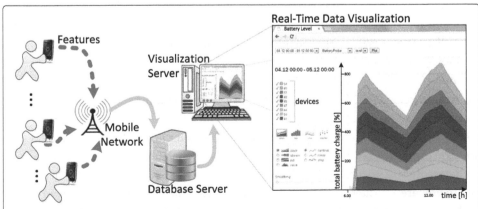

Figure 2 CoenoFire: smartphone based data collection framework. Raw smartphone sensor data is saved to the SD-Card and features are transmitted via the mobile network to enable real-time monitoring of performance metrics and system status, e.g. battery level.

For data collection, we used the Sony Xperia Active smartphone which is dust and water-resistant, has a 3-inch capacitive touchscreen and a built-in ANT-radio (http://www.thisisant.com). ANT is a low power wireless protocol that was developed to connect fitness devices such as heart-rate-belts and pedometers with sport watches; however, in this work we use it for proximity estimation. We developed an Android app to continuously record data of the phone's built-in sensors. Therefore, we extended the funf-open-sensing-framework [35] to also detect nearby devices by transceiving ANT-radio messages and to save the raw sensor data locally to the memory card.

Data was recorded from the following built-in sensors: acceleration and orientation sensors were used to measure body movement, the barometer measured atmospheric pressure and was used to infer whether individuals were on the same floor level and ANT-radio messages were sent and received to find out which team member was in proximity to another one.

As our goal was to sense team behaviors, all devices carried by the team members needed to be synchronized to allow comparison of the sensor signals across team members. Therefore, we measured the offset between system time and a common reference time each 5 min using the network time protocol. With this approach, we were able to achieve a time synchronisation across devices with a maximum time difference of 500 ms. To enable remote monitoring, we configured the framework to upload every five minutes a subset of calculated features, such as the battery level to a central server. Because we used the smartphone as a sensing platform, we installed our app as the default home-screen and blocked all soft buttons. In this way, our app was always visible and the use of the smartphone was restricted to our data collection.

At the back-end, we ran one web server to receive and store the data from the smartphones in a central database. A second web server provided a web-based user interface that offered real-time monitoring of the system. A screen shot of the web interface showing the battery status of the devices is presented in the right of Figure 2. The interface also allows visualization of real time data of the firefighters' movement and speech activity.

Experimental study

In order to validate our approach, we tested it in a sample of firefighting teams completing a training scenario. The study was conducted in cooperation with the Zurich fire department and approved by the Ethics committee of the University of Zurich. Written consent from all participants was obtained prior to data collection.

Scenario

In cooperation with the training instructors, we designed the difficult level of the training scenario to be challenging for the firefigthers in order to maximize differences in team coordination and performance. Impressions of the scenario are shown in Figure 3. The scenario involved a fire on the third floor of an apartment building at which teams arrived with two fire trucks. The building had to be accessed via the roof. Thus, the firefighters had to prepare a turntable ladder. A first troop entered the building and navigated blindly to the source of the fire. On their way the troop detected an unconscious dummy person. As a first priority, this person had to be evacuated. After that, the fire had to be extinguished, which could either be done by the first troop or by a second troop depending

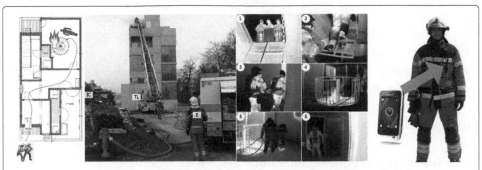

Figure 3 Impressions of the training scenario. Firefighters had to enter through a roof window and navigate in low-visibility to a fire on the third floor, rescue an unexpected dummy person and extinguish the fire.

on the decision of the incident commander (IC). The scenario ended when the fire was extinguished.

Setting and procedure

The scenario took place in a burn building, a multi-story training facility that allows for a highly realistic simulation of fire incidents. During training sessions, firefighters were confronted with actual fires, extreme heat, high humidity and thick smoke restricting visibility. Trainings were performed using standard equipment including vehicles, protection suits, and self-contained breathing apparatus (SCBA). We informed the participants about the study two weeks prior to data collection during their morning reports. Upon arrival at the trainings site, participants were again informed about the study, and completed the consent form and a personal background questionnaire. They also received a briefing about the scenario from a training instructor. Then, the first trial was conducted. Each firefighter carried one smartphone in the left jacket pocket of his protection suit (see Figure 3). We videotaped all trials using two regular cameras to record outside and a thermographic camera to record inside the building. After the scenario, they completed the coordination questionnaire (see below) and received a technical debriefing about their performance. Team members switched roles and started the next scenario after a short break.

Measurement of perceived coordination

Perceived explicit and implicit coordination were measured via self-report after each trial. To assess explicit coordination we used three items of the German translation of the sub-scale coordination of the transactive memory scale [36]. A sample item is "Our team worked together in a well-coordinated fashion". The scale had a high reliability ($\alpha = .80$). In absence of a validated scale, we developed five items to assess implicit coordination based on its definition. Sample items included "We automatically adjusted our working styles to each other" and "We understood each other blindly". The scale had a high reliability ($\alpha = .87$). All items were answered on a 5-point scale ranging from 1 = "strongly disagree" to 5 = "strongly agree".

Data set

In total 51 professional firefighters from the Zurich Fire Brigade participated in our study. All participants were male, aged 35 ± 10 years. They completed a simulated fire incident in teams of 7-9 members. The data collection was conducted on four consecutive days. We recorded 18 training runs of the described scenario. Most firefighters took part in more than one trial because of the limited overall sample size. However, we made sure that participants switched their roles after each trial to ensure variation. In five trails one smartphone partially failed recording; in additional three runs one firefighter did not participate in the study. This left us with 10 complete runs totaling to over 2 h of training data.

Extraction of team coordination indicators

In the following, we present how we extract team coordination indicators from automatically sensed team networks. First, we describe how moving subgroups are detected to derive the sub-group network. Second, we describe how temporal activity alignment is quantified to extract the activity alignment network. Third, we detail how team coordination indicators are extracted from the team networks.

Detection and visualization of moving sub-groups

In our previous work [34], we have shown how moving sub-groups within teams can be detected from radio-based proximity data obtained with smartphones. The detected sub-groups can be visualized in the form of narrative charts to display which team members were in sub-groups at each point in time and show how sub-groups merge and split over time. The narrative chart presented in Figure 4a illustrates the moving sub-groups of firefighters during the described training scenario. The chart allows for example to identify the points in time when the first (1) and second troop (3) reached the top of the turntable ladder and when the first troop entered the building (2). As can be seen in the narrative chart the lines representing the members of the first troop (T1a, T1b, T1c) split from the other lines (other team members) at time point (1) when the first troop forms a sub-group and uses the turntable ladder to reach the roof window. At time point (2) two members (T1a, T1b) of the first troop enter the building and team member T1c remains outside on the top of the ladder. In the narrative chart this is shown by the splitting of the yellow line from the orange and purple lines. At time point (3) members of the second troop (T2a, T2b) climb the turntable ladder and join team member T1c which is shown in the chart by the merging of the red and brown lines with the yellow line.

Having detected moving sub-groups, we are able to calculate a sub-group network that summarizes which team member was for how long in a sub-group with another team member. Thus, the sub-group network captures the overall spatial structure of the team during a mission. In Figure 4a the corresponding sub-group network is presented on the right of the narrative chart. The network graphs highlights three sub-groups that belong to the first and second troop that enter the building via the turntable ladder as well as the ground support team that includes the incident commander, turntable ladder operator and the engineer. In the graph darker links between nodes correspond to team members that were longer than 60% of the mission together in a sub-group.

In the following we briefly describe our method to detect moving sub-groups using radio-based proximity data. Please refer to [34] for more details. We follow a two stage approach to detect moving sub-groups: We first calculate the proximity matrix D^t for consecutive time intervals t of length $L = 5$ s. Each binary element D_{ij}^t indicates

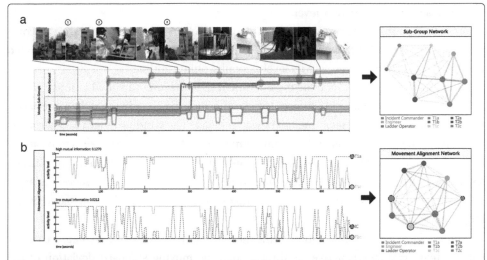

Figure 4 Measuring the sub-group and movement alignment networks. a) Narrative chart represents proximity dynamics of a team. Each colored line represents a team member, close lines indicate moving sub-groups. Team members are either on ground level or above ground level. The sub-group network summarizes how long each team member was in a sub-group with which each other team member. Darker links indicate pairs that were together in a sub-group for more than 60% of the mission. **b)** Examples of high and low mutual information between two activity level signals. Activity level signals change more often simultaneously in the top graph as opposed to those shown in the bottom graph. Consequently, mutual information is higher for signals shown in the top graph. The movement alignment network summarizes how well team members aligned their activity levels in time. Darker links indicate pairs of team members that showed higher motion alignment than 60% of all other pairs in the data set.

whether device i received any ANT message of device j during time interval t. Considering proximity to be undirected, we further symmetrize the proximity matrix to obtain D^t_{sym}.

In the second stage, moving sub-groups are clustered from the proximity data. Clusters are first identified independently from the symmetrized proximity matrices of each time interval and secondly, the clustering output is smoothed by applying a temporal filter, so that clusters last for at least 10 s. We cluster each symmetrized proximity matrix D^t_{sym} using the single-link criterion. As a result, if group member A is connected with B and B with C, but not with A, all three devices are still clustered into one group.

Using only radio based proximity information might lead to individuals on different height levels to be clustered into one group. To address this problem, we added height information derived from the atmospheric pressure sensor. If the absolute atmospheric pressure difference between two devices is greater than a predefined threshold, the two devices are considered to be on different height levels and are thus not clustered to the same sub-group. To obtain the sub-group network, we average the clustering results over all time intervals.

As the ANT-radio protocol operates in the 2.4 GHz band, radio signals are particularly influenced by the surrounding environment. In our experiments, we observed that depending on the relative orientation and environment of the individuals, the maximal transmit distance varied in the range of 1 m to 20 m. In [34] we evaluated our algorithm to detect moving sub-groups of firefighters during the described training scenario by comparing the results to a manually annotated ground truth. On average, team members were assigned to the correct sub-group with 95% accuracy.

Temporal alignment of activity level

In order to capture the temporal aspect of coordination in teams, we measure and compare activity levels of individual team members. Thus, we assume that well coordinated team members change their activity level at similar points in time.

We define the activity level to be the fraction of time that an individual is active within a moving window of length L. The activity level increases when individuals become active and decreases as soon as team members stop moving. The window length L determines the slope of the activity level and the minimum time that an individual needs to be active to reach the maximum activity level. The value of L also affects the temporal resolution, a small value requires individuals to change their activity closer in time, whereas a larger value allows for a delay between activity changes, as the activity level is calculated over a longer period.

Figure 5 illustrates the calculation of the motion activity level. In a first step, we detect when a team member is active, by thresholding the moving standard deviation of the linear acceleration magnitude. When a predefined threshold is exceeded, motion activity is detected (top in Figure 5). In a second step, the motion activity level is calculated as the percentage of time that motion activity was detected within a hopping window of length L and step size S (bottom in Figure 5). For further processing, the continuous activity level is linearly quantized into 10 discrete activity levels $\{0..9\}$.

In order to compare two motion activity level signals $X, Y \in \{0..9\}$ of two team members, we use the mutual information as similarity measure. In general, mutual information measures the dependency between two random variables, that is how much information two variables share and is defined as:

$$I(X, Y) = \sum_{x \in X} \sum_{y \in Y} p(x, y) \log \frac{p(x, y)}{p(x)p(y)} \tag{1}$$

The dependency between X and Y is expressed by the joint distribution $p(x, y)$ and compared to the joint distribution when independence is assumed, in which case $p(x, y) = p(x)p(y)$. Thus, $I(X, Y)$ is zero if and only if X and Y are independent.

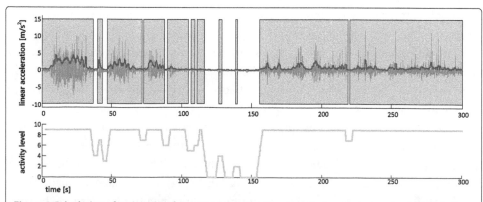

Figure 5 Calculation of activity level. Top: Linear acceleration magnitude and moving standard deviation (pink), rectangles indicate segments in which the standard deviation exceeds the activity detection threshold. Bottom: Activity level calculated on a hopping window ($L = 5$ s, $S = 200$ ms).

Two examples of activity level alignment that occurred during the firefighting training scenario are presented in Figure 4b. The two activity levels presented in the top graph belong two team members from the first troop (T1a, T1b), whereas the activity levels shown in the bottom graph belong to team member T1b and the incident commander. While the activity levels of the troop members change often together in time and are well aligned, the activity levels of the troop member T1b and the incident commander are not well aligned in time. Consequently, the observed mutual information is higher between the activity levels of the troop members as opposed to those of troop member T1b and the incident commander.

In order to summarize the temporal alignment for the whole team, the mutual information between all pairs of activity levels are calculated. This results in the activity alignment network. An example is presented on the right side of Figure 4b. As can be seen, troop member T1b had highest activity alignment with troop member T1a and lowest with the incident commander.

Team coordination indicators

On each of the extracted team networks (sub-group network and activity alignment network), we calculate network density and degree centralization in order to characterize the global network structure. In summary, we extract the following team coordination indicators from the team networks:

- **Density of the sub-group network** measures how long team members were on average in sub-groups. As the sub-group network captures the spatial distribution of team members, a high density indicates that many team members were together for a long time, whereas a low density indicates that team members were mostly on their own.
- **Degree centralization of the sub-group network** measures how differently team members were part of a sub-group. A high degree centralization indicates that there was at least one well connected large group and one other small group.
- **Density of the activity alignment network** measures how well team members aligned their activity level on average. It can thus be seen as an overall measure of how coordinated a team moved.
- **Degree centralization of the activity alignment network** measures how differently the team members aligned their activity levels with that of others. It can thus be seen as an overall measure of how differently team members' motions were coordinated.

In the following, we give the definition of network density and centralization. Degree centrality of a node in the network captures how well each node (team member) in the network is connected to other nodes (other team members). Degree centrality of node i is defined by

$$d_i = \frac{1}{N-1} \sum_{j \neq i} a_{ij},$$

with $a_{ij} \in [0..1]$ being an element of the adjacency matrix defining the network and $i, j \in [1..N]$, with N being the number of nodes in the network. Network density D is the average degree centrality and thus captures how well nodes in the network are connected with each other. Network density is given by

$$D = \frac{1}{N}\sum_i^N d_i.$$

Degree centralization DC measures how central its most central node (highest degree) is in relation to how central all the other nodes are. Thus, it is a measure of degree variation and is zero in a homogeneously connected network where each node has the same degree and one in a star network. Degree centralization is defined by

$$DC = \frac{1}{N-1}\sum_i^N |d^* - d_i|,$$

with d^* being the maximum degree observed in the network.

Evaluation of team coordination indicators

Correlation analysis

In order to evaluate our approach, we correlated the proposed coordination indicators derived from the sensor data with three validation criteria. We used perceived implicit and explicit coordination to validate the indicators. Explicit coordination includes those actions intentionally used for team coordination and is achieved by means of verbal communication. By contrast, implicit coordination refers to the anticipations of others members' actions and the dynamic adjustment of one's own actions accordingly, without the need for overt communication [37].

We additionally used time to complete the training mission as objective validation criteria. As time is critical in firefighting our reasoning was that well coordinated teams would be faster.

Our findings reveal significant relationships between both subjective and objective validation criteria as can be seen from Table 1. Figure 6 shows the relationships graphically. In summary, we find:

- Degree centralization of the sub-group network is highly negatively correlated with completion time and positively with implicit team coordination. That is, the centralization of the sub-group network decreased with completion time (compare Figure 6a) and increased with perceived implicit coordination (compare Figure 6c). In other words, faster teams showed a higher degree of centralization in the

Table 1 Linear correlation analysis: relationship between team coordination indicators and outcome measures team performance and experienced coordination (implicit and explicit) ($N = 10$, $L = 5$ s)

Network	Metric	Completion time		Impl. coordination		Expl. coordination	
		r	p	r	p	r	p
Sub-group	Density	+0.207	0.567	−0.609	0.062	−0.587	0.074
	Centralization	−0.841**	0.002	+0.644*	0.044	+0.427	0.219
Movement-alignment	Density	−0.824**	0.003	+0.657*	0.039	+0.415	0.233
	Centralization	−0.356	0.313	+0.411	0.238	+0.569	0.086

Notes: *$p < 0.05$, **$p < 0.01$.

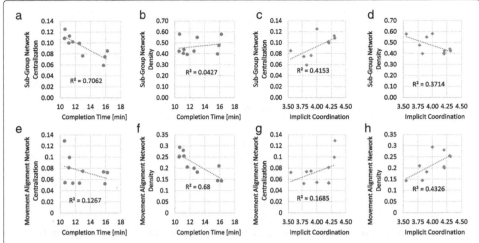

Figure 6 Linear trend lines. Relationship between team coordination indicators and completion time and experienced implicit coordination ($N = 10, L = 5$ s).

sub-group network, meaning that team members were more heterogeneously connected, e.g. some firefighters were in well connected sub-groups for a long time, whereas others were longer on their own or part of a small sub-group.

- Density of activity alignment networks is highly negatively correlated with completion time and positively with implicit coordination. That is, the density of the movement alignment network decreased with completion time (compare Figure 6f) and increased with perceived implicit coordination (compare Figure 6h). Thus, faster teams showed more alignment of their activity levels and perceived their implicit coordination as better than slower teams.

The finding that faster teams had a sub-group network with higher degree of centralization makes sense, because the chosen scenario demanded teams to split into at least three sub-groups of different size: the troop that went inside the building, the firefighter on top of the ladder that helped with the fire hose and the remaining team members on the ground outside the building. Thus, faster teams organized their spatial structure more efficiently than slower teams.

In terms of activity alignment, the results showed that faster teams exhibited higher temporal movement coordination. This finding seems reasonable as it indicates that firefighters in faster teams worked well together and aligned their movements accordingly. Thus, faster teams moved on average more synchronously than slower teams.

The correlation analysis did not indicate any significant relationships between the proposed team coordination indicators and perceived explicit coordination. This is likely due to the fact that the proposed coordination indicators measure spatial and temporal aspects and did not include direct verbal communication which is essential for explicit coordination.

Visual analysis of team networks

To further analyse the correlation results, we visually inspect the team networks. In Figure 7 the sub-group networks of the teams are presented. As can be seen, faster teams

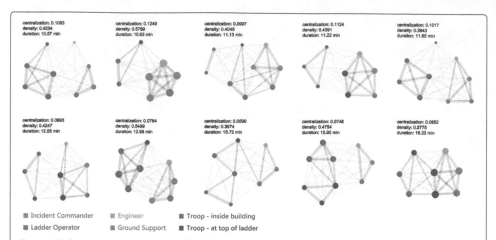

■ Incident Commander   ■ Engineer   ■ Troop - inside building
■ Ladder Operator   ■ Ground Support   ■ Troop - at top of ladder

Figure 7 Sub-group networks sorted from fastest team (top left) to slowest team (bottom right). Each team member is represented by a node which size is proportional to its degree. Degree expresses how long a team member was on average in a sub-group with each other team member. Roles are indicated by different colors. Links between nodes represent the time that the corresponding team members were in one sub-group, nodes of team members which were longer in the same sub-group are shown to be closer together. Sub-group networks of faster teams are more heterogeneous, whereas slower teams have more homogeneously connected networks. This indicates that faster teams split more quickly into the task demanded sub-groups and thus were better spatially coordinated.

tended to have one firefighter on top of the ladder (red circle) and two well connected sub-groups, the troop and the remaining firefighters on ground. The observed high degree centralization stems from the fact that faster teams split quickly into these three groups so that the firefighter on top of the ladder was relatively long alone, which is the reason for the low degree (small circle). As the other firefighters were part of a sub-group, their respective degrees were higher (larger circle). Due to this difference in the individual degrees the overall degree centralization of the network is high. While not being statistically significant, it can also be observed from the networks, that slower teams showed higher density, meaning that their team members stayed longer in well connected sub-groups, which indicates that they needed more time to split into the required sub-groups.

The movement alignment networks of all groups are presented in Figure 8. As can be seen, faster teams (top row) have better connected networks and thus higher network density. Further, the networks show that the highest activity coordination occurred between members that worked close together such as the troop inside the building. Troop members of faster teams had higher alignment between their activity levels (represented by bigger circles) than those of slower teams (represented by smaller circles).

Discussion

The aim of the current paper was to introduce smartphone based behavior sensing and data processing as a means to automatically observe team coordination processes in realistic environments. To this end, we described the method, its theoretical background and reported the findings of a validation study. Our method consists of three steps: First, individual activity level and proximity between team members is measured with the integrated sensors of smartphones. Second, individual data streams are processed and compared with each other to derive motion alignment and sub-group networks

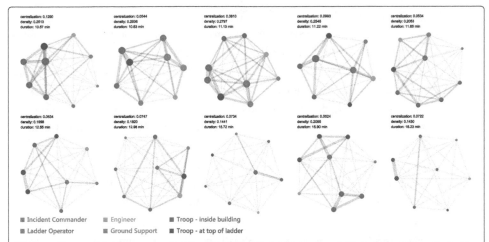

Figure 8 Movement alignment networks sorted from fastest team (top left) to slowest team (bottom right). Size of a node corresponds to its degree. Degree expresses the average activity coordination with all other team members. Roles are indicated by different colors. Link width corresponds to activity coordination between two team members, nodes of team members which better aligned their motion activity levels are shown to be closer together. Movement alignment networks of faster teams are highly connected, whereas slower teams have less connected networks. This indicates that faster teams had better temporal coordination.

which capture team coordination processes. Third, to derive team coordination indicators we used social network analysis to quantify temporal and spatial coordination on the team level. In a firefighting training scenario, we have validated the team coordination indicators by investigating their link to team performance and experienced team coordination.

Implications

We see four main implications of our method:

- First, we provide a method that is capable of continuously monitoring team coordination processes in a variety of settings. Thereby, we provide a new measurement tool for team research.

- Second, the smartphone allows to capture different types of networks that are beyond classical self-report based social networks that focus on content such as advice, information or friendship. We introduced proximity based sub-groups and motion activity alignment as contents. Moreover, the smartphone data has a high temporal resolution (in the order of seconds) and thus captures changes in network structure over time.

- Third, the smartphone-based behavior sensing approach enables easier data collection as no user input is required. In addition, the smartphone-based approach offers a higher degree of anonymity than videos, which potentially increases the willingness to participate in a study.

- Finally, our approach bears the potential to open up new settings for team research. The smartphone can be used in settings where traditional behavioral observation is not feasible. For example, firefighters can be monitored during real incidents. In earlier work [33], we have shown that a smartphone-based data collection approach is feasible in such settings.

Practical implications

Our proposed team sensing approach also has potential implications for practitioners. Instructors of first responder teams can use the smartphone during training to collect objective data on team processes. These data could then serve as additional input for debriefing and thus enables data supported training feedback. Even more so, as the data can be illustrated using different graphs. For example, the narrative chart (compare Figure 4) can be used to get a quick overview of when sub-groups formed and disbanded over the course of a mission.

As the smartphone allows for continuous, real-time assessment of teams, it could also be used during actual missions to monitor performance and coordination. This has a large potential for error prevention. For example, using radio-based proximity data, mission commanders can detect when a team member moves out of sight of the rest of the team without relying on GPS or any installed infrastructure. Being alone may pose a threat to this person because it will be more difficult for his teammates to recognize potential dangers and to provide timely backup. As smartphones are widely used, it would not be difficult to implement such a monitoring system.

Limitations

In order to detect moving sub-groups over time, we make use of radio based proximity estimation. The accuracy of nearby device detection dependents on architectural constraints and consequently varies across locations. Experiments showed that the maximum detection distance varies between 1 m to 20 m. This accuracy proved to be good enough for the detection of moving sub-groups in the firefighting scenario. We therefore believe our method to be also applicable to other first responder teams. Having room-level accuracy, the approach is also useful to track white-collar workers in office buildings in order to capture their co-location networks, which could be used to identify important persons in a social network. However, in a social event in which individuals stand close together the spatial resolution is likely not to be sufficient to reliably detect social interaction. In such scenarios, the used technique can only give rough proximity cues.

Further, we measured temporal coordination as simultaneous change in activity level. As the activity level captures the amount of body movement, it is only a rough estimate of action coordination. For firefighting teams and most likely also for other first responder teams, the simultaneous change in body movement is clearly related to team coordination because in such teams it is important to move together to solve the task. For white-color workers in an office building this simultaneous change in movement however has no clear meaning. In typical office work, body movement itself is not a driving process behind team performance.

Conclusion

We proposed a set of team coordination indicators that can be measured with the built-in sensors of smartphones. We demonstrated the validity of our approach in firefighting teams performing a realistic training scenario and investigated the link between the coordination indicators and team performance as well as experienced team coordination. Our method enables researchers to capture temporal and spatial team coordination automatically and objectively. However, to prove the generality of the approach, future studies have to be carried out in different architectural configurations and with other types of teams.

Competing interests
The authors declare that they have no competing interests.

Authors' contributions
This work is a joint effort between ETH Zurich and University of Zurich. Collaboration has been established within the interdisciplinary SNSF project "Micro-level behavior and team performance". The different partners have contributed to different parts of this work. All authors were heavily involved in the data recording part which includes system design and deployment but also management and coordination task and establishing the required contacts. All authors have contributed to this document and given the final approval. Detailed contributions (in alphabetic order): Experiment planning: MB, SF, KJ, GT. System deployment: MB, SF. Evaluation: SF. Manuscript: MB, SF, KJ, GT. Acquisition of funding: MB, KJ, GT. All authors read and approved the final manuscript.

Acknowledgements
The authors would like to thank all members of the Zurich fire brigade for their participation and support throughout the experiments. We are grateful to Bert Arnrich and to Bertolt Meyer for their help in designing this study. We thank Anna-Lena Köng, Laura Fischer and Nadja Ott for their help with the data collection and for behavioral coding. This work was funded by the SNSF interdisciplinary project "Micro-level behavior and team performance" (grant agreement no.: CR12I1_137741).

Author details
[1]Wearable Computing Laboratory, ETH Zurich, Gloriastrasse 35, 8092 Zurich CH, Switzerland. [2]Department of Psychology, University of Zurich, Binzmuehlestrasse 14, 8050 Zurich CH, Switzerland.

References
1. Salas E, Cooke NJ, Rosen MA (2008) On teams, teamwork, and team performance: Discoveries and developments. Hum Factors 50(3):540–547
2. Cohen SG, Bailey DE (1997) What makes team work: group effectiveness from the shop floor to the executive suite. J Manag 23(3):239–290
3. Moreland RL, Fetterman JD, Flagg JJ, Swanenburg K (2010) Behavioral assessment practices among social psychologists who study small groups. In: Then A Miracle Occurs: Focusing on Behavior in Social Psychological Theory and Research. Oxford University Press, New York, pp 28–53
4. Rosen MA, Bedwell WL, Wildman JL, Fritzsche BA, Salas E, Burke CS (2011) Managing adaptive performance in teams: guiding principles and behavioral markers for measurement. Hum Res Manag Rev 21(2):107–122
5. Brannick MT, Prince C (1997) An overview of team performance measurement. In: Team Performance Assessment and Measurement: Theory, Methods, and Applications. Lawrence Erlbaum Associates, London, pp 3–16
6. Kozlowski SWJ, Bell BS (2003) Work groups and teams in organizations. In: Handbook of Psychology: Industrial and Organizational Psychology vol. 12. Wiley, London, pp 333–375
7. Guastello SJ, Guastello DD (1998) Origins of coordination and team effectiveness: a perspective from game theory and nonlinear dynamics. J Appl Psychol 83(3):423–437
8. Lane ND, Miluzzo E, Lu H, Peebles D, Choudhury T, Campbell AT (2010) A survey of mobile phone sensing. IEEE Commun Mag 48(9):140–150
9. Burtscher MJ, Manser T, Kolbe M, Grote G, Grande B, Spahn DR, Wacker J (2011) Adaptation in anaesthesia team coordination in response to a simulated critical event and its relationship to clinical performance. Br J Anaesth 106(6):801–806
10. Burtscher MJ, Wacker J, Grote G, Manser T (2010) Managing non-routine events in anesthesia: the role of adaptive coordination. Hum Factors 52(2):282–294
11. Stachowski AA, Kaplan SA, Waller MJ (2009) The benefits of flexible team interaction during crises. J Appl Psychol 94(6):1536–1543
12. Crawford ER, LePine JA (2013) A configural theory of team processes: accounting for the structure of taskwork and teamwork. Acad Manage Rev 38(1):32–48
13. Wasserman S, Faust K (1994) Social network analysis: methods and applications. Cambridge University Press, New York
14. Knoke D, Yang S (2008) Social network analysis. Quantitative applications in the social sciences, vol. 154. Sage, Thousand Oaks, CA
15. Balkundi P, Harrison DA (2006) Ties, leaders, and time in teams: Strong inference about network structure effects on team viability and performance. Acad Manag 49(1):49–68
16. Sparrowe RT, Liden RC, Wayne SJ, Kraimer ML (2001) Social networks and the performance of individuals and groups. Acad Manag 44(2):316–325
17. Zohar D, Tenne-Gazit O (2008) Transformational leadership and group interaction as climate antecedents: a social network analysis. J Appl Psychol 93(4):744–757
18. Houghton RJ, Baber C, McMaster R, Stanton NA, Salmon P, Stewart R, Walker G (2006) Command and control in emergency services operations: a social network analysis. Ergonomics 49(12-13):1204–1225
19. Pentland A (2008) Honest Signals: How They Shape Our World. The MIT Press, Cambridge
20. Eagle N, Pentland A (2005) Reality mining: sensing complex social systems. Pers Ubiquitous Comput 10(4):255–268
21. Farrahi K, Gatica-Perez D (2008) What did you do today?: Discovering daily routines from large-scale mobile data. In: Proc. Int. Conf. ACM Multimedia

22. Chon Y, Lane ND, Li F, Cha H, Zhao F (2012) Automatically characterizing places with opportunistic crowdsensing using smartphones. In: Proc. Int. Conf. Ubiquitous Computing (UbiComp)

23. Rossi M, Amft O, Tröster G (2012) Recognizing daily life context using web-collected audio data. In: Proc. Int. Symp. Wearable Computers (ISWC)

24. Choudhury T, Pentland AS (2003) Sensing and modeling human networks using the sociometer. In: Proc. Int. Conf. Symposium on Wearable Computers (ISWC)

25. Wyatt D, Bilmes J, Choudhury T (2008) Towards the automated social analysis of situated speech data. In: Proc. Int. Conf. Ubiquitous Computing (UbiComp)

26. Rossi M, Amft O, Tröster G (2012) Collaborative personal speaker identification: a generalized approach pervasive and mobile computing. Pervasive Mobile Comput 8:180–189

27. Rachuri KK, Mascolo C, Rentfrow PJ, Longworth C (2010) EmotionSense: A mobile phones based adaptive platform for experimental social psychology research. In: Proc. Int. Conf. Ubiquitous Computing (UbiComp)

28. Lu H, Frauendorfer D, Rabbi M, Mast MS, Chittaranjan GT, Campbell AT, Gatica-Perez D, Choudhury T (2012) StressSense: Detecting stress in unconstrained acoustic environments using smartphones. In: Proc. Int. Conf. Ubiquitous Computing (UbiComp)

29. Rabbi M, Ali S, Choudhury T, Berke E (2011) Passive and in-situ assessment of mental and physical well-being using mobile sensors. In: Proc. Int. Conf. Ubiquitous Computing (UbiComp)

30. Do TMT, Gatica-Perez D (2011) Human interaction discovery in smartphone proximity networks. Pers Ubiquitous Comput 17(3):413–431

31. Olguin D, Gloor PA, Pentland AS (2009) Capturing individual and group behavior with wearable sensors. In: AAAI Symp. Human Behavior Modeling

32. Feese S, Arnrich B, Rossi M, Burtscher M, Meyer B, Jonas K, Tröster G (2013) Towards monitoring firefighting teams with the smartphone. In: Proc. Int. Conf. Pervasive Computing and Communications (PerCom): WorkInProgress

33. Feese S, Arnrich B, Burtscher M, Meyer B, Jonas K, Tröster G (2013) CoenoFire: Monitoring performance indicators of firefighters in real-world missions using smartphones. In: Proc. Int. Conf. Ubiquitous Computing (UbiComp)

34. Feese S, Arnrich B, Burtscher M, Meyer B, Jonas K, Tröster G (2013) Sensing group proximity danamics of firefighting teams using smartphones. In: Proc. Int. Symp. Wearable Computers (ISWC)

35. Aharony N, Pan W, Ip C, Khayal I, Pentland A (2011) Social fMRI: Investigating and shaping social mechanisms in the realworld. Pervasive Mobile Comput 7:643–659

36. Lewis K (2003) Measuring transactive memory systems in the field: scale development and validation. J Appl Psychol 88(4):587–604

37. Rico R, Sanchez-Manzanares M, Gil F, Gibson C (2008) Team implicit coordination processes: a team knowledge-based approach. Acad Manage Rev 33(1):163–184

7

All capacities modular cost survivable network design problem using genetic algorithm with completely connection encoding

Huynh Thi Thanh Binh[*] and Son Hong Ngo

* Correspondence: binh.
huynhthithanh@hust.edu.vn
School of Information and
Communication Technology, Hanoi
University of Science and
Technology, Hanoi, Vietnam

Abstract

We study the survivable network design problem (SNDP) for simultaneous unicast and anycast flows in networks where the link cost follows All Capacities Modular Cost (ACMC) model. Given a network modeled by a connected, undirected graph and a set of flow demands, this problem aims at finding a set of connections with a minimized network cost in order to protect the network against any single failure. This paper proposes a new Genetic Algorithm with an efficient encoding to solve the SNDP in networks with ACMC model (A-SNDP). Our encoding scheme is simple and allows large search space. Extensive simulation results on real large topology instances show that the proposed algorithm is much more efficient than the Tabu Search and other conventional Genetic Algorithm in terms of minimizing the network cost.

Keywords: Survivable network design; All capacities modular cost; Anycast; Unicast; Genetic algorithm

Introduction

There are many types of connection for data transmission over the Internet. The most popular type of connection is from one node to another, which is called unicast. An anycast connection is also from one node to another, the difference is that the destination node has a one or many replicated servers which back up for it. Anycast has in recent years become increasingly popular for adding redundancy to many Internet services [1–3]. Anycast connection is currently used in many applications such as Domain Name Service (DNS), Web Service, Overlay Network, peer-to-peer (P2P) systems, Content Delivery Network (CDN), software distribution. The popularity of anycast technology will increase in the near future, since many new services that use both unicast and anycast paradigms are being developed.

In the Internet, any network failure can cause serious consequences, e.g., a single link failure affected more than 30,000 users and it takes 12 hours to fix [3]. Therefore, the design of survivable networks is a crucial problem. For the commnunication networks, the research in [4] presented detailed information on protecting as well as restoring them with specifies techniques such that organization time and money can be saved. Also, in the survivable network design problem (SNDP) with simultaneous unicast and anycast flows, the common objective is to minimize the network cost to protect network against failures. To guarantee the survivability, we adopt the protection approach [5–10] in that each connection must include a working path and a link-disjoint backup path. The working path is used for data transmission in failure-free state of the network. If there is a single link failure on the working path, the failed connection is then switched to the backup path.

In [5] Gładysz et al. have considered the SNDP for networks using ACMC (All Capacities Modular Cost) link cost model (here after called by A-SNDP). In the ACMC model, a link has many bandwidth levels, each level has a corresponding cost. Many flow demands can go through the same link thus the link cost is defined as the total of required bandwidth from all demands on that link. The network cost is defined as the total of all link cost. The A-SNDP problem is defined as follows. Given a network modeled by an undirected graph where the link cost follows ACMC model and a set of survivable flow demands between node pairs with correspon-ding bandwidth and type of connection (anycast or unicast), this problem aims at finding a set of connection for all flow demands such that the network cost is minimized. The authors in [5] have also proposed a heuristic for A-SNDP using Tabu Search. However, their result is still far from optimal approach.

Genetic algorithm (GA) has been proved effective on NP-hard problem [11]. There have been a lot of research works on using GA approach to solve NP-hard problem, particularly in net-work design problem [9,12]. In our previous work [12], we have developed a genetic algorithm for A-SNDP called CDE-GA that uses Connection Database Encoding for individual representation. However, this encoding method is complex and search space is not diverse enough, thus it limits the performance of GA approach in solving A-SNDP problem.

In this paper, we propose new individual encoding scheme called Complete Connection Encoding (CCE) with genetic algorithm for solving A-SNDP. CCE encoding is simple, and it helps to create more new individuals and enlarge the search space to find better solution in large network instances. We then design the evolution operators using CCE and simulate our proposed algorithm with three typical network instances (Polska, Germany, Atlanta) and two large instances (Germany50, America). We compare the results with Tabu Search [5] and CDE-GA. Results obtained in experimentation show that our proposed algorithm are much better than the compared algorithms in terms of minimizing network cost.

The rest of this paper is organized as follows. Section "Problem description and related works" describes problem and the related works. Our new approach to encode individual and the proposed GA algorithm to solve A-SNDP is shown in Section "Genetic algorithm for solving A-SNDP". Experimental results are given in Section "Experimental results". The paper concludes with Section "Conclusion" by discussion and future works.

Problem description and related works

The SNDP is generally presented in [13] that considers both economics and reliability in telecommunication network design. The SNDP has to guarantee the survivability of a network system against single or multiple failures and also to minimize the network cost. In both cases, single [5–10] and multiple failures [14], the most popular way mentioned in the literature is the single backup path approach. The main idea of this method is as follows: Each connection has a working path and a backup path, if there is a single link failure on the working path, the failed connection is then switched over its backup path [5–10]. In this work, we consider the protection network from any single failure and assume that one backup path is dedicated for one working path. The approach of using shared backup path [13] is not considered in the scope of this paper.

The A-SNDP problem is described as follows. Given an undirected graph G = (V, E) and a set of customer demand between node pairs with corresponding bandwidth and type of connection (anycast or unicast). Like a unicast connection, an anycast connection is also from one node to another, the difference is that the destination node has one or many replicated servers which back up for it (see Figure 1). In this problem, the cost of a link follows All Capacities Modular Cost model [3], that means a link has many bandwidth levels, each level has a corresponding cost. Many flow demands can go through the same link thus the cost of a link is defined as the total of required bandwidth from all demands on that link. The goal is to find a set of connection for all demands such that the network cost (NCost) is minimized:

$$NCost = \sum_i c_i$$

where $c_i = C_k$, if $B_{k-1} < \sum_j Rij < B_k$

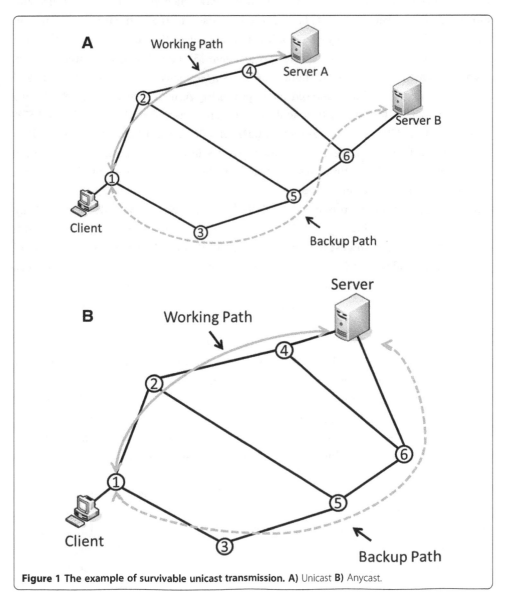

Figure 1 The example of survivable unicast transmission. A) Unicast **B)** Anycast.

here, c_i is the cost of link i; B_k and C_k is bandwidth and corresponding cost in level k; R_{ij} is the required bandwidth from the demand j on the link i.

In the literature, there are many papers focus on minimizing the network cost for SNDP problem (see [5,9,15]) and references therein). They use branch – and – bounds or branch – and – cut methods to find optimal solution. These methods can only use for networks with small number of nodes. For larger networks, they have proposed many heuristics such as evolutionary algorithms, tabu search and simulated annealing. In [9], Nissen and Gold applied the evolution strategy (ES) to solve this problem. It is shown by the authors that when using ES, a larger population can achieve better result than a smaller one by avoiding or delaying convergence on local suboptimal. However, this algorithm is applied in the network which has only unicast flows.

With the network which has both anycast and unicast flows, Walkowiak et al. presented a heuristic algorithm for solving A-SNDP [16]. The main idea of this algorithm is based on Flow Deviation method [15] and Local Search algorithm [17]. They achieved a very good result with small networks such as the Polska instance and showed that the average gap of the proposed heuristic to the optimal result is around 7.11%. Furthermore, they also built a Tabu Search algorithm based on hill climbing method with some heuristics to solve this problem [5]. Experiments on three network instances which are Polska (12 nodes, 36 links), Germany (17 nodes, 52 links) and Atlanta (26 nodes, 82 links) showed many promising results. In particular with Polska network (smallest instances), they achieve the average gap to optimal results is 2.57% for 70% anycast/30% unicast case and 2.00% for 80% anycast/20% unicast case. It is observed that by using TS, even on a small network instance like Polska, there is still a significant gap to the optimal result, therefore, the result obtained by Tabu Search algorithm can be further improved.

In [18], Huynh et al. proposed the FBB heuristic (FBB1 and FBB2) for solving A-SNDP. The main idea of FBB1 is based on the use of redundant bandwidth corresponding with paid cost level in each link and that of FBB2 is the combination of FBB1 and the Tabu Search algorithm (TS). Experiments conducted on three network instances (Polska, Germany and Atlanta) show that FBB1 and FBB2 have better result than that of TS [5]. However, the improvement of FBB in compared with TS is still not significant.

In [12], Binh et.al proposed a new algorithm called CDE-GA based on Genetic Algorithm for solving A-SNDP. A new characteristic of this algorithm is to use a new encoding called Connection Database based Encoding (CDE). They also experimented on three instances which are Polska, Germany and Atlanta network [5,16]. With each instance, they randomly create 10 test sets that are different from the content of customers' demands. The results show that the proposed approach is quite effective with A-SNDP. On the big instances (likely Germany and Atlanta network), CDE-GA has much better results than Tabu Search. However, on the small network (likely Polska network), the deviation of the results found by CDE-GA and the results found by Tabu Search is not significant. Other drawback of CDE-GA is that in the mutation operator, only the identification of backup path is changed so it is difficult to create more new paths, thus it limits the search space of GA approach in solving A-SNDP problem.

In the next section, we develop our new Genetic Algorithm by proposing a new scheme to encode an individual for solving the A-SNDP. This scheme is expected to improve the effectiveness in terms of network cost when adopting GA for this problem, especially on large scale network instances.

Genetic algorithm for solving A-SNDP
Individual representation

In the design of a Genetic Algorithm, the encoding is the most important task. There are some methods to encode each individual in a population, such as binary encoding, integer encoding... In this paper, we propose a new encoding mecha-nism, called Complete Connection Encoding (CCE) to encode individuals in GA. An individual built by CCE is presented as follows: Each individual T (i.e. a complete solution) is a set of substrings. Each substring T_i, represents a flow demand i and has two parts: the working path and the backup path. Illustration of an individual is shown in Figure 2.

To initialize an individual T, we create each of its substring T_i in turn. The working path of T_i is built by using a path finding algorithm. After that, all the link of this path will be deleted from the graph to find the backup path of T_i. using the same path finding algorithm. Therefore, to initiate an individual that represents a solution of A-SNDP, we need the time is $O(|D|.n^2)$ where n is the number of nodes.

Genetic operators

Crossover operator We apply two different crossover operators: one-point crossover and path crossover. In one-point crossover, we combine the substrings from $T_1 .. T_i$ with $T'_{i+1}...T'_n$ to create the child. In path crossover, we combine the working path of the first parent T with the backup path of the second parent T' to create the child T_{child} (see Figure 3). With the second type of crossover, sometimes, the working path and the corresponding backup path are not link-disjoint anymore. Thus, we have to check the child again and if any substring violates the link-disjoint condition, it will be replaced by the corresponding substring from its parent.

Mutation operator We choose some individuals in the current population randomly. Then, with each selected indivi-dual, we choose one substring i randomly and replace its working path as well as backup path by other couple of link-disjoint paths satisfying the demand i.

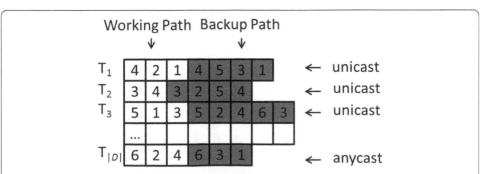

Figure 2 An example representing an individual built by CCE, where each row represents a solution for a demand; |D| is number of flow demands.

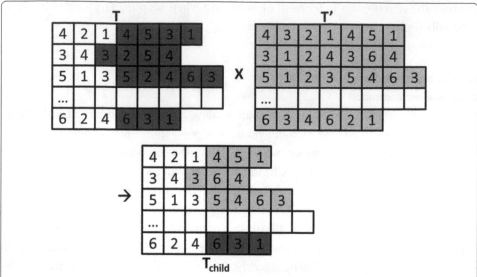

Figure 3 Illustration of the path crossover operator between parent T and T', which reproduces the child T_child.

Structure of genetic algorithm for solving A-SNDP

Below is pseudo-code of our proposed algorithm. In line 4, 7 and 14, *noGeneration, noCrossover* and *noMutation* stand for the number of generation, the number of crossover operator and the number of mutation operator, respectively.

```
1.  Procedure CCE-GA
2.  Begin
3.      initPopulation(P) /*Init a population*/ current = 0
4.      While(current < noGeneration) {
5.          Population child = Ø
6.          h = 0
7.          While(h < noCrossover) {
8.          T₁, T₂ ← SelectParent(P)
9.              T' = Crossover(T₁, T₂)
10.             child = child U T'
11.             h = h + 1
12.         }
13.         m = 0
14.         While(m < noMutation) {
15.             T ← SelectParent(P)
16.             T' = Mutation(T)
17.             child = child U T'
18.             m = m + 1
19.         }
20.         P = P U child
21.         P = Selection(P)
22.         current = current + 1
23.     }
    End.
```

Table 1 Topology instances for experiments

Parameters	Networks				
	Polska	Germany17	Atlanta	Germany50	TA2
Nodes	12	17	26	50	65
Links	36	52	82	176	216
Unicast/Anycast	65/12	119/13	234/22	80/20	80/20

Experimental results

We run our proposed algorithm (CCE-GA) independently and compare its performance with the Tabu Search [5] and CDE-GA [12]. All the programs are run on a machine with Intel Core 2 Duo U7700, RAM 2GB, Windows 7 Ultimate, and are installed by C++ and Java language.

Problem instances

In our experiments, we used five real world instances including the Polska, Germany17, Atlanta, Germany50 and America (TA2) topologies. All can be downloaded from http://sndlib.zib.de [19]. With each instance, we fix the number of flow demands and randomly create 10 test sets which are different from the content of customers' demands (see Table 1).

Parameters setting

For both CDE-GA and CCE-GA, the number of individual is 300 and the number of generation is 300. This is based on our observation from experiments that when we used larger values, the result is not better. In CCE-GA, we set the one-point crossover probability to 17% and the path crossover probability is also 17%. The selection of crossover probability value is tuned after many experiments with the range from 10% to 50%. The mutation rate is set to a small value (3%). Experiment is repeated 10 times for each test set.

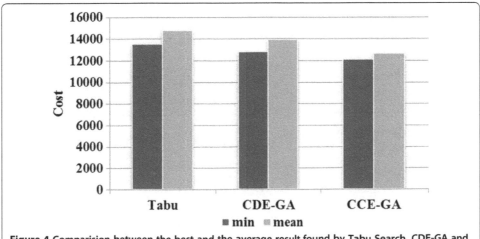

Figure 4 Comparision between the best and the average result found by Tabu Search, CDE-GA and CCE-GA on Polska network.

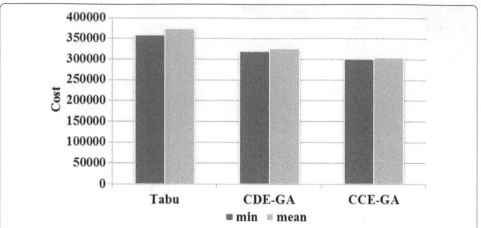

Figure 5 Comparision between the best and the average result found by Tabu Search, CDE-GA and CCE-GA on Germany17 network.

Result and discussion

Figures 4, 5, 6, 7 and 8 show the computational results of three compared algorithms on five network instances. For each network, we compare the minimum and the average network cost found. It is notable that the minimum and the average result found by CCE-GA are better than the one found by Tabu Search and CDE-GA on almost problem instances. For example in the Figure 4 (Polska network), the minimum network cost found by CCE-GA are 11% and 6% better than Tabu Search and CDE-GA, respectively.

The average cost found by CCE-GA are 15% and 10% better than Tabu Search and CDE-GA, respectively. The same results can be observed in Figure 8; The best network cost found by CCE-GA are 8% and 4% better than Tabu Search and CDE-GA, while the average network cost found by CCE-GA are better than Tabu Search and CDE-GA about 7% and 6%.

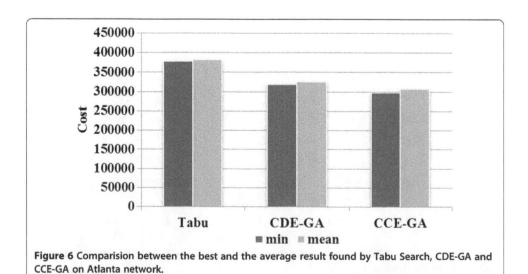

Figure 6 Comparision between the best and the average result found by Tabu Search, CDE-GA and CCE-GA on Atlanta network.

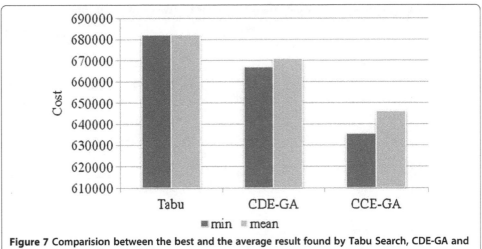

Figure 7 Comparision between the best and the average result found by Tabu Search, CDE-GA and CCE-GA on Germany50 network.

These above results prove the efficiency of Genetic Algorithms over Tabu Search for this problem. These results also demonstrate the efficiency of our new encoding scheme because it helps to increase the performance of CCE-GA in compare with CDE-GA. As we have explained in previous section, the new encoding scheme can exploit a larger search space. Therefore it can find a better result than that of CDE-GA.

To demonstrate the efficiency of CCE-GA over CDE-GA on large scale networks, we present the detail results on a small network (Polska, Table 2) and on a larger network (TA2, Table 3). For Polska network, the average cost found by CCE-GA are better than that found by CDE-GA on 8/10 problem instances (except the test #3 and the test #5) For TA2 network, the average cost found by CCE-GA are always better than that of CDE-GA. This is because the CDE-GA only works well on small network but not for large scale network. We also observe that for all test sets, the minimum cost found by CCE-GA is much better than that of CDE-GA.

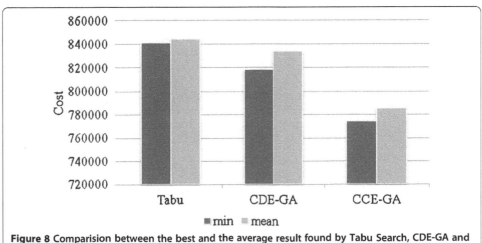

Figure 8 Comparision between the best and the average result found by Tabu Search, CDE-GA and CCE-GA on TA2 network.

Table 2 The best and average results found on polska network after 10 running times

Test #	Cost	Tabu	CDE-GA	CCE-GA
1	Min	13550	12812	12130
	Mean	14777	13923	12653
2	Min	14962	13898	13200
	Mean	15270	14670	13860
3	Min	14010	12218	12722
	Mean	15511	13289	13309
4	Min	11226	11484	10792
	Mean	12616	12359	11045
5	Min	14654	13176	14054
	Mean	13691	14318	14690
6	Min	12714	12480	11464
	Mean	12899	13262	11866
7	Min	16238	15850	15326
	Mean	17160	16709	16305
8	Min	12038	12298	12168
	Mean	12320	13099	12719
9	Min	12042	11846	11186
	Mean	12990	12386	11939
10	Min	15284	14590	13570
	Mean	15284	15300	14556

Table 3 The best and average results found on ta2 network after 10 running times

Test #	Cost	Tabu	CDE-GA	CCE-GA
1	Min	894440	850640	848320
	Mean	905968	880571	862527
2	Min	843280	836120	785480
	Mean	850613	837814	785480
3	Min	835280	817800	781480
	Mean	842613	817800	781480
4	Min	841280	822120	798640
	Mean	842613	827586	813037
5	Min	858440	836120	806960
	Mean	861756	844252	814589
6	Min	825280	806120	779800
	Mean	827413	810386	789364
7	Min	816120	799800	778640
	Mean	818986	808289	786980
8	Min	841280	832120	784960
	Mean	844280	835773	794862
9	Min	831280	814960	771480
	Mean	834746	821565	784582
10	Min	841280	818640	774320
	Mean	844480	834137	785542

Table 4 The comarision of the average running time (in second) found by tabu search, cde-ga and cce-ga

	Polska	Germany17	Atlanta	Germany50	TA2
CCE-GA	18	21	95	1951	26216
CDE-GA	13	21	78	941	13232
TabuSearch	1	5	36	666	6514

To compare the tested algorithms in terms of running time, we calculate the average running time of all 10 test sets for each algorithm. Table 4 shows that CCE-GA takes much more running times in compare with Tabu Search and CDE-GA. But if the running time for Tabu Search, CDE-GA is increased, the best result is not improved.

The above observation can be explained more clearly in Figures 9 and 10, which show the convergence rate of CDE-GA and CCE-GA on TA2 network. Here, because the gap of the convergence rate between CDE-GA and CCE-GA is too large from the first generation to 14th generation so we draw from the 15th generation. It is notable that CCE-GA converge more quickly than CDE-GA from the 15th generation. cost over the failures.

Conclusion

In this paper, we proposed a new algorithm called CCE-GA for solving A-SNDP. This algorithm uses a new simple encoding scheme called Completely Connection Encoding (CCE) to enlarge the search space to find better solution in large network instances. Experiments are conducted on real network topologies on show that our proposed approach is very efficient in solving A-SNDP. On the big instances, such as Atlanta, Germany50 and TA2 networks, the best and average result found by CCE-GA are much better than CDE-GA and Tabu Search. However, CCE-GA takes much more running times in compare with Tabu Search and CDE-GA to find best result. But if the running time for Tabu Search, CDE-GA is increased, the best result is not improved.

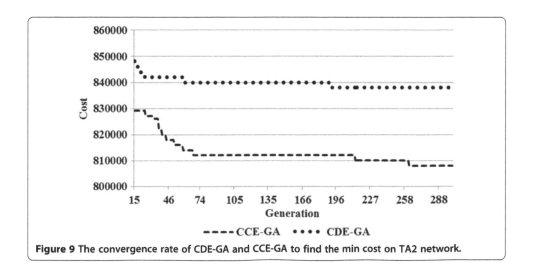

Figure 9 The convergence rate of CDE-GA and CCE-GA to find the min cost on TA2 network.

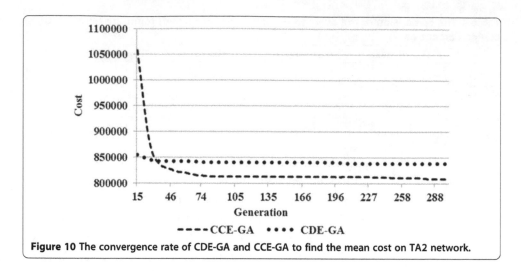

Figure 10 The convergence rate of CDE-GA and CCE-GA to find the mean cost on TA2 network.

In the future, we are planning to improve this algorithm for solving bigger instances in a reasonable time. Moreover, we hope that we can find the other approach with better results for A-SNDP.

Competing interests

The authors declare that they have no competing interests.

Authors' contributions

HTTB carried out the design, simulation and drafting the algorithms. SHN participated the design, acquisition of data and helped to draft the manuscript. Both authors read and approved the final manuscript.

Acknowledgment

This work was supported by the project *"Models for next generation of robust Internet"* funded by the Ministry of Science and Technology, Vietnam under grant number 12/2012-HD-NDT.

References

1. Johnson D, Deering S (1999) Reserved IPv6 Subnet Anycast Addresses. RFC 2526
2. Ballani H, Francis P (2005) Towards a global IP anycast service. In: SIGCOMM'05. New York, USA, pp 301–312
3. Walkowiak K (2003) Anycast Communication – A New Approach to Survivability of Connection-Oriented Networks. In: Communications in Computer and Information Science. Springer, Berlin, pp 378–389
4. Vasseur J, Pickavet M, Demeester P (2004) Network Recovery: Protection and Restoration of Optical, SONET-SDH, IP and MPLS. Morgan Kaufmann, San Francisco
5. Gładysz J, Walkowiak K (2010) Tabu Search Algorithm for Survivable Network Design Problem with Simultaneous Unicast and Anycast Flows. In: Intl Journal Of Electronics And Telecommunications, vol 56. Versita Publisher, Warsaw, pp 41–48, no. 1
6. Walkowiak K (2008) A Flow Deviation Algorithm for Joint Optimization of Unicast and Anycast Flows in Connection-Oriented Networks. In: Osvaldo Gervas, Computational Science and Its Applications – ICCSA 2008, LNCS, vol 5072. Springer, Perugia, Italy, pp 797–807
7. Walkowiak K (2006) A New Function for Optimization of Working Paths in Survivable MPLS Networks. In: Computer and Information Sciences – ISCIS 2006. Springer, Istanbul, pp 424–433
8. Grover W (2004) Mesh-based Survivable Networks: Options and Strategies for Optical, MPLS, SONET and ATM Networking. Prentice Hall PTR, Upper Saddle River, New Jersey
9. Nissen V, Gold S (2008) Survivable network design with an evolution strategy. In: Success in Evolutionary Computation. Springer, Berlin, pp 263–283
10. Sharma V, Hellstrand F (2003) Framework for MPLS-based recovery. RFC 3469
11. Michalewicz Z (1995) Genetic Algorithms + Data Structures = Evolution Programs, Thirdth edn. Springer
12. Huynh Thi Thanh B, Son Hong N, Nguyen Ngoc D (2013) Genetic Algorithm for Solving Survivable Network Design with Simultaneous Unicast and Anycast Flows. In: the Proceedings of the Eighth International Conference on Bio-Inspired Computing: Theories and Applications. BIC-TA, China, pp 1237–1247
13. Kerivin H, Ridha Mahjoub A (2005) Design of survivable networks: A survey. J Netw 46:1–21
14. Jozsa BG, Orincsay D, Kern A (2003) Surviving Multiple Network Failures Using Shared Backup Path Protection. In: Proceedings of the Eighth IEEE International Symposium on Computers and Communications. Kiris-Kemer, Turkey, June 30-July 03, 2003, pp. 1333
15. Pioro M, Medhi D (2004) Routing, Flow, and Capacity Design in Communication and Computer Networks. Morgan Kaufmann Publishers, San Francisco, CA, USA

16. Gladysz J (2009) Krzysztof Walkowiak: Optimization of survivable networks with simultaneous unicast and anycast flows. Poland, ICUMT, pp 1–6
17. Battiti R, Brunato M, Mascia F (2008) Reactive Search and Intelligent Optimization 1st. Springer, New York, USA, p 182
18. Huynh Thi Thanh B, Pham Vu L, Nguyen Ngoc D, Nguyen Sy Thai H (2012) Heuristic Algorithms for Solving Survivable Network Design Problem with Simultaneous Unicast and Anycast Flows. In: The Eight International Conference on Intelligence on Computing, ICIC-2012. Huangshang, China, pp 137–145
19. Orlowski S, Wessäly R, Pióro M, Tomaszewski A (2010) SNDlib 1.0-Survivable Network Design Library. Networks 55(3):276–286

8

Context-aware recommender for mobile learners

Rachid Benlamri[*] and Xiaoyun Zhang

* Correspondence: rbenlamr@
lakeheadu.ca
Department of Software
Engineering, Lakehead University,
955 Oliver Rd, Thunder Bay, ON P7B
5E1, Canada

Abstract

As mobile technologies become widespread, new challenges are facing the research community to develop lightweight learning services adapted to the learner's profile, context, and task at hand. This paper attempts to solve some of these challenges by proposing a knowledge-driven recommender for mobile learning on the Semantic Web. The contribution of this work is an approach for context integration and aggregation using an upper ontology space and a unified reasoning mechanism to adapt the learning sequence and the learning content based on the learner's activity, background, used technology, and surrounding environment. Whenever context change occurs, the system identifies the new contextual features and translates them into new adaptation constraints in the operating environment. The proposed system has been implemented and tested on various mobile devices. The experimental results show many learning scenarios to demonstrate the usefulness of the system in practice.

Keywords: Ubiquitous learning; Context modeling and management; Semantic web; Ontology design; Mobile learning

Introduction

The Semantic Web is an extension of the current web, whereby content is given well defined meaning so that it can be understood and processed by both software agents and humans [1]. Semantic Web provides an infrastructure with the potential to efficiently reason with content that is defined at the semantic level with formalized knowledge [2-6]. The challenge in an information-rich world is not only to make information available to people at any time, any place, and in any form, but also to offer the right content to the right person in the right way [7-9]. In particular, in the context of mobile learning, if such approach is to be adopted, many research efforts are needed to close the gap between learning strategies, knowledge discovery, and context perception and management on the Semantic Web [10]. These efforts would lead to a Semantic Web that has the potential to revolutionize the way learning services available on the web are discovered, adapted, and delivered to mobile users based on their context. To achieve this goal, we need to formally describe not only web-content, but also the various system stakeholders including content producers, content consumers, and surrounding context. This approach is adopted in this paper by integrating learner's knowledge, domain knowledge, and context knowledge. At the semantic level, meta-information and reasoning mechanisms are used to integrate these knowledge components, thus making it possible to infer the learning sequence that suits learner's profile and experience, and the learning content that suits their activity, used technology and surrounding environment.

In this paper we deal with learning in a mobile environment. Although, much progress has been made in the field of mobile services [11-15], we believe that more research is needed in the area of mobile learning. This is mainly due to the fact that most existing systems have been designed with focus on technology only [16], while they should equally address knowledge representation and learning strategies' aspects for mobile learning. In particular, several obstacles still hinder personalization of mobile learning services, such as: (i) current mobile learning services act as passive components rather than active components that can be embedded with context awareness mechanisms; (ii) existing approaches for service discovery neglect contextual information on surrounding environment; and (iii) lack of context modeling and reasoning techniques that allow integration of various contextual features for better personalization. In this paper, an attempt is made to solve some of the above mentioned problems, aiming to build a mobile recommender system with semantic-rich awareness information. Our goal is to develop services capable of providing content recommendations tailored to the learner's background, context, and task at hand. Mobile learners expect to access such learning services from various ubiquitous setups (workplace, home, on the move, etc.) with different operational characteristics such as varying network bandwidth and limited resources on mobile devices [17]. Also, it is important to note that the operational environment of a mobile setting changes frequently. It is therefore necessary to consider a proactive context awareness mechanism that can sense both system-centric and learner-centric context and adapts the accessed services accordingly at run-time. In such setup, context aggregation can be made possible using a shared ontology space and a unified reasoning mechanism. In particular, whenever context change occurs, the system identifies the new contextual features and translates them into new adaptation constraints in the operating environment. The contribution of this paper can be summarized into three points. First, a shared ontology space for capturing, integrating and modeling contextual knowledge at a higher level based on learner context, activity context, device context and environment context. Second, a method for structuring semantic knowledge about subject-domain in such a way to enable provision of content at different granularity levels to suit learners with various background and skills. Finally, a model for run-time context management that translates context changes into system-centric and learner-centric adaptations for better personalization.

The remainder of this paper is organized as follows. Section 2 reviews related work and discusses the main challenges for developing context-aware mobile learning systems. The overall system design and architecture, including context modeling are presented in section 3. Section 4 discusses the reasoning mechanisms used to deal with context integration and management. The experimental results are discussed in section 5, and finally, conclusions are drawn and further research work is suggested.

Background and related work

Research in the field of personalized learning has been dominated by the use of ontologies and related Semantic Web technologies [18-28]. Ontology is a representation of a set of concepts within a domain and the relationships between those concepts [18]. It is used to reason about the properties of that domain. Ontology concepts are defined in terms of classes which are extended with properties. These are commonly encoded using ontology languages such as the Web Ontology Language (OWL). In particular, ontology-based approaches have been widely used for context modeling and management [8-12]. A variety of ontologies have been adopted to model knowledge about subject domains, users, resources, and other contextual elements of the user surroundings [8,29-34]. In such setups, reasoning techniques are usually applied on metadata derived from a single ontology. However, real-life learning systems require simultaneous use of knowledge derived from multiple ontologies. Cross-ontology reasoning presents many challenges. One major challenge is related to disparity and semantic mismatching between related context elements across ontologies [35,36]. A solution to this problem is efficient integration of various ontologies into an upper ontology space capable of capturing and modeling information related to the global shared knowledge at a higher semantic level, and thus simplifying cross-ontology reasoning. Another problem of concern with ontology based approaches is their inappropriateness to reasoning with uncertainty. It should be noted that not all context elements are perceived with precision. Some of the context elements are quantized with uncertainty leading to certain ambiguity while defining and reasoning with context, [37]. This problem can be dealt with by integrating various reasoning models that may combine probabilistic, rule-based and logic reasoning techniques [38-40].

In addition to the above-mentioned problems, research in mobile learning recommenders has its own challenges. The task of a mobile learning recommender can be considered, to a certain extent, as a knowledge management task to support the learner's current activity. This is because the goal for mobile learning is not always long term learning, but, in many cases, an on-demand learning process triggered by immediate real-world needs. In such learning environment, the context of the learner matters, and the system should be able to capture the learner's profile, learner's context, task at hand, and the environment in which learning occurs. This knowledge is important to provide context-aware delivery methods that can generate content that meets the immediate learning goals. Other challenges that need to be addressed to develop robust mobile learning recommenders are those related to (i) the limited-resource mobile technology; (ii) low-bandwidth and unsecured wireless communication; (iii) heterogeneous context management and (iv) personalized content retrieval. This paper attempts to solve some of the problems related to the last two challenges, heterogeneous context management and personalized content retrieval, making use of the progress made in ubiquitous computing and the Semantic Web respectively. Before describing our system, we first overview recently published work in the field of ontology-based content retrieval and adaptation for e/m-learning. We then particularly focus on work in m-learning recommenders.

Dolog and Nejdl [33] have used knowledge extracted from four different ontologies (subject, user, resource, and link ontology) to realize personalized access to resources on the Semantic Web. Subject and resource ontologies are used to provide explicit semantic about information resources and the way they fit to user queries and goals. However, user and link ontologies are used to provide additional means for deciding which links to show, hide, and annotate according to the learner's background. The focus of their work is mainly around learner-centric adaptations. Another system that relies on learner modeling is the European Union project, Learning In Process (LIP) [41]. LIP aims to provide immediate learning content on demand for knowledge intensive organizations through incorporating context into the design of learning systems. A matching procedure is presented to suggest personalized learning content based on user's current competency gap. The matching process tries to find relevant learning objects for a given user context by computing a similarity measure between the current user context abstraction and the ontological metadata of each learning object.

In the field of mobile learning, many approaches were adopted to develop context-aware learning services. These vary from simple systems relying solely on device content adaptation [42], to complex infrastructures for generating context aware mobile learning applications [43]. Yarandi et al.[44] have developed a mobile learning system with four modules to enable courseware management, course content adaptation, test evaluation and course recommendation mediation. The system is used to learn new natural languages. The course recommendation mediator selects suitable learning material by traversing the courseware knowledgebase according to pedagogical rules and ontological user profiles. The recommendation mediator is guided using results provided by the course-test evaluation module. Course material consists of learning objects with various granularity and their associated learning activities (writing, reading, speaking and listening). Each activity retains a learning objective, a difficulty-level, a suggested time for completion, and is associated a test score based on a probabilistic model. In a similar study, Benlamri et al. [45] have developed a combined model based on probabilistic learning techniques and ontologies to enable context processing and management in a mobile learning environment. The system uses Naïve Bayesian classifiers to deal with context elements that are quantized with uncertainty. Naïve Bayesian classifiers are used to recognize high level contexts in terms of their constituent atomic context elements involving uncertainty. Recognized contexts are then interpreted as triggers of actions yielding web service discovery and adaptation in order to achieve personalized instruction that best match the learner's needs and the operating environment. Mobiglam [46] is another mobile learning framework that is based on Bayesian techniques. Unlike the systems mentioned above, Mobiglam allows users to access resources and other learning services through Virtual Learning Environments (VLEs) such as Moodle and WebCT. Device adaptations are provided by a J2ME application installed on the client devices, while adaptation of VLE content is done on the server side through a decision engine relying on a Bayesian learning algorithm.

Unlike the systems described above, Mobilearn [43] is a complete infrastructure developed by a consortium of European universities in collaboration with MIT and Stanford to build mobile learning applications. Mobilearn is based on the Open Mobile-access Abstract Framework (OMAF). The latter is built upon two technologies – an extended version of the MIT-OKI (Open Knowledge Initiative) which provides an open and extensible architecture for learning technology [47] – and the IMS-ALF (Abstract Learning Framework) which provides an abstract representation of interoperable services and their interfaces [48]. The goal is to build a framework that can provide various specifications (i.e. various mobile applications) based on the used services, according to the open architecture approach.

Another challenge of mobile learning is its human computer interface (Mobile HCI) aspect, and especially the provision of context-aware communication and interaction. For instance, a mobile device that support a number of network adaptors, and equipped with some sensors such a GPS (Global Positioning System) unit, a network bandwidth sensor, and a smart card for user-authentication, can provide useful context-aware functionalities that allow one to adapt the behavior of the system according to the sensed wireless network, position in space (location-awareness), unexpected network interruptions, and security threats respectively. Such system becomes able to select what content to show and how to show it based on the learner's activity and surrounding environment. An example system with such capability is the MObile PErsonal Trainer, MOPET [49]. The latter monitors users' positions and other physiological parameters in outdoor sports activities to present functionalities such as location-aware maps augmented with visualizations of users' performance, or context-aware fitness advice and 3D demonstrations of exercises. Mobile learning systems should exhibit these capabilities to achieve efficient context-aware communication and interaction.

Although our approach builds on many of the techniques described above, it differs from previous work in several aspects. First, unlike the above mentioned approaches, the proposed system tries to build a global context view out of a large set of heterogeneous contextual information, including knowledge about the learner, learning domain, learning activity, used technology, and surrounding environment. Second, unlike the systems described in [33,41,44] which use separate ontologies for reasoning with domain knowledge and context knowledge respectively, our approach uses a shared upper ontology space that permits reasoning with the entire system-centric and learner-centric contexts, thus enabling efficient context integration and adaptation. Finally, an important aspect of our approach is the ability for reasoning under uncertainty. It should be noted that not all contextual information around the learner can be quantized with certainty, yet the semantic web models are logic based with facts either being true or false. One possible solution to this problem is to simplify contextual data, which is fundamentally continuous or uncertain, down to symbolic discrete assertions. However, this process may introduce errors which can further propagate globally when repeatedly used in the reasoning process. To deal with this issue we opted for uncertainty representations like fuzzy logic which uses non-linear combination functions. Fuzzy logic uses min/max to combine values, so repeat combination of the same information does not introduce significant errors [50] in the reasoning process.

System design and architecture

The overall system architecture is presented in Figure 1. The core of the proposed system is based on a Run Time Environment (RTE) designed to maintain consistent behavior across variations in the operating environment. The aim is to provide learning services adapted to the learner's global context. Therefore, the main function of the RTE is to coordinate and facilitate integration and aggregation of the main context components as they emerge from the learner's interaction with the system. To achieve such complex task, we structured the RTE into three hierarchical levels as shown in Figure 2. At the lower level of the hierarchy is the context sensing layer which is provided by a collection of hardware and software sensors that continuously probe the wireless network features, temporal-spatial data, device features, and users' background and preferences. The context sensing layer generates quantized and non-quantized raw data whose values are numeric values, boolean values, and literals, and most of which are time-stamped. To transform this context data into meaningful context information

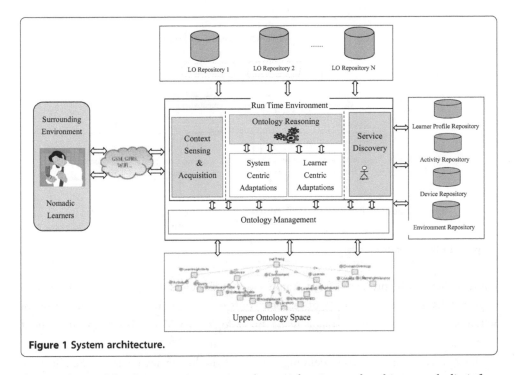

Figure 1 System architecture.

that can be used by the reasoning engine, the raw-data is translated into symbolic information. The mapping is achieved by the context perception layer through computation, inference and learning techniques. The context perception layer is independent from the context sensing technology in the sense that it provides an abstract context representation through the use of ontologies. At the higher level, is context adaptation layer, where learning services are discovered and learning content is adapted based on perceived context. The upper ontology space describing knowledge about all context components is incremented with subject-domain ontology knowledge, and used as a unified knowledge base for system reasoning. The result of the reasoning process is a set of extracted metadata used for learning services discovery and adaptation based on system-centric context (i.e. device and environment context) and learner-centric context (i.e. learner and activity context). In particular, the extracted metadata is used to personalize both the learning path and the learning content in order to match the learner's background, prerequisite requirements, previous tasks, available network bandwidth, network security, and other connectivity issues. Each of these adaptations is controlled by context-adaptation logic in the form of ontology reasoning.

Context acquisition and representation

Context is any information that can be used to characterize the situation of an entity, where an entity can be a person, a place, a physical or a computational object [51]. Context information can be classified into atomic context and composite context. Atomic context elements are associated with raw data that is either sensed or profiled. Composite context on the other hand can be derived from atomic context elements through computation, inference, or learning techniques. Example of computed composite context is user's age, or time to accomplish a learning task. Example of inferred composite context is inference of media type that can be played by a handheld device based on current network bandwidth and available memory. Finally, learned context is

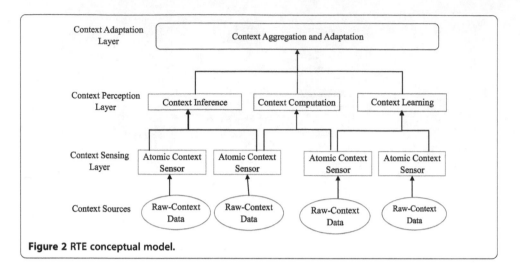

Figure 2 RTE conceptual model.

context that can be predicted from atomic context elements using prior knowledge and a probabilistic model. Example of learned context used in this study is prediction of wireless network bandwidth-range using fuzzy logic as will be shown in subsequent sections.

Many researchers have tried defining context at the higher level such as Schilit et al. [18] who decompose context into three categories – computing context – user context – and physical context. In this study, a fourth dimension of context is introduced to deal with activity context. The inclusion of activity context in a mobile setting is motivated by the fact that the needs of mobile users regarding information access are quite different from those of stationary users [52]. Usually, mobile users' needs are mainly about personalized content that is highly sensitive to their immediate environment and task at hand. Therefore, activity context will significantly improve service discovery and learning content adaptation to user needs and context.

In this study we divide context into four context groups – Learner context – Activity context – Device context – and Environment context. Figure 3 shows the way these four context categories extend each other for better context integration and service adaptation. Learner context is the main source for provisioning personalization. It also extends activity context by providing information such as learner's background, preferred language(s), and learner's schedule. Activity context however deals with accessed services; consumed learning resources; adopted learning sequences; and other subject-

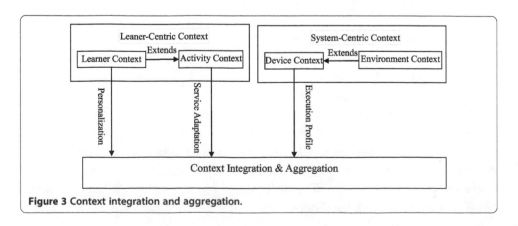

Figure 3 Context integration and aggregation.

domain related knowledge. It uses subject-domain ontology as the main backbone for service adaptation and content management. Device context on the other hand is the main source for determining the software and hardware capabilities of used devices, and hence is used for setting the right execution profile for the accessed services. Information such as used operating system, screen resolution, and available memory are crucial to target metadata that allow discovery of services that can run on such devices. Finally, environment context deals with information such as temporal and spatial contextual information, network bandwidth, and other quality service features including security. Environment context extends device context by adjusting the execution profile of accessed services. For example, in determining the media type of the resources that can run on the used device at a specific point in time, we may not solely depend on the capabilities of the used device, but we should also take into consideration current network bandwidth and network security for instance.

Figure 2 shows the main components of the context acquisition system. At the lower level, a set of software and hardware services are used to sense and collect atomic context data from different sources. Whenever the learner logs into the system, the latter identifies the used device type, and then retrieves its static features from the associated device profile stored in a device profile repository (see Figure 1) which is based on the CC/PP (Composite Capabilities / Preference Profiles) standard [53]. It also senses the user's location, network channel used for connecting the learner; its connection speed (i.e. maximum theoretical speed), and the current available bandwidth [54]. It should be noted that while connection speed provides a good idea of the capabilities of the used network adapter (i.e. its upper bound limit), it does not help predict the actual network bandwidth which might be substantially less if the network is overloaded. So, ideally, the available bandwidth should be continuously monitored to report bandwidth changes as they occur. However, the process of continuously sensing and updating such dynamic context element is time and resource consuming, especially in a mobile computing environment where system resources are very limited [14]. To deal with this problem, we rather predict current network bandwidth based on previously sensed values. This is done using a fuzzy logic approach as described in section 4.1.

Table 1 shows some of the atomic context data used in this study. Each atomic context is defined by a 4-tuple (*Source_Id, Feature_Id, Absolute_Value, Symbolic_Value*). *Source_Id* refers to one of the above-mentioned four categories of context. *Feature_Id*

Table 1 Example of Atomic Context Properties

Source_ID (Type)	Feature_ID (Type)	Absolute_Value	Symbolic_Value
1 (Device)	1 (Memory Size)	Kbytes	{Small, Medium, Large}
1 (Device)	2 (Screen Res.)	(length, width)	{Low, Medium, High}
1 (Device)	3 (OS)	String	{Linux, Symbian, …}
1 (Device)	4 (Media)	String	{Text, Image, Audio, Video}
2 (Environment)	1 (Net. Bandwidth)	Kbps	{Low, Medium, High}
2 (Environment)	2 (Ne.Security)	Boolean	{Secured, NonSecured}
2 (Environment)	3 (Time)	Date-time	{Current(yyyy:mm:dd;hh:mm:ss)}
3 (Learner)	1 (Authentication Info.)	String	{Username, Password}
3 (Learner)	2 (Language)	String	{English, French, …}
4 (Activity)	1 (Query)	String	{keyword, Domain-concept}

identifies the atomic context within the context group, *Absolute_Value* is the actual value of the atomic context, and *Symbolic_Value* is the associated symbolic representation of the actual value that is used for context reasoning. The focus of this paper is on the way context data is perceived, integrated and recognized for better personalization of the learning process.

Ontology-based context modeling

At the semantic level, we define context information using an upper ontology space that includes four interrelated sub-ontologies – learner ontology – activity ontology – device ontology – and environment ontology, in addition to a domain ontology that is used to define the subject domain of interest. Thus, context aggregation is enabled using a shared ontology space and a unified reasoning mechanism across these sub-ontologies. Figure 4 shows the upper ontology space which encompasses the four context sub-ontologies and the domain ontology. Various core ontology classes describing basic ontology concepts (e.g. *Device*, *LearningResource*), role concepts (e.g. *Learner*), and role holders (e.g. *LearningActivity*), are used to interrelate concepts among the combined sub-ontologies. As shown in Figure 4, the five sub-ontologies are blended along the many properties that link various classes to form the upper ontology space. The following sections describe in details each of these sub-ontologies as well as the relationships between them.

3.2.1 Domain ontology

Domain ontology is expressed in terms of a hierarchy of subject topics, each of which is described by a set of concepts and their relationships. The class *concept* is the ontology's core class as shown in Figure 5. Concepts are related along the properties *HasPrerequisite*, *Is-a*, *HasPart*, and *HasNececassaryPart* to describe the prerequisite, is-a, part-whole, and necessary part-whole dependencies between the various concepts respectively. While these properties are important authoring tools for defining concepts' fragments (sub-concepts) at any desirable granularity level, they are also crucial to guiding learners in building their learning paths. In addition to the above mentioned

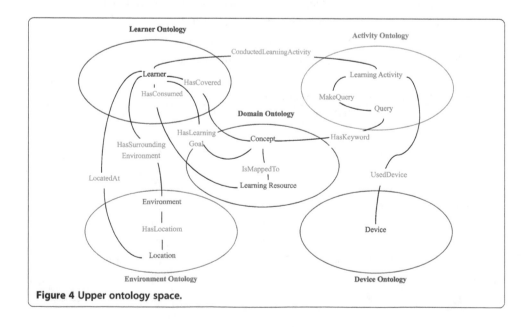

Figure 4 Upper ontology space.

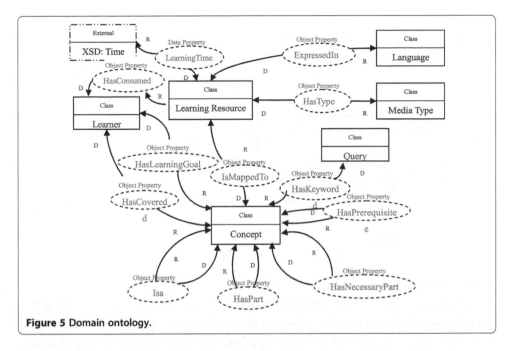

Figure 5 Domain ontology.

properties, we use the class property *IsMappedTo* to annotate learning resources with ontology concepts. This property along with *HasKeyword* and *HasLearningGoal* properties, which associate keywords input by the learner to most related ontology concepts and learning goals, are very useful for retrieving learning resources by mapping their metadata to ontology concepts, thus allowing resource sharing. Another important property is *LearningTime* which associates learning resources with the typical learning time it takes a learner to consume them. This feature enables time-constrained learning by restricting the search for those learning resources that fall within the learner's allotted time. Time constrained learning is crucial in mobile learning which is time-dependent in nature. In this study, we opted for the IEEE LOM (Learning Object Metadata) standard [55] to represent learning resources. LOM introduces a base schema that abstracts data elements for learning resources into metadata with nine categories capable of describing content granularity, learning time, and semantic relationship between described concepts.

3.2.2 Learner ontology

Learner ontology is used to capture knowledge about the learner, thus enabling the system to discover, adapt, and deliver the most relevant learning resources based on their needs, background, and preferences. As shown in Figure 6, learner ontology is related to domain ontology along *HasCovered* and *HasConsumed* properties which link learners to covered concepts and consumed learning resources respectively. In particular, when a new learning path is constructed, all consumed learning resources are automatically discovered and removed for better personalization, and further learning resources are suggested to fulfill the learning goal. The latter is captured through the *HasLearningGoal* property which associates learners to one or more concepts they are interested in. Finally, the property *ConductedLearningActivity* is used to track previously conducted learning interactions by a particular learner. Other properties are also used to determine learner's location, preferred language(s), surrounding environment, and available learning time.

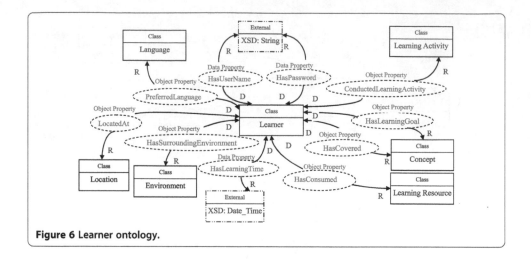

Figure 6 Learner ontology.

3.2.3 Activity ontology

Activity ontology is used to capture knowledge about a learning activity (i.e. set of user interactions) conducted by a learner over a period of time using a specific handheld device. Knowledge embedded in this ontology allows the system to infer history of all user interactions with the system, including queries made by the learner and used devices. It also allows the system to recover from wireless network disconnections, which could be frequent in a mobile environment, by identifying the most recent learning activity and restoring most recent learning context. Figure 7 shows the main concepts used in activity ontology along with their relationships with other ontology concepts. The property *UsedDevice* links learning activities to devices that were used to conduct them. Device is deliberately linked to learning activity as learners may use different devices in their various interactions with the system. The property *MakeQuery* allows inferring all queries made during a learning interaction with the system. Queries are linked to concepts along the *HasKeyword* property. The system is designed to help learners use ontology vocabulary to compose their queries. The data property *QueryTime* is used to time stamp all queries made by the learner in order to infer the order in which ontology concepts were covered and their respective learning resources were consumed. This important temporal feature is crucial to organize and adjust the learning path

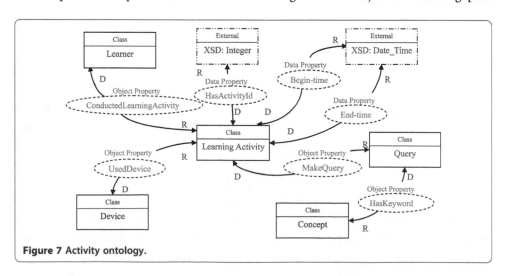

Figure 7 Activity ontology.

every time a new query is made or a new learning resource is invoked by the learner. Information such as begin-time and end-time of a learning activity can also be retrieved from the ontology to track the most recent interaction with the system, and to deal with the learner's available time.

3.2.4 Device ontology

Device ontology is used to capture knowledge about used devices and their hardware and software capabilities as well as their limitations. This knowledge is very useful for discovery of learning services whose execution profile matches the characteristics of the used device. Our device ontology is conforming to the CC/PP standard [53]. The latter is an industry standard for describing a delivery context, a set of attributes that characterizes the capabilities of the access mechanisms and the preferences of the user. Using CC/PP, allows separating content-design from content-delivery. CC/PP represents device capabilities using two-level hierarchy consisting of hardware and software attributes. As shown in Figure 8, the device ontology is based on the CC/PP components, *HasSoftwareProfile* and *HasHardwareProfile*. These two ontology classes define knowledge related to the software-centric and hardware-centric features of a device. For instance, information about device operating system, supported applications, and screen resolution are essential to discover learning services whose software and hardware requirements match device capabilities. Other properties embedded in the device ontology can also be used for personalization. For example, the property *SupportedLanguage* is used to infer whether the used device supports a language preferred by the learner. Learner ontology and device ontology are linked along property *UsedDevice* which enables inferring which device is used by a particular learner during a specific learning activity.

3.2.5 Environment ontology

Environment ontology formally describes the knowledge about a learner environment which consists mainly of temporal and spatial contextual features, as well as networking, security, and connectivity issues. Figure 9 shows the main ontology classes and their relationships. The property *HasLocation* links the Environment class to the current learner's location, while the properties *HasWirelessNetwork*, *IsSecured* and *Has-Bandwidth* describes the wireless Network the learner is connected to, its security status, and its current bandwidth. These contextual elements are crucial to infer and

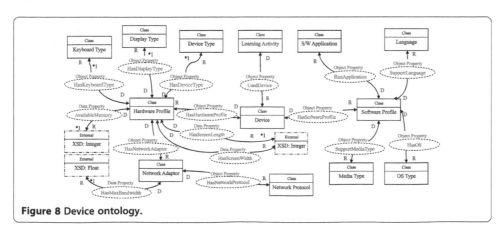

Figure 8 Device ontology.

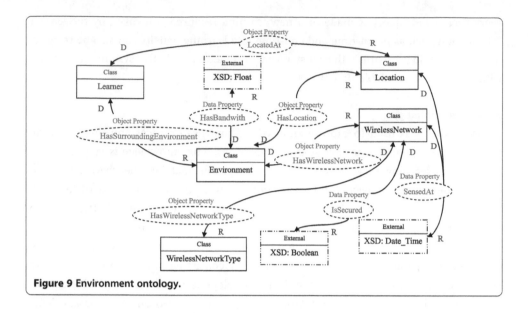

Figure 9 Environment ontology.

adjust learning content that is compatible, in terms of size, media-type, and security with the technological set-up that characterizes the surrounding environment.

Ontology reasoning

Understanding the importance and the role of tacit knowledge is key element to formulating knowledge management strategies for mobile-learning systems. Unlike explicit knowledge that is coded knowledge, tacit knowledge is knowledge that is embedded in system actors (i.e. learners and other dynamic context elements) [56] and which is difficult to be shared and distributed. In this study, the upper ontology space, built out of the five integrated sub-ontologies is used in such a way to allow tacit knowledge related to learners and their context to be defined at the semantic level and used to a great extent in the personalization process. In particular, knowledge in the upper ontology space is structured in such a way to allow building a conceptual learner model out of a sequence of learning activities by linking a user's conceptualization to particular subject domain ontology. This constitutes the key design aspect of our upper ontology space to enable personalized learning. A learning activity is characterized by user interactions, through which contextual information related to the user's surroundings, as well as concepts covered, queries performed, and learning resources consumed are stored and used as knowledge facts to enable further inferences aiming to achieve better adaptation. Thus, the perceived context and the accessed domain information are efficiently used for building a personalized learning path that is aware of the learner's interaction history, preferences, background knowledge, and operating environment. The used approach models the learner at the semantic level by providing a formal learner's conceptualization defined in OWL, and thus allows reasoning upon it in order to infer the learner's understanding of the subject domain. The reasoning is performed in terms of SWRL (Semantic Web Rule Language) rules that are applied on knowledge represented in the OWL-DL (Description Logics) ontology. It should be noted here that reasoning in systems integrating DL ontologies and rules is a very hard task [56]. This is mainly due to undecidability of reasoning in such systems. This is particularly the case for those systems integrating DL ontologies with recursive or hybrid rules [57,58]. So, bridging the discrepancy in these two knowledge representations is a challenging problem. Many studies [57-60] have shown that to avoid undecidability of reasoning, practically all decidable approaches to integrating ontologies and rules should impose specific conditions which restrict the interaction between the rules and the ontology. In this work, we adopt a similar decidable reasoning approach by adhering to restrictions, such as avoiding recursive and hybrid rules. In particular, we use the SWRL-Jess Bridge, a bridge that provides the infrastructure for incorporating the Jess rule engine into Protégé-OWL to execute SWRL rules. The system also relies on some SWRL-built-in libraries, which include an implementation of the core SWRL built-ins, as well as mathematical built-ins, to support the use of complex expressions in rules, reasoning with temporal information and querying OLW ontologies.

The sequence of steps given below illustrates the personalization process adopted by our system in a typical learning scenario where a learner submits a query in a specific subject domain area and receives a planned learning sequence fulfilling the learning goal. This learning scenario is also depicted graphically in Figure 10.

1. When the learner logs in, his background, preferences, and previous learning activity are retrieved.
2. The learner uses the domain ontology vocabulary to query the system.
3. The subject-domain ontology related to the learner's query is identified and retrieved.
4. Based on the learner's query, the system infers the related ontology concept(s) and identifies those concepts that are part of prerequisite knowledge, core-knowledge, and related knowledge using *HasPrerequisite*, *HasNecessaryPart*, and *HasPart* properties respectively.
5. Next, the system uses the perceived device and environment atomic context elements to infer metadata that adapts the search for those learning resources that are suitable for the system-centric context.

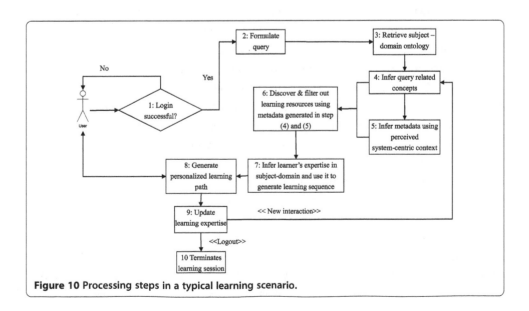

Figure 10 Processing steps in a typical learning scenario.

6. The metadata generated in (4) dealing with related domain ontology concepts, and the system-centric metadata generated in (5) are then used to discover and filter out learning resources from various learning repositories.

7. The system will then determine the learner's expertise in the subject-domain (i.e. tacit knowledge) by inferring previous learning activities, covered concepts, adopted learning paths, and consumed learning resources. This knowledge is used to build a personalized learning sequence that is aware of the learner's history and available learning time. Thus, the newly constructed learning sequence consists of optimized system-centric learning resources to fulfill the current learner's activity and goals.

8. The personalized learning sequence is then provided to the learner for navigation.

9. Based on the newly selected concept, learner's expertise is automatically updated and the personalized learning path is re-adjusted by resuming processing from step (4).

10. The learning activity terminates when either the learner logs out the system, or when all domain concepts related to current activity have been covered.

The above strategy strives to meet the best personalized learning path by dynamically updating the learning sequence based on the learner interactions with the system and surrounding environment. Below, we give a detailed description of the various system-centric adaptations and learner-centric adaptations used in the personalization process. We also provide the algorithm used to help navigate a learning path.

4.1 System-centric adaptation

In a mobile environment it is important for the system to consider system-centric adaptations to cope with the lack of resources in used devices and the unsecured low-bandwidth wireless network. Thus, system-centric adaptations aim at filtering out those learning resources that can efficiently be transmitted over the network and properly run on used devices. These adaptations are triggered by the context monitoring process which identifies context changes and proactively performs actions such as restricting media type and pruning large learning resources from the learning path in case of low network bandwidth. A number of inference rules have been developed to operate on perceived device and environment atomic context elements to achieve this goal. The diagram shown in Figure 11 describes the logical steps used to achieve the main system-centric adaptations considered in this study.

When the learner logs into the system, first, the system senses the used network adaptor and retrieves its connection speed. Connection speed is an attribute that is straightforward to obtain and it represents the maximum theoretical speed for the used wireless adapter [56]. Knowing the type of the network connection, such as IEEE 802.11 or GPRS, gives our reasoning engine the insight that allows it to make some adaptation choices related to media-type and size of resources that are to be retrieved. This is achieved by taking into account the available bandwidth and device features. For example, if the network connection is IEEE 802.11, the system does not need to sense the network bandwidth and does not need to make any restrictions on media type because the available bandwidth is stable and large enough to handle all type of resources. However, if the sensed connection is GPRS, the system adapts the media-type and size based on the available bandwidth as explained below. For example, for a GPRS

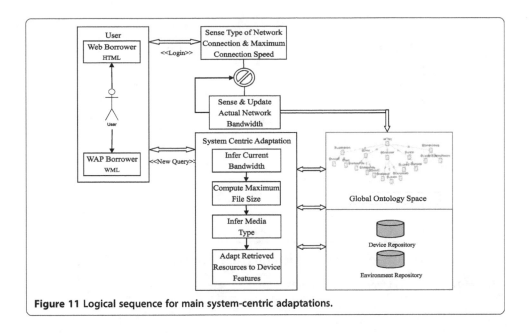

Figure 11 Logical sequence for main system-centric adaptations.

connection with a maximum connection speed of 48 kbps, the actual network bandwidth is usually less than 48 kbps due to traffic on the network [54]. Ideally, the system should continuously sense and update the current network bandwidth whenever bandwidth change occurs. However, the process of continuously sensing and updating the ever changing bandwidth is time and resource consuming as it involves sending data packets through the network. To solve this problem, we only sense the actual bandwidth at some points in time, and we use a fuzzy logic approach in conjunction with SWRL rules to predict the available bandwidth between these points. Also, to reason with bandwidth, we translate the predicted current bandwidth into meaningful symbolic values such as *low*, *medium*, and *high* bandwidth. Fuzzy logic is also used to predict the maximum size of learning resources that can be communicated without incurring long delays. For instance, we only search for learning resources with text type if a mobile device, operating on a GPRS network for instance, has very low bandwidth. However, we can extend media type to image and video if the network bandwidth is high and the available device memory is large. We also perform other checks to adapt to features such as screen resolution, used operating system, and network security. Below we describe the fuzzy logic approach used to predict media type and size and we give a full scenario to illustrate all system-centric adaptations.

We make use of the fuzzy logic truth values in conjunction with SWRL rules to allocate symbolic value to the predicted current network bandwidth. Figure 12 shows the membership function for network bandwidth. This is used to predict the network bandwidth using the fuzzy qualifying linguistic variables such as *low*, *medium*, and *high*. Note that *Maxband* which stands for maximum bandwidth is associated with the maximum connection speed of the used wireless adaptor. The symbol $\mu_A(x)$ represents a truth value that is between 0 and 1. Based on the membership function given in Figure 12, $\mu_A(x)$ can be computed by (1).

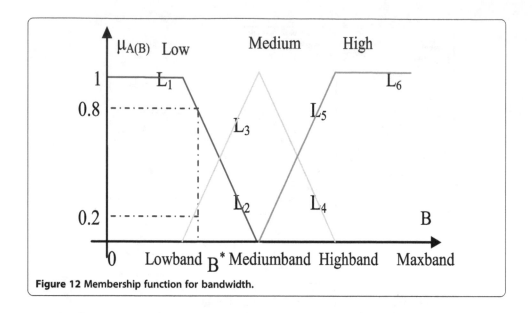

Figure 12 Membership function for bandwidth.

$$L_1 : \mu_A(b) = 1$$
$$L_2 : \mu_A(b) = -\frac{b-Mediumband}{Mediumband-Lowband}$$
$$L_3 : \mu_A(b) = \frac{b-Lowband}{Mediumband-Lowband}$$
$$L_4 : \mu_A(b) = -\frac{b-Highband}{Highband-Mediumband} \tag{1}$$
$$L_5 : \mu_A(b) = \frac{b-Mediumband}{Highband-Mediumband}$$
$$L_6 : \mu_A(b) = 1$$

In Rule-Set-1 we describe the SWRL rules that are used to infer the truth values of classified symbolic network bandwidth given in (1). For the sake of space we only give *TruthValueRule1* and *TruthValueRule2* which are respectively related to L_1 and L_2 of (1), and which are used to infer the truth values associated to low network bandwidth. The abstract SWRL syntax which is consistent with the OWL specification is rather verbose and not particularly easy to read [61]. Instead, we use a relatively informal "human readable" form where both antecedent and consequent are conjunctions of atoms with variables prefixed with a question mark (e.g., ?x), and which may also include functional notations as shown in Rule-Set-1. The latter shows the two above-mentioned rules which use the property *UsedDevice(?act,?dev)* which associates a learner identified by an activity identifier *act* to their handheld device *dev*, and the data properties *HasBandwidth* and *MaxBandwidth* which describe respectively the current network bandwidth and maximum connection speed of a used handheld device.

Rule-Set-1 SWRL rules for fuzy logic truth values
TruthValueRule1
ActivityID(?act) ∧ UsedDevice(?act, ?dev)∧ HasBandwidth(?dev, ?b) ∧ HasNetworkAdaptor(?dev, GPRS) ∧MaxBandwidth(?dev,?Maxband) ∧ swrlb:multiply(?Lowband,?Maxband, 0.25) ∧ swrlb:lessThanOrEqual(?b, ?Lowband)→ProbLow(?dev, 1.0) ∧ NetworkBandwidth(?dev, "Low").

TruthValueRule2

ActivityID(?act) ∧ UsedDevice(?act, ?dev) ∧ HasBandwidth(?dev, ?b) ∧ HasNetworkA-daptor(?dev, GPRS) ∧ MaxBandwidth(?dev,?Maxband) ∧ swrlb:multiply(?Lowband,? Maxband,0.25) ∧ swrlb:multiply(?Mediumband, ?Maxband, 0.5) ∧ swrlb:greaterThan(?b, ?Lowband) ∧ swrlb:lessThanOrEqual(?b, ?Mediumband) ∧ swrlb:subtract (?z1, ?Med-iumband, ?b) ∧ swrlb:subtract(?z2, ?Mediumband,?Lowband) ∧ swrlb:divide(?z, ?z1, ? z2)→ProbLow (?dev, ?z) ∧ NetworkBandwidth(?dev, "Low")

The following real-life scenario illustrates the way we apply the SWRL rules shown in Rule-Set-1. For instance, let's assume that *Irene* is using the "Motorola W270" mobile device model, called here *MotoW270* which supports a maximum connection speed of 32.0 kbps. Let's also assume that the value (x^*) which represents the most recently sensed network bandwidth is found to be around 18.0 kbps. This is fluctuating between medium to high bandwidth with respect to the maximum connection speed as shown in Figure 12. When *TruthValueRule4* and *TruthValueRule5* are applied, facts (*A2*) and (*B2*) are inferred, resulting into the addition of four statements to the list of facts as shown in Rule-Set-2. These new facts reveal the probabilities for the predicted current bandwidth which were found to be 0.75 for medium bandwidth and 0.25 for high bandwidth.

The inferred probabilities associated with current bandwidth are then used to determine the maximum allowable resource size. The aim here is to target resources which have reasonable size, as it is not practical to offer the learner a large learning resource (e.g. few Mbytes) if the used device operates on a low bandwidth (e.g. few kbps). So, we conducted few experiments on three devices with different capabilities to identify some typical threshold values related to resource sizes that can be used for specific bandwidth ranges. The used devices are a basic Nokia phone emulator, a Sony-Ericson W830C and an HTC-S261 smartphone which have a maximum bandwidth of 32kpbs, 48 kbps and 120 kbps respectively. We used these devices to request learning resources of different media type and size under a network bandwidth varying from 8 kbps to 120 kbps. Based on these experiments, we have adopted the following assumptions aiming to keep a reasonable response time. If a mobile device has a connection speed less than 32 kbps, we should not consider resources that exceed 500Kbytes. However, if the connection speed was between 32 kbps to 66 kbps, then resources over 1Mbytes should not be considered. We used these threshold values along with the previously inferred symbolic values associated with current network bandwidth to predict the maximum allowable resource size.

Rule-Set-2 Examples of truth value inferences
Ontology related facts

A1) before applying TruthValueRule4

ActivityID(Irene) UsedDevice(Irene, MotoW270) HasBandwidth(MotoW270, 18.0) HasNetworkAdaptor(MotoW270, GPRS) MaxBand(MotoW270, 32.0) swrlb:multiply (?Highband,32.0,0.75) swrlb:multiply(?Mediumband, 32.0, 0.5) swrlb:greaterThan(18.0, 16.0) swrlb:lessThanOrEqual(18.0, 24.0) swrlb:subtract(?z1, 24.0, 18.0) swrlb:subtract (?z2, 24.0, 16.0) swrlb:divide(?z, 6.0, 8.0)

B1) before applying TruthValueRule5

UsedDevice(Irene, MotoW270) HasBandwidth(MotoW270, 18.0) HasNetworkAdaptor (MotoW270, GPRS) MaxBand(MotoW270, 32.0) swrlb:multiply(?Highband,32.0,0.75) swrlb:multiply(?Mediumband, 32.0, 0.5) swrlb:greaterThan(18.0, 16.0) swrlb:lessThanOr Equal(18.0, 24.0) swrlb:subtract(?z1, 18.0, 16.0) swrlb:subtract(?z2, 24.0, 16.0) swrlb:divide (?z,2.0,8.0)

OInferred facts

A2) after applying TruthValueRule4

ProbMedium(MotoW270, 0.75) NetworkBandwidth(MotoW270, "Medium")

B2) after applying TruthValueRule5

ProbHigh(MotoW270, 0.25) NetworkBandwidth (MotoW270, "High")

It should be noted that the system is designed in such a way that the maximum tolerable response time, that depends on the user's activity and the nature of requested resources, can be easily modified to accommodate learners with more or less restrictive time constraints. Figure 13 shows the main components of the used fuzzy system which consists of singleton fuzzifier, product inference engine, fuzzy rule base, and center average defuzzifier. The system starts with a fuzzification of the input variable, then rule evaluation, followed by aggregation. The latter is the process of unification of the outputs of all rules. The last step of the fuzzy system is defuzzification to obtain a crisp output [50]. Figure 14 shows the membership function for resource size.

The three fuzzy sets *Low, Medium,* and *High* describing predicted network bandwidth are used as an input space in the fuzzy system to predict the maximum allowable resource size. We also define three fuzzy sets *Small, Medium,* and *Large* as the output space (resource size) as shown in Figure 14. Note that we use *SmallSize, MediumSize,* and *LargeSize* to refer to center average values for *small, medium, and large* fuzzy sets respectively. The fuzzy rule base consists of three simple rules as shown below.

R^1: if network bandwidth *(B)* is *Low* then resource size *(Z)* is set to *Small*
R^2: if network bandwidth *(B)* is *Medium* then resource size *(Z)* is set to *Medium*
R^3: if network bandwidth *(B)* is *High* then resource size *(Z)* is set to *High*

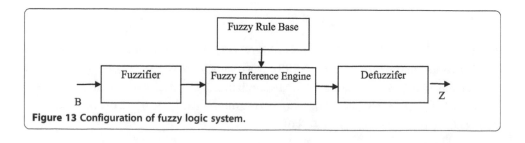

Figure 13 Configuration of fuzzy logic system.

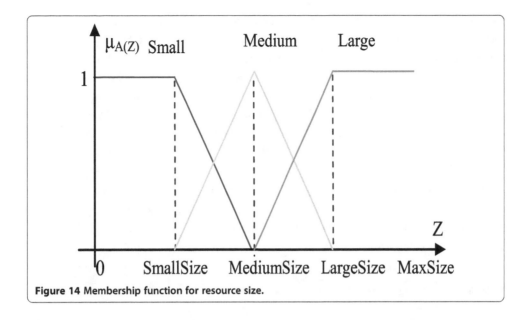

Figure 14 Membership function for resource size.

Suppose that the fuzzy set F^k in the fuzzy rule base R^k is normal with center $\bar{y}^k$. Then the crisp output from the fuzzy system with singleton fuzzifier, product inference engine, center average defuzzifier, and rule base R^k where, R^k is defined as follows: **if** x_1 is A_1^k and... and x_n is A_n^k, **then** y is F^k, $k = 1,...N$ is given by [50]:

$$y^* = \frac{\sum_{k=1}^{N} \bar{y}^k \left(\prod_{i=1}^{n} \mu_{A_i^k}(x_i^*) \right)}{\sum_{k=1}^{N} \left(\prod_{i=1}^{n} \mu_{A_i^k}(x_i^*) \right)} \tag{2}$$

In our case, (2) results into:

$$Z^* = \frac{\sum_{i=1}^{3} \bar{Z}_i * \mu_{A^i}(B^*)}{\sum_{i=1}^{3} \mu_{A^i}(B^*)}$$
$$= \frac{SmallSize * \mu_{Low}(B^*) + MediumSize * \mu_{Medium}(B^*) + LargeSize * \mu_{Large}(B^*)}{\mu_{Low}(B^*) + \mu_{Medium}(B^*) + \mu_{Large}(B^*)} \tag{3}$$

In Rule-Set-3, we show the SWRL rule (*ResourceSizeRule*) associated with equation (3). In *ResourceSizeRule*, the data properties *ProbLow*, *ProbMedium*, and *ProbHigh* are those probabilities obtained in *TruthValueRules* (see Rule-Set-1). To show how these rules are applied in our system, we provide a real-life scenario. Let's assume that our learner *Irene* is using a GPRS connection with a maximum connection speed of 32 kbps. This connection speed delimits the maximum resource size to 500Kbytes as described above. These assumptions are represented by facts (*A1*) in Rule-Set-3. When *Resource SizeRule* is applied, fact (*A2*) is inferred resulting into the addition of statement *Resource Size(MotoW270, 281.25)* to the list of facts. Indeed, since the previously sensed network bandwidth was 18 kbps, our system chooses not to exchange resources over 281.25Kbytes as deduced from the set of inferences shown in Rule-Set-3.

Rule-Set-4 describes the SWRL rules used to select the media type of retrieved learning resources based on predicted current bandwidth. The data properties *Network Bandwidth* and *AvailableMemory* represent respectively the current bandwidth and available device memory. In *MediaRule1-to-3*, the system sets the media type to the appropriate format (i.e. text, image, video) based on the value of predicted current network bandwidth. The system also sets the maximum allowable resource size, as computed in Rule-Set-3, based on the device's available memory. If the size of the device memory is smaller than the maximum allowable media size computed in Rule-Set-3, then *AllowedResourceSizeRule1* sets the maximum media size to the device memory size; otherwise the maximum media size remains unchanged as stated in *AllowedResourceSizeRule2*.

Rule-Set-3 SWRL rule and inferences for determining maximum allowed resource size
ResourceSizeRule

ActivityID(?act) ∧ UsedDevice(?act, ?dev) ∧ ProbLow(?dev, ?Tl) ∧ ProbMedium(?dev,? Tm) ∧ ProbHigh(?dev, ?Th) ∧ MaxSize(?dev, ?Maxsize) ∧ swrlb:multiply(?Lowsize, 0.25, ?Maxsize) ∧ swrlb:multiply(?Mediumsize,0.5,?Maxsize) ∧ swrlb:multiply(?Largesize, 0.75, ?Maxsize) ∧ swrlb:multiply(?l, ?Lowsize, ?Tl)∧swrlb:multiply(?m, ?Mediumsize,? Tm) ∧ swrlb:multiply(?h, ?Largesize, ?Th) ∧ swrlb:add(?z1, ?l, ?m, ?h) ∧ swrlb:add(?z2, ? Tl, ?Tm, ?Th) ∧ swrlb:equal(?z2, 1) ∧ swrlb:divide(?z, ?z1, ?z2) → FileSize(?dev, ?z)

Ontology related facts

A1) before applying *ResourceSizeRule*

ActivityID(Irene)
UsedDevice(Irene, MotoW270)
ProbLow(MotoW270, 0.0)
ProbMedium(MotoW270, 0.75)
ProbHigh(MotoW270, 0.25)
MaxSize(MotoW270, 500)
swrlb:multiply(?Lowsize, 0.25, 500.0) swrlb:multiply(?Mediumsize, 0.5, 500.0) swrlb: multiply(?Largesize, 0.75, 500.0) swrlb:multiply(?l, 125.0, 0.0) swrlb:multiply(?m, 250.0, 0.75) swrlb:multiply(?h, 375.0, 0.25)
swrlb:add(?z1, 0.0, 187.5, 93.75)
swrlb:add(?z2, 0.0, 0.75, 0.25)
swrlb:divide(?z, 281.25, 1)

Inferred facts

A2) after applying *ResourceSizeRule*

FileSize (MotoW270, 281.25)

To show how the above rules are applied we use the previous scenario of learner *Irene* who is using device *MotoW270* operating at a bandwidth of 18.0 kbps to access the system services. Following the reasoning shown in Rule-Set-2, the system infers a bandwidth fluctuating between medium to high as shown in facts (*A1*) and (*B1*). When applying *MediatypeRule2* and *MediatypeRule3*, facts (*A2*) and (*B2*) are respectively inferred and added to the list of facts as shown in Rule-Set-5. In (*C1*), *AllowedResource SizeRule2* is applied to compare the maximum allowed resource size previously inferred in Rule-Set-3 with the device's available memory, leading to the addition of statement *AllowedSize(MotoW270*, 281.25) to the list of inferred facts as shown in (*C2*). The outcome of the ontology reasoning for this scenario is that all types of media can be selected for delivery, while their size should not exceed 281.25Kbytes for them to be efficiently ported on to the used device, and thus avoiding long communication delays.

Rule-Set-4 SWRL rules for media type and resource size selection

MediaRule1

ActivityID(?act) ∧ UsedDevice(?act,?dev) ∧ NetworkBandwidth(?dev,"Low") →HasMediaType(?dev, Text)

MediaRule2

ActivityID(?act) ∧ UsedDevice(?act, ?dev) ∧ NetworkBandwidth(?dev,"Medium") → HasMediaType(?dev, Text) ∧ HasMediaType(?dev, Image)

MediaRule3

ActivityID(?act) ∧ UsedDevice(?act, ?dev) ∧ NetworkBandwidth(?dev, "High") → HasMediaType(?dev,Text) ∧ HasMediaType(?dev,Image) ∧ HasMediaType(?dev,Video)

AllowedResourceSizeRule1

ActivityID(?act) ∧ UsedDevice(?act, ?dev) ∧ FileSize(?dev,?Size) ∧ AvailableMemory(?dev,?MemorySize) ∧ swrlb:lessThan(?MemorySize,?Size) → AllowedSize(?dev,?MemorySize)

AllowedResourceSizeRule2

ActivityID(?act) ∧ UsedDevice(?act,?dev) ∧ FileSize(?dev,?Size) ∧ AvailableMemory(?dev,?MemorySize) ∧ swrlb:greaterThanOrEqual(?MemorySize, ?Size) → AllowedSize(?dev,?Size)

Rule-Set-5 Inferences for media type selection

Ontology related facts

A1) before applying MediatypeRule2

ActivityID(Irene)
UsedDevice(Irene, MotoW270) NetworkBandwidth(MotoW270,"Large")

B1) before applying MediatypeRule3

ActivityID(Irene)
UsedDevice(Irene, MotoW270) NetworkBandwidth(MotoW270,"Large")

C1) before applying AllowedResourceSizeRule2

ActivityID(Irene)

UsedDevice(Irene, MotoW270) FileSize(MotoW270, 281.25) AvailableMemory(MotoW270, 1024.0) swrlb:greaterThanOrEqual(1024.0, 281.25)

Inferred facts

A2) after applying MediatypeRule2

HasMediaType(MotoW270,Text)
HasMediaType(MotoW270,Image)

B2) after applying MediatypeRule3

HasMediaType(MotoW270,Text)
HasMediaType(MotoW270,Image)
HasMediaType(MotoW270,Video)

C2) after applying AllowedResourceSizeRule2

AllowedSize(MotoW270,281.25)

Another type of adaptation considered in this study is language adaptation that takes into account the language preferred and used by the learner. *LanguageRule* in Rule-Set-6 establishes a constraint represented by the relationship *SearchLanguage* that associates a language with a specific learner activity. The property *PreferredLanguage(?act, ?lan)* links an activity identifier *act* to a preferred language *lan*. The property *Support Language(?dev, ?lan)* links learner's handheld device *dev* to its support language *lan*. For instance, let's assume French is the preferred language for learner *Irene*. Let's also assume that English and French are languages supported by the used device *MotoW270*. When applying *LanguageRule1*, as shown by (*A1*) in Rule-Set-6, we can infer (*A2*) that is *SearchLanguage (Irene, French)*, confirming that French can be used as a search language because it is supported by the used device. The knowledge base developed in this study also includes rules that deal with other system-centric adaptations such as network security, operating system compatibility, and screen resolution.

Rule-Set-6 SWRL rule for language adaptation
LanguageRule
ActivityID(?act) ∧ UsedDevice(?act,?dev) ∧ PreferredLanguage(?act, ?lan) ∧ SupportLanguage(?dev, ?lan) → SearchLanguage(?act, ?lan)

Ontology related facts

A1) before applying *LanguageRule*

ActivityID(Irene)
UsedDevice(Irene, MotoW270)
PreferredLanguage(Irene, French) SupportLanguage(MotoW270, English) Support Language(MotoW270, French)

A2) after applying *LanguageRule*

SearchLanguage(Irene, French)

Rule-Set-7 SWRL rules for learning sequence construction

***SimilarResourceRule1*: ConductedLearningActivity(?L,?act) ∧ MakeQuery(?act,?Q) ∧**
HasKeyword(?Q,?C) ∧ IsMappedTo(?C,?LR) ∧ HasLearningTime(?L, t) ∧
LearningTime(?LR, ?t1) ∧ swrlb:greaterThanOrEqual(?t, ?t1) → SimilarLR(?act,?LR)

***SimilarResourceRule2*:** ConductedLearningActivity(?L,?act) ∧ MakeQuery(?act,?Q) ∧
HasKeyword(?Q,?C) ∧ Has(?C,?Ci) ∧ ¬Covered(?L,?Ci) ∧ IsMappedTo(?Ci,?LRi) ∧
¬Consumed(?L,?LRi) ∧ HasLearningTime(?L, t) ∧ LearningTime(?LRi, ?t1) ∧ swrlb:
greaterThanOrEqual(?t, ?t1) → SimilarLR(?act,?LRi)

***SimilarResourceRule3*:** ConductedLearningActivity(?L,?act) ∧ MakeQuery(?act,?Q) ∧
HasKeyword(?Q,?C)∧ Isa(?C,?Ci)∧¬ Covered(?L,?Ci)∧ IsMappedTo(?Ci,?LRi)∧ ¬Con-
sumed(?L,?LRi) ∧ HasLearningTime(?L, t) ∧ LearningTime(?LRi, ?t1) ∧ swrlb:great-
erThanOrEqual(?t, ?t1) → SimilarLR(?act,?LRi)

PrerequisiteResourceRule: ConductedLearningActivity(?L,?act)∧MakeQuery(?act,?Q)∧
HasKeyword(?Q,?C)∧ HasPrerequisite(?Q,?Ci)∧ ¬ Covered(?L,?Ci)∧ IsMappedTo(?
Ci,?LRi) ∧¬Consumed(?L,?LRi) ∧ HasLearningTime(?L, t) ∧ LearningTime(?LRi, ?t1) ∧
swrlb:greaterThanOrEqual(?t, ?t1) → PrerequisiteLR(?act,?LRi)

CoreResourceRule1: ConductedLearningActivity(?L,?a) ∧ MakeQuery(?act,?Q) ∧
HasKeyword(?Q,?C)∧ HasNecessaryPart(?Q,?Ci) ∧ ¬Covered(?L,?Ci)∧ IsMappedTo(?
Ci,?LRi)∧ ¬ Consumed(?L,?LRi) ∧ HasLearningTime(?L, t) ∧ LearningTime(?LRi, ?t1) ∧
swrlb:greaterThanOrEqual(?t, ?t1) → CoreLR(?act,?LRi)

CoreResourceRule2: ConductedLearningActivity(?L,?a) ∧ MakeQuery(?act,?Q) ∧
HasKeyword(?Q,?C) ∧ IsNecessaryPartOf(?Q,?Ci) ∧ ¬Covered(?L,?Ci) ∧ IsMappedTo
(?Ci,?LRi) ∧ ¬ Consumed(?L,?LRi) ∧ HasLearningTime(?L, t) ∧ LearningTime(?LRi, ?t1)
∧ swrlb:greaterThanOrEqual(?t, ?t1) → CoreLR(?act,?LRi)

NonCoreRelatedResourceRule1: ConductedLearningActivity(?L,?act) ∧ MakeQuery(?
act,?Q) ∧
HasKeyword(?Q,?C) ∧ HasPart(?Q,?Ci) ∧ ¬Covered(?L,?Ci) ∧ IsMappedTo(?Ci,?LRi)
∧ ¬Consumed(?L,?LRi) ∧ HasLearningTime(?L, t) ∧ LearningTime(?LRi, ?t1) ∧ swrlb:
greaterThanOrEqual(?t, ?t1) → NonCoreRelatedLR(?act,?LRi)

NonCoreRelatedResourceRule2: ConductedLearningActivity(?L,?act)∧MakeQuery(?
act,?Q)∧HasKeyword(?Q,?C) ∧ IsPartOf(?Q,?Ci)∧ ¬Covered(?L,?Ci)∧ IsMappedTo(?Ci,?
LRi)∧ ¬Consumed(?L,?LRi) ∧ HasLearningTime(?L, t) ∧ LearningTime(?LRi, ?t1) ∧
swrlb:greaterThanOrEqual(?t, ?t1) → NonCoreRelatedLR(?act,?LRi)

4.2 Learner-centric adaptation
The best personalization of learning is the one that supplements domain knowledge
with the learner's tacit knowledge. This approach is adopted in the learner-centric
adaptation process to produce ontology-compliant learning sequence aware of the
learner's background and task at hand. As shown in Figure 10, first, the system infers
concepts related to the learner's query using knowledge embedded in the subject domain
ontology. This is done to ensure that the initial learning sequence is ontology compliant.

Then, knowledge related to learner's context is used to avoid reiterated covered concepts and consumed learning resources. In Rule-Set-7, we show the rules used to derive the initial learning sequence. First, the reasoning engine uses *Similar ResourceRule1-to-3* to check for resources that are directly related to concept(s) in the learner's query. Second, *PrerequisiteResourceRule* is applied to infer prerequisite knowledge based on *HasPrerequisite* relationship. Third, the reasoner checks for core knowledge using *CoreResourceRule* which is based on the necessary part-whole (*HasNecessaryPart*) relationship, thus inferring sub-concepts that should be covered to completely understand the queried concept(s). Finally, the learning sequence is complemented with non-core related knowledge inferred using *Non CoreResourcesRule1&2* which are based on *HasPart* and its reciprocal relationship *IsPartOf*. Each of the above-mentioned rules checks whether the time needed to consume the recommended resource is within the learner's available time. It also checks for already covered concepts and consumed resources which are automatically eliminated from the learning sequence. Thus, making use of tacit knowledge retrieved from the learner profile.

Rule-Set-8 example of learning sequence construction
Ontology related facts

A1) before applying *SimilarResourceRule1:*

ConductedLearningActivity(Irene,A1) MakeQuery(A1, Logical Express)
HasKeyword(Logical Express, C_{28})
IsMappedTo(C_{28},LR_{28a})IsMappedTo(C_{28}, R_{28b})

B1) before applying *CoreResourceRule1*

ConductedLearningActivity(Irene,A1) MakeQuery(A1, Logical Express)
HasKeyword(Logical Express, C_{28})
HasNecessaryPart(C_{28},C_{29})
HasNecessaryPart(C_{28},C_{30})
HasNecessaryPart(C_{28},C_{31})
HasNecessaryPart(C_{28},C_{32})
¬Covered(Irene,C_{31})
¬Covered(Irene,C_{32})
IsMappedTo(C_{31},LR_{31a})
IsMappedTo(C_{31},LR_{31b})
IsMappedTo(C_{32},LR_{32a})
¬Consumed(Irene,LR_{31b})
¬Consumed(Irene, LR_{32a})

C1) before applying *NonCoreRelatedResourceRule2:*

ConductedLearningActivity(Irene,A1)

MakeQuery(A1, Logical Express)

HasKeyword(Logical Express, C_{28})

IsPartOf(C_{28},C_5)

¬Covered(Irene,C_5)

IsMappedTo(C_5,LR_{5a})

IsMappedTo(C_5,LR_{5b})

IsMappedTo(C_5,LR_{5a})

¬Consumed(Irene,LR_{5a})

¬Consumed(Irene, LR_{5c})

Inferred facts

A2) after applying *SimilarResourceRule1*

SimilarLR(A1, LR_{28a})

SimilarLR(A1, LR_{28b})

B2) after applying *CoreResourceRule1*

CoreLR(A1,LR_{31b})

CoreLR(A1,LR_{32a})

C2) after applying *NonCoreRelatedResourceRule2*

NonCoreRelatedLR (A1,LR_{5a})

NonCoreRelatedLR (A1,LR_{5c})

To illustrate the reasoning mechanism adopted in the learner-adaptation process, we use a real life learning scenario based on the C++ Programming ontology shown in Figure 15. Let's assume that learner *Irene* wants to learn about "logic expressions" of the C++ programming language. This query has similar keywords with the ontology

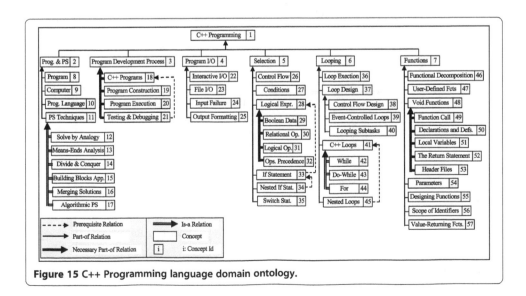

Figure 15 C++ Programming language domain ontology.

concept C28 which describes "Logical_Expression" as shown in Figure 15. The reasoning engine is invoked by firing *SimilarResourceRule1* which operates on facts (*A1*) and infers (*A2*) as shown in Rule-Set-8. The results of this inference consist of mapping learning resources *LR28a* and *LR28b* to concept *C28*. Facts (*A2*) are then added to the knowledge base. It should be noted here that concept *C28* does not have any similar or prerequisite concepts in the C++ ontology. Therefore, the application of *SimilarResourceRule2&3* and *PrerequisiteResourceRule* do not produce any useful results in this case. However, when applying *CoreResourceRule* on facts (*B1*), concepts *C29(Boolean_data)*, *C30(Relational_Operators)*, *C31(Logical_Operators)*, and *C32* (*Operators_Precedence*) are inferred as core knowledge that need to be offered to the learner to fully understand the queried concept (i.e. *Logical_Expressions*). We also infer that concepts *C29* and *C30* have already been covered by Irene in previous studies, thus, the reasoner automatically eliminates them from the learning sequence. The system also infers that learning resources (*LR31a*, *LR31b*) and *LR32a* are mapped to concepts *C31* and *C32* respectively, and that learning resources *LR31b* and *LR32a* have not been consumed by *Irene*. These resources are therefore prescribed to *Irene* and facts (*B2*) are added to the knowledge base. Finally, *NonCoreResourceRule2* is applied on facts (*C1*) to infer (*C2*) which states that concept *C28(Logical_Expression)* is part of *C5*(Selection), and that *LR5a* and *LR5c* which correspond to concept *C5* have not been consumed by *Irene* so far, and therefore can be prescribed to her as non-core related knowledge. The learning sequence resulting from the application of the above mentioned rules produces the learning sequence shown in Figure 16 where the type of each learning resource (e.g. core, non-core, prerequisite, etc.) is clearly specified to the learner.

The learning path navigation algorithm, described below, is triggered once the learner starts interacting with the initially recommended learning sequence. The invocation of any learning resource leads to updating the list of consumed learning resources, and generating a new sub-learning path associated with the newly invoked concept. The new path is then added to the global learning path as shown in step 10 of the

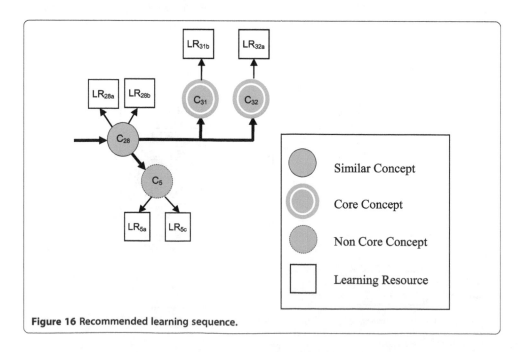

Figure 16 Recommended learning sequence.

Learning_path_Navigation algorithm. The new sub-learning path is constructed by the *learning_path_generation* procedure, which first infers core concepts associated with the newly invoked concept and appends their respective resources. Then, for each core concept, it infers resources to fulfill their prerequisite knowledge. The learning path thus, grows dynamically as the learner invokes new concepts. However, when the learner makes a backward move, the corresponding sub-learning path is completely pruned from the global learning path. The learning session terminates when the learner either logs out of the system or consumes all prescribed learning resources.

Experimental results

To illustrate the ontology reasoning mechanisms used in this study, we provide a number of scenarios that demonstrate the various system-centric and learner-centric adaptations. For system-centric adaptations, we devised an experiment where three mobile phones with different software and hardware capabilities were used to query concepts related to C++ programming language. Table 2 shows the software and hardware features of the used devices while Figure 17 shows the list of learning resources returned for each device after applying the various system centric rules described in section 4.1. The first device used in this experiment is an emulator for a Nokia phone with basic features and limited resources. The reasoning engine recognizes the limitations of the Nokia phone and the limited network bandwidth (8.0 kbps) sensed during the experiment, and returns a set of learning resources in text format, not exceeding 125Kbytes as shown in Figure 17.a. Figure 17.b shows the learning resources retrieved for the Sony Ericsson W830C which has more capabilities than the Nokia phone. These include resources of image media type in addition to text resources not exceeding 250Kbytes due to the limited sensed bandwidth. However, Figure 17.c shows the learning resources retrieved for the HTC S621 Smartphone which can support all types of media. Based on the sensed bandwidth and the predicted maximum resource size, the system was able to retrieve larger resources of various media types.

To demonstrate some of the learning centric adaptations used in this study, we show an experiment where Irene is working on a C++ programming assignment as part of her first programming course. Being a novice programmer, Irene is confused about the syntax of "C++ Loops". So, she used her mobile device "HTC S621 Smartphone" to query the system using "C++ Loops". Irene's available learning time is set to 15 minutes.

Table 2 Experimental Mobile Devices

Feature	Basic Nokia Phone Emulator	Sony Ericsson W830C	HTC S621 Smartphone	Samsung S4 Smartphone
Operating system	Symbian	Sony Ericsson Java	Windows Mobile 6	Android 4.2.2
Available Memory	256.0kbytes	6.0Mbytes	32.0Mbytes	64GB
Connection Speed	32.0 kbps	48.0 kbps	120.0 kbps	150Mbps
Screen Resolution	128×96 pixels	320×240 pixels	320×240 pixels	1920×1080
Browser	WAP 2.0	WAP 2.0	Internet Browser	Internet Browser
Keyboard Type	Virtual	Virtual	Real	Virtual
Media Type	Text, Image	Text, Image, Video	Text, Image, Video	Text, Image, Video
Display Type	Monochrome	256 k Colors	65536 Colors	16 M Color Depth
Network Adaptor	GSM 1900	GPRS, EDGE	Wifi/GPRS/EDGE	Wifi/GPRS/EDGE/HSPA

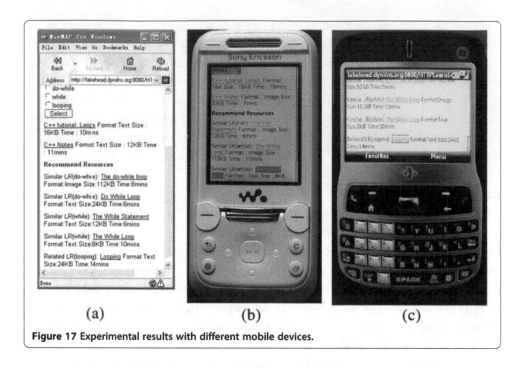

(a)   (b)   (c)

Figure 17 Experimental results with different mobile devices.

Once logged in, the system tracks her previous login sessions, covered concepts, consumed learning resources, and previously conducted learning interactions. Then, the system proceeds with system-centric rules to adapt the search for learning resources, taking into account the limitations of the used device and surrounding environment. Irene's query is then used to reason with the related subject-domain ontology to infer those concepts that are part of similar knowledge, prerequisite knowledge, core-knowledge, and related knowledge, using *Is-a, HasPrerequisite, HasNecessaryPart*, and *HasPart* properties respectively. Consequently, the ontology concepts *For, Do-While*, and *While* are inferred and classified as "similar knowledge" to C++ Loops, while concept *Looping* is inferred and classified as "related knowledge". As shown in Figure 15, the C++ ontology does not have prerequisite or core concepts associated with C++ Loops. Thus, the learning sequence suggested by the system for this scenario is C41 (C ++ Loops) → C44 (For) → C43 (Do-While) → C42 (While) → C5 (Looping) as shown in Figure 18.b. The system will then starts searching for learning resources associated with the inferred ontology concepts to build a personalized learning path. The learning path construction process uses the learner-centric rules described in section 5.2 to remove already covered concept and consumed learning resources. It also uses the learner's available time (i.e. 15 minutes) to suggest only those learning resources that can fit within the allotted time. Figure 18 shows Irene's interactions with the system for this learning scenario. The suggested learning resources for this case are a video about C++ loops from YouTube Pocket and a text tutorial about While loop as shown in Figure 18.

An additional experiment was conducted to show both system-centric and learner-centric adaptations using an ontology related to photography. The photography ontology edited using Protégé software is shown in Figure 19. In this scenario we assume that Irene would like to purchase a camera as a gift for her friend. On her way to the shopping mall she used our system to get some technical background about cameras in

Figure 18 Learning scenario for C++ loops query.

order to make the right purchase decision. She queries the system with the keyword "camera". This experiment is conducted using three different devices, the openwave simulator to emulate a Nokia phone with basic features, the Sony-Ericson W830C, and a Samsung S4 Smartphone. The capabilities and features of these devices vary from simple to sophisticated respectively as shown in Table 2. Irene's available learning time in this case is 20 minutes. For each experiment, first, system-centric adaptations rules are applied to select learning resources that can be played on the used device. Second, learner-centric adaptations rules are applied to infer concepts related to the user's query, taking into account the available learning time. The suggested learning concepts are inferred in the following order: similar knowledge, prerequisite knowledge, core knowledge, and then, related knowledge. In our experiment, the ontology concept *Digital Camera* and *Film Camera* are inferred as "similar knowledge" of concept *Camera*. The concept *Photography Equipment* is inferred as "related knowledge". Thus, the

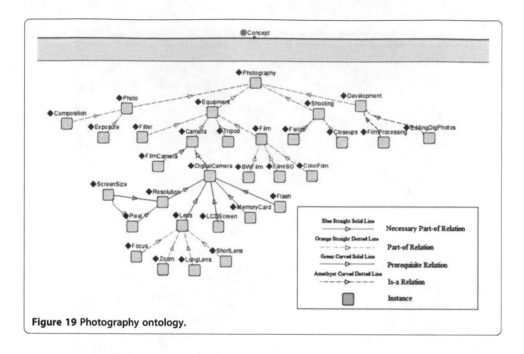

Figure 19 Photography ontology.

resulting learning sequence is (*Camera*) → (*DigitalCamera*) → (*FilmCamera*) → (*Equipment*). The learning resources associated with these concepts, as shown in Figure 20, are based on device capabilities and environment context as determined by the various adaptation rules. In this case, Irene is particularly interested in *Digital Cameras.* By choosing *Digital Camera,* further related concepts (*Resolution, Lens, LCD Screen, Memory Card, and Flash)* are inferred from the ontology and suggested for learning. Irene can then deepen her knowledge about any of these features before making a purchase decision. It can be seen in Figure 20 that resources suggested using the openwave emulator are mainly small text-based resources, while more image- and video-based resources are suggested for the Samsung S4 smartphone. The images for the Samsung are taken using the Samsung screenshot utility. Each time Irene interacts with the system, the learning resources associated with consumed concepts are removed and the learning path is updated accordingly as shown in Figure 20. Due to limited space we could not show all Irene's interactions, however, details of the above mentioned learning scenarios can be viewed in videos provided at http://unite.lakeheadu.ca/mlearning.

Conclusion

In this paper, a personalized mobile learning system that provides lightweight services adapted to both system-centric and learner-centric context is proposed. In particular, an attempt was made to solve two challenging problems related to context-aware mobile learning. These are heterogeneous context perception and integration at the semantic level, and context-aware content discovery and adaptation at run-time. To deal with context heterogeneity, an upper ontology space is used to define a higher level unique semantic view of the learning scenario. We showed that knowledge embedded in the upper ontology can homogeneously be used to enable a unified reasoning mechanism that operates on facts instantiated by the perceived heterogeneous context elements. The paper also addressed the problem of context that is perceived with ambiguity by using fuzzy logic in conjunction with semantic web based reasoning. The

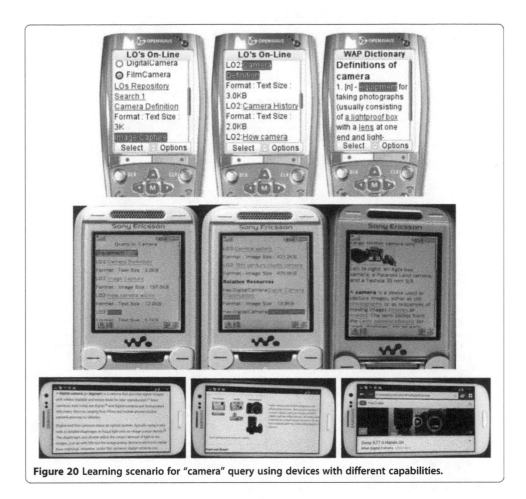

Figure 20 Learning scenario for "camera" query using devices with different capabilities.

proposed system is characterised by the fact that the reasoning engine translates context changes as they occur into new content adaptation constraints in the operating environment, thus enabling context-aware personalized learning services. A number of learning scenarios have been used to demonstrate the main functions of the proposed system. The experimental results have shown that the system successfully adapts the learning content based on the learner's context and surrounding environment.

This research work can be extended in many ways. One possible extension is the use of Mashup technology to make it possible to use multiple search agents in order to retrieve learning resources from multiple repositories, thus enhancing learning-content provision. In addition, we are currently working towards the provision of secured lightweight learning services. Trusted web-services are crucial for mobile learning applications such as those related to telemedicine or corporate learning.

Competing interests
The authors declare that they have no competing interests.

Authors' contributions
The authors have significantly contributed in the research described in this manuscript. RB has made substantial contribution to the conception and design of the overall system developed in this research, while XZ has contributed in the design of the context acquisition and ontology, and has implemented most parts of the system. XZ has performed data acquisition and initial analysis of results, while RB has helped in the data analysis and significantly contributed in the interpretation of results. RB has drafted the manuscript and revise it critically for important intellectual content. XZ has helped drafting sections 3 and 4 of the manuscript. Both authors read and approved the final manuscript.

Acknowledgment

This research work is supported by the Natural Sciences and Engineering Research Council of Canada (NSERC).

References

1. Teo CB, Gay RKL (2006) A knowledge-driven model to personalized e-Learning. ACM J Educ Resour Comput 6 (1):39–53
2. Davies J, Lytras M, Sheth A (2007) Semantic web based knowledge management. IEEE Internet Comput 10:14–16
3. Zouaq A, Nkambou R (2010) A Survey of Domain Ontology Engineering: Methods and Tools. In: Nkambou, Bourdeau, and Mizoguchi (ed) Advances in Intelligent Tutoring Systems. Springer-Verlag, Berlin Heidelberg. pp 103–119
4. Wu J (2010) An Ontology-Based Context Awareness Approach in Autonomous Mobile Learning. In: Proc. of Int. Conference on e-Business and e-Government ICEE2010, Guangzhou, China
5. Henze N, Dolog P, Nejdl W (2004) Reasoning and ontologies for personalized e-Learning in the semantic web. Educ Technol Soc 7(4):82–97
6. Benlamri R, Berri J, Atif Y (2006) A Framework for ontology-aware instructional design and planning. J E-Learn Knowl Soc 2(1):83–96
7. Huang T, Cheng S, Huang W (2009) A blog article recommendation generating mechanism using an SBACPSO algorithm. Expert Syst Appl 36(7):10388–10396
8. Yu Z, Nakamura Y (2007) Ontology-based semantic recommendation for context-aware e-Learning. Proc. Int. Conf. Ubuquitous and Intelligence Computing - UIC'2007. Lecture Notes in Computer Science 4611:898–907
9. Sudhana KM, Raj VC, Suresh RM (2013) An ontology-based framework for context-aware adaptive e-learning system. In: Proc. of the 3rd Int. Conference on Computer Communication and Informatics (ICCCI'2013), Chennai, India
10. Chia Y, Tsa FS, Tiong AW, Kanagasaba R (2011) Context-Aware Mobile Learning with a Semantic Service-Oriented Infrastructure. In: Proc. of 25th IEEE Int. Conference on Advanced Information Networking and Applications, Biopolis, Singapore
11. Hsu C, Hwang G, Chang C (2013) A personalized recommendation-based mobile learning approach to improving the reading performance of EFL students. Comput Educ 63(4):327–336
12. Weal MJ, Michaelides DT, Page K, de Roure DC, Monger E, Gobbi M (2012) Semantic annotation of ubiquitous learning environments. IEEE Trans Learn Technol 5(2):143–156
13. Dorn C, Dustdar S (2007) Sharing hierarchical context for mobile web services. Distr Parallel Databases 21(1):85–111
14. Bellavista P, Corradi A, Montanari R (2006) A mobile computing middleware for location and context aware Internet data services. ACM Trans Internet Technol 6(4):356–380
15. Wan N (2013) Conceptualizing m-learning literacy. Int J Mobile Blended Learn 5(1):1–20
16. McCalla G (2004) The ecological approach to the design of e-Learning environments: Purpose-based capture and use of information about learners. J Interact Media Educ 7:1–23
17. Mukherjee A, Saha D, Jha S (2003) Location management in mobile wireless networks. In: Handbook of Wireless Internet, Borko Furht Ed. Cat. No. 7006. CRC Press LLC, Florida, USA
18. Schilit B, Adams N, Want R (1994) Context-aware computing applications. In: Proc. of The IEEE Workshop on Mobile Computing Systems and Applications. IEEE Xplore, Santa Cruz, California, USA
19. Bu Y, Li J, Chen S, Tao X, Lv J (2005) An enhanced ontology based context model and fusion mechanism. Proc. Of the Int. Conf on embedded and ubiquitous computing. Lect Notes Comput Sci 3824:920–929
20. Dolog P, Henze N, Nejdl W, Sintek M (2004) The Personal Reader: Personalizing and Enriching Learning Resources Using Semantic Web Technologies. In: Proc. of 3rd Int. Conf. Adaptive Hypermedia and Adaptive Web-based Systems, Netherlands
21. Jeremic AZ, Jovanovic J, Gasevic D (2013) Personal learning environments on the social Semantic Web. J Semantic Web 4(1):23–51
22. Baldoni M, Baroglio C, Henze N (2005) Personalization for the Semantic Web. Proc. of Reasoning Web Conf. Lect Notes Comput Sci 3564:173–212
23. Kay J (2008) Life-Long Learning, Learner Models and Augmented Cognition. Proc. Int. Conf. Intelligent Tutoring Systems. Lect Notes Comp Sci 5091:3–5
24. Niu WT, Kay J (2008) Pervasive personalization of location information: personalized context ontology. Proc. Int. Conf. Adaptive hypermedia and adaptive Web-based systems. Lect Notes Comp Sci 5149:143–152
25. Siorpaes K, Simperl E (2010) Human intelligence in the process of semantic content creation. World Wide Web J 13(2):33–59
26. Dagger D, Wade VP, Conlan O (2004) Developing active learning experiences for adaptive personalized eLearning. Proc. Of Int. Conf. Adaptive hypermedia and adaptive Web-based systems. Lect Notes Comp Sci 3137:55–64
27. Conlan O, Wade VP (2004) Evaluation of APeLS - an adaptive eLearning service based on the multi-model, metadata-driven approach. Proc. Of Int. Conf. Adaptive hypermedia and adaptive Web-based systems. Lect Notes Comp Sci 3137:291–295
28. Yee KY, Ang WT, Tsai FS, Kanagasabai R (2009) OntoMobiLe: A Generic Ontology-Centric Service-Oriented Architecture for Mobile Learning. In: Proc. of 10th Int. Conference on Mobile Data Management, May 18–20, 2009, Taipei, Taiwan
29. Jimenez W, Vallina CPA, Gutierrez JMA, de Pablos PO, Gayo JEL (2013) Emergent Ontologies by Collaborative Tagging for Knowledge Management. In: de Pablos PO (ed) Advancing Information Management Through Semantic Web Concepts and Ontologies. IEEE Xplore, USA, pp 54–69
30. Zoua A, Ga D, Sevi C, Hatala M (2011) Towards open ontology learning and filtering. Inf Syst 36(7):1064–1081
31. Park J, Cho W, Rho S (2010) Evaluating ontology extraction tools using a comprehensive evaluation framework. Data Knowl Eng 69:1043–1061

32. Denaux R, Dolbear C, Hart G, Dimitrova V, Cohn AG (2011) Supporting domain experts to construct conceptual ontologies: a holistic approach. J Web Semantics 9(2):113–127

33. Dolog P, Nejdl W (2007) Semantic web technologies for the adaptive web: Methods and strategies of web personalization. In: The Adaptive Web. Lect Notes Comput Sci 4321:697–719

34. Jovanovic J, Gasevic D, Brooks C (2007) Using semantic web technologies to analyze learning content. IEEE Pervasive Comput 11(5):45–53

35. Krummenacher R, Kopecky J, Strang T (2005) Sharing context information in semantic spaces. Proc. Int. Workshop On the Move to Meaningful Internet Systems. Lect Notes Comp Sci 3762:229–232

36. Hage WRV, Katrenko S, Schreiber G (2005) A method to combine linguistic ontology-mapping techniques. Proc. 4th Int. Semantic Web Conference – ISWC'05. Lect Notes Comp Sci 3729:732–744

37. Mantyjarvi J, Seppanen T (2003) Adapting applications in handheld devices using fuzzy context information. Interact Comput 15(4):521–538

38. Pan JZ, Stoilos G (2005) f-SWRL: a fuzzy extension of SWRL. Journal on data semantics VI: special issue on emergent semantics. Lect Notes Comp Sci 3697:829–834

39. Tho QT, Hui SC, Fong ACM, Cao TH (2006) Automatic fuzzy ontology generation for semantic web. IEEE Trans Knowl Data Eng 18(6):842–856

40. Huang Y, Huang T, Wang K, Hwang W (2009) A Markov-based recommendation model for exploring the transfer of learning on the Web. Educ Technol Soc 12(2):144–162

41. Schmidt A (2008) Impact of Context Awareness on the Architecture of Learning Support Systems. In: Pahl C (ed) Architecture Solutions for e-Learning Systems. Idea Group Publishing, USA, pp 306–319

42. Hanaf HF, Samsudin K (2012) Mobile learning environment system (MLES): the case of android-based learning application on Undergraduates' learning". Int J Adv Comput Sci Appl 3(3):63–66

43. Hsu T, Ke H, Yang Y (2006) Knowledge-based mobile learning framework for museums. Electron Libr 24(5):635–648

44. Yarandi M, Jahankhani H, Tawi A (2012) An Ontology-based Adaptive Mobile Learning System Based on Learners' Abilities. In: Proc. of the Global Engineering Education Conference. Marrakech, Morocco, pp 17–20

45. Benlamri R, Zhang X, Berri J (2007) Proactive mobile learning on the semantic web. In: Int. Workshop on Ubiquitous Computing WUC'07, Portugal

46. Meawad FE, Stubbs G (2006) A framework for Interoperability with VLEs for Large Deployment of Mobile Learning. In: Proc. 4th IEEE Int. Workshop on Wireless, Mobile, and Ubiquitous Technology in Education WMUTE'06, IEEE Xplore, USA.

47. Kumar V, Merriman J, Thorne S (2002) What is the Open Knowledge Initiative? Eduworks Corporation white paper, September 20, 2002, http://mit.edu/oki

48. IMS Abstract Learning Framework white paper (2002) Revision July 31, 2002. http://www.imsglobal.org

49. Buttussi F, Chittaro L (2008) MOPET: A context-aware and user-adaptive wearable system for fitness training. Artif Intell Med 42(2):153–163

50. Ross TJ (2005) Fuzzy Logic with Engineering Applications, 2nd edn. John Willey and Sons Eds, New York.

51. Yang SJH (2008) Context aware ubiquitous learning environment for peer-to-peer collaborative learning. Educ Technol Soc 9(1):188–201

52. Benlamri R, Atif Y, Berri J (2008) An ontology-based approach for context-aware mobile learning. In: Advances in Ubiquitous Computing: Future Paradigms and Directions. Idea Group Publishing, USA, pp 23–44

53. CCPP Composite Capabilities Preference Profiles (2007). W3C (World Wide Web Consortium) standard, http://www.w3.org/Mobile/CCPP/

54. Cooper F (2007) Adapting to Available Network Bandwidth. Intel Software Network, Mobilizing Applications, 28 February https://software.intel.com/en-us/articles/mobilizing-applications-adapting-to-available-network-bandwidth-code-sample

55. IEEE LOM (2002) IEEE Learning Object Metadata Standard. http://ltsc.ieee.org/wg12/20020612-Final-LOM-Draft.html

56. Derballa V, Pousttchi K (2004) Extending knowledge management to mobile workplaces. In: Proc. Sixth International Conference on Electronic Commerce. Delft, The Netherlands

57. Rosati R (2006) The limits and possibilities of combining Description Logics and Datalog. In: Proc. 2nd Int. Conf. on Rules and Rule Markup Languages for the Semantic Web (RuleML'06), Georgia, USA, November 10–11, 2006

58. Rosati R (2008) On combining description logic ontologies and nonrecursive datalog rules. Proc. Of 2nd Int. Conf. On Web reasoning and rule systems. Lect Notes Comp Sci 5341:13–27

59. Mei J (2006) DatalogDL: datalog rules parameterized by description logics. Can Semantic Web Springer Series Semantic Web Beyond 2:171–187

60. Motik B, Sattler U, Studer R (2005) Query answering for OWL-DL with rules. J Web Semantics 3(1):41–60

61. Horrocks L, Boley PFH, Tabet S, Grosof B, Dean M (2004) SWRL: A semantic web rule language combining OWL and RuleML. W3C Member Submission, 21 May 2004, http://www.w3.org/Submission/SWRL/#2

9

A review on stochastic approach for dynamic power management in wireless sensor networks

Anuradha Pughat[*†] and Vidushi Sharma[†]

* Correspondence:
anuradha.pughat@gmail.com
†Equal contributors
School of Information and
Communication Technology,
Gautam Buddha University, Greater
Noida, India

Abstract

Wireless sensor networks (WSNs) demand low power and energy efficient hardware and software. Dynamic Power Management (DPM) technique reduces the maximum possible active states of a wireless sensor node by controlling the switching of the low power manageable components in power down or off states. During DPM, it is also required that the deadline of task execution and performance are not compromised. It is seen that operational level change can improve the energy efficiency of a system drastically (up to 90%). Hence, DPM policies have drawn considerable attention. This review paper classifies different dynamic power management techniques and focuses on stochastic modeling scheme which dynamically manage wireless sensor node operations in order to minimize its power consumption. This survey paper is expected to trigger ideas for future research projects in power aware wireless sensor network arenas.

Keywords: Wireless sensor networks; Stochastic approach; Dynamic power management; Markov model

Introduction

A wireless sensor network (WSN) consists of mostly tiny, resource-constrained, self-organized, low power, low cost and simple sensor nodes which are organized in a cooperative manner. The sensor nodes can sense, communicate and control the surrounding environment. They can provide interaction between the users (human being), physical environment and embedded computers in order to perform some specific operation. They follow IEEE 802.15.4 as basis standard for lower layers (physical and medium access control) and other standards like ZigBee, ISA100.11a etc. as upper layer (application, routing) protocols. WSNs have wide application bandwidth emerging the areas of agricultural, medical, military, environmental, industrial control, monitoring, civil and mechanical, etc. Target tracking and continuous monitoring in WSNs are important energy hungry problems with a large spectrum of applications, such as surveillance [1], natural disaster relief [2], traffic monitoring [3] and pursuit evasion games, and so forth. A wide range of wireless sensor network applications helps in transforming human lives in various aspects of intelligent living technology. These attractive applications have generated a great interest amongst industrialists and researchers [4].

Several multifunctional sensor nodes in specified area work for any specified tasks continuously without any internal interruption. Collectively sensor nodes connect with the pan-coordinator or sink nodes through the gateway and helps in forwarding the information to users through the network as depicted in Figure 1. Usually, a sensor node receives then processes and route the data to the next level nodes. The power manager as a part of micro-operating system (μ. OS), controls and manage the on/off and power down states of the components of sensor node (e.g. Embedded processor, memory, RF transceiver) to enable power management.

DPM is referred to as an operating system-level algorithm/technique which is used to control the power and performance parameters of a low power system, by increasing idle time slots of its devices and switching the devices to low power mode. Broadly, the ultra-low-power components of the sensor node make the node energy efficient by implementing dynamic power management policies to achieve longer lifetime [5]. The total power dissipation of sensor node can be modelled with static and dynamic power dissipation. Static power consumption is the result of leakage current flow in ultra-low power components of sensor node that can be reduced at design time by using static techniques. The static power can be reduced using synthesis and compilation at design time, whereas the dominate part such as dynamic power is the result of switching power consumption that can be reduced by selectively switching or shutting down hardware components on a sensor node. The switching or dynamic power consumption decreases quadratically with supply voltage (i.e. power gating) and linearly with the reduction in the working frequency (i.e. clock gating). Further, more the power modes of a component more is the saving of energy in a sensor node. To maximize the lifetime of the battery, the power consumption of sensor node components should reduce. Hence, the power management problem minimizes switching power or the power consumption of components. Switching power is defined as the power required for the component to change over from low power mode to high power mode and vice versa. The stochastic modelling is used for studying DPM in a wireless sensor network for power management [6,7]. Emphasis on the system model for power management shows the basic requirements for sensor node components and demands for power management.

The rest of this paper is organized as follows. Next section illustrates the abstract system model for dynamic power management and the system component requirements are identified. The section 3 classifies the major policies such as greedy schemes, time-out schemes, predictive schemes, stochastic schemes, dynamic scaling schemes, switching and scheduling schemes with their pros and cons. A brief discussion on other state

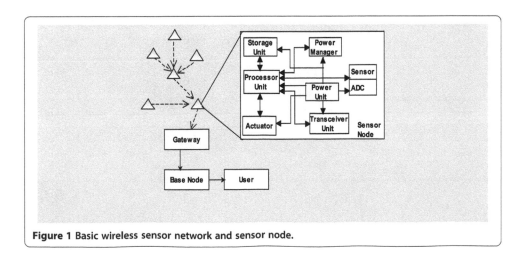

Figure 1 Basic wireless sensor network and sensor node.

of the art on discrete time and continuous time techniques is also presented. In section 4, the power consumption issues in continuous time Markov model and semi Markov model have been analyzed in detailed case studies 1 & 2 respectively. It also provides some background about existing stochastic models for dynamic power management as described in the literature, aiming at their stiff and weak points in wireless sensor network applications [8]. Apart from this, it highlights the important key areas, challenges and lacuna in managing the power dynamically using power aware stochastic modelling techniques, which gives future direction for research in the WSN area. Finally, section 5 concludes the entire paper and states about the Author's future interest and investigation.

Basic power management system model

The operating system level dynamic power management schemes take the knowledge of application requirement and present states of power manageable devices and then switch the devices into different power modes for the next state. The unused components turn off if idle period is large. Today, DPM trends a Markov process in which stochastic models can analyze the power and performance in the system. The system model consists of a power manager (PM), a service provider (processor), a service requestor (input from sensors) and a service request queue (memory) as shown in Figure 2. The activity of different devices in WSN may be in discrete time, continuous time and event driven also that affect the battery lifetime. The temporal event behavior over the entire sensing region, R, can be assumed as a Poisson process with an average event rate. The power manager tracks the states of service provider, service requester, service queue and gives command signals to control the power modes of the system and power management components those are idle and waiting for the next command. The power manager can be a component of the software or hardware module. We can implement a suitable stochastic modelling approach at the Operating System (OS) level to achieve better energy efficiency at lower cost. Stochastic scheme or Markov Decision Policy (MDP) models a system and its workload [9,10]. Here, consider the workload is the arrival of the request and the information associated with it. Existing analysis and modelling of DPM schemes [11,12] have been accepted with the length of the queue of waiting tasks as a parameter of latency measurement. However, the deadline of task execution is important latency or performance parameter in Markov models. Dynamic power management obtains the

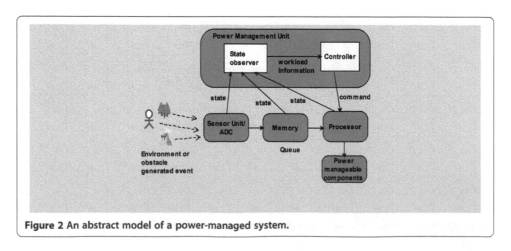

Figure 2 An abstract model of a power-managed system.

correct power switching time after observing the workload and system component states at a performance cost [13]. Therefore, the basic need of DPM is embedded operating system (micro-operating system in case of sensor node) the power management components which support different power states, e.g. active, sleep and idle.

The switching between different power modes increases latency and degrades performance, which results the power and latency trade-offs. The authors presented the basic idea behind dynamic power management and the resulting power and performance trade-off space in wireless sensor network.

Ideally, a power manageable component with more than two power down states and its switching to deep sleep state can reduce more power consumption. Moreover, switching from power down to power up states and vice versa, require finite transition time and overhead of storing processor state before turning the device into low power mode or off. Deeper sleep state requires larger waking up time and which in turn increases the latency. Hence, there is a great need of an optimized DPM scheme that can reduce power consumption with performance constraints and gain performance with power constraints for power source limited applications in wireless sensor networks.

Dynamic power management

Some important factors that affect the sensor node life are the power consumption in different modes of operation, switching cost to power down modes and time duration of the processor in each mode [14]. A class of major dynamic power management policies such as greedy schemes, time-out schemes, predictive schemes, stochastic schemes, dynamic scaling schemes, switching and scheduling schemes respectively have been presented in Figure 3. The greedy (always ON) and timeout policies are heuristic policies. The timeout scheme shuts down a power manageable component after a fixed inactive time (T). Time out policy outperforms only when the idling duration is very large, but it costs for waiting period dissipation [15]. Predictive scheme is another type of heuristic scheme. It first predicts the future arrival time and nature, then directs the system for next state and makes it idle if the predicted time duration is more than break-even time [16,17]. Thus, predicted time determines the switching of the components to the low

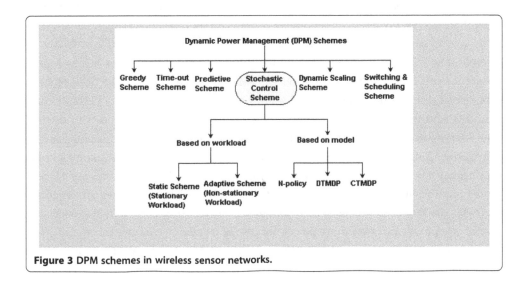

Figure 3 DPM schemes in wireless sensor networks.

power state. The authors have introduced adaptive filters for workload prediction to make the state changes of the power manageable devices on the basis of the predicted time. They have used workload traces, taking different processors for different time slots in a daytime. A performance metric is defined for efficiency of observations. A workload prediction scheme does not deal with a generalized system model and they are not suitable for providing an accurate tradeoff between power saving and performance reduction. Therefore, stochastic techniques are required to mitigate the limitations of predictive techniques. The stochastic policies are better in terms of the power delay trade-off than heuristic policies [18].

Static approach has a priori knowledge of different power manageable component states and stationary workload. Adaptive approach accounts for non-stationary nature of the workloads and uses policy pre-characterization, parameter learning and policy interpolation in taking the determination for power down states of parts [19]. Adaptive Markov Control Process for non-stationary workloads are online adaptation DPM schemes for non-stationary workloads or real-life systems [20].

In discrete time Markov decision policy (DTMDP), the power manager takes the decision for next state at discrete time intervals regardless of the input nature. A discrete time, finite state Markov decision model for power-managed systems are proposed for giving the exact solution using linear optimization problem in polynomial time [21]. This discrete time Markov model takes decision for the next state at every defined discrete interval of time. Therefore, it is not suitable for continuous monitoring or event driven processes. In discrete finite horizon Markov decision process (MDP), the sensor's battery discharge process as an MDP is modelled stochastically and characterized the optimal transmission strategy [22]. The scheme can be generalized for the decentralized case with the stochastic game theory technique. Generally, network lifetime analysis models in the literature assume average node power consumption. A discrete time Markov model for a node with a Bernoulli distribution of arrival process and phase-type distribution of service time has been validated for single and multi-hop network [23]. Observations tell that, these schemes have limitations in terms of architectural modification.

A continuous time Markov decision policy (CTMDP) is event driven and the decision taken can change only at event occurrence. A wrong decision can increase energy overhead than energy saving. The continuous time Markov models [11] need all the stochastic processes as exponential processes. These models overcome the problems in discrete time methods. Continuous time modelling is complex and does not give good results for real time systems. Therefore, semi-Markov model reduces the need of strict exponential distribution. Time indexed semi Markov Decision Process (TISMDP) combines the advantages of event driven Semi Markov Decision process model with discrete time Markov decision process (DTMDP) model, but limited to non-exponential arrival distribution coupled with non-uniform transition distribution [24]. The multiple non-exponential processes require a more flexible model and the Time-indexed semi-Markov models can be one of its solution. A model with multiple non-exponential processes increases the model as well as system complexity. Nevertheless, the non-stationary nature of work loads can save more power because of its adaptive nature scheme [9]. The N-policy gives accumulation of N events and then processing to make the system more energy efficient.

Other techniques such as dynamic scaling [13], decreases the power consumption of the system components by operating them at different low voltage and frequency levels during active phase. The switching and scheduling schemes help in power saving by controlling idle periods of the system [25]. The sleep state policy also improves energy efficiency to the greatest extent [26]. The anticipated workload of the different subsystems and the estimation of the task arrival rate at the scheduler are crucial preconditions for a DPM technique. Various cases of filters as estimation techniques are investigated [27,28]. These filters are predicting based which trace the past N number of tasks at scheduler and define the work load of the microcontroller for the next observation point. In a more precise estimation process, the workload of every hardware component is first observed and then the future load on the sensor node can be determined. This is particularly useful for selective switching. The scheduler can give the appropriate workload information regarding input events and event counter counts frequency and time-period of hardware employed by each task [29]. A stochastic sleep scheduling (SSS) with and without adaptive listening scheme is proposed and proved better in terms of energy consumption and delay reduction at the network level for S-MAC. This scheme is applicable for high node scalability and stochastic sensor sleep period [30]. The energy efficiency can be improved in the routing layer to enhance the network lifetime. Several energy efficient routing algorithms for wireless sensor network are discussed which assume arrival of the input as a stochastic process [31]. The authors have shown improvement in wireless sensor network lifetime introducing dynamic power management policy in broadband routing [32], target tracking [33] and other applications [34-37]. It is remarked that instead of energy efficiency improvement in routing protocols, power management can also improve energy efficiency. An OS-directed, event based, predictive power management technique [38] is proposed for single node energy efficiency improvement. PowerTOSSIM [39], mTOSSIM [40] and eSENSE [41] are easily available platform for sensor node life estimation.

Stochastic optimal control approach

Stochastic schemes are based on Markov decision policies which a power manager uses to direct the power manageable devices about the state change. Established in the memory-less property of Markov decision policy, power manager considers only present state of the devices for taking next state decisions. Here, the term "State" is the power mode of the device. The main function of stochastic approaches is the development and analysis of a system model to direct the system components for suitable operating mode to achieve the maximum power savings. The wireless sensor nodes observe the presence of the random inter-arrival of events on their input. Therefore, the input pattern follows any one of the exponential distribution, Pareto distribution, uniform distribution, normal distribution, Bernoulli distribution and Poisson distributions for modelling [42]. A paper on controllable Markov decision model provides heuristic and stochastic policies with linear programming optimization [43]. This work gives the importance to workload statistics for two, three and four state system model. It establishes that the delay in attending an event decreases with increase in timeout duration but the power consumption increases.

The advanced Partially Observable Markov Decision Process (POMDP) enabled the Hidden Markov model and event arrival distribution by causing modifications in the likelihood of the observed input sequence and optimizing it [44]. The paper focused on the Hidden Markov model (HMM) modelling of the service requester and the rest of the system (including service provider and service queue) is modelled in DTMDP. The authors compared the achieved results for HMM with other models and found 65.4% higher than earlier. In accumulation and fire (A&F) policy based model, the power manager can be entirely shut down when the service provider (SP) is activated. However, the A&F policy does not involve updating tasks [45,46]. This reduces average power dissipation. The PM latency is extremely small. A finite state Markov model for the server that minimizes the workload demand during energy minimization at the cost of reliability in hosting clusters is presented [47]. Thus, the hierarchical approaches are required to scale down the large systems consisting of a number of servers.

It is found through literature review that the power manager (PM) is the component which dissipates negligible power. Therefore, there is a need of policy that can consider power consumption of power manager along with the other component power on the system. Markov model based policies are not proven globally optimum for stationary Markovian workload. The accuracy of Markov models for non-stationary workload increases by incorporating a number of power states in the Markov chain. Different techniques of dynamic power management have their different implementation approach depending on the application requirement. The power consumption depends on the workload pattern and the states of the different components on the sensor node. The non-geometric transition times of the states and their complex cost functions can also be improved adding more states into a Markov chain of power managed system. However, this can increase the complexity of the system. Finally, constrained by the coarse-grain power management policy, one can search for a refined policy for the states inside each sensor node component dynamically.

Case study 1

A new continuous-time Markov decision processes shown in Figure 4 can overcome the shortcomings of reviewing models and form the new fine grain Markov model for DPM system in wireless sensor networks. The power saving can be achieved by decreasing the number of shutdown and wake up processes. Here, batch processing accumulates on 'k' number of events and the system fires at activation time. In this scheme, all the event requests arrive and serviced according to the first-in, first-out (FIFO) sequencing. The event arrival behaves as stochastic processes as an exponential distribution with mean $1/\lambda$. Consider, the event occurrence as a signal received by the sensor node that has a value greater than a predetermined threshold value (V_{th}). Usually, the incoming events or requests have non-stationary distribution in space and time and represents a probability distribution function independently as $p_{xy}^{(x,y)}$. Assume, an event arrives at the input of a sensor node in the region, R. Then equation (1) represents the probability of event detection by sensor node k (p_{ek}) that is above the threshold level. A paper shows adaptive event detection with time varying Poisson processes [48].

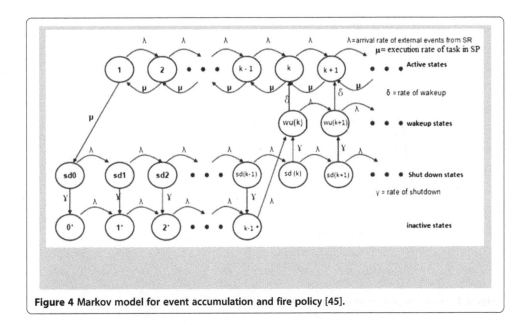

Figure 4 Markov model for event accumulation and fire policy [45].

$$p_{ek} = \frac{\displaystyle\int_{C_k} p_{XY}^{(x\,y)} dx\, dy}{\displaystyle\int_{R} P_{XY}^{(x\,y)} dx\, dy} \qquad (1)$$

The authors of this paper have assumed individual task execution as a Poisson distribution and the n + 1 task execution as Erlang distribution. A system can process a new arrived task only when its processor comes out of the current state (for example, wake up state Wu (k) to active state). The task execution introduces delay by increasing the time of task accumulation and then batch processing reduces the power consumption. The average power consumption in this policy is the sum of power consumption in service provider (processor) and control unit (power manager, task manager and memory unit). The stochastic model analysis includes the following parameters:

Inactive mode power consumption-0 W
Inactive mode start-up energy-4.75 J
Transition time from inactive to active-5 Sec
Active mode power consumption-1.9 W
Active mode start-up energy-0 W
Transition time from active to inactive-0 W
Accumulation limit (k) -4
Task execution rate (greedy policy) -100,1000
Task execution rate (A&F policy) -100

The control unit of accumulation and fire policy ((without batch processing or k = 1)) consumes more power than greedy policy because of processing overhead Figure 5. The average power consumption of the A&F policy is less than greedy policy Figure 6. Therefore, the average power use of the sensor node with inclusion of A&F policy will be lesser than the greedy policy but performance cost increases.

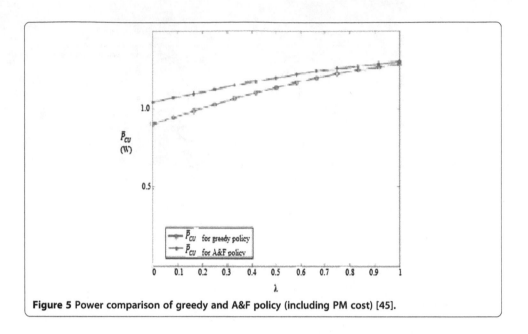

Figure 5 Power comparison of greedy and A&F policy (including PM cost) [45].

Case Study 2

A Markov model represents memory-less system. Therefore, the present states and inputs at that time determine the next power states of the system. However, in the embedded Markov model, a semi Markov process represents the next state of the system components. It does not only take the present states, but considers the time a system spends in that state to determine the probability of the system being in low power mode. A semi Markov model for power consumption and lifetime analysis is developed and implemented [49]. The model is implemented on schedule driven Mica2 and Telos motes and analyzed using following parameters for both the motes-

Event arrival rate range:150.000/hr. - 12960000.000/hr.

Average number of jobs per event:1.666667e + 000/event

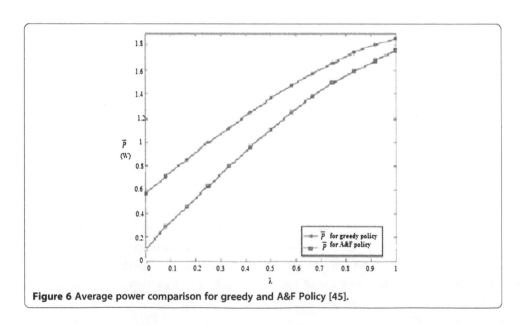

Figure 6 Average power comparison for greedy and A&F Policy [45].

Event duration:1 Sec

Duty cycle range:0.010 - 0.900

Duty period:5 Sec

Simulation results are conducted on Matlab and represented in Tables 1 and 2 for Telos and Mica2 motes. Table 1 represents power consumption and lifetime of a system model which has five different power states ($S_0 - S_4$). The state S_0 is corresponding to lowest power state and saves more power whereby state S_2 is found to be the most power consuming states. This reflects the need of power management and switching of system components from sleep to communication and vice versa whenever required. Simultaneously, the listening power state duration should also be minimized. However, operating the system and its components in various power states increases latency, switching and energy overheads. Thus, the energy saving should always be greater than energy overheads. The table clearly indicates that the Telos motes are more energy efficient and live longer than mica2 motes. It also relates the life of a sensor node with the event detection. Lesser detection probability means the node is in low power or sleep state in most of the time and the communication unit is OFF more often. The lifetime of a sensor node increases to a great extent when detection probability decreases. But this increases event missing rate. Thus, the choice of power mode and duration of any power state depends on the application in case of wireless sensor networks. Table 2 shows the power breakdown for two motes at different values of duty cycle. When duty cycle has a minimum value, most of the time a node remains in sleep mode with maximum sleep power breakdown. It decreases as the duty cycle increases. Telos mote takes more power in transmitting and reception than mica2 mote. However, they consume less power in different processing states. The active, idle, transmission and reception power breakdown, increases with increase in duty cycle as presented in Table 2. The idle power breakdown, increases to a great extent with the duty cycle increase.

Apart from this, it is observed that the solution to stochastic modelling technique becomes complex when the number of power states in the model increases. Table 3 depicts the modelling requirements for stochastic modelling techniques for dynamic power management. With state of the art, the stochastic nature of event arrival distribution, service time distribution and transition time distribution are taken as normal, uniform, exponential, Poisson, Pareto, Gaussian and Erlang distributions. The number of states in the model and processor used previously in many stochastic models is

Table 1 Power consumption and lifetime between Mica2 and Telos motes

	Mica2 mote	Telos mote
Power states	**Power consumption (mW)**	
S_0 (sleep)	8.309	0.007
S_1 (processing)	68.00	15.927
S_2 (communication)	93.50	50.926
S_3 (idle)	17.60	0.104
S_4 (listening)	53.00	40.705
Detection probability	**Lifetime (days)**	
Detection probability = 1	0.837	14.986
Detection probability = 0.210	2.124	107.130

Table 2 Comparison of power breakdown for mica2 and Telos motes

Power Breakdown (mW)

	Mica2 mote			Telos mote		
	Duty cycle= 0. 01	Duty cycle= 0. 455	Duty cycle= 0.9	Duty cycle= 0. 01	Duty cycle= 0. 455	Duty cycle= 0. 9
Active state	0.472	1.597	3.312	0.111	0.374	0.776
Sleep state	8.164	4.871	1.104	0.007	0.004	0.001
Idle state	0.157	6.773	14.204	0.001	0.040	0.084
Transmission state	0.145	0.491	1.018	0.079	0.267	0.554
Reception state	0.004	0.013	0.027	0.003	0.010	0.021

presented in the table which can be helpful for quick selection of the model for any particular application.

Observations and challenges

The state of art in this paper tells about the important key points, challenges and lacuna in stochastic modelling for dynamic power management. Based on the in depth survey, the following observations and challenges give the future research direction.

- The continuous time (event driven) model does not need synchronization pulse at each interval of time, as in case of discrete time system model.

Table 3 Modeling requirement for stochastic processes

Process name	Application	Event arrival distribution	Service time distribution	Transition time distribution	Processor	Model states
DTMDP [21]	Laptop, desktop computer	Exponential	Geometric	Bell-shaped	ARM SA-1100	Two
DTMDP [50]	Security, health care	-	Geometric	-	ATmega12	Four
DTMDP [51]	Tracking	-	-	-	MSP430	Eight
CTMDP [43]	-	Exponential, Pareto, uniform, normal	Exponential, uniform	Exponential	-	Four
CTMDP [11]	Portable devices	Poisson	Exponential	Exponential	-	Three
CTMDP [52]	-	Gaussian	Exponential	Gaussian	-	Three
CTMDP [45,46]	Portable systems	Exponential	Erlang	Poisson	-	Four
DTMDP, CTMDP [53]	-	Deterministic, exponential, Erlang, uniform, Pareto	Uniform	Exponential	-	Five
SMDP [54]	Camera node platform	Poisson	Arbitrary	Arbitrary	MSP430 and MS360LP	Five
TISMDP [55]	Telnet, web browser	Exponential, Pareto	Exponential	Non-exponential, uniform	-	Three
TISMDP [24]	Laptop, smart Badge	Pareto	Exponential	Uniform	-	Three

- The mission critical applications require the immediate service (high priority) queue and regular service (lower priority) queue.
- Stochastic modelling outperforms over other dynamic power management techniques, but the solution of modelling becomes complex with the increase in the number of parameters used.
- Pareto distribution is more suited for modelling event arrival when idle periods are long [10].
- A stochastic modelling for dynamic power management along with dynamic voltage and frequency scaling will be the effective way of power consumption reduction in wireless sensor networks.
- Consider the parameters such as delay in servicing an event, the number of waiting tasks, clock frequency, power manager delay, state transition time, detection probability and task execution deadline etc. as performance measure parameters.
- Stochastic modelling for non-stationary service request needs improvement and directs toward future research area.
- The knowledge gained from literature review is useful in the development of dynamic power management technique/algorithm for power hungry applications, e.g. continuous monitoring and detection of critical and emergency applications.
- The cost of power manager needs to be evaluated for actual power consumption measurement in complete system.
- The components other than processor should be working on scale down the voltage and frequency for achieving the more flexibility in modeling.

Conclusion

After in depth survey of power management techniques during the last two decades, this paper gives a brief review of papers which can be helpful in making decision for power management policy selection for wireless sensor network. The stochastic schemes as the Markov decision model helps in reducing the power consumption in wireless sensor network and thus, increases the sensor node life. The implementation and execution of dynamic power management policies are possible at operating system/software level. Thus, the energy efficiency of a sensor node can increase without requiring any specific power management hardware. This paper provides a brief study of Markov models. The work on specific stochastic modelling techniques for power and performance trade-offs in wireless sensor network will be investigated and upgraded in our future report. The need of power management tends towards a quest to design simpler, energy efficient, optimized and flexible modelling techniques which itself are less power consuming and need less memory to fulfil the requirement of wireless sensor network environment.

Competing interests
The authors declared that they have no competing interests.

Author's contributions
Both the authors, AP and VS, have equally contributed in sequence designing and drafting the manuscript. All authors have read and approved the final manuscript.

Acknowledgement
The author's would like to thank Gautam Buddha University for providing workplace, support and resources.

References

1. Valera M, Velastin SA (2005) Intelligent distributed surveillance systems: a review. In: IEE Proceedings of Vision, Image, and Signal Processing, Institution of Engineering and Technology (IET). 152(2):192–204, doi:10.1049/ip-vis:20041147
2. Wang Z, Li H, Shen X, Sun X, Wang Z (2008) Tracking and Predicting Moving Targets in Hierarchical Sensor Networks. In: IEEE International Conference on Networking, Sensing and Control. Sanya, IEEE, 1169-1173. Available: http://dx.doi.org/10.1109/icnsc.2008.4525393
3. Li X, Shu W, Li M, Huang HY, Luo PE, Wu MY (2009) Performance evaluation of vehicle-based mobile sensor networks for traffic monitoring. IEEE Trans Vehicle Tech 58:1647–1653
4. Song AJ, Lv JT (2014) Remote Medical Monitoring Based on Wireless Sensor Network. Applied Mechanics and Materials. Trans Tech Publ 556–562:3327–30
5. Otis B, Rabaey J (2007) Wireless Sensor Networks. Ultra-Low Power Wireless Technologies for Sensor Networks. Springer, US, 10.1007/978-0-387-49313-8_1
6. Chandrakasan A, Sinha A (2004) Dynamic Power Management in Sensor Networks. Handbook of Sensor Networks. CRC Press LLC, 2000 N.W. Corporate Blvd., Boca Raton, Florida 28 Jul 2004. doi:10.1201/9780203489635.sec7
7. Fallahi A, Hossain E (2007) QoS provisioning in wireless video sensor networks: a dynamic power management framework. IEEE Wirel Commun 14(6):40–9
8. Power-Aware Wireless Sensor Networks (2003) Wireless Sensor Network Designs. John Wiley & Sons, Ltd, pp 63–100. doi:10.1002/0470867388.ch3
9. Simunic T, Benini L, De Micheli G (2001) Energy-efficient design of battery-powered embedded systems. IEEE Transactions on Very Large Scale Integration (VLSI) Systems 9(1):15–28
10. Wang X (2007) Dynamic power optimization with target prediction for measurement in wireless sensor networks. Chinese J Mechanical Engineer 43(08):26
11. Qiu Q, Pedram M (1999) Dynamic power management based on continuous-time Markov decision processes. In: Proceedings of the 36th ACM/IEEE conference on Design automation conference–DAC, ACM Press, New Orleans, Louisiana, United States
12. Ren Z, Krogh BH, Marculescu R (2005) Hierarchical Adaptive Dynamic Power Management. IEEE Trans Comput 54(4):409–20
13. Simunic T, Benini L, Acquaviva A, Glynn P, De Micheli G (2001) Dynamic voltage scaling and power management for portable systems. In: Proceedings of the 38th annual Design Automation Conference. ACM, New York, NY, USA, pp 524–529
14. Estrin D, Heidemann J, Xu Y (2001) Geography-informed energy conservation for Ad-hoc routing. In: Proceedings of the ACM/IEEE International Conference on Mobile Computing and Networking, ACM, New York, USA, pp 70–84, Jul 2001
15. Zamora NH, Kao J-C, Marculescu R (2007) Distributed Power-Management Techniques for Wireless Network Video Systems. In: Design, Automation & Test in Europe Conference & Exhibition, Apr 2007. Nice Acropolis, France, IEEE. Available from: http://dx.doi.org/10.1109/date.2007.364653
16. Srivastava MB, Chandrakasan AP, Brodersen RW (1996) Predictive system shutdown and other architectural techniques for energy efficient programmable computation. IEEE Transactions on Very Large Scale Integration (VLSI) Systems 4:42–55
17. Hwang C-H, Wu AC-H (1997) A predictive system shutdown method for energy saving of event-driven computation. In: Proceedings of IEEE/ACM international conference on Computer-aided design, Digest of Technical Papers (ICCAD '97). IEEE Computer Society Press, Washington, Brussels, Tokyo, pp 28–32, Nov 1997
18. Shen Y, Li X (2008) Wavelet Neural Network Approach for Dynamic Power Management in Wireless Sensor Networks. In: International Conference on Embedded Software and Systems. 29-31 Jul 2008, Sichuan, IEEE, 376-381. doi:10.1109/icess.2008.36
19. Wu K, Liu Y, Zhang H, Qian D (2010) Adaptive power management with fine-grained delay constraints. In: 3rd International Conference on Computer Science and Information Technology 9-11 Jul 2010, Chengdu, IEEE, 2:633-637. doi:10.1109/iccsit.2010.5565140
20. Chung EY, Benini L, Bogliolo A, Lu Y-H, Micheli GD (2002) Dynamic power management for nonstationary service requests. IEEE Trans Comput 51(11):1345–1361
21. Benini L, Bogliolo A, Paleologo GA, Micheli GD (1999) Policy optimization for dynamic power management. IEEE Transactions Computer-Aided Design Integrated Circuits and Systems 18(6):813–833
22. Kobbane A, Koulali MA, Tembine H, Koutbi ME, Benothman J (2012) Dynamic power control with energy constraint for multimedia wireless sensor networks, IEEE ICC 2012 - Ad-hoc and Sensor networking Symposium. 518-522, 10-15 Jun 2012, Ottawa, Canada, IEEE, doi:10.1109/ICC.2012.6363971
23. Wang Y, Vuran MC, Goddard S (2010) Stochastic Analysis of Energy Consumption in Wireless Sensor Networks. In: Proceedings of 7th Annual IEEE Communications Society Conference on Sensor Mesh and Ad Hoc Communications and Networks (SECON), pp 1–9 Boston, MA, 21-25 Jun 2010, IEEE, doi:10.1109/SECON.2010.5508259
24. Simunic T, Benini L, Glynn P, Micheli GD (2000) Dynamic power management for portable systems. In: Proceedings of 6th International Conference on Mobile Computing and Networking, pp 11-19, Boston, MA, ACM, 1 Aug 2000.
25. Mei J, Li K, Hu J, Yin S, H-M, Sha E (2013) Energy-aware pre-emptive scheduling algorithm for sporadic tasks on DVS platform. Microprocessors and Microsystems. Elsevier BV 37(1):99–112
26. Lin C, He Y, Xiong N (2006) An Energy-Efficient Dynamic Power Management in Wireless Sensor Networks. In: Fifth International Symposium on Parallel and Distributed Computing, Jul 2006. pp 148–154, Timisoara, Romania, IEEE doi:10.1109/ispdc.2006.8
27. Sinha A, Chandrakasan A (2001) Dynamic power management in wireless sensor networks. IEEE Des Test 18(2):62–74
28. Zhang D, Miao Z, Wang X (2013) Saturated Power Control Scheme for Kalman Filtering via Wireless Sensor Networks. WSN Scie Res Publ Inc 05(10):203–207
29. Isci C, Martonosi M (2003) Runtime power monitoring in high-end processors: Methodology and empirical data. In: Proceedings of the 36th annual IEEE/ACM International Symposium on Microarchitecture MICRO 36. IEEE Computer Society Pub, Washington, DC, USA, p 93

30. Zhao Y, Wu J (2010) Stochastic sleep scheduling for large scale wireless sensor networks. In: IEEE International Conference on Communications, ICC 2010, Cape Town, 23–27 May 2010, pp 1-5, IEEE, doi:10.1109/ICC.2010.5502306

31. Haq U, Riaz, Norrozila, Sulaiman, Muhammad, Alam (2013) A Survey of Stochastic processes in Wireless Sensor Network: a Power Management Prospective In: Proceedings of 3rd International Conference on Software Engineering & Computer Systems (ICSECS - 2013), Universiti Malaysia Pahang, Available from: http://umpir.ump.edu.my/5011/

32. Sausen PS, Spohn MA, Perkusich A (2008) Broadcast routing in Wireless Sensor Networks with Dynamic Power Management. IEEE Symposium on Computers and Communications, 6-9 July 2008, pp 1090-1095, Marrakech, IEEE doi:10.1109/iscc.2008.4625620

33. Li G-J, Zhou X-N, Li J, Zhu J-H (2013) Distributed Targets Tracking with Dynamic Power Optimization for Wireless Sensor Networks. Sensors Letter. Am Sci Publ 11(5):907–910

34. Passos RM, Coelho CJN, Loureiro AAF, Mini RAF (2005) Dynamic Power Management in Wireless Sensor Networks: An Application-Driven Approach. Second Annual Conference on Wireless On-demand Network Systems and Services. pp 109-118, 19-21 Jan 2005, IEEE doi:10.1109/wons.2005.13

35. Halawani Y, Mohammad B, Al-Qutayri M, Saleh H (2013) Efficient power management in wireless sensor networks. IEEE 20th International Conference on Electronics, Circuits, and Systems (ICECS), Dec 2013. 8-11 Dec. 2013, pp 72-73, Abu Dhabi, IEEE, doi:10.1109/icecs.2013.6815350

36. Lee DH (2013) Yang WS (2013) The N-policy of a discrete time Geo/G/1 queue with disasters and its application to wireless sensor networks. Appl Mathematical Modelling Elsevier BV 37(23):9722–9731

37. Zhang Y (2011) An Energy-Based Stochastic Model for Wireless Sensor Networks. WSN Sci Res Publ Inc 03(09):322–328

38. Benini L, Bogliolo A, Micheli GD (2000) A survey of design techniques for system-level dynamic power management. IEEE Trans Very Large Scale Integr Syst 8(3):299–316

39. Perl E, Catháin AÓ, Carbajo RS, Huggard M, Mc Goldrick C (2008) PowerTOSSIM z. In: Proceedings of the 3rd ACM workshop on Performance monitoring and measurement of heterogeneous wireless and wired networks - PM2HW2N, ACM Press, pp 35-42, ACM New York, NY, USA. doi:10.1145/1454630.1454636

40. Mora-Merchan JM, Larios DF, Barbancho J, Molina FJ, Sevillano JL, León C (2013) mTOSSIM: A simulator that estimates battery lifetime in wireless sensor networks, Simulation Modelling Practice and Theory. Elsevier BV 31:39–51

41. Liu H, Chandra A, Srivastava J (2006) eSENSE: energy efficient stochastic sensing framework for wireless sensor platforms. In: 5th International Conference on Information Processing in Sensor Networks. pp 235-242, ACM New York, NY, USA, doi:10.1109/ipsn.2006.243752

42. Heyman DP (1975) Queueing Systems, Volume 1: Theory by Leonard Kleinrock John Wiley & Sons, Inc. New York Wiley-Blackwell 6(2):189–190

43. Qiu Q, Qu Q, Pedram M (2001) Stochastic modeling of a power-managed system-construction and optimization. IEEE Transactions Comput-Aided Design Integrated Circuits Syst 20(10):1200–1217

44. Tan Y, Qiu Q (2008) A framework of stochastic power management using hidden Markov model. In: Proceedings of the conference on Design, automation and test in Europe-DATE'08, ACM Press. Date: August 2008 UK Performance Evaluation Workshop. pp 92-97, ACM New York, NY, USA, doi:10.1145/1403375.1403402

45. Chen Y, Xia F, Shang D, Yakovlev A (2008) Fine grain stochastic modelling and analysis of low power portable devices with dynamic power management. UK Performance Evaluation Workshop (UKPEW) Aug 2008, Imperial College London, DTR08-09, pp 226-236, http://ukpew.org/2008/papers/dynamic-power-management

46. Chen Y, Xia F, Shang D, Yakovlev A (2009) Fine-grain stochastic modelling of dynamic power management policies and analysis of their power–latency trade-offs. IET Software. Inst Engineer Technol (IET) 3(6):458–469

47. Guenter B, Jain N, Williams C (2011) Managing cost, performance, and reliability tradeoffs for energy-aware server provisioning In: Proceedings of IEEE INFOCOM. 10-15 Apr 2011, pp 332-1340, Shanghai, IEEE. doi:10.1109/infcom.2011.5934917

48. Ihler A, Hutchins J, Smyth P (2006) Adaptive event detection with time-varying Poisson processes. In: Proceedings of the 12th ACM SIGKDD International conference on knowledge discovery and data mining, ACM New York, NY, USA, pp 207–216

49. Jung D, Teixeira T, Savvides A (2009) Sensor node lifetime analysis. TOSN. Assoc Comput Machinery (ACM) 5(1):1–33. doi:10.1145/1464420.1464423

50. Munir A, Gordon-Ross A (2012) An MDP-Based Dynamic Optimization Methodology for Wireless Sensor Networks. IEEE Transac Parallel Distributed Systems 23(4):616–625

51. Kang H, Li X, Moran PJ (2007) Power-Aware Markov Chain Based Tracking Approach for Wireless Sensor Networks. In: Proceedings of the IEEE Wireless Communications and Networking Conference. Hong Kong, 11–15 Mar 2007, pp 4209–4214. doi:10.1109/wcnc.2007.769

52. Xu D, Wang K (2014) Stochastic Modeling and Analysis with Energy Optimization for Wireless Sensor Networks. International Journal of Distributed Sensor Networks. Hindawi Publishing Corporation 2014:1–5

53. Norman G, Parker D, Kwiatkowska M, Shukla S, Gupta R (2005) Using probabilistic model checking for dynamic power management. Springer Sci Business Media 17(2):160–176. doi:10.1007/s00165-005-0062-0

54. Jung D, Teixeira T, Barton-Sweeney A, Savvides A (2007) Model-Based Design Exploration of Wireless Sensor Node Lifetimes. In: Proceedings of the European Conference on Wireless Sensor Networks (EWSN), Springer-Verlag, Berlin Heidelberg, Aug 2006. pp 277–292. doi:10.1007/978-3-540-69830-2_18

55. Simunic T, Benini L, Glynn P, De Micheli G (2001) Event-driven power management. IEEE Transactions Comput-Aided Design Integrated Circ Systems 20(7):840–857

10

The BAU GIS system using open source mapwindow

Balqies Sadoun[*], Omar Al-Bayari, Jalal Al-Azizi and Samih Al Rawashdeh

* Correspondence:
balqiessadoun@yahoo.com
Department of Surveying and
Geomatics Engineering, AL-Balqa'
Applied University, Al-Salt, Jordan

Abstract

"BAU GIS" is an efficient and flexible Geographic Information System (GIS) that supports manipulation, analysis, and viewing of geospatial data and associated attribute data in various GIS data formats. "BAU GIS" system is a stand-alone application, developed using (Map Window Open Source GIS) and (visual basic 10.0). It has been designed and developed to address the need for a GIS programming tool that could be used in engineering research and project software, without requiring end users to purchase a complete GIS system, or become a GIS experts. It is both a GIS modeling system, and a GIS application programming interface (API); all in a convenient redistributable package. The **BAU GIS** application is free and extensible GIS that can be used as an open-source alternative to desktop GIS, in order to distribute data to others and to develop and distribute custom spatial data analysis tools.

Keywords: GIS; Web interface; Open source GIS (OSGIS); MapWindow; Application Programming Interface (API)

Introduction

Due to the advancement in the computing technology and the rising need for GIS applications [1-3], more and more scientists are developing free of charge software packages and tools which are very useful for those who cannot afford to buy commercial expensive software packages. Then, the main purpose is to serve the groups that are working in Meta Data management and who publish their works on the World Wide Web for all interested users. As part of the "Geomatics Engineering Department" who is interested in GIS and its application, we decided the development of this software to be used by our students and all interested groups.

The advancement of computers and computing capabilities created great deal of data (Meta data) and vice versa specialized groups in its management. Famous scientists are working hardly in the area of data organization and management as it is becoming the real problem. GIS is a great system for Meta data management. Its applications are numbered and proved to be efficient in real life and in case of catastrophes (as in Catherina storm in the USA). All commercial Software are expensive and you have to buy add on for special applications which make them more expensive. We decided to develop an OSGIS and add on to be used for free. We randomly used MapWindow to design our OSGIS then test it against the commercial GIS, where it proved complete functionality and reliability.

MapWindow: is a mapping tool, a GIS modeling system, and a GIS application programming interface (API), which was developed at Utah State University by Daniel P. Ames and his team. It was developed to address the need for a GIS programming tool for research and projects, without the need to purchase GIS systems, or become GIS expert. It is used to distribute data and develop custom spatial data analysis tools [4-6]. Developers can write Plug-ins to add additional functionality (models, special viewers, and hot-link). Handlers and data editors can pass these to users. It includes standard GIS data visualization features as well as database functions such as attribute table editing, shape file editing and data converters. Dozens of standard GIS formats are supported, including Shape files, GeoTIFF, ESRI format, ASCII and binary grids [7,8]. It includes a complete ActiveX component to instantly add GIS capabilities to the user's existing software product [9,10]. Additional geo-processing components are available for .NET-compatible environments and languages. Components of MapWindow are:

1. MapWinGIS: This is an ActiveX control, which may be placed into any project in any programming language that supports ActiveX. This is the main map component - if the user wanted to write a program that displayed shape data, for example, the user could use this control for the display portion of the user's program.
2. MapWin Interfaces: Also called the "Plug-in Interface". It is a .dll file, which will allow the user to write the user's own plug-ins to the main application. This may be done from any programming language, which supports the creation and use of Microsoft .NET 2.0 Dynamic Link Libraries (dlls).
3. MapWinGeoProc: This is a .NET library of geoprocessing functions, including tools for managing projections, clipping and buffering.

Setting up the Development Environment: Using Microsoft Visual Basic 2010 Express Edition, the Visual Studio development environment main window is presented in order to select Windows Form Application and to give a name (BAU GIS) to the web site. Then the process can continue to the tool box and all Windows Forms collapsible menu then to Map Control.

BAU GIS Development:

A. The first form is the "frmIntro" which is the introduction frame in BAU GIS (Figure 1). This form "frmIntro" includes: Images from BAU and two labels in the bottom of the form.
B. The second frame is the "frmMain" form, which is the main frame in BAU GIS (Figure 2). All other frames are connected to "frmMain." These are used to apply some commands and display results. The "frmMain" of the BAU OSGIS form consists of the following parts:
   - **Main menu:** Consists of five titles to give a specific command to work (See Figure 3).
   - **Standard toolbar:** It consists of (14) icons; each gives a specific task to be worked in BAU OSGIS (See Figure 4).

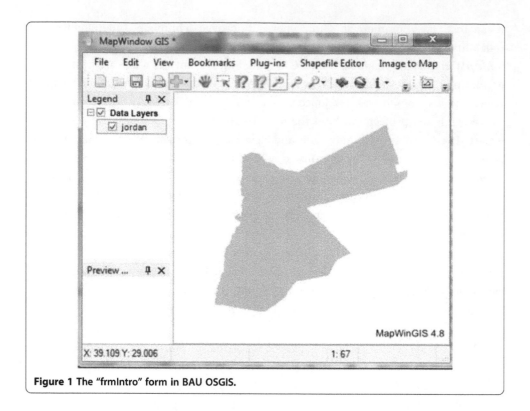

Figure 1 The "frmIntro" form in BAU OSGIS.

- **Main Map:** This is the utmost important part as most of the results will be displayed in this object. On main map you can do several functions and set general display properties (display Map layer, tracking layer etc.).
- **Legend:** This is needed in order to clarify the symbols used to represent features on the map. Legend consists of examples of the symbols on the map with labels containing explanatory text. When you use a single symbol for the features in a layer, the layer is labeled with the layer name in the legend. User can open attribute for the layer or show properties, etc. (Figure 5).

C. There are many other forms like Error dialog, form about dialog, form plug-in, form choose projection, form project setting and others which are related to form main (See Figure 6).

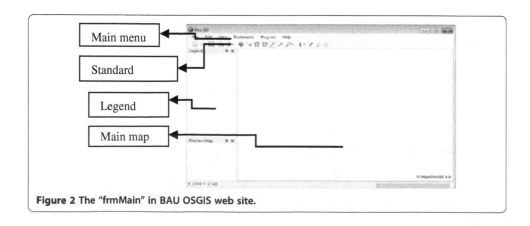

Figure 2 The "frmMain" in BAU OSGIS web site.

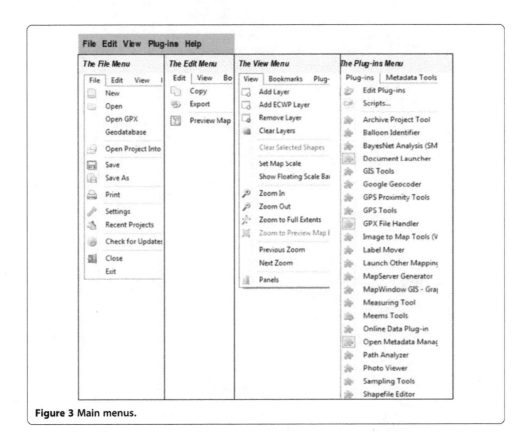

Figure 3 Main menus.

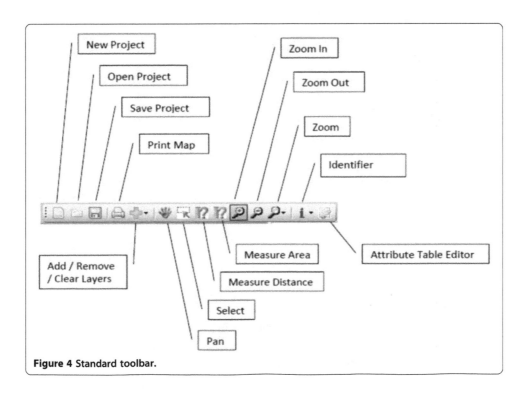

Figure 4 Standard toolbar.

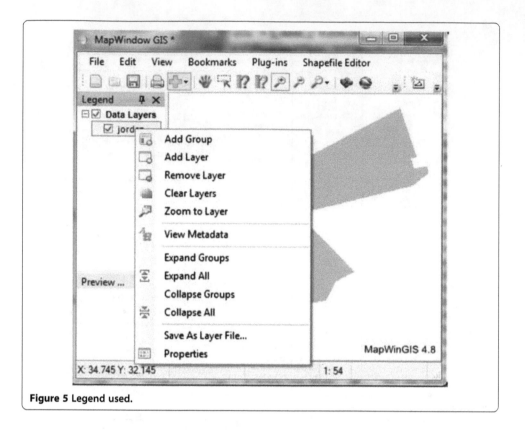

Figure 5 Legend used.

Figure 6 Other forms related to main frame.

Writing the code:

Classes: we wrote nearly 100 classes to use for all forms that are related in main form such as class: application, projection, draw, menu, layer, identified layer, etc. (See Figure 7).

Codes: Some codes are meant for class application and description such as the code for measuring the area of a polygon. Other codes are written for drawing line, point, polygon with respect to the shape file that are selected from legend to start editing, etc.

Module: We wrote 20 modules to use for all forms that are related to main form such as module main, module application, among others; see Figure 8.

Running BAU GIS: When the "frm intro" appears, it starts to load other forms that are related to "form main" such as "forms of plug in" etc. (Figure 1). After loading the main form, the form of the welcome screen will appear. Only the standard toolbars will appear in the main form (new, open, save, print, add data, pan, select, measure area, measure distance, zoom in, zoom out, zoom, identify, and query). If you want to show other toolbars related to main form you should press plug-ins from the main menu and choose what you need to work with.

Important contents of the plug-in menu:

- GIS tool: It is the function that includes the processes that are needed to build a GIS such as: assigning projection to grid or image or raster, Georeferencing an image or grid, generating a contour shape file and other processes (See Figure 9).

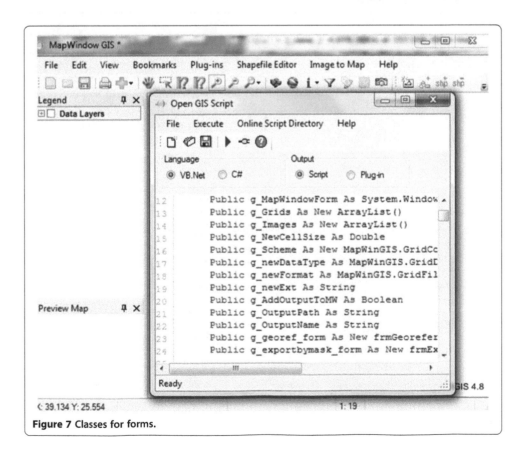

Figure 7 Classes for forms.

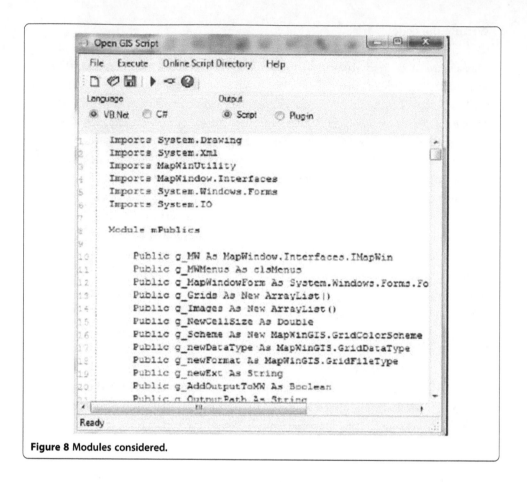

Figure 8 Modules considered.

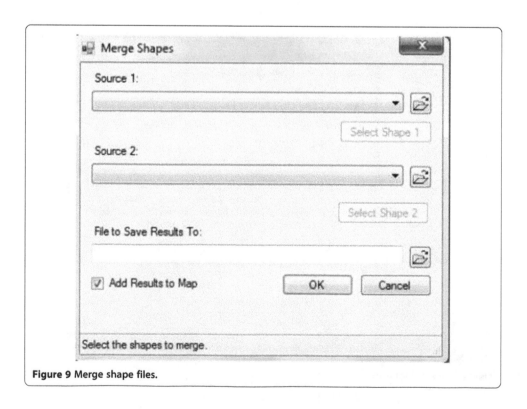

Figure 9 Merge shape files.

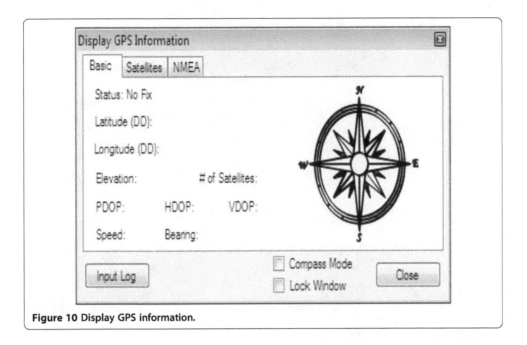

Figure 10 Display GPS information.

– GPS Tool: This includes processes that should be applied when the GPS instrument is connected into a computer in order to process data, start logging track, draw GPS location on map, and display GPS information; see Figure 10.

– Image to map tools: This tool used to convert image to map registration by using least square method and to rectify image by using another original rectified image (See Figure 11).

– Path analyzer: This is designed to draw the path of the selected feature in shapefile by determining the Digital Elevation Model (DEM) of the rectified image and drawing this path as a profile to make other processes on shapefile (see Figure 12). The plug-in menu is very important.

– Shapefile editor: It is used to create shapefile and start editing the shapefile. It includes other processes that are related to shapefile such as snapping, edit vertices, and merge of features.

– Measuring tools: These include function for measuring distance, and area for the selected features in the shapefile.

– Map Window graph tools: This is meant to allow drawing graphs using one field in the attribute field of the shapefiles (see Figure 13).

The reason for designing and developing this program is to fulfill the need of mainly our students in their GIS projects. Moreover, we posted the material on the web for all other public users.

Up on the application using our OSGIS we propose the following suggestions to address in future work:

– Download Mapwindow open source program.
– Create a new VB.Net Class Library project using Microsoft Visual Studio. Make a Right-click on the class in Solution Explorer and select "Properties". Select the References page and click the "Add" button at the bottom of that form, then select

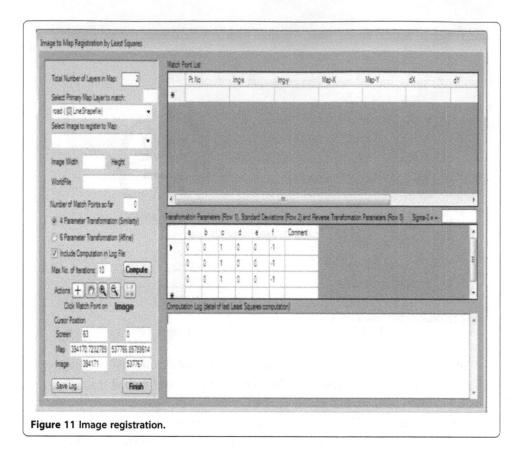

Figure 11 Image registration.

the Browse tab and navigate to the location of and select the MapWinGIS.ocx and MapWininterfaces.dll; typically, found in C:\ProgramFiles\MapWindow\ as shown in Figure 14.

– In the compile settings, sometimes it is useful to set the build path to your MapWindow "Plug-in" sub-directory or sub-directory within it, such as C:\ProgramFiles\MapWindow\Plugins\PathAnalyzer directory. This will save you

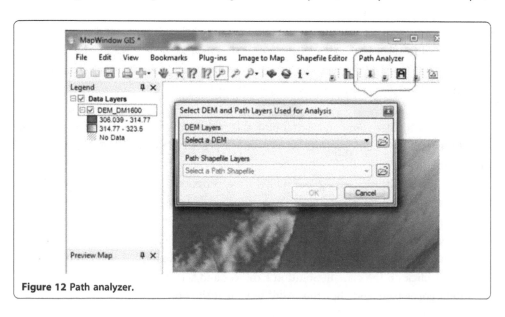

Figure 12 Path analyzer.

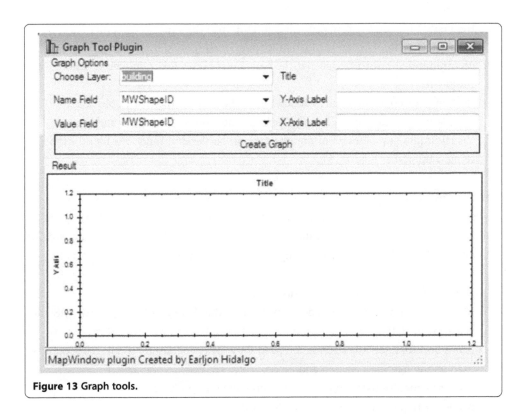

Figure 13 Graph tools.

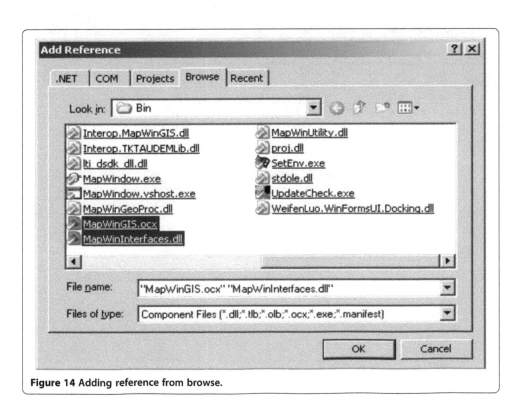

Figure 14 Adding reference from browse.

the task of having to copy your plug-in DLL into the Plug-in directory for MapWindow in order to load when it runs. If using this, it is strongly recommended not to forget that the path must be set for both Debug and Release properties.

− Back in your code, after the "Public Class..." line; insert the line Implements "MapWindow.Interfaces.IPlugin". Then, hit enter on that interface and see how Visual Studio populates all of the interface properties and functions found in the IPlugin Interface (Figure 15).

Conclusions

To conclude, the "BAU GIS" is a Programmable GIS system, which supports manipulation, analysis, and viewing of geospatial data and associated attribute data in several standard GIS data formats. Basically, It has the following features and capabilities:

− It uses an open Source Map Window soft.
− It is a standalone application, developed using Map Window Open Source GIS and visual basic 10.0.
− It has been designed to address the need for a GIS programming tool that could be used in engineering research and project software.
− It doesn't require users to purchase a complete GIS package.
− It doesn't require users to become GIS experts.
− It is a GIS modeling system and GIS application programming interface (API) all in one convenient redistributable package.

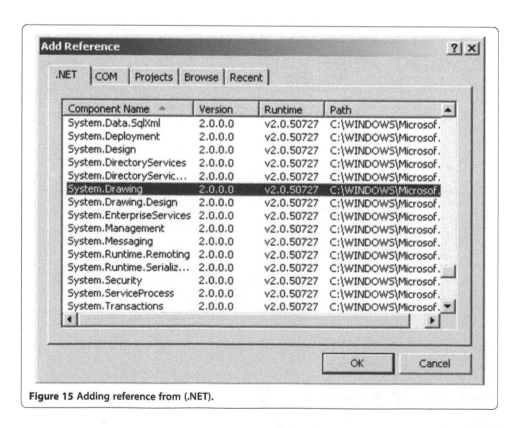

Figure 15 Adding reference from (.NET).

Finally, the BAU **GIS** application is free and extensible which can be used as: an Open-Source alternative to desktop GIS systems, in order to distribute data to others and to develop and distribute custom spatial data analysis tools. For example, a researcher or a company may want to deploy a tool that lets users build and interact with maps of GPS data overlaid on USGS quad maps. One approach is to build the tool as an extension to popular GIS software, and then require users to purchase that software to run the extension. Alternatively, the user/company could use BAU GIS as a platform and build a specialized application that does the needed function and then give it or sell it directly to end user with no need for third party software purchase.

Abbreviations
GIS: Geographical information system; API: Application programming interface; BAU: Al-Balqa' applied university; OSGIS: Open Source GIS Services; VB.NETL: Visual Basic implemented on the .NET Framework; DEM: Digital elevation model.

Competing interests
The authors declare that they have no competing interests.

Authors' contributions
BS devised the scheme, analyzed the results and written almost all the paper. OA-B helped in the design of the technique in the programming and in the analysis process. JA-A helped in collecting data and making some plots. SAR helped in the analysis and verifying the results. All authors read and approved the final manuscript.

Authors' informations
B. Sadoun is a full professor of Geomatics Engineering and Surveying at the Al-Balqa' Applied University, Jordan. She obtained her M.S. and Ph.D. degrees from the Ohio State University, Columbus, Ohio, USA. She has published over seventy five (75) refereed journal and conference papers.
Omar Al-Bayari is an associate professor of Geomatics Engineering ad Surveying at the Al-Balqa' Applied University, Jordan.
J. Al-Azizi is a student at the Geomatics Engineering ad Surveying Department at the Al-Balqa' Applied University, Jordan.
Al Rawashdeh is an associate professor of Geomatics Engineering and Surveying at the Al-Balqa' Applied University, Jordan.

Acknowledgements
We would like to thank Al-Balqa' Applied University for partial support of this work by allowing us to use the University facilities to conduct the work.

References
1. ArcGIS for Desktop. http://www.esri.com/software/arcgis/about/gis-for-me.html
2. Arc/Info: Full featured Geographic Information System (2010). http://en.wikipedia.org/wiki/ArcInfo
3. Google Earth (2005). http://en.wikipedia.org/wiki/Google_Earth
4. Appleman D (1998) Developing COM/ ActiveX Componfent with visual basic 6, 1st edn. SAMS, United States
5. MapWindow GIS Open Source Project, 1998-2014. http://www.mapwindow.org/
6. Ames DP (2007) MapWinGIS Reference Manual: a function guide for the free MapWindow GIS ActiveX map component. Lulu.com,Morrisville
7. GIS Fundamentals; a First Text on Geographic Information Systems, 3rd edn. New York, Eider Press.
8. An Extensible, Interface-Based, Open Source GIS Paradigm: MapWindow 6.0 Developer Tools for the Microsoft Windows Platform. Free and Open Source Software for Geoinformatics (FOSS4G), Cape Town.
9. Getting Started with MapWindow 6 Harold (Ted) Dunsford Jr. Mark Van Orden Jiří Kadlec October 2009. http://mapwindow6.codeplex.com/documentation
10. Dunsford HA Jr, 2010: Design and development of an extensible, interchangeable component architecture for open -source geographic information systems, Idaho State University, 2010, p 278; 3407289

11

Performance evaluation of WMN-GA system for different settings of population size and number of generations

Admir Barolli[1], Shinji Sakamoto[2,3,4,5,6], Tetsuya Oda[2,3,4,5,6], Evjola Spaho[2,3,4,5,6]*, Leonard Barolli[2,3,4,5,6] and Fatos Xhafa[2,3,4,5,6]

*Correspondence:
evjolaspaho@hotmail.com
[2]Canadian Institute of Technology,
Zayed Center, Rr. Sulejman Delvina,
Tirana, Albania
[3]Graduate School of Engineering,
Fukuoka Institute of Technology
(FIT), 3-30-1 Wajiro-Higashi,
Higashi-Ku, Fukuoka, 811-0295
Fukuoka, Japan
Full list of author information is
available at the end of the article

Abstract

Wireless Mesh Networks (WMNs) distinguish for their low cost nature that makes them very attractive for providing wireless Internet connectivity. Such infrastructures can be used to deploy community networks, metropolitan area networks, municipal and corporative networks, and to support applications for urban areas, medical, transport and surveillance systems. The main issues in WMNs are achievement of network connectivity and stability as well as QoS in terms of user coverage. In this paper, we deal with the effect of changes in population size and number of generations for node placement problem in WMNs for Normal distribution of mesh clients. We consider two population sizes 8 and 512 and for every population size the number of generations are 200 and 20,000. As evaluation metrics we used size of giant component and number of covered users. The simulation results have shown that the increase of the population size results in better performance. Best results are obtained for the number of generation 20,000. However, when the number of generation is increased, the computation time is also increased.

Keywords: Wireless mesh networks; Genetic algorithms; Population size; Size of giant component; Number of covered users

Introduction

Wireless Mesh Networks (WMNs) are applicable in deployment of medical, transport and surveillance applications in urban areas, metropolitan, neighboring communities and municipal area networks. At the heart of WMNs are the issues of achieving network connectivity and stability as well as QoS in terms of user coverage. These issues are very closely related to the family of node placement problems in WMNs, such as mesh router nodes placement. Node placement problems have been long investigated in the optimization field due to numerous applications in location science (facility location, logistics, services, etc.) and classification (clustering). In such problems, we are given a number of potential facilities to serve costumers that are connected to facilities aiming to find locations such that the cost of serving all customers is minimized. In traditional versions of the problem, facilities could be hospitals, polling centers, fire stations serving to a number of clients and aiming to minimize some distance function in a metric space between clients and such facilities.

Facility location problems are thus showing their usefulness to communication networks, and more especially from WMNs field. WMNs [1,2] are currently attracting a lot of attention from wireless research and technology community due to their importance as a means for providing cost-efficient broadband wireless connectivity. WMNs infrastructures are currently used in developing and deploying medical, transport and surveillance applications in urban areas, metropolitan, neighboring communities and municipal area networks [3]. WMNs are based on mesh topology, in which every node (representing a server) is connected to one or more nodes, enabling thus the information transmission in more than one path. The path redundancy is a robust feature of this kind of topology. Compared to other topologies, mesh topology needs not a central node, allowing networks based on such topology to be self-healing. These characteristics of networks with mesh topology make them very reliable and robust networks to potential server node failures. In WMNs mesh routers provide network connectivity services to mesh client nodes. The good performance and operability of WMNs largely depends on placement of mesh routers nodes in the geographical deployment area to achieve network connectivity, stability and user coverage. The objective is to find an optimal and robust topology of the mesh router nodes to support connectivity services to clients.

For most formulations, node placement problems are shown to be computationally hard to solve to optimality [4-7], and therefore heuristic and meta-heuristic approaches are useful approaches to solve the problem for practical purposes. Several heuristic approaches are found in the literature for node placement problems in WMNs [8-12].

Genetic Algorithms (GAs) have been recently investigated as effective resolution methods. Mutation operator is one of the GA ingredients.

In this paper, we present the implemented system: Wireless Mesh Network - Genetic Algorithm (WMN-GA) system and investigate the effect of population size and number of generations in the node placement problem in WMNs considering giant component and number of covered users.

The rest of the paper is organized as follows. In Section 'Proposed and implemented WMN-GA System' is shown the proposed and implemented WMN-GA system. The simulation results are given in Section 'Simulation results'. We end the paper in Section 'Conclusions' with conclusions.

Proposed and implemented WMN-GA System

In this section, we present WMN-GA system. Our system can generate instances of the problem using different distributions of client and mesh routers.

The GUI interface of WMN-GA is shown in Figure 1. The left site of the interface shows the GA parameters configuration and on the right side are shown the network configuration parameters.

For the network configuration, we use: distribution, number of clients, number of mesh routers, grid size, radious of transmission distance and the size of subgrid.

For the GA parameter configuration, we use: number of independent runs, GA evolution steps, population size, population intermediate size, crossover probability, mutation probability, initial methods, select method.

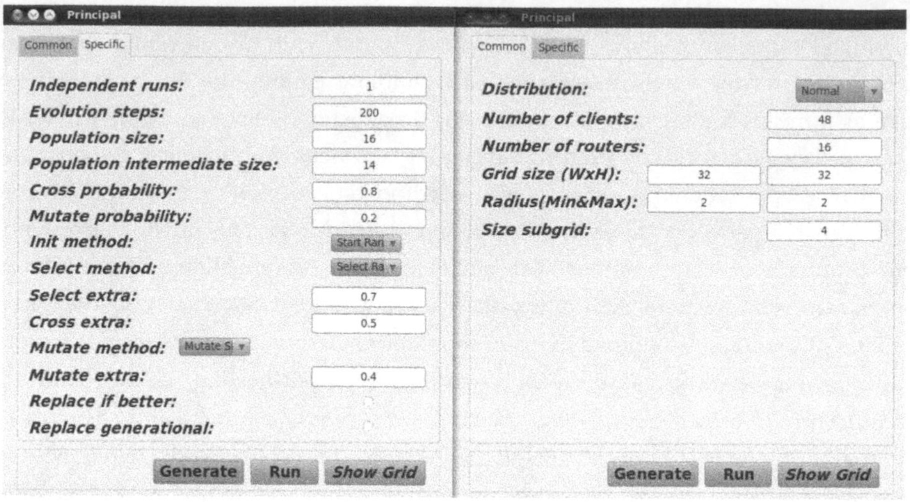

Figure 1 GUI tool for WMN-GA system.

Genetic algorithms

Genetic Algorithms (GAs) [13] have shown their usefulness for the resolution of many computationally combinatorial optimization problems. For the purpose of this work we have used the *template* given in Algorithm 1.

Algorithm 1 Genetic Algorithm Template

Generate the initial population P^0 of size μ;
Evaluate P^0;
while not termination-condition **do**
    Select the parental pool T^t of size λ; $T^t := Select(P^t)$;
    Perform crossover procedure on pairs of individuals in T^t with probability p_c; $P_c^t := Cross(T^t)$;
    Perform mutation procedure on individuals in P_c^t with probability p_m; $P_m^t := Mutate(P_c^t)$;
    Evaluate P_m^t ;
    Create a new population P^{t+1} of size μ from individuals in P^t and/or P_m^t ;
    $P^{t+1} := Replace(P^t; P_m^t)$
    $t := t + 1$;
end while
return Best found individual as solution;

We present next the particularization of GAs for the mesh router nodes placement in WMNs (see [14] for more details).

Encoding

The encoding of individuals (also known as chromosome encoding) is fundamental to the implementation of GAs in order to efficiently transmit the genetic information from parents to offsprings.

In the case of the mesh router nodes placement problem, a solution (individual of the population) contains the information on the current location of routers in the grid area as well as information on links to other mesh router nodes and mesh client nodes. This information is kept in data structures, namely, `pos_routers` for positions of mesh router nodes, `routers_links` for link information among routers and `client_router_link` for link information among routers and clients (matrices of the same size as the grid area are used). Based on these data structures, the size of the giant component and the number of users covered are computed for the solution.

It should be also noted that routers are assumed to have different radio coverage, therefore to any router could be linked to a number of clients and other routers. Obviously, whenever a router is moved to another cell of the grid area, the information on links to both other routers and clients must be computed again and links are re-established.

Selection operators

In the evolutionary computing literature we can find a variety of selection operators, which are in charge of selecting individuals for the pool mate. The operators considered in this work are those based on *Implicit Fitness Re-mapping* technique. It should be noted that selection operators are generic ones and do not depend on the encoding of individuals.

- *Random Selection*: This operator chooses the individuals uniformly at random. The problem is that a simple strategy does not consider even the fitness value of individuals and this may lead to a slow convergence of the algorithm.
- *Best Selection*: This operator selects the individuals in the population having higher fitness value. The main drawback of this operator is that by always choosing the best fitted individuals of the population, the GA converges prematurely.
- *Linear Ranking Selection*: This operator follows the strategy of selecting the individuals in the population with a probability directly proportional to its fitness value. This operator clearly benefits the selection of best endowed individuals, which have larger chances of being selected.
- *Exponential Ranking Selection*: This operator is similar to Linear Ranking but the probabilities of ranked individuals are weighted according to an exponential distribution.
- *Tournament Selection*: This operator selects the individuals based on the result of a tournament among individuals. Usually winning solutions are the ones of better fitness value but individuals of worse fitness value could be chosen as well, contributing thus to avoiding premature convergence. Particular cases of this operator are the *Binary Tournament* and *N-Tournament Selection*, for different values of *N*.

Crossover operators

The crossover operator selects individuals from the parental generation and interchanging their *genes*, thus new individuals (descendants) are obtained. The aim is to obtain descendants of better quality that will feed the next generation and enable the search to explore new regions of solution space not explored yet.

There exist many types of crossover operators explored in the evolutionary computing literature. It is very important to stress that crossover operators depend on the chromosome representation. This observation is especially important for the mesh router nodes problem, since in our case, instead of having strings we have a grid of nodes located in a certain positions. The crossover operator should thus take into account the specifics of mesh router nodes encoding. We have considered the following crossover operators, called *intersection operators* (denoted `CrossRegion`, hereafter), which take in input two individuals and produce in output two new individuals (see Algorithm 2).

Algorithm 2 Crossover Operator

1: **Input:** Two parent individuals P_1 and P_2; values H_g and W_g for height and width of a small grid area;

2: **Output:** Two offsprings O_1 and O_2;

3: Select at random a $H_g \times W_g$ rectangle RP_1 in parent P_1. Let RP_2 be the same rectangle in parent P_2;

4: Select at random a $H_g \times W_g$ rectangle RO_1 in offspring O_1. Let RO_2 be the same rectangle in offspring O_2;

5: Interchange the mesh router nodes: Move the mesh router nodes of RP_1 to RO_2 and those of RP_2 to RO_1;

6: Re-establish mesh nodes network connections in O_1 and O_2 (links between mesh router nodes and links between client mesh nodes and mesh router nodes are computed again);

7: **return** O_1 and O_2;

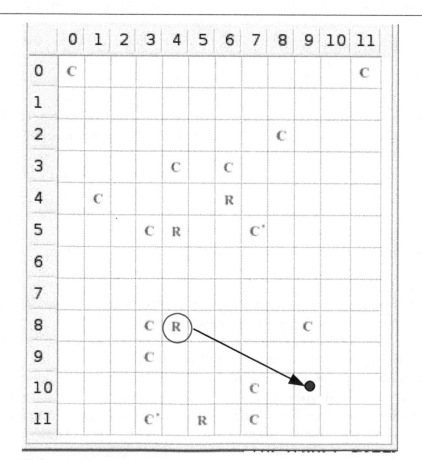

Figure 2 Single mutate operator.

Mutation operators for mesh routers nodes placement in WMNs

Mutation operator is one of the GA ingredients. Unlike crossover operators, which achieve to transmit genetic information from parents to offsprings, mutation operators usually make some small local perturbation of the individuals, having thus less impact on newly generated individuals.

Crossover is "a must" operator in GA and is usually applied with high probability, while mutation operators when implemented are applied with small probability. The rationale is that a large mutation rate would make the GA search to resemble a random search. Due to this, mutation operator is usually considered as a secondary operator.

In the case of mesh routers node placement, the matrix representation is chosen for the individuals of the population, in order to keep the information on mesh router nodes positions, mesh client positions, links among routers and links among routers and clients. The definition of the mutation operators is therefore specific to matrix-based encoding of the individuals of the population. Several specific mutation operators were considered in this study, which are move-based and swap-based operators.

SingleMutate

This is a move-based operator. It selects a mesh router node in the grid area and moves it to another cell of the grid area (see Figure 2).

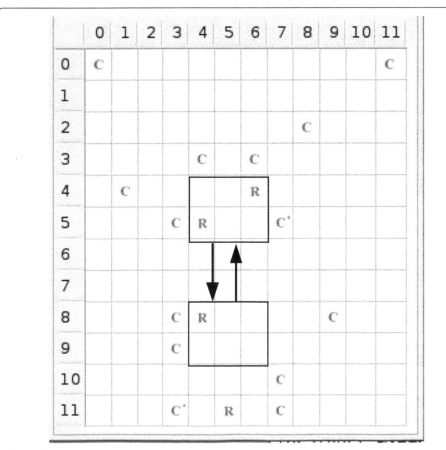

Figure 3 Rectangle mutate operator.

RectangleMutate

This is a swap-based operator. In this version, the operator selects two "small" rectangles at random in the grid area, and swaps the mesh routers nodes in them (see Figure 3).

SmallMutate

This is a move-based operator. In this case, the operator chooses randomly a router and moves it a small (*a priori* fixed) number of cells in one of the four directions: up, down, left or right in the grid (see Figure 4). This operator could be used a number of times to achieve the effect of SingleMutate operator.

SmallRectangleMutate

This is a move-based operator. The operator selects first at random a rectangle and then all routers inside the rectangle are moved with a small (*a priori* fixed) numbers of cells in one of the four directions: up, down, left or right in the grid (see Figure 5).

Simulation results

We carried out many simulations to evaluate the performance of WMNs using WMN-GA system. In this work, we consider the population size (n). We consider two parameters, m and n and the relation between them is: $n \triangleq 2^m$, $m \triangleq \{m \in Z \mid 0 \leq m \leq 12\}$ and $1 \leq n \leq 4096$. The grid size is considered 32×32. There are many distribution methods,

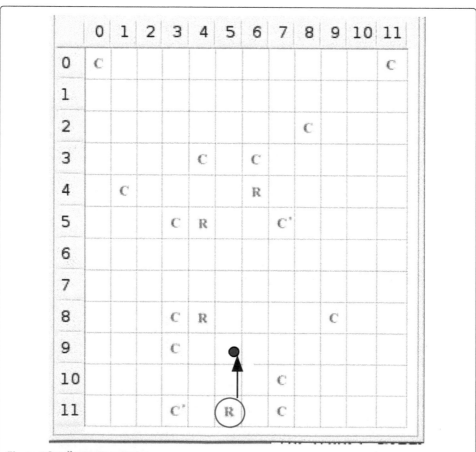

Figure 4 Small mutate operator.

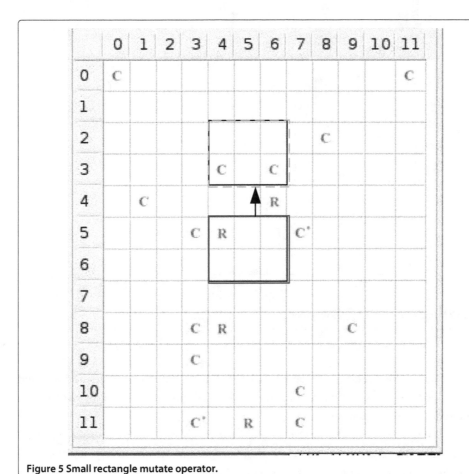

Figure 5 Small rectangle mutate operator.

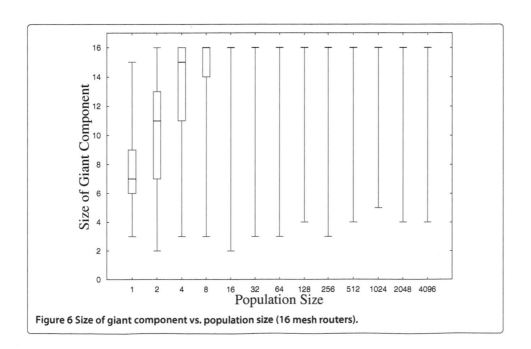

Figure 6 Size of giant component vs. population size (16 mesh routers).

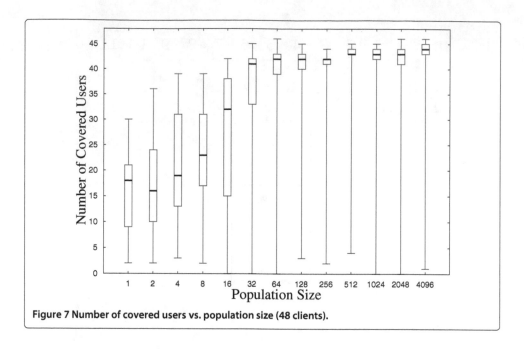

Figure 7 Number of covered users vs. population size (48 clients).

but we take in consideration only the normal distribution. As selection method we used linear ranking and as mutation method we used single mutation. The crossover rate is considered 0.8 and the mutation rate 0.2.

We used box plots to analyze the range of data values. The bottom and top of the box are the 25th and 75th percentile (the lower and upper quartiles, respectively), and the band near the middle of the box is the 50th percentile (the median). The ends of the whiskers represent the minimum and maximum of all the data.

In Figure 6 is shown the size of giant component vs. population size. In this case, the number of mesh routers is considered 16.

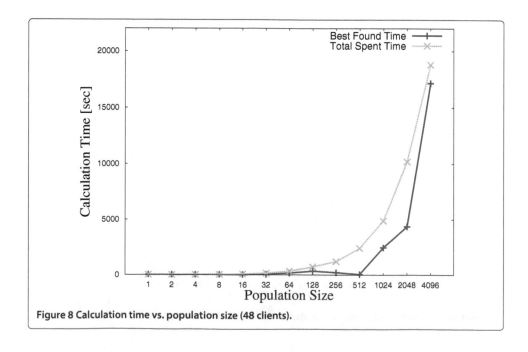

Figure 8 Calculation time vs. population size (48 clients).

In Figure 7 is shown the number of covered users vs. population size. The number of clients is considered 48. We can see that with the increase of the population size, the size of giant component and the number of covered users is increased. The maximal number of users covered is 45 and this is reached for population size 32.

In Figure 8 is shown calculation time vs. population size. We measured the calculation time for 48 clients. As can be seen from the graph, the computational time is high and it increases almost exponentially. However, until the population size is 512 the calculation time is very small. For this reason, we made extensive simulations for population sizes: 8 and 512 considering number of generations 200 and 20,000.

In Figure 9 are shown the simulation results for population size 8 and number of generations 200. In Figure 9(a) is shown the size of giant component vs. population size. In this

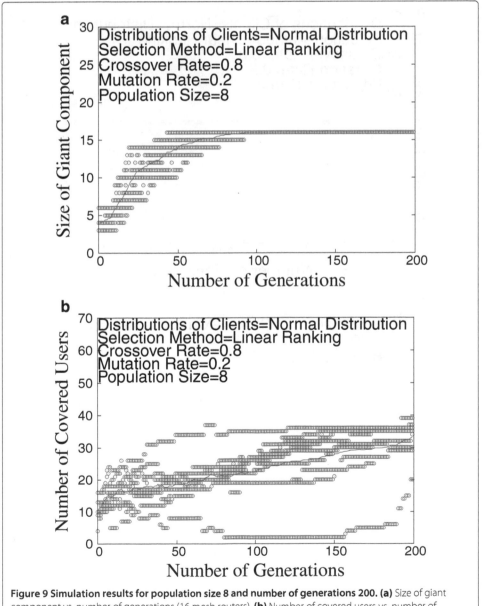

Figure 9 Simulation results for population size 8 and number of generations 200. (a) Size of giant component vs. number of generations (16 mesh routers). **(b)** Number of covered users vs. number of generations (48 clients).

case, the number of mesh routers is considered 16. In Figure 9(b) is shown the number of covered users vs. population size. The number of clients is considered 48.

In Figure 10, we increased the population size to 512 and the number of generations is 200. In Figure 10(a) is shown the size of giant component vs. population size and in Figure 10(b) is shown the number of covered users vs. population size.

If we compare Figure 9(a) and Figure 10(a), we can see that in both cases all 16 mesh routers are connected with each other. Comparing the results for population sizes: 8 and 512 (Figure 9(b) and Figure 10(b)), we can see that with the increase of the population size, the performance of WMN is increased and the mesh routers can cover more mesh clients.

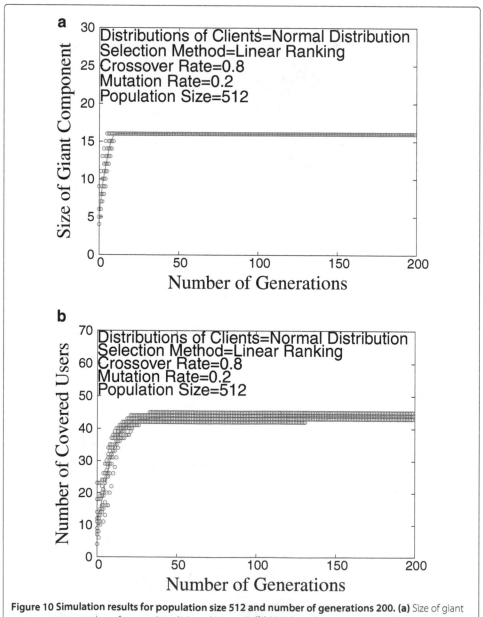

Figure 10 Simulation results for population size 512 and number of generations 200. (a) Size of giant component vs. number of generations (16 mesh routers). **(b)** Number of covered users vs. number of generations (48 clients).

We made other simulations by changing the number of generations to 20,000. In Figure 11 and Figure 12 are shown the simulation results for the population size 8 and 512, respectively. In both cases, the connectivity between all routers is established (see Figure 11(a) and Figure 12(a)) and the number of covered users is almost the same (see Figure 11(b) and Figure 12(b)).

From the results, we can see that the best results are obtained when the number of generation is 20,000. Thus, for higher number of generations and larger population size, the system has better performance.

Conclusions

In this work, we carried out simulations with WMN-GA system to see effect of changes in population size and number of generations for node placement problem in WMNs.

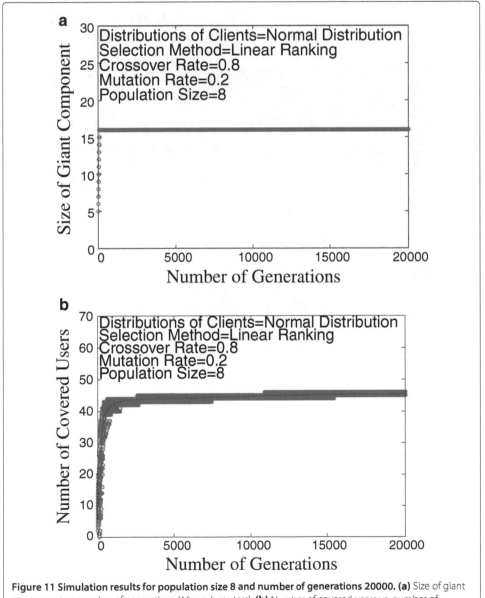

Figure 11 Simulation results for population size 8 and number of generations 20000. (a) Size of giant component vs. number of generations (16 mesh routers). **(b)** Number of covered users vs. number of generations (48 clients).

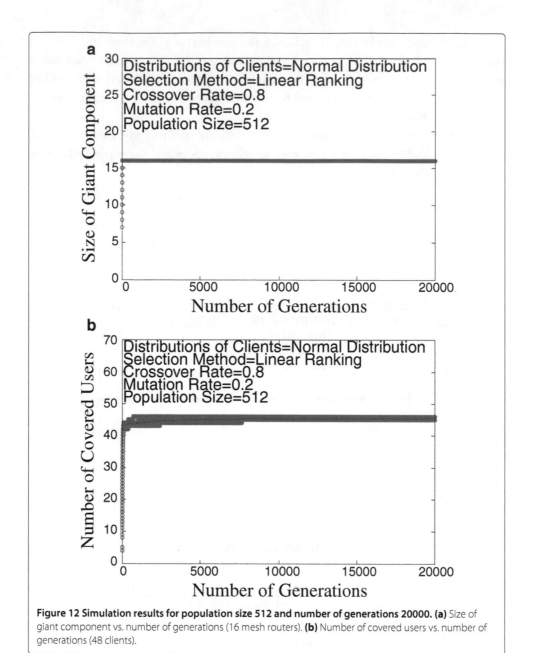

Figure 12 Simulation results for population size 512 and number of generations 20000. (a) Size of giant component vs. number of generations (16 mesh routers). **(b)** Number of covered users vs. number of generations (48 clients).

We considered two population sizes: 8 and 512, and for every population size the number of generations was 200 and 20,000. As evaluation metrics, we used the size of giant component and number of covered users. From the simulations we found out the following results.

- With the increase of the population size, the size of giant component and the number of covered users is increased.
- When the number of clients is 48, the computational time is high and it increases almost exponentially.
- When the number of generation is increased to 20,000, we obtained better results.
- For larger population sizes and higher number of generations the system performance is better. However, the computation time is increased.

- The computational time is highly increased with the increasing of the population size, for the same number of generations.

In the future work, we would like to evaluate the performance of WMN-GA system for different parameters and different distributions of mesh routers and clients.

Competing interests
The authors declare that they have no competing interests.

Authors' contributions
AB, SS and TO perticipated in: the design and implementation of WNN-GA system; analysis and interpretation of data and in the draft of the manuscript. ES, LB and FX pericipated in: the conceptation and design of the system; the discussion and evaluation of the proposed system and in giving the final approval of the version to be published. All authors read and approved the final manuscript.

Acknowledgements
This work is supported by a Grant-in-Aid for Scientific Research from Japanese Society for the Promotion of Science (JSPS). The authors would like to thank JSPS for the financial support.

Author details
[1]Faculty of Business and Technologies, Department of Information Technology, Kristal University, Autostrada Tirane - Durres, Km 3, Tirana, Albania. [2]Canadian Institute of Technology, Zayed Center, Rr. Sulejman Delvina, Tirana, Albania. [3]Graduate School of Engineering, Fukuoka Institute of Technology (FIT), 3-30-1 Wajiro-Higashi, Higashi-Ku, Fukuoka, 811-0295 Fukuoka, Japan. [4]Fukuoka Institute of Technology (FIT), 3-30-1 Wajiro-Higashi, Higashi-Ku, Fukuoka, 811-0295 Fukuoka, Japan. [5]Department of Information and Communication Engineering, Fukuoka Institute of Technology (FIT), 3-30-1 Wajiro-Higashi, Higashi-Ku, Fukuoka, 811-0295 Fukuoka, Japan. [6]Department of Languages and Informatics Systems, Technical University of Catalonia, C/Jordi Girona 1-3, 08034 Barcelona, Spain.

References
1. Akyildiz IF, Wang X, Wang W (2005) Wireless mesh networks: a survey. Comput Network 47(4): 445-487
2. Nandiraju N, Nandiraju D, Santhanama L, He B, Wang J, Agrawal D (2007) Wireless mesh networks: current challenges and future direction of web-in-the-sky. IEEE Wireless Comm 14(4): 79–89
3. Chen C-C, Chekuri C Urban wireless mesh network planning: the case of directional antennas. Tech Report No. UIUCDCS-R-2007-2874, Department of Computer Science, University of Illinois at Urbana-Champaign, 2007
4. Garey MR, Johnson DS (1979) Computers and intractability -a guide to the theory of NP-completeness. Freeman, San Francisco
5. Lim A, Rodrigues B, Wang F, Xua Zh (2005) k-center problems with minimum coverage. Theor Comput Sci 332(1–3): 1–17
6. Amaldi E, Capone A, Cesana M, Filippini I, Malucelli F (2008) Optimization models and methods for planning wireless mesh networks. Comput Networks 52: 2159–2171
7. Wang J, Xie B, Cai K, Agrawal DP (2007) Efficient Mesh Router Placement in Wireless Mesh Networks. In: Mobile adhoc and sensor systems. MASS-2007, Pisa, Italy, pp 9–11
8. Muthaiah SN, Rosenberg C (2008) Single Gateway Placement in Wireless Mesh Networks In: Proc. of 8th International IEEE Symposium on Computer Networks, Turkey. (ISCN), Istanbul, Turkey, pp 4754–4759
9. Zhou P, Manoj BS, Rao R (2007) A gateway placement algorithm in wireless mesh networks. In: Proc. of the 3rd International Conference on Wireless Internet (Austin, Texas, October 22–24, 2007). ICST (Institute for Computer Sciences Social-Informatics and Telecommunications Engineering), Brussels, pp 1–9
10. Tang M (2009) Gateways placement in backbone wireless mesh networks. Int J Comm Netw Syst Sci 2(1): 45–50
11. Franklin AA, Siva C, Murthy R (2007) Node placement algorithm for deployment of two-tier wireless mesh networks. In: Proc. of IEEE Global Communications Conference GLOBECOMM (2007), Washington DC, USA, pp 4823–4827
12. Vanhatupa T, Hännikäinen M, Hämäläinen TD (2007) Genetic algorithm to optimize node placement and configuration for WLAN planning. In: Proc. of 4th International Symposium on Wireless Communication Systems, pp 612–616
13. Holland J (1975) Adaptation in natural and artificial systems. University of Michigan Press, Ann Arbor
14. Xhafa F, Sanchez C, Barolli L (2010) Genetic algorithms for efficient placement of router nodes in wireless mesh networks. In: Proc. of IEEE International Conference on Advanced Information Networking and Applications, Perth, Australia, pp 465–472

12

Fairness scheme for energy efficient H.264/AVC-based video sensor network

Bambang AB Sarif[1*], Mahsa T Pourazad[1,2], Panos Nasiopoulos[1], Victor CM Leung[1] and Amr Mohamed[3]

* Correspondence:
bambangs@ece.ubc.ca
[1]Electrical and Computer
Engineering Department, University
of British Columbia, 2332 Main Mall,
Vancouver, BC V6T 1Z4, Canada
Full list of author information is
available at the end of the article

Abstract

The availability of advanced wireless sensor nodes enable us to use video processing techniques in a wireless sensor network (WSN) platform. Such paradigm can be used to implement video sensor networks (VSNs) that can serve as an alternative to existing video surveillance applications. However, video processing requires tremendous resources in terms of computation and transmission of the encoded video. As the most widely used video codec, H.264/AVC comes with a number of advanced encoding tools that can be tailored to suit a wide range of applications. Therefore, in order to get an optimal encoding performance for the VSN, it is essential to find the right encoding configuration and setting parameters for each VSN node based on the content being captured. In fact, the environment at which the VSN is deployed affects not only the content captured by the VSN node but also the node's performance in terms of power consumption and its life-time. The objective of this study is to maximize the lifetime of the VSN by exploiting the trade-off between encoding and communication on sensor nodes. In order to reduce VSNs' power consumption and obtain a more balanced energy consumption among VSN nodes, we use a branch and bound optimization techniques on a finite set of encoder configuration settings called configuration IDs (CIDs) and a fairness-based scheme. In our approach, the bitrate allocation in terms of fairness ratio per each node is obtained from the training sequences and is used to select appropriate encoder configuration settings for the test sequences. We use real life content of three different possible scenes of VSNs' implementation with different levels of complexity in our study. Performance evaluations show that the proposed optimization technique manages to balance VSN's power consumption per each node while the nodes' maximum power consumption is minimized. We show that by using that approach, the VSN's power consumption is reduced by around 7.58% in average.

Keywords: Component; Video sensor network; H.264/AVC; Power consumption; Computation and communication trade-off; Fairness

Introduction

The advances in VLSI, sensors and wireless communication technologies have provided us with miniature devices that have low computational power and communication capabilities. These devices can be organized to form a network called wireless sensor network (WSN). A WSN is typically used to measure physical attributes of the monitored environment and send the information to a central device that usually has unlimited resources. The information gathered at the central device, usually called the sink node, can be used by human operator or any additional machine/software to perceive the condition of the monitored environment and provide some action if necessary. Due to the ad-hoc nature of the deployment, the information sent to the sink is usually performed in a multi-hop wireless communication fashion.

Considering that visual information can significantly improve the perceived information gathered from the sensed environment, there is a growing interest in incorporating video applications and transmissions over WSN [1-3]. Wireless video sensor network (VSN) has the potential to improve the ability to develop user-centric surveillance applications to monitor and prevent harmful events [4,5]. VSNs offer an alternative to several existing surveillance technologies because it can be implemented in an ad-hoc manner, customized to user requirements, and implemented on locations that are lacking infrastructure. However, unlike the conventional WSNs, VSNs require a large amount of resources for encoding and transmitting the video data. Therefore, maximizing the power efficiency of coding and transmission operations in VSNs is very important.

Video nodes in VSNs share the same wireless medium in order to send their encoded video to the sink node. Since the bandwidth allocated for the network is limited, there is an issue of fairness of bandwidth allocated per each VSN node. Allocating the same bitrate to each video node guarantees the fairness in terms of bitrate and the quality of the encoded video, given that each node is using the same video encoding parameter settings and configurations. However, in many VSN deployment scenarios, nodes further from the sink usually need to relay their data through intermediate nodes. Therefore, the total energy consumption of nodes that are closer to the sink will be greater than the nodes further. More balanced energy consumption among VSN nodes is achieved by allocating different fairness ratio per each node in the VSN. It has to be noted that this has to be done without sacrificing the quality of the transmitted video of any node. To this end different fairness ratios are assigned to VSN nodes such that the tradeoff between encoding complexity and compression performance is exploited. Since encoding complexity and compression performance (in terms of bit rate) determine the required power for coding and transmission respectively, assigning different fairness ratio per each node will affect the distribution of power consumption in a VSN. To the best of our knowledge this idea has not been studied in details in the existing literature on VSN.

In order to exploit the trade-off between computation and communication of a video stream, an understanding on how the encoder works along with its impact on the compression performance is necessary. H.264/AVC is the current most widely used ITU and MPEG video coding standard [6,7]. There is a number of published research works on H.264/AVC's performance in literature [8,9]. However, the focus of most of the existing studies is mainly on determining the optimal coding configuration without considering the total energy consumed for encoding and transmission. One of the earlier studies on H.264/AVC power consumption in a VSN is presented in [10]. In this study, the trade-off between encoding and transmission energy consumption for only two configuration settings of H.264/AVC are investigated. In another study [11], the researchers compares the total energy consumption of some video encoders including H.264/AVC using the same configuration settings as the ones used in [10]. The study in [10] was further extended by [12] through including more configuration settings of H.264/AVC encoder for investigating the trade-off between encoding and transmission energy consumption in a VSN. Furthermore, in [12] some encoder parameters that can affect the performance of the encoder in terms of bitrate and computational complexity were highlighted. In order to take advantage of the trade-off between encoding and transmission energy consumptionin, a table called configuration ID (CID) was proposed, that includes several encoder configuration settings to compress a video with almost similar quality in terms of peak signal to noise ratio (PSNR), at different bitrate and compression complexity level. Unlike the *CommonConfig* approach used in [10] [11], where all VSN nodes have the same encoding configuration, the proposed scheme in [12], assigns different CIDs to different nodes in order to exploit the trade-off between communication and computation. The analysis of the energy consumption fairness of the VSN showed that by assigning different configuration setting parameters to each node, the node's maximum energy consumption of VNSs can be reduced [13]. One of the common drawbacks of the existing studies is using the same video resource for all VSN nodes. While this seting may show some aspects of the video encoding process and trade-off in a VSN, it does not reflect the real life setting of a VSN deployment, where different VSN nodes capture the scene from different point of view and thus the complexity of captured content is not consistent over different nodes. Note that the performance of a video encoder in terms of computational complexity and bitrate depends on both the encoding configuration and temporal and spatial complexity of content. That brings the problem of exploiting the trade-off between computation and communication in a VSN into a different level of difficulty.

In this paper, we propose an algorithm to reduce the maximum power consumption VSN nodes by extending our previous work in [12] and [13]. We use a branch and bound optimization techniques on a finite set of CID options and a fairness-based scheme in order to reduce VSNs' power consumption and obtain a more balanced energy consumption among VSN nodes. Furthermore, in order to simulate a realistic VSN implementation, we use a variety of real life captured content in our analysis. We also study the effect of spatial and temporal complexity of the videos on the VSN's encoding performance. In order to perform the analysis, the captured videos are classified into different content complexity classes. Then some of these videos are used for training and the rest for testing the performance of our algorithm. Also, to evaluate the performance of the proposed algorithm in a more realistic scenario, the VSN used in this study has a more complex network topology than the one used in [12,13].

The rest of the paper is organized as follows: Section Video capturing and encoding settings describes the video capturing and encoding settings used in this paper, Section Video content classification presents the video content classification methodology, Section VSN Power consumption modelling and formulation describes the energy consumption model for the VSN used in the paper, experiments and results are provided in Section Experiments and results, and conclusions are and future works are discussed in Section Conclusions.

Video capturing and encoding settings

The complexity of the captured content by the VSN nodes depends on the activities of the scene where VSN is deployed. This in turn will also affect the encoding complexity and bitrate of the encoded video at each VSN node. In order to mimic realistic VSN applications, we have installed nine cameras in one of our labs. The cameras are installed

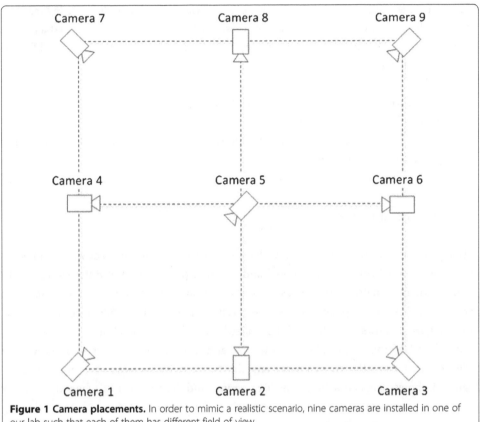

Figure 1 Camera placements. In order to mimic a realistic scenario, nine cameras are installed in one of our lab such that each of them has different field of view.

such that each of them has different field of view as shown in Figure 1. Some of the cameras' field of view overlaps one another. The scene arrangement is such that the motion and activities are not centered in the middle of the field and the content captured by each camera is different. With the assumption that most important activities occur around the entrance door in a surveillance system, the middle camera (see camera 5 in Figure 2) is directed towards the door. To capture representative VSN data with different temporal and spatial complexity levels, we modify the layout of the lab to

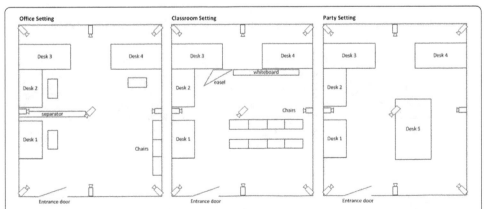

Figure 2 The setting of the room for video capturing process. To capture representative data, we modify the layout of our lab to represent three different scenes: office (left), classroom (middle) and party (right).

represent three different scenes, namely "office", "classroom", and "party". Figure 2 illustrates the layout of different scene settings. To have a representative database with different activity levels, each scene is captured several times based on four different settings as follows:

1. The level of activity of all the people in the room is high, and the total number of people is between six to eight.
2. Three or more people moving around the room, while the total number of people in the room is around six.
3. Couple of people walking around the room, while the total number of people in the room is around five.
4. Three or four people walking in the room.

Using the nine cameras installed, we have captured four different activity settings for the three scenes ("office", "classroom" and "party"), producing 108 different videos to be used for our analysis. Each video is 10s length and downsampled to 15 frame per seconds (fps) 416×240 pixels to mimic the requirement of a decent video sensor network. Figure 3 shows snapshots of the "office" scene from camera2 and camera4 when activity level of the scene falls into the first and third settings. As it is observed the video content from the two cameras and the two activity scenarios are not the same. Figure 4 shows snapshots from the "classroom" and "party" scenes when the activity level of the scene falls into the second setting. For ease of referencing, the following video identification is used: *<camera-id__scene-setting__activity-level>*. Hence, *camera2_party_act1* means the video captured by camera2 in the "party" scene when the activity level of the scene falls into the first setting.

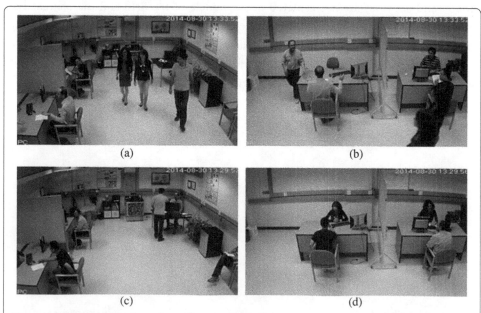

(a)   (b)

(c)   (d)

Figure 3 Some snapshots from the "office" scene. The first row show the snapshots of the "office" scene in the first activity settings from: **(a)** camera2 and **(b)** camera6. The two cameras produced different contents when the activity level of the scene falls into the third setting as shown in **(c)** camera2 and **(d)** camera6.

Fairness scheme for energy efficient H.264/AVC-based video...

207

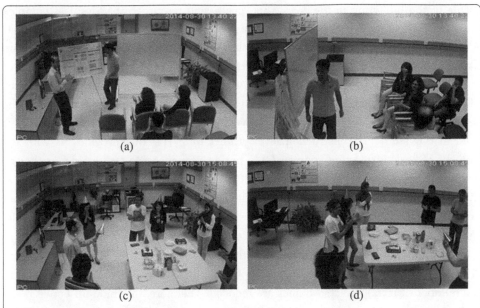

Figure 4 Some snapshots from the "classroom" and "party" scene. The first row shows the snapshots of the "classroom" scene from **(a)** camera2 and **(b)** camera4. On the other hand the second row show the snapshots of the "party" scene from **(c)** camera2 and **(d)** camera4.

For encoding the videos captured at each node, we use the most widely used video coding standard H.264/AVC [6]. The video coding standard comes with a number of different encoding tools that can be configured to suit a wide range video applications. The performance of the H.264/AVC encoder in terms of computation requirement (complexity) and bitrate depends on the setting parameters used to encode the video. One of the encoding parameters is group of picture (GOP) size. GOP size determines the number of inter-frame coded picture within a successive video stream. In inter-frame prediction process, each block within a current frame is predicted by the most similar block from previously coded reference frames. This is in contrast with the intra-frame prediction technique, in which blocks of pixels are predicted from its neighboring pixels within the same frame. The inter-frame prediction technique produces lower bitrate than intra-frame prediction; while the encoding complexity of inter-frame coding is much higher than the later. As it is observed by increasing the GOP size, the number of inter-frame coded pictures increases, therefore the bitrate of the coded video is reduced at the cost of higher encoding complexity. Note that the complexity and bitrate of inter-frame prediction can be controlled by adjusting the search range (SR) of motion estimation process. The SR determines the size of searching area in the reference frame to find the best match to be used for inter prediction. Increasing the SR may result in better compression performance at the cost of increased complexity. However this observation is quite content dependant and there are cases where increasing the value of SR does not provide significant benefit in terms of compression performance [12]. Quantization parameter (QP) is another encoding parameter that regulates how much spatial detail is saved. In fact, the quality of the encoded video in terms of peak signal to noise ratio (PSNR) depends largely on the QP value. When QP value is very small, the residue signal is preserved more and the quality of compressed video is high, at the cost of higher complexity and bitrate.

Due to the limitation in the energy and processing resources of VSNs, less complex encoder configurations are deployed. To this end, we use the baseline profile of H.264/AVC that is suitable for low complexity applications. Therefore, only I and P frames are used (no B-frame). The other encoding settings used in this paper include the use of context-adaptive variable-length coding (CAVLC) entropy coding, one reference frame, SR equal to eight, while the rate distortion optimization (RDO), rate control, and the deblocking filter are disabled. The H.264/AVC reference encoder software (JM 18.2) is used in our study. The instruction level profiler *iprof* [14] that provides us with the number of basic instruction counts (IC) to perform an encoding task is used as the encoding complexity measure. The benefit of using IC as the measure of complexity is threefold. Firstly, IC is more accurate than the commonly used encoding time. The other benefit of using IC is the fact that IC is agnostic to the device architecture. In addition, IC can be used to estimate the encoding power consumption of the video node.

From our earlier work, we learned that the IC increases as the GOP sizes increases [12]. For a specific QP, however, increasing the GOP size will also reduce the bitrate as the number of intra predicted frames are reduced. Therefore, the trade-off between encoding and transmission power consumption can be controlled by managing the GOP size. This information were translated into a tabular format as shown in Table 1. It has to be noted that the table only shows the value of GOP size used for the corresponding configuration ID (CID). The remaining encoder setting parameters are the same, i.e., as mentioned in the previous paragraphs.

Figure 5(a) shows the complexity and bitrate plot of the CIDs defined in Table 1 for different QP values for *camera2_party_act2* video. As it is observed, when CID value is small, the compression performance of the encoder is sacrificed such that the bitrate is high. However, this is compensated by having a low encoding complexity. On the other hand, using bigger CID means increasing the encoder complexity to gain a better compression performance. Figure 5(a) also shows that reducing the value of QP will increase both the encoder complexity and bitrate. Therefore, the bitrate of the encoded video and the complexity of the encoding process depend on the CID and QP used. It has to be noted that although the GOP sizes gap for CID = 6 (GOP = 32) and CID = 7 (GOP = 64) is very high, i.e., the GOP size gap is 32, the different in complexity (bitrate) between these two CIDs is very small. Moreover, the values used in Table 1 shows a relation between the GOP size and the CID, i.e., $CID = log_2(2^*GOP)$. This shows that the CID values represent an encoder parameter, i.e., the GOP size, whose values affect the complexity and bitrate of the encoder. We also want highlight that the bitrate

Table 1 Configuration ID (CID)

CID	GOP
1	1
2	2
3	4
4	8
5	16
6	32
7	64

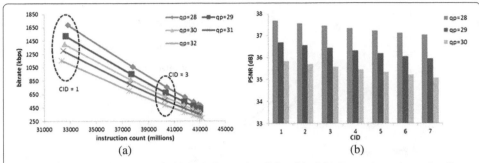

Figure 5 Complexity, bitrate, and video quality trade-off. Part **(a)** of this figure shows the trade-off between complexity (in terms of instruction counts) and bitrate of *camera2_party_act2* video encoded with different CID and QP values. It can be seen that the smaller CID value entails high bitrate but low encoding complexity. On the other hand, encoding the video with a smaller QP value (to get better video quality) increases computation complexity and bitrate. Part **(b)** of the figure shows that for the same value of QP, the video quality is almost the same, regardless of the CID used to encode the video.

(complexity) is monotonously decrease (increase) with the increase of CID value. In terms of the encoded video quality, Figure 5(b) shows that for the same QP, the quality of the encoded video is almost the same in terms of PSNR, i.e., the different is less than 0.5 dB, regardless of the CID value used to encode the video.

Video content classification

Since the cameras in a VSN can have different field of views, the content captured by each camera in a VSN will be different. For example, Figure 6(a) shows the complexity and bitrate of videos captured by three different cameras in the "party" scene at the same activity level while Figure 6(b) shows the complexity and bitrate of videos captured by camera2 in the "party" scene at different activity levels. On the other hand, Figure 7 shows the complexity and bitrate of videos captured by camera2 in different scenes. It can be seen from these figures that the bitrate and encoding complexity of the videos captured by each camera depends on the content complexity of the scene. The video that contain more objects and with higher motion will have a higher bitrate than the video that has less objects and motion. Consequently, the total bitrate generated by the captured scenes that have high spatial and temporal detail will be bigger

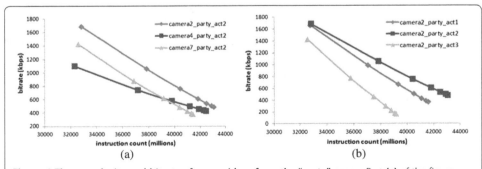

Figure 6 The complexity and bitrate of some videos from the "party" scene. Part **(a)** of the figure shows the complexity and bitrate of videos from camera2, camera4, and camera7 in the second activity setting. On the other hand, part **(b)** of the figure shows the complexity and bitrate of videos captured by camera2 in different activity settings. The videos are encoded with QP equal to 28 while the CID value is varied.

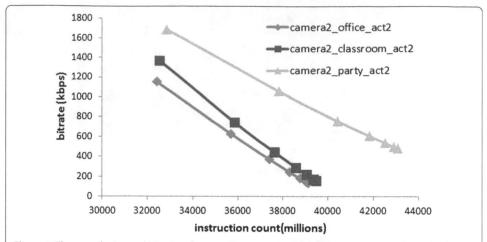

Figure 7 The complexity and bitrate of some videos captured at different scene settings. The figure shows the complexity and bitrate of videos from camera2 captured at different scenes. The videos are encoded with QP equal to 28 while the CID value is varied.

than the ones obtained from the scenes with lower spatial and temporal detail. Ideally, we need to find the nodes' optimal bitrate allocation for each possible scene. However, this approach is not practical. In this regard, we assume that if we can obtain the optimal bitrate ratio allocation for the worst scenario, i.e., when the nodes' bitrate is high, we can use that information as an initial guide for us to allocate the configuration settings for the other scenarios. Thus, in this paper, the scenes with higher content will be used for the training set while the remaining scenes are use as the test set. In order to find the scenes that have higher activity content, we need to formulate a methodology to classify each camera and scene into different content complexity level. For that purpose, we use the ITU-T recommendation that includes the use of spatial information unit (SI) and temporal information unit (TI) that is defined as follow [15]:

$$SI = \max_{time}\left\{std_{space}[Sobel(F_n)]\right\} \tag{1}$$

$$TI = \max_{time}\left\{std_{space}[F_n - F_{n-1}]\right\} \tag{2}$$

SI and TI measure the spatial and temporal activity level of videos. In this regard, Figure 8 shows the SI and TI values of camera1, camera2, camera5, and camera9. It can be seen from this figure that for the same scene, each camera has different spatial and temporal activity level. Consequently, Table 2 shows the SI values of all videos while Table 3 shows the TI values, respectively.

In order to classify the scenes into different content complexity level, the following procedure is used:

1. Classify each video from a scene into different SI and TI classes using the following threshold:

$$
\begin{aligned}
t1 &= mean(CC) - 0.5^*std(CC) \\
t2 &= mean(CC) + 0.5^*std(CC) \\
CC &= \{SI, TI\}
\end{aligned}
\tag{3}
$$

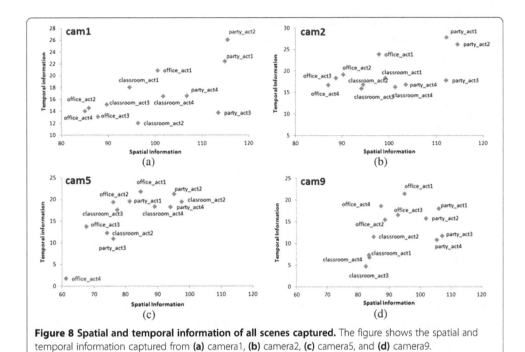

Figure 8 Spatial and temporal information of all scenes captured. The figure shows the spatial and temporal information captured from **(a)** camera1, **(b)** camera2, **(c)** camera5, and **(d)** camera9.

Using (3), we found that the value of $t1$ and $t2$ for SI are 87.85 and 98.95, respectively. On the other hand, the value of $t1$ and $t2$ for TI are 14.32 and 19.04, respectively. For example, if a specific video's SI is less than $t1$, the video is classified as *low-SI_video*. If the video's SI is higher than $t2$, it is classified as *high-SI_video*. If the video's SI is between $t1$ and $t2$, the video is classified as *medium-SI_video*.

2. Based on the SI(TI) classes of the videos, we classify the scene into different SI(TI) classes using the following rules:
   a. The SI(TI) class of a scene is equal to the majority of SI(TI) classes of all videos from that scene
   b. If no majority is found, the scene is classified as medium SI(TI) scene

Table 2 Spatial Information unit (SI) of all videos

Scene	cam1	cam2	cam3	cam4	cam5	cam6	cam7	cam8	cam9
office_act1	100.52	97.83	88.92	76.17	84.60	89.95	85.73	95.06	94.98
office_act2	85.83	90.26	85.90	71.24	76.14	84.45	85.20	90.06	88.62
office_act3	87.78	88.68	89.78	74.30	67.62	91.16	89.93	90.80	92.75
office_act4	84.97	87.01	87.96	71.40	61.17	89.97	83.85	87.36	87.43
classroom_act1	94.62	99.18	96.73	89.56	97.46	96.04	92.03	88.12	83.59
classroom_act2	96.30	94.46	96.30	91.46	74.07	88.83	92.74	85.52	84.99
classroom_act3	89.67	94.11	90.04	85.71	77.42	87.03	88.94	85.85	82.55
classroom_act4	101.69	101.21	94.74	92.68	89.08	94.57	91.86	89.19	83.64
party_act1	114.85	112.10	116.85	99.60	81.27	104.73	104.60	110.79	105.97
party_act2	115.40	114.49	107.53	90.61	95.06	101.31	104.56	111.56	101.90
party_act3	113.43	112.04	113.87	99.02	76.15	96.36	107.40	111.86	107.08
party_act4	106.64	103.51	111.48	89.54	93.97	95.22	101.28	102.44	105.30

Table 3 Temporal Information unit (SI) of all videos

Scene	cam1	cam2	cam3	cam4	cam5	cam6	cam7	cam8	cam9
office_act1	20.91	23.88	18.15	25.59	21.83	26.44	14.93	21.35	21.51
office_act2	14.59	19.21	18.46	22.00	19.43	23.26	17.33	15.10	15.47
office_act3	13.10	18.34	18.77	20.77	13.73	20.90	17.04	17.20	16.51
office_act4	14.05	16.76	16.21	17.74	1.74	15.87	14.55	18.08	18.60
classroom_act1	18.05	18.39	18.42	17.47	19.47	19.56	11.04	11.21	7.38
classroom_act2	12.04	16.78	12.75	15.14	12.25	13.82	13.85	7.60	11.58
classroom_act3	15.18	15.88	11.79	13.76	17.64	14.98	9.65	11.07	4.75
classroom_act4	16.52	16.24	13.41	15.65	18.40	17.46	11.22	12.04	6.79
party_act1	22.45	27.82	21.44	27.15	19.59	21.93	17.15	18.27	17.98
party_act2	26.10	26.24	19.76	17.66	21.24	26.86	22.29	22.67	15.76
party_act3	13.75	17.83	14.74	17.05	10.92	15.01	13.93	13.50	11.72
party_act4	16.59	16.78	17.00	13.17	18.25	15.32	11.10	13.31	10.83

Figure 9 shows an example on how to obtain the *office_act1* and *classroom_act1* scenes' classes. Using the above rule, the *office_act1* is classified as *medium-SI_high-TI_scene*. On the other hand, scene *classroom_act1* is classified as *medium-SI_medium-TI_scene*. Figure 10 shows the classes of all the scenes.

Scenes with high SI will generally produce videos with higher bitrate than the scenes that have lower SI. This is especially true for CID equal to one that corresponds to using GOP size equal to one, i.e., the video is intra-frames coded. Therefore, the configuration settings that is suitable for a specific SI class may not be suitable to be used for the other SI class. Based on this assumption, the scenes are arranged into three different sets, namely scenes that have high SI, scenes that have medium SI and scenes that have low SI. In each of these sets, the scene with the highest TI will be selected as the training scene. For example, in Figure 10, the scenes having medium SI are the *office_act1*, *office_act3*, *classroom_act1*, *classroom_act2*, and *classroom_act4*. Out of these five scenes, the scene that has the highest TI class, i.e., *office_act1*, is selected as the training scene for the medium SI scenes. If there is more than one candidate for the training scene, the scene that has the biggest average TI will be selected as the training scene. Henceforth, the training set for the high SI scenes is the *party_act2*, the training set for the medium SI scenes is the *office_act1*, and the training scene for the low SI

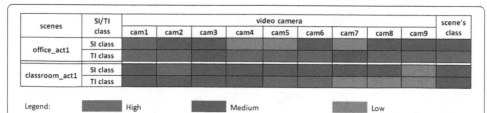

Figure 9 SI (TI) class of office_act1 and classroom_act1 scenes and their corresponding scene's class. This figure shows an example on how we can obtain the scene's class. Consider the office_act1 scene. Using equation (3), the SI classes of camera1 to camera9 are high, medium, medium, low, low, medium, low, medium, and medium. Since the SI class's majority is medium, office_act1 scene is classified as a scene with medium SI. Furthermore, office_act1 also falls into a scene with high TI. Thus, the office_act1 is classified as a medium-SI_high-TI scene. Using the same approach, classroom_act1 scene is classified as a medium-SI_medium-TI scene.

	SI Class		
	Low	Medium	High
High TI	N/A	Office_act1	Party_act1 Party_act2
Medium TI	Office_act2 Office_act4	Office_act3 Classroom_act1 Classroom_act4	Party_act4
Low TI	Classroom_act3	Classroom_act2	Party_act3

Figure 10 Scene's classes. The scenes shown in bold are the training scenes for their respective SI class.

scenes is the *office_act2*. The training scenes are shown in bold in Figure 10. Correspondingly, Table 4 shows the training scenes and their corresponding test scenes.

VSN Power consumption modelling and formulation

The encoding power consumption of a VSN node depends on the CID value assigned to that node. However, since some nodes need to relay their data through intermediate nodes, the node's communication power consumption depends on both the CID value assigned to that node and the way the encoded data is relayed in the network. This problem can be formulated as an optimization procedure. For this purpose, the following video sensor node model is used in this paper. All the nodes, including the sink, are assumed to be statically deployed in the deployment area. It is assumed that a standard medium access control (MAC) protocol is applied to resolve the link interference problem. The network is modeled as an undirected graph $G(N,L)$ where N is the set of nodes and L is the set of links. The nodes are identified such that the first node is the closest node to the sink while the Nth node is farthest one. The sink has unlimited source of energy. However, the total information flow to the sink is constrained by the bandwidth of the network.

Node i can communicate with node j if a link between those nodes ($L_{ij} \in L$) exists. Sensor node i can capture and encode video, and then generate video traffic with a source rate R_i. Furthermore, each node can also relay the traffic from upstream nodes. The flow conservation law at each node is then:

$$\sum r_{ij} - \sum r_{ki} = R_i \qquad (4)$$

Table 4 Training and test scenes

Scene's SI class	Training scene	Test scene	Test scene label
High	party_act2	party_act1	VS1
		party_act3	VS2
		Party_act4	VS3
Medium	office_act1	classroom_act1	VS4
		classroom_act2	VS5
		classroom_act4	VS6
		office_act3	VS7
Low	office_act2	office_act4	VS8
		classroom_act3	VS9

Here, r_{ij} denotes the outgoing rate at L_{ij} while r_{ki} denotes incoming rates at L_{ki}, and $L_{ij}, L_{ki} \in L$.

The sum of transmission rate of all the nodes is constrained to be equal to the bandwidth available (B):

$$\sum_{i=1}^{N} R_i \leq B \tag{5}$$

The bitrate allocated to a node itself is obtained using the relation $R_i = R\{CID_i, QP_i\}$, where R is the bitrate of the video for the pair of CID and QP used by the node.

A generally used energy consumption model for a wireless communication transmitter and receiver as presented in [16] is used in this paper. The total transmission power consumption of node i is the sum of all power consumed to transmit data to other nodes within its transmission range. The transmission power consumption is calculated as follow:

$$P_{ti} = \sum \left(a + \beta \cdot d_{ij}^{n} \right) \cdot r_{ij} \tag{6}$$

where, P_{ti} is the transmission power consumption of node i, α and β are constant coefficients, η is the path loss exponent, and d_{ij} is the distance between node i and node j. The total reception power consumption of node i is the sum of all power consumed to receive data from other nodes, as formulated below, where λ is a constant coefficient:

$$P_{ri=} \sum \lambda \cdot r_{ki}. \tag{7}$$

The energy depleted to execute that task can be calculated as the multiplication of the total number of cycles to execute that task and the average energy depleted per cycle. Therefore, the average power consumption required to encode a sequence is estimated as [12]:

$$P_{ei} = \frac{k_i \cdot CPI \cdot E_c \cdot F_r}{N_f} \tag{8}$$

where, κ_i is the total number of instructions to encode the video for node i, CPI is the average number of cycles per instruction of the CPU, E_c is the energy depleted per cycle, N_f is the number of frames and F_r denotes the frame rate of the video sequence. The value of κ_i is obtained using the following relation $\kappa_i = IC\{CID_i, QP_i\}$, where IC is the instruction count provided by *iprof* for the pair of CID and QP values used. Since we want each node to produce video with almost similar quality, all nodes have to use the same QP, thus, $QP_i = QP$, $\forall i \in N$.

The total energy dissipation at a sensor node consists of the encoding power consumption (P_e), the transmission power consumption (P_t) and the reception power consumption (P_r):

$$P_i = P_{ei} + P_{ti} + P_{ri} \tag{9}$$

In a VSN-based monitoring or surveillance applications, the system lifetime is usually denoted by the time on which the first node consumes all of its energy resource. This means, the objective is to minimize the maximum energy consumption among all nodes, i.e., minimize P_{net} where $P_i \leq P_{net}, \forall i \in N$. This optimization problem is then shown as follow.

Optimization minimizePower(CID)

minimize P_{net}

subject to:

$$P_i \leq P_{net}$$

$$P_i = P_{ei} + P_{ti} + P_{ri}$$

$$P_{ei} = K_i \cdot CPI \cdot E_{ec} \cdot F_r / N_f$$

$$K_i = IC\{CID_{i,} QP\}$$

$$\sum r_{ij} - \sum r_{ki} = R_i, \forall k \in N, k \neq i, \forall j \in N, j \neq i$$

$$R_i = R\{CID_i, QP\}$$

$$P_{ti} = \sum \left(a + \beta \cdot d_i^n\right) \cdot r_{ij}$$

$$P_{ri} = \sum \lambda \cdot r_{ki}, \forall k \in N, k \neq i$$

$$\sum R_i \leq B$$

In order to find the configuration settings per each node that minimizes the energy consumption, we need to evaluate all possible CID combinations in the VSN. Let v_i denotes the different CIDs that can be used by node i, then $V = \{v_1, v_2, ..., v_N\}$ denotes the vector of possible CID that can be selected by the nodes in a VSN. The combination of all CIDs that needs to be evaluated is then given by $C(V,N)$, where C denotes the combinatorial operation. The number of possible combinations increases with the number of node. For example, when the number of nodes is equal to three, the number of possible CID combinations that needs to be evaluated is equal to 343. However, when the number of nodes is increased to nine, the number of possible CID combination is equal to 7^9. We can reduce the search space for the optimization problem by focusing on the fact that all nodes share the same wireless bandwidth (2) such that the bitrate allocated per each node is equal to a portion of the total bandwidth. Therefore, the problem of assigning the CIDs to all nodes can be viewed as the problem of assigning fairness ratio to each node in the VSN.

Common approach

A common approach for setting encoding parameters of VSN nodes is to use the same configuration settings over all nodes. We call this approach *CommonConfig* algorithm. This approach has been used by [10] and [17] to analyze the VSN power consumption of Intra only configuration and Inter Main Profile with GOP size of 6 and frame-type sequence of I-P-B-P-B-P-I. The authors in [11] also have used *CommonConfig* algorithm for Intra only configuration in their analysis. In order to implement the *CommonConfig* algorithm while still being fair with the implementation reported in the literature, we try to assign the same CID to all nodes such that the bandwidth constraint is not violated.

It has to be noted that, the analysis performed in [10, 11, 17] assume that each VSN node uses the same video. Therefore, by implementing the algorithm *CommonConfig*, each node will have the same bitrate and encoding complexity. However, if the video source for each video is different, assigning the same CID to each node will not guarantee the same bitrate is allocated to each node. The amount of bitrate allocated to each node will then depend on the content complexity of the video captured by the node. To guarantee some fairness measure for the VSN nodes, one can allocate the same bitrate per each node. In this regard, the end-to-end fairness constraint, i.e., the maximum percentage of the total bitrate that can be sent to the sink by each node, is formulated as follow [18]:

$$R_i \leq \rho_i \cdot \sum\nolimits_{j=1}^{N} R_j \tag{10}$$

With this constraint, each node i can only generate a flow to the sink that is lower than a fraction of ρ_i of the sum of the bitrate of all nodes. According to (5) the sum of all bitrate has to be less than the bandwidth of the network (B). When all nodes use the same fairness constraints that is equal to $\rho_{fair} = \rho_i = 1/N$, each node will be allocated equal transmission rate. In this condition, the network is called to use the *MaximumFairness* scheme, as shown below.

Algorithm MaximumFairness(f_{ratio})

% N: number of node

for $i= 1: N$
    $CID_i \leftarrow getCID(\rho_i, 0)$
end

minimizePower(CID)

In the algorithm shown above, the procedure *getCID* is a procedure to assign a node with a specific CID, where $R\{CID_i, QP\}/B < \rho_i$, and R is the bitrate allocated for node i when using the corresponding CID. Note that, $f_{ratio} = \{\rho_1, \rho_2, ..\rho_N\}$, N is the number of nodes, and $\rho_i = 1/N$.

Proposed optimization-based minimum energy VSN

For a VSN that has a large number of nodes, an exhaustive search to find the best CID allocation is not feasible. In this paper, we try to solve the problem as an optimization framework based on the finite set of CIDs defined in Table 1. The CIDs represent encoder configuration labels and are related with the GOP size as explained in Section Video capturing and encoding settings. It has to be noted that, the value of bitrate (complexity) is monotonously decreasing (increasing) with the increase of the CID label. Consider an example of *cam1_office_act4* video. Assuming that QP equal to 28, for CID equal to one, the bitrate of the video is equal to 1161 kbps while the encoding complexity is 32470 million of instructions. On the other hand, when the CID is equal to four, i.e., GOP = $2^3 = 8$, the bitrate of the video is 195 kbps while the encoding complexity is 37411 million of instructions. In addition, when the CID is equal to seven, i.e., GOP size is 64, the bitrate of the encoded video is 78.85 kbps while the encoding complexity for that configuration is 38115 million of instructions. Thus, selecting smaller CID corresponds to using smaller

GOP size and lower encoding complexity but higher bitrate. Consider a simple VSN example consisting of two nodes where node B sends its data to node A, and then node A sends its own data and the relayed data to the sink. For simplicity, assume that both node A and B have the same video source, i.e., *cam1_office_act4* video, and the configuration setting available for both nodes are either CID equal to one or CID equal to seven. Table 5 shows the four possible configurations for node A and B along with the nodes' power consumption associated with the possible CID combinations. Here PE, PT, and PR denote the power consumption for encoding, transmission and reception respectively using a particular CID for a specific video. The table shows that if both nodes use the same CID, the power consumption of node A will be higher than that of node B. However, if the nodes are using different CIDs, we can exploit trade-off between encoding complexity and bitrate to minimize the node's maximum power consumption. The example shown in the Table is for a simple VSN with two nodes. However, the number of possible CID combinations increases exponentially with the increase of the number of nodes.

Furthermore, it should be noted that the value of CID is bounded to be integral. On the other hand, the value of r_{ij} and r_{ki} that determine the routing of data from and to node i in (6) and (7) are rational numbers. An optimization problem involving mixed linear and integer variables is NP-complete, where some of the solutions are intractable. However, there are algorithms that can be used to provide a near optimal solution for this kind of optimization problem. These algorithms mostly work by solving the relaxed linear programming and then adding some linear constraints that drive the solution towards being integer without excluding any integer feasible points. Branch and bound [19] is considered one such algorithm. Using branch and bound algorithm, the optimization procedure can be terminated early and as long as a solution that satisfies the stopping criteria is found. Therefore, a feasible, not necessarily optimal solution can be obtained. In this paper, the branch and bound approach is implemented by using the following steps: 1) solve the bounded optimization problem 2) call a recursive procedure to perform branch and bound until a solution is found or termination criteria are satisfied. The bounded optimization problem is shows as follow.

Optimization minimizePowerBounded$(CID^{u-bound}, CID^{l-bound})$

minimize P_{net}

subject to:

$$P_i \leq P_{net}$$
$$P_i = P_{ei} + P_{ti} + P_{ri}$$
$$P_{ei} = \kappa_i \cdot CPI \cdot E_{ec} \cdot F_r / N_f$$
$$\kappa_i = IC\{CID_i, QP\}$$
$$\sum r_{ij} - \sum r_{ki} = R_i, \forall k \in N, k \neq i, \forall j \in N, j \neq i$$
$$R_i = R\{CID_i, QP\}$$
$$P_{ti} = \sum (\alpha + \beta \cdot d_i^{\eta}) \cdot r_{ij}$$
$$P_{ri} = \sum \lambda \cdot r_{ki}, \forall k \in N, k \neq i$$
$$\sum R_i \leq B$$
$$CID_i \leq CID_i^{u-bound}$$
$$CID_i \geq CID_i^{l-bound}$$

The difference between this algorithm and *minimizePower* optimization described in Section VSN Power consumption modelling and formulation, is the fact that the CID

Table 5 Node's power consumption for a simple scenario

CID (A,B)	Node A's power consumption				Node B's power consumption			
	Encoding	Transmit.	Relay	Receive	Encoding	Transmit.	Relay	Receive
(1,1)	PE(1)	PT(1)	PT(1)	PR(1)	PE(1)	PT(1)	N/A	N/A
(7,7)	PE(7)	PT(7)	PT(7)	PR(7)	PE(7)	PT(7)	N/A	N/A
(7,1)	PE(7)	PT(7)	PT(1)	PR(1)	PE(1)	PT(1)	N/A	N/A
(1,7)	PE(1)	PT(1)	PT(7)	PR(7)	PE(7)	PT(7)	N/A	N/A

values are given as upper and lower bounds instead of a specific value. Note that, since the CID value represent the configuration label, whenever the optimization procedure needs to lookup the values of the complexity and bitrate, the CID value needs be rounded to the nearest integer. If the CID provided by the bounded optimization does not satisfy the integrality constraint, the *RecursiveBranchBound* procedure will be called to perform branch and bound approach to find the solution, as shown below.

Procedure RecursiveBranchBound *(Power, CID^{u_bound}, CID^{l_bound})*

% ε: integrality constraint

[*TPower, status, TCID*]←**minimizePowerBounded(** CID^{u_bound}, CID^{l_bound})
if *status≤0* or *TPower>Power*

    return [*TPower, status, TCID*]

end

% if TCID satisfy integrality constraint
if (*TCID* – **round**(TCID) <ε
    status=1
    if *TPower<Power*
       CID← round(*TCID*)
       Power←*TPower*
    end
    return [*TPower, status, CID*]
end

% solution is not feasible → solve the first branch
$CID^{u\_bound\_1}$=**floor**(*TCID*)

[*TPower, status, CID*] ←**RecursiveBranchBound** *(Power,* $CID^{u\_bound\_1}$ *,* CID^{l_bound})

% solution is not feasible → solve the second branch
$CID^{l\_bound\_1}$=**ceil**(*TCID*)

[*TPower, status, CID*] ←**RecursiveBranchBound** *(Power,* CID^{u_bound} *,* $CID^{l\_bound\_1}$)

If a solution that satisfies the integrality constraint cannot be found, the problem will be divided into two sub-problems by defining new upper and lower bounds followed by call to the recursive functions. Note that, the integrality constraint ε is the error between the CID and the rounded integral value of the CID. In order to illustrate the proposed approach, consider an example of a four node

VSN. Assume that the configuration options available for these nodes are $1 \le CID \le 4$ and the integrality constraint is equal to 0.2. Assume that the proposed algorithm proceed as shown in Table 6 (please see Figure 11 for the illustration of this example). The UB and LB shown in the table are the CID's upper and lower bounds for the corresponding search space respectively. Finally the best solution will be selected from the candidate solutions that satisfy the integrality constraint, i.e., $CID_i = \{3, 2, 2, 1\}$ or $CID_i = \{2, 1, 1, 1\}$.

Fairness-based CID allocation for the test Set

The scenes' content complexity affects the overall VSN's power consumption. Ideally, in order to find the best solution, the VSN nodes' optimal bitrate for each possible scene has to be calculated. However, this approach is not practical since the scene's activity captured by a VSN changed with time while the algorithm to find the optimal solution requires some significant computation. Thus, following our assumption mentioned in Section Video content classification, we will attempt to find the optimal fairness ratio allocation only for the training sets. The optimal fairness ratio allocation obtained from the training sets will be used as an initial guess to allocate the CID for the test videos. However, since the content of the video of the training set and the test set are not exactly the same, we need to perform some adjustment procedure while assigning the nodes' CID in the test sets. Hence, the algorithm *FairnessBased* CID allocation is shown below.

Algorithm FairnessBased(f_{ratio})

```
% fratio = {ρ₁, ρ₂,.., ρₙ}
% B: Bandwidth of the network

overflow = 0
for i=N:-1:1
    CIDᵢ ← getCID(ρᵢ, 0)
    ρᵢ' ← R{CIDᵢ, QP}/B
    if CIDᵢ is {}
        CIDᵢ = 7
        overflow = overflow + (R{CIDᵢ, QP} − ρᵢ*B)
    else
        if overflow>0
            CIDᵢ ← getCID(ρᵢ', 0)
            overflow = overflow − (ρᵢ*B − R{CIDᵢ, QP})
        end
    end
end

checkBandwidthConstraint(CID)
minimizePower(CID)
```

In the above algorithm, the *getCID* procedure returns the highest possible CID option that can be allocated to node i with fairness ratio equal to ρ_i. For example, if the possible CIDs that can be allocated to node i are either six or seven, the *getCID* procedure

Table 6 Example of the progression of the proposed MILP-based optimization for a four node VSN

	Bounds	Solution found
Step 1	UB = {4,4,4,4}	SOL = {3.5, 2.75, 2, 1.75}
	LB = {1,1,1,1}	
Recursive 1	UB = {4,4,4,4}	NA
	LB = {4,3,3,2}	
Recursive 2	UB = {3,2,2,1}	SOL = {2.75, 1.75, 1.75, 1}
	LB = {1,1,1,1}	
Recursive 2.1	UB = {3,2,2,1}	SOL = {3, 2, 2, 1}
	LB = {3,2,2,1}	
Recursive 2.2	UB = {2,1,1,1}	SOL = {2,1,1,1}
	LB = {1,1,1,1}	

will return CID equal to six. However, in some cases, the *getCID* procedure may not be able find a suitable CID with fairness ratio allocation ρ_j to be allocated to node *j*. In this regard, the node will need to be assigned the highest CID possible according to Table 1, i.e., it will use the configuration with the lowest bitrate. Then, a variable named *overflow* is updated with the difference between the allocated bitrate (obtained using a lookup table R{CID_j, QP}) with the supposed maximum bitrate for that node, i.e., ρ_j*B. Note that, the variable *overflow* is used to record the accumulative amount of bitrate that are borrowed from the other nodes. On the other hand, if an appropriate CID is available while the value of *overflow* variable is positive, another call to the procedure *getCID* with a lower fairness ratio is performed to get another CID. This is performed so that we can 'pay back' the outstanding bitrate 'debt'. The *overflow* variable is then updated accordingly. In the chance that the *overflow* variable is still positive after the CID allocation for all nodes have been performed, a procedure *checkBandwidthConstraint* is then called to adjust the CID allocation per each node. Starting from the node furthest from the sink, the procedure checks whether assigning a higher CID to that node can reduce the variable *overflow* to be less than or equal to zero. After that, the nodes' power consumption is calculated using the *minimizePower* procedure as discussed in Section VSN Power consumption modelling and formulation.

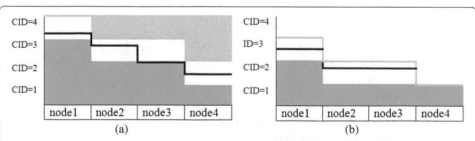

Figure 11 Example of how the proposed optimization based approach proceeds. This figure shows an example of CID allocation for a four node VSN. Part **(a)** of the figure shows the initial step where the solution obtained is shown as the dark bold line. Since the solution violates the integrality constraint, the search space is divided into two new spaces, colored with green and yellow. Then, recursive calls with new boundaries are executed. Following the assumption shown in Table 6, the new solution is shown as the dark bold line in **(b)**. Here two new search spaces are created. Note that, in this figure, the upper and lower bound for the yellow colored space is the same.

The VSN's power consumption can be reduced further by adjusting the CID allocated on some of the nodes. The following shows the adjustment procedure that is performed on two nodes, e.g., the last node and the first node.

Algorithm FairnessBased_withAdjustment(f_{ratio})

% fratio = $\{\rho_1, \rho_2,.., \rho_N\}$
% N: number of node

$\{Power, CID\}$ ←**FairnessBased**(f_{ratio})
$TCID$←CID

% adjust the last node
for i= CID_N+ 1:1:7
    $TPower$←**minimizePower**($TCID$)
    if $TPower$<$Power$
        $Power$←$TPower$
        CID←$TCID$
    end
    $TCID_N$ = i
end

% adjust the first node
for i= CID_1–1: –1:1
    $TPower$←**minimizePower**($TCID$)
    if $TPower$<$Power$
        $Power$←$TPower$
        CID←$TCID$
    end
    $TCID_1$ = i
end

In this algorithm, the *perturb* procedure checks whether altering the CID allocation of a specific node can reduce the VSN's power consumption. For example, if node i is assigned to use CID equal to four, the *perturb* procedure will check whether assigning CID equal to three or five to node i reduces the VSN's power consumption further.

Experiments and results

This section elaborates on our experiment settings for evaluating the performance of our proposed approach. To ensure the efficiency of our proposed scheme, our experiment results are compared with the CommonConfig and MaximumFairness approaches.

Experiments settings

Figure 12 shows the network topology analyzed in this paper. In this figure, the dark node is the sink node while the blank nodes are the video node. Each node is given an identification number according to its distance to the sink. Therefore, the distance between node1 to the sink is smaller than the distance between node2 to the sink. It is assumed that each video node located at a specific location in the topology illustrated in

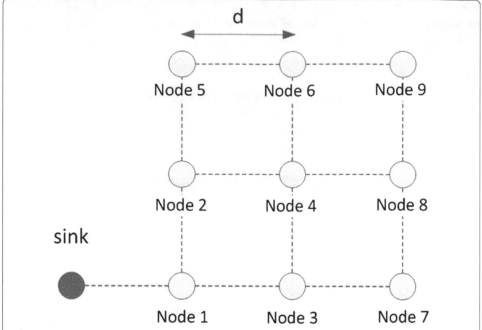

Figure 12 Network topology used. The dark node is the sink node while the blank nodes are the video node. Each node is given an identification number according to its distance to the sink. Therefore, node1 is closer to the sink than node2, and so on. Each video node located at a specific location in the topology illustrated in this is attached to the camera located at the same location shown in Figure 1.

Figure 12 is attached to the camera located at the same location shown in Figure 1. Therefore, node1 will be using the video captured by camera1; node2 will be using the video captured by camera4, and so forth. The H.264/AVC software, JM version 18.2 is used to generate the CID lookup table of encoding complexity and bitrate of all videos. The QP value used in this paper ranges from 28 until 36.

Two separate sets of experiments were performed. The first set of experiment is conducted on the training set. The objective is to compare the results obtained by the proposed optimization technique with the ones obtained using the *CommonConfig* and *MaximumFairness* approaches. From this experiment, we will obtain the fairness ratios of the training set that minimize the node's maximum energy consumption. We will compare the energy consumption obtained using that approach with the one obtained using the *CommonConfig* and *MaximumFairness* approaches. To this end the parameters shown in Table 7 are used.

Performance evaluation of the proposed algorithms for the training scenes

In order to find the minimum power consumption with the highest possible video quality, we need to find the minimum QP for each content complexity class. To do this, starting from the lowest QP, a procedure to check the possibility to allocate CIDs to all the nodes is performed using the *MaximumFairness* approach. Since each scene has different SI (TI) complexity class, the minimum QP value for each scene may also be different. For example, for scene *party_act2*, the minimum QP that can be used to allocate the CID using the maximum fairness approach is equal to 36. However, the

Table 7 Parameters used

Parameters	Description	Value
α	Energy cost for transmitting 1 bit	0.5 J/Mb
β	Transmit amplifier coefficient	$1.3 \cdot 10\text{-}8$ J/Mb/m^4
λ	Energy cost for receiving 1 bit	0.5 J/Mb
η	Path loss exponent	4
CPI	XScale average cycle per instruction [20]	1.78
E_c	Energy depleted per cycle for imote2 [10]	1.215 nJ
B	Network Bandwidth	2 Mbps
d	Distance between node	5m
ε	Integrality constraints for the optimization based algorithm	0.2

minimum QP for scene *office_act2* is 28. Once the minimum QP for a scene is obtained, we execute the optimization-based approach on the corresponding training scene. It should be noted that for the optimization-based approach, we repeat the experiment eight times to find the best solution. For the purpose of the analysis, we compare the performance of the algorithm against the *CommonConfig* and *MaximumFairness* approaches mentioned in Section Common approach. Figure 13 shows the bitrate allocated using the compared techniques. Figure 13(a) shows the bitrate allocation for the training scenes obtained using the *CommonConfig* algorithm. The figure shows that the difference between the highest bitrate and the lowest bitrate allocated in each scene is as follow: 129.85 kbps for the high SI training scene (*party_act2*), 115.87 kbps for the medium SI training scene (*office_act1*)

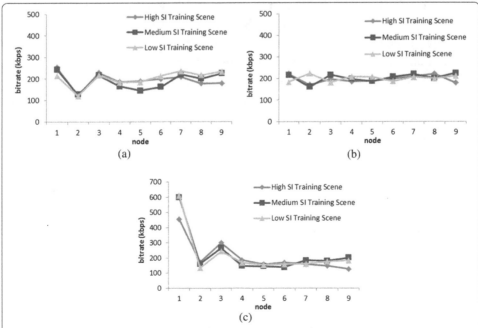

Figure 13 Bitrate allocated per each node in all training scenes. Part **(a)** of the figure shows the bitrate allocated by the *CommonConfig* approach. Part **(b)** of the figure shows the bitrate allocated by the *MaximumFairness* approach. The figure shows that the bitrate allocated per each node is roughly the same. On the other hand, **(c)** shows the bitrate allocated by the proposed optimization based.

and 115.08 kbps for the low SI training scene (*office_act2*), respectively. The algorithm *CommonConfig* does not regulate the bitrate assigned per each node since the algorithm only concern about using the same configuration for each node. Thus, the bitrate assigned to each node does not follow any trend. However, the *MaximumFairness* approach allocates roughly the same bitrate per each VSN node for any training scene used as shown in Figure 13(b). Given that the content captured by each camera in each training scene is not the same, there are some variations in the bitrate assigned to each node. However, the difference between the highest bitrate and the lowest bitrate allocated in each scene is not significant, i.e., 50.37 kbps for the high SI training scene (*party_act2*), 63.85 kbps for the medium SI training scene (*office_act1*) and 41.64 kbps for the low SI training scene (*office_act2*), respectively. On the other hand, the proposed optimization-based approach takes into account the node's total power consumption in allocating the bitrate for each node. As Figure 13(c) shows, the proposed technique allocates different bitrate to each node such that the nodes closer to the sink have generally higher bitrate than the nodes that are farther from the sink. The different between the maximum and minimum bitrate allocated in each scenes has become more significant, equaling to 327.73 kbps for the high SI scene, 471.56 kbps for the medium SI scene and 476.59 kbps for the low SI training scene, respectively. It can also be seen in this figure that node2 is allocated with smaller bitrate than the other nodes. The reason behind this behavior is the fact that node2 corresponds to camera4 (see Figure 1), which according to Table 2 and Table 3 has lower content complexity level than the other cameras.

It should be noted that assigning a higher bitrate to a node is equal to using a lower CID that exhibit lower encoding complexity. Therefore, the nodes that are assigned to have higher bitrate will have lower encoding power consumption. This will balance out the increase in the transmission power consumption with having higher bitrate. Indeed, the plot shown in Figure 14 clarifies the trend in case of the high SI scene. Note that the communication power consumption shown in this figure is the sum of transmission and reception power consumption. Figure 14(a) shows that by using the algorithm *CommonConfig*, each node consume almost the same encoding power consumption. In the *MaximumFairness* approach (see Figure 14(b)), each node was assigned roughly the same bitrate. However, nodes that are closer to the sink consume more energy because they need to relay the data from the other nodes. On the other hand, Figure 14(c) shows that the proposed optimization-based approach manages to balance the total energy consumption of each node in the VSN. Even though the nodes closer to the sink still consume more energy for communication, these nodes have lower encoding power consumption than those that are farther from the sink. This trend is also observed in the medium SI and low SI training scenes. Table 8 shows the P_{net} (nodes' maximum power consumption), P_{avg} (average maximum power consumption) and $STD(P_i)$ (standard deviation of nodes' power consumption) of the three algorithms. It is interesting to see that the *CommonConfig* algorithm manages to perform better than the *MaximumFairness* algorithm. This shows that assigning the same bitrate to each node does not help in reducing the VSN's power consumption. On the other hand, Table 8 also shows that the optimization-based approach manage to have lower P_{net} and P_{avg} as compared to the other algorithms. The algorithm is also better in regard of balancing out the power consumption among all nodes as measured in terms of standard deviation of nodes' power consumption. This shows that by regulating the bitrate and nodes' encoder configuration such that the nodes' power consumption is

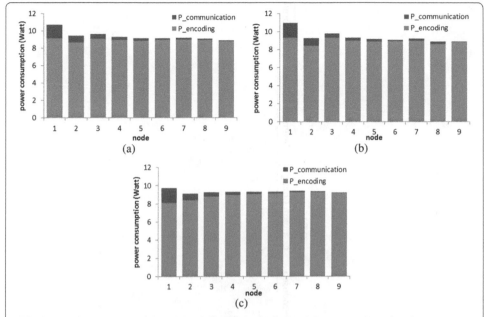

Figure 14 Node's power consumption profile for the high SI training scene. Note that the communication power consumption shown in this figure consists of transmission and reception power consumption. Part **(a)** of the figure shows the node's power consumption profile using the *CommonConfig* algorithm. Using this technique, the encoding power consumption per each node are almost the same. Part **(b)** of the figure shows the node's power consumption profile obtained using the *MaximumFairness* approach. Using this algorithm, the bitrate allocated per each node are roughly the same. However, nodes closer to the sink spend more energy for communication due to relaying other nodes' data. It can be seen that node1 consume the highest energy as compare to the other nodes. On the other hand, **(c)** shows node's power consumption profile obtained by the optimization-based technique that is not only more balanced but also has a smaller P_{net} than the one obtained by the *CommonConfig* and *MaximumFairness* approaches.

balanced, we can obtain lower VSN's power consumption than the other algorithms. Furthermore, Table 9 shows the fairness ratio allocation of the training scenes.

Performance of the fairness based algorithms for the test scenes

Using the fairness ratio obtained from the training scenes, the fairness based algorithm explained in Section Fairness-based CID allocation for the Test Set will be used to allocate the VSN nodes' CID for all test scenes. Our initial experiments show that the fairness-based with adjustment algorithm managed to obtain lower P_{net}, P_{avg} and STD (P_i) than the propsoed fairness-based allocation algorithm. Therefore, from this point forward, we will only compare the proposed fairness-based with adjustment with the other techniques mention in Section Common approach. In this regard, Table 10 shows the P_{net}, P_{avg} and STD(P_i) of the three algorithms for all test scenes. It can be seen from the table that the proposed fairness with adjustment algorithm proves to perform better than the other techniques. Correspondingly, Figure 15 compares the value of the P_{net}, P_{avg} and STD(P_i) obtained by the three algorithms in all test cases. Furthermore, Table 11 shows the percentage of P_{net}, P_{avg} and STD(P_i) improvement obtained by the proposed techniques against the common approach for all test cases used. It can be seen here that the amount of power consumption reduction obtained by the proposed fairness-based with adjustment technique is in the range of 5.06% to 10.48%, averaging into 8.18% improvement against the *MaximumFairness* algorithm. On the other hand,

Table 8 P_{net}, P_{avg} and STD(P_i) of the training scenes

Training sequence	P_{net}			P_{avg}			STD(P_i)		
	Common Config	Maximum Fairness	Proposed	Common Config	Maximum Fairness	Proposed	Common Config	Maximum Fairness	Proposed
party1_act2	10.73	10.95	9.73	9.40	9.39	9.31	0.54	0.64	0.18
office_act1	10.25	10.45	9.53	9.03	9.03	9.38	0.49	0.57	0.09
office_act2	9.97	10.06	9.35	8.80	8.83	9.19	0.47	0.48	0.09

Table 9 Fairness ratio allocation obtained from each training scenes

Training sequence	node1	node2	node3	node4	node5	node6	node7	node8	node9
party1_act2	0.243	0.092	0.160	0.100	0.085	0.090	0.084	0.079	0.068
office_act1	0.296	0.079	0.131	0.082	0.071	0.063	0.090	0.089	0.099
office_act2	0.307	0.068	0.122	0.085	0.078	0.080	0.081	0.089	0.092

the percentage of P_{net} reduction against *CommonConfig* algorithm is in the range 4.24% to 9.67%, averaging into 6.97% improvement. Thus, the average improvement of the proposed algorithm against the common approach is around 7.58%. This result is encouraging since it shows that by using the fairness ratio obtained from the videos with higher activity level; we are still able to reduce the maximum power consumption by around 7.58% than the *CommonConfig* and *MaximumFairness* approaches. Since VSN's energy is usually limited, reducing the energy consumption by 7.58% means that we are increasing the lifetime of the sensor network by 7.58%. In addition to that, except for test scene VS1 and VS4 the proposed algorithm also manage to slightly reduces the average power consumption. On the other hand, the standard deviation of nodes' power consumption is also reduced by more than 40% on average.

Future work

In order to improve the result obtained in this paper, there are some considerations that can be included into our framework. The first and notable extension is to directly incorporate the effect of spatial and temporal information of the videos into the

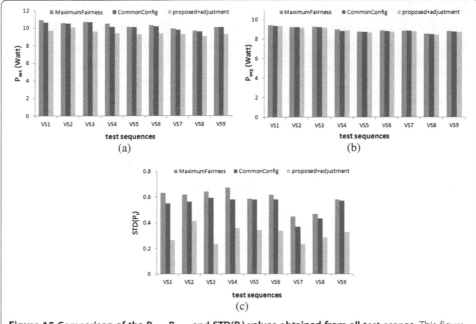

Figure 15 Comparison of the P_{net}, P_{avg}, and STD(P_i) values obtained from all test scenes. This figure compares the P_{net}, P_{avg}, and STD(P_i) values obtained by the **(a)** *CommonConfig* **(b)** *MaximumFairness* **(c)** proposed approaches It can be seen that the proposed approaches produce smaller P_{net}, P_{avg}, and STD(P_i) in all test cases.

Table 10 Performance of the different techniques in all test cases

Test scenes	CommonConfig			MaximumFairness			Proposed		
	P_{net}	P_{avg}	$STD(P_i)$	P_{net}	P_{avg}	$STD(P_i)$	P_{net}	P_{avg}	$STD(P_i)$
VS1	10.61	9.32	0.55	10.87	9.41	0.63	9.73	9.35	0.26
VS2	10.47	9.18	0.56	10.56	9.19	0.62	10.03	9.14	0.41
VS3	10.63	9.22	0.59	10.71	9.24	0.64	9.60	9.16	0.24
VS4	10.11	8.78	0.58	10.48	8.99	0.67	9.40	8.89	0.36
VS5	10.08	8.73	0.58	10.08	8.77	0.59	9.28	8.66	0.34
VS6	10.14	8.79	0.58	10.29	8.87	0.62	9.38	8.76	0.34
VS7	9.73	8.84	0.37	9.91	8.83	0.45	9.29	8.78	0.23
VS8	9.55	8.51	0.43	9.64	8.52	0.47	9.04	8.43	0.29
VS9	10.06	8.76	0.57	10.07	8.80	0.58	9.24	8.69	0.33

optimization framework. In this paper, the effect of spatial and temporal information is implemented indirectly through the process of classifying the videos into different scenes' classes. We are currently working on to develop a model for encoding complexity and bitrate that incorporate the spatial and temporal information. By using a model, we can remove the use of tabular information of configuration ID that is used in this paper. Another consideration that could be addressed is the power consumption minimization during or at the point of the transmission. For example, one can implement an importance based scheduling approach such that only select nodes are allowed to send their data to the sink. Some other practical considerations that could be included from this study is to consider the effect of camera orientation into the VSN power consumption and whether the nodes are implemented for indoor or outdoor environment. We are also considering the possibility to use the new encoding standard HEVC for our future work. However, it has to be noted that HEVC encoder's complexity is higher than that that of H.264/AVC encoder. HEVC utilizes more advanced and complex features compared to H.264/AVC. In order to implement our approach to the HEVC-based VSNs, we need to first investigate the trade-off provided by different encoding parameters of HEVC and generate a CID table customized for HEVC, and then tune our scheme accordingly.

Table 11 Percentage of improvement of the proposed algorithm against the other techniques

Test scenes	Improvement against CommonConfig (%)			Improvement against MaximumFairness (%)		
	P_{net}	P_{avg}	$STD(P_i)$	P_{net}	P_{avg}	$STD(P_i)$
VS1	8.33	−0.29	51.92	10.48	0.72	58.20
VS2	4.24	0.41	26.68	5.06	0.48	33.54
VS3	9.67	0.63	60.32	10.30	0.88	63.30
VS4	7.01	−1.29	38.01	10.23	1.04	46.57
VS5	7.88	0.83	40.86	7.97	1.29	41.32
VS6	7.50	0.41	41.89	8.83	1.29	45.48
VS7	4.60	0.63	36.85	6.28	0.53	47.90
VS8	5.40	0.96	33.65	6.21	1.05	38.81
VS9	8.12	0.73	42.56	8.24	1.20	43.33

Conclusions

This paper analyzed the problem of minimizing the VSN's power consumption by exploiting the video encoder's performance trade-off while also considering the different content and scene settings on which a VSN can be implemented. For the purpose of the analysis, a large number of real-life captured videos of simulated VSN scenes settings with different activity levels are used in this paper. The scenes are classified according to its content complexity on which the higher activity level scenes are used as the training set. The proposed optimization technique to minimize the node's maximum power consumption is then used on the training sets. We have shown that the proposed optimization procedure performs better than the *CommonConfig* and *MaximumFairness* approaches such that VSN's power consumption per each node was balanced while the nodes' maximum power consumption is minimized. We have also shown in this paper that the fairness ratio allocated per each node affects the distribution of power consumption in a VSN. In particular, by assuming that the fairness ratio of nodes closer to the sink are higher than the nodes that are farther from the sink, the VSN's power consumption is reduced.

The fairness ratio obtained by the proposed optimization-based approach is then used in the proposed fairness-based encoder complexity and bitrate allocation algorithm for the test scenes. The results show that the amount of power consumption reduction obtained by the proposed techniques varies according to the test sequences used. In general, the improvement obtained by the fairness based with adjustment technique is 8.18% on average against the *MaximumFairness* algorithm and 6.97% on average against *CommonConfig* algorithm. In addition to that, the proposed algorithm also shows better performance in terms of nodes' average power consumption and standard deviation of nodes' power consumption.

Abbreviations
WSN: Wireless sensor network; VSN: Video sensor network; CID: Configuration ID; PSNR: Peak signal to noise ratio; FPS: Frames per second; GOP: Group of pictures; SR: Search range (in motion estimation); QP: Quantization parameter; IC: Instruction counts; SI: Spatial information unit; TI: Temporal information unit; CPI: Cycle per instruction.

Competing interests
The authors declare that they have no competing interests.

Authors' contributions
This work is a joint effort between the University of British Columbia and Qatar University. All authors have contributed to this document and given the final approval. All authors read and approved the final manuscript.

Acknowledgment
This work was supported by the NPRP grant # NPRP 4-463-2-172 from the Qatar National Research Fund (a member of the Qatar Foundation). The statements made herein are solely the responsibility of the authors.

Author details
[1]Electrical and Computer Engineering Department, University of British Columbia, 2332 Main Mall, Vancouver, BC V6T 1Z4, Canada. [2]TELUS Communications Inc, 555 Robson St, Vancouver, British Columbia V6B 3K9, Canada. [3]Computer Science and Engineering Department, Qatar University, Doha, Qatar.

References
1. Akyildiz F, Melodia T, Chowdhury KR (2007) A survey on wireless multimedia sensor networks," Computer Networks. The International Journal of Computer and Telecommunications Networkin 51(4):921–960
2. Ren X, Yang Z (2010) "Research on the key issue in video sensor network", presented at the Computer Science and Information Technology (ICCSIT), 2010 3rd IEEE International Conference on. Chengdu 7:423–426
3. Seema A, Reisslein M (2011) Towards efficient wireless video sensor networks: a survey of existing node architectures and proposal for a flexi-WVSNP design. Communications Surveys & Tutorials, IEEE 3:462–486

4. Chen J, Safar Z, Sorensen JA (2007) Multimodal Wireless Networks: Communication and Surveillance on the Same Infrastructure. Information Forensics and Security, IEEE Transactions on 2(3):468–484

5. R"aty TD (2010) Survey on Contemporary Remote Surveillance Systems for Public Safety," Systems, Man, and Cybernetics, Part C. Applications and Reviews, IEEE Transactions on 40(5):493–515

6. Wiegand T, Sullivan GJ, Bjontegaard G, Luthra A (2003) Overview of the H.264/AVC video coding standard. IEEE Transactions on Circuits and Systems for Video Technology 13(7):560–576

7. Richardson E (2010) The H.264 Advanced Video Compression Standard, Second Editionth edn. John Wiley & Sons, Ltd

8. H. K. Zrida, A. C. Ammari, M. Abid, and A. Jemai, Complexity/Performance Analysis of a H.264/AVC Video Encoder, in Recent Advances on Video Coding, InTech, Rijeka, Croatia, 2011.

9. Ostermann J, Bormans J, List P, Marpe D, Narroschke M, Pereira F et al (2004) Video coding with H.264/AVC: tools, performance, and complexity. IEEE Circuits and System Magazine 4(1):7–28

10. J. J. Ahmad, H. A. Khan, and S. A. Khayam, "Energy efficient video compression for wireless sensor networks," Information Sciences and Systems, 2009. CISS 2009. 43rd Annual Conference on, Baltimore, MD, 2009, pp. 629 – 634.

11. Imran N, Seet BC, Alvis C, Fong M (2012) A comparative analysis of video codecs for multihop wireless video sensor networks. Multimedia Systems 18(5):373–389

12. B. A. B. Sarif, M. T. Pourazad, P. Nasiopoulos, and V. C. M. Leung, "Encoding and communication energy consumption trade-off in H.264/AVC based video sensor network," World of Wireless, Mobile and Multimedia Networks (WoWMoM), 2013 IEEE 14th International Symposium and Workshops on a , pp.1,6, Madrid, 4-7 June 2013.

13. B. A. B. Sarif, M. T. Pourazad, P. Nasiopoulos, and V. C. M. Leung, "Analysis of Energy Consumption Fairness in Video Sensor Networks." Poster presented at 2013 Qatar Foundation Annual Research Forum Proceedings, ICTSP 02. Qatar, Nov. 2013.

14. P. M. Kuhn, "A Complexity Analysis Tool: iprof (version 0.41)," ISO/IEC JTC1/SC29/WG11/M3551, Dublin, Ireland, July 1998.

15. ITU-T, "Subjective video quality assessment methods for multimedia applications," P.910, April 2008.

16. T. S. Rappaport, Wireless communications: principles and practice, 2nd ed. Prentice Hall, 2001.

17. S. Ullah, J. J. Ahmad, J. Khalid, and S. A. Khayam, "Energy and distortion analysis of video compression schemes for Wireless Video Sensor Networks," Military Communication Conference, MILCOM 2011, Baltimore, MD, Nov. 2011, pp. 822 – 827.

18. B. Krishnamachari and F. Ordonez, "Analysis of Energy-Efficient, Fair Routing in Wireless Sensor Networks through Non-linear Optimization," in IEEE Vehicular Technology Conference, 2003 IEEE 58th, vol.5, Orlando, Florida, Oct. 2003, pp. 2844 – 2848.

19. J. Clausen, "Branch and Bound Algorithms - Principles and Examples," University of Copenhagen, Mar. 1999.

20. D. Chinnery and K. Keutzer, Closing the Power Gap between ASIC & Custom: Tools and Techniques for Low Power Design, 1st edition. Springer, 2007.

13

Performance analysis of E-shaped dual band antenna for wireless hand-held devices

Balamurugan Rajagopal[1*] and Lalithambika Rajasekaran[2*]

* Correspondence:
megalaimurugan@yahoo.com;
srlalithambika@gmail.com
[1]Assistant Director (Administration),
All India Council for Technical
Education, New Delhi, India
[2]Post Graduate Engineer, Anna
University (Regional Centre
Coimbatore), Tamil Nadu, India

Abstract

Due to evolution in wireless applications, the high performance dual band handsets were blooming in the market. In this paper, a compact dual band E shaped planar inverted F antenna is presented, which is suitable for GSM application in handheld devices. Here, antenna is described for GSM (900 MHz and 1800 MHz), which covers (831 MHz – 973 MHz and 1700 MHz – 1918 MHz) 10 dB bandwidth. The designs and simulations are performed using Finite Difference Time Domain (FDTD) technique based General Electro Magnetic Simulator – Version 7.9 (GEMS-7.9). The performance analysis of E-shaped antenna also includes real world interaction between antenna element and Spherical human head model composed of three layers, skin, skull and brain. The simulated results including, S-Parameter, radiation pattern, current distributions and Specific absorption rate, thermal distributions have validated the proposed E shaped antenna design as useful for compact mobile phone devices with comparatively low average Specific Absorption Rate in market.

Keywords: Dual band antenna; GSM (Global System for Mobile communication); PIFA (Planar Inverted F-antenna); S - Parameter; Specific Absorption Rate (SAR); Finite Difference Time Domain (FDTD); General Electro Magnetic Simulator (GEMS)

Introduction

Over last decade, the evolution of wireless communication devices has increased rapidly to fulfill the requirement of high performance mobile portable devices which includes smart phones, Tablets, Notebooks etc. The handset antenna which, plays a transceiver role in mobile phone handset, should be optimized for better performance. In addition to the electrical requirements, the design of a handset antenna has to take into account the resulting exposure of the user. However, there has also been increase in concern regarding ill effects of Radio Frequency (RF) emitted by mobile phone antennas. These adverse health effects can be assessed by measuring power coupled to human tissue and thermal change, by using dosimetry called Specific Absorption Rate. The international commission on non-ionizing radiation protection and IEEE provides radiation level limit for the consumer products in free space.

Now a days variety of multiband internal antennas are reported, which are highly preferred for slim mobile phone due to their compactness [2,7]. The following literature survey shows the implication of dual band antenna in mobile phone communications. Dual band antenna (MIMO) can be used for LTE band (0.746 – 0.787 GHz) and the M-WiMAX (2.5 – 2.69 GHz). It consists of two identical elements, each of which is 15×13.25 mm^2. The minimum separation between two elements is 0.5 mm [14]. Novel coplanar waveguide fed planar monopole antenna with dual-band operation for Wi-Fi and 4G LTE. It's operating bands consists of 2.3 – 3.0 GHZ, 4.7 to 5.9 GHz are achieved by carefully optimizing the position and size of a smiling slot. Antenna is characterized in terms of return loss, radiation pattern, and measurement in anaerobic champers [16].

A connected E-shaped and U-shaped dual band patch antenna for operating frequencies 2.46 GHz and 4.9 GHz is designed and the bandwidth variation is analyzed by changing the height of substrate, bridge width etc. for different wireless LAN applications. The simulation studies are performed using GEMS simulation software [21]. A compact planar inverted E-shaped dual band antenna is designed over PCB board of $10 \times 5 \times 4$ mm^3 and good performance characteristics observed at 2.4 GHz and 5.5 GHz makes this antenna suitable for mobile device applications [22].

In many commercial wireless applications, PIFA and PMA are extensively used because it is simple, compact with good radiation pattern with sufficient Bandwidth. Normally, the electrical characteristics of handset antenna mainly depend on the ground plane on which the antenna is fabricated and also on the phone casing. The bandwidth of the antenna element increases, if the casing also resonates at operating frequency. Bandwidth and radiation characteristics make the 2G dual band antenna suitable to be used for Wi-Fi and 4G LTE applications in the 2.4 GHz to 2.7 GHz band and also 5.1 GHz to 5.875 GHz band [13]. Currently, GSM (Global System for Mobile Communication) is a standard protocol for digital mobile communication used for phone calls and transmission of text messages, which is addressed in this paper [3].

In this paper, E shaped PIFA with dual band 900/1800 MHz has been introduced [2]. The design considerations and simulated results for the Proposed E shaped antenna such as, return loss, radiation pattern and current distributions were also analyzed. Further, the performance analysis of E shaped antenna is described by considering the real world environment in which, mobile phone is expected to operate. The near field environment are created with mobile phone model which includes antenna element, battery, exterior plastic shell and three layered human head model. Simulation and performance analysis of proposed E shaped antenna are performed using FDTD based GEMS simulator [11].

Section Numerical modelling includes the modeling technique and the modeling of antenna and near field interactive devices. Section Performance analysis of antenna in free space involves parametric analysis of E shaped antenna and current distributions in free space. Section Influence of near field on antenna performance discusses the influence of near field environment when antenna is in close proximity to a human head model. Finally, section Conclusion provides conclusion.

Numerical modelling

Maxwell's equations can be solved in the time whereas for frequency domain many EM simulation techniques available using FDTD [17,18]. If the problem size grows, FDTD approach provides excellent scaling and the Broadband output can be obtaining using time domain approach. FDTD leads other computational methods say Finite Element method, Method of Moments etc. when the number of size of computational space increases. For studying, biological effects of Electromagnetic radiation from Wireless devices FDTD is better, which is the technique employed in our work. Further, FDTD also provides accurate results of the filed penetration into biological tissues.

Numerical formulation using FD-TD technique

In this work, finite difference time domain technique is used throughout the work, which can be formulated using Maxwell's curl equations,

$$\nabla \times E(r, t) = -\partial B(r, t)/\partial t \tag{1}$$

$$\nabla \times H(r, t) = J(r, t) + \partial D(r, t)/\partial t \tag{2}$$

Where, the equation involves electric field strength (E) and electric flux density (D), magnetic field strength (H) and magnetic flux density (B), electric current density (J) and electric charge density (ρe). Current density produces magnetic field around it. From the curl equation, we observed that the time derivative of the E-field depends on the change of the H-field across space. Hence, the value of the E-field can be computed if we know its previous value and the space-derivative of the H-field, which in turn is time-stepped and if initial field value, initial conditions and boundary conditions are known [4]. The FDTD technique divides the computational space into a Cartesian co-ordinate's grid of voxels and then allocates the components of the electric and magnetic fields as every E field is surrounded by H field and vice versa. This scheme is known as Yee lattice. If, the current changes over time, alternating magnetic field causes alternating electric field, which in turn causes another magnetic field, results in the creation of propagating electromagnetic wave of higher frequency.

There are certain commercially available EM simulators (say SEMCADx, GEMS etc.) which employ FDTD technique for computation. The computational performance of SEMCADx is as follows (Min grid size (mm) is 300, Computational domain is 14.2 M cells; Simulation time is <15 min, Simulation Speed is 300 M cells/s [19,20].

A FDTD based electromagnetic simulator (GEMS version −7.9) is used throughout the work. The FDTD modeling including head and hand model consists of 739675 cells. The convergence of the simulated solutions has been checked for every 100 time steps and the solutions are set to be converged for S- parameter calculations.

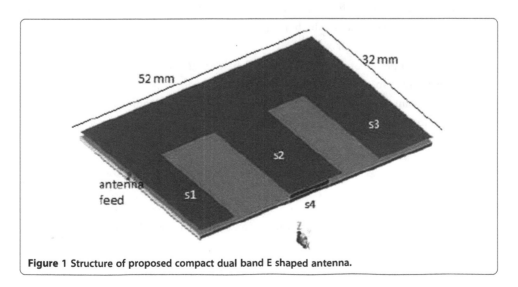

Figure 1 Structure of proposed compact dual band E shaped antenna.

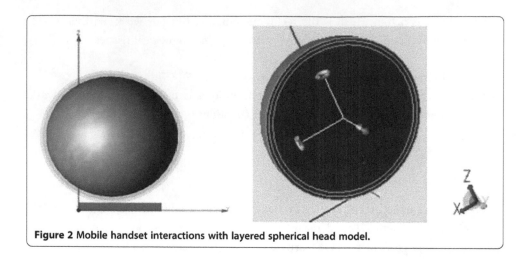

Figure 2 Mobile handset interactions with layered spherical head model.

E - shaped antenna design

The configuration of proposed E shaped antenna is shown in Figure 1. In general, traditional PIFA [1,4] is composed of metal strip, feeding line and shorting structure. The Antenna element has rectangular ground plane (52 mm × 32 mm). The radiating element composed of feed line (52 mm × 12 mm), patch S_1 (20 mm × 8 mm), patch S_2 (12 mm × 20 mm), patch S_3 (12mm × 20 mm). There is free space (height = 1.8 mm) between the antenna top plate and the substrate.

The substrate material used is of thickness t = 2 mm. The dimension of the shorting plate (S4) is 10 mm × 1.8 mm. The distance between the feeding and the shorting plate is 27 mm [6]. The radiating E element is modeled as perfect electric conductor. The excitation port is modeled as lumped port with internal resistance being 50 Ω. Maximum working frequency of 3 GHz is allowed for performance analysis of radiating antenna.

Handheld device model and user head model

In order to meet the expected handset performance in this work, we not only contend with designing antennas but also in need mitigating the RF interaction with the near field environment, which influences the E-shaped antenna performance. Figure 2 shows the hand held device model which is in close proximity to spherical human head model.

The device composed of E shaped antenna, battery (20 mm × 25 m × 2.5 mm) and plastic cover (80 mm × 45 mm × 5 mm) which, encloses all the components. The dielectric constant used for the plastic cover is 4.4. The antenna and battery were modeled as metal materials [10]. The spherical head model consisting of three layers

Table 1 Properties of human tissues

Tissue	Brain diameter (mm)		Skull thickness (mm)		Skin thickness (mm)	
Human adult	160.1		8.9		7.2	
Tissue density (Kg/m3)	1030		1085		1010	
Operating frequency	0.9 GHz	1.8 GHz	0.9 GHz	1.8 GHz	0.9 GHz	1.8 GHz
Permittivity	55.0	53.0	8.0	8.0	34.5	32.5
conductivity	1.23	1.7	0.11	0.16	0.6	0.52

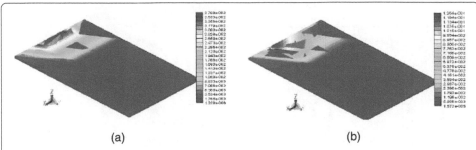

Figure 3 (a) & (b): current distribution in ground plane for 0.9 GHz, 1.8 GHz respectively. Surface current in the ground plane is higher near feeding point.

skin, skull and brain (as shown in Table 1) [8] is selected for the simulation study. The conductivity, permittivity and density of tissues which is a function of frequency (as shown in Table: 1) are an important factor in power coupled to human tissues [12]. The phone model is placed at three different distances from the side of the head and simulated results were compared for analysis.

Performance analysis of antenna in free space

The design objective is a dual band portable handheld device antenna suitable for 900/1800 MHz GSM application. We optimize the design through simulation using General Electro – Magnetic Simulator (GEMS), a commercial software package based on Finite Difference Time Domain(FDTD) technique [10].

Current distributions

While using the handset, the pulsed current flows from the battery to radiating element. This excitation gives rise to magnetic field around the handset.

Figure 3 shows the current distributions in ground plane at 900 MHz and 1800 MHz respectively. The excitation of feeding port at right end of the E - shaped Antenna shows high magnitude surface current at the proximity of feeding point and becomes almost zero near the open end. This coupled current also affects the antenna performance by inducing heat around the handset device.

Figure 4 shows the current distributions in radiating E-shaped radiating element at 900 MHz and 1800 MHz respectively. The excitation of feeding port induces high magnitude surface current in proximity of feed but weak or null current in the area far from the feed [5]. Further, the weak surface current on the ground plane ensures the

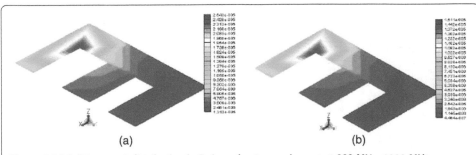

Figure 4 (a) & (b): current distribution in E shaped antenna element at 900 MHz, 1800 MHz respectively. Lower surface currents other than feeding point ultimately reduces power coupled.

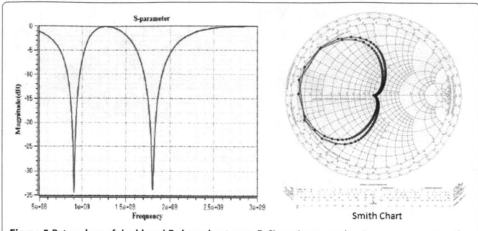

Figure 5 Return loss of dual band E shaped antenna. E- Shaped antenna showing two resonant modes at 0.9 GHz and 1.8 GHz operating frequency.

better antenna performance by reducing the specific absorption rate (SAR), where power coupled to human tissues when antenna is in proximity to users head. Since, the mobile handset is usually held close to the human body during the operation, it is necessary to analyze the current distribution as a function of distance (in section Influence of near field on antenna performance).

S- parameter

The simulated S parameter and smith chart representation for the dual band E shaped antenna is shown in Figure 5. Simulations were carried out using GEMS, a FDTD based simulator [7]. The results indicate the return loss better than 25 dB which can be seen above. It is observed that the 10 dB bandwidth covers 831 MHz – 973 MHz and 1700 MHz – 1918 MHz. This satisfies the required bandwidth for GSM 850/900/1800 MHz when compared to other proposed antennas as in [2,7].

Bandwidth is one of the very important characteristics which make the 2G dual band antenna suitable to be used for 4G LTE applications. For example, the 10 dB bandwidth of proposed antenna covers LTE band-19 of NTT Docomo (Japan) which has uplink of (830–845) MHz and downlink of (875–890) MHz and LTE band-3 of NTT Docomo (Japan) has uplink of (1764–1784) MHz and downlink of (1859–1879) MHz. Similarly, FAReastone (Taiwan) covers LTE band-3 with uplink (1735–1755) MHz and downlink

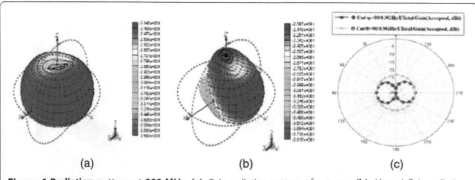

Figure 6 Radiation pattern at 900 MHz. (a): Gain radiation pattern of antenna, **(b)**: Altered Gain radiation pattern due to human head interaction, **(c)**: Polar plot of Gain pattern.

Performance analysis of E-shaped dual band antenna for wireless...

237

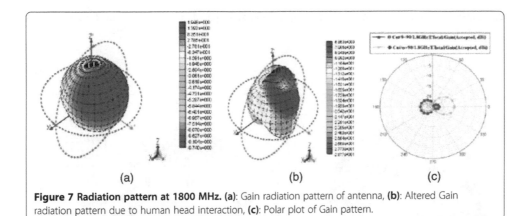

Figure 7 Radiation pattern at 1800 MHz. (a): Gain radiation pattern of antenna, **(b)**: Altered Gain radiation pattern due to human head interaction, **(c)**: Polar plot of Gain pattern.

of (1830–1850) MHz. Hence, the proposed antenna can also be employed for 4G LTE applications [15].

3D- radiation pattern

Figures 6 and 7, represents the simulated 3D gain radiation pattern and polar plot of dual band E-shaped antenna gain at operating frequencies 900 MHz and 1800 MHz. Figure 6a; Figure 7a shows that, the radiation pattern were symmetrical about broad side direction

The antenna radiates possibly in all direction to cover the range. However, it radiates more in positive Z - direction, since reflected by the ground plane. The user head in Z direction acts as obstacle and absorbs certain amount of radiated power in Z direction thereby decreasing the efficient performance of E- antenna. Figures 6(b) and 7(b) show the altered radiation pattern due to human head interaction which absorbs certain amount of power radiated by phone, there by impacting mobile phone E-antenna performance [9].

Influence of near field on antenna performance

Specific Absorption Rate is the subject of strict regulation for health protection. This section focuses to describe the impact of human head model interaction with mobile phone handset [8].

Specific absorption rate

SAR is the rate at which the RF energies are absorbed by a given mass of material, as evidenced by a rise in material temperature. The SAR distribution on head model is

Table 2 SAR averaged over 1 g and 10 g tissue when exposed to handheld device

Model	Placement of mobile handset device with respect to head model					
	Placed near (d = 0 mm)		d = 5 mm		d = 10 mm	
	0.9 GHz	*1.8 GHz*	*0.9 GHz*	*1.8 GHz*	*0.9 GHz*	*1.8 GHz*
1-g SAR (W/Kg)	6.87	23.5	2.36	19.69	1.009	13.8
10-g SAR (W/Kg)	3.65	15.95	1.38	10.09	0.632	7.68
Max SAR (W/Kg)	1.004	24.604	0.354	19.88	0.154	13.55
Average SAR (W/Kg)	0.067	0.438	0.041	0.432	0.027	0.418

calculated by assessing the E field coupled density (ρ) of the brain tissue layers and its conductivity (σ).

$$SAR = \left(\sigma |E|^2\right)/(\rho) \qquad\qquad (3)$$

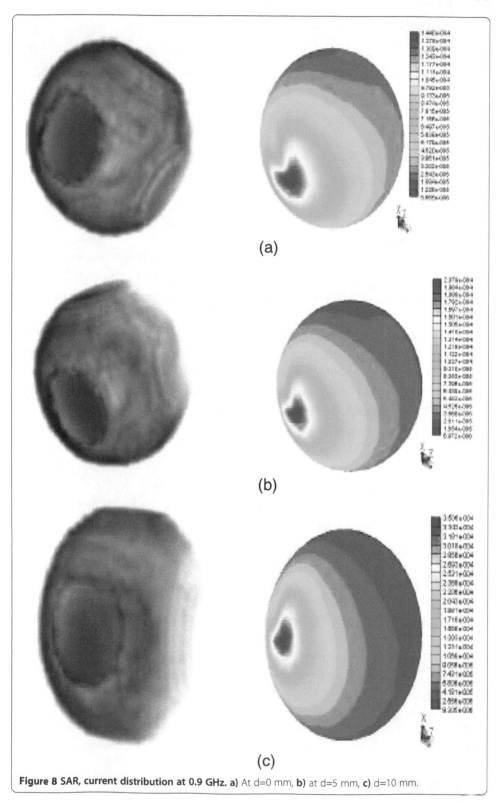

Figure 8 SAR, current distribution at 0.9 GHz. a) At d=0 mm, **b)** at d=5 mm, **c)** d=10 mm.

SAR is averaged over tissue masses of 1 or 10 g tissue [5]. The human body which is a good conductor acts like a receiving antenna, absorbs the EM energy from the space. The tissues which are composed of different salts and organic compounds owns its

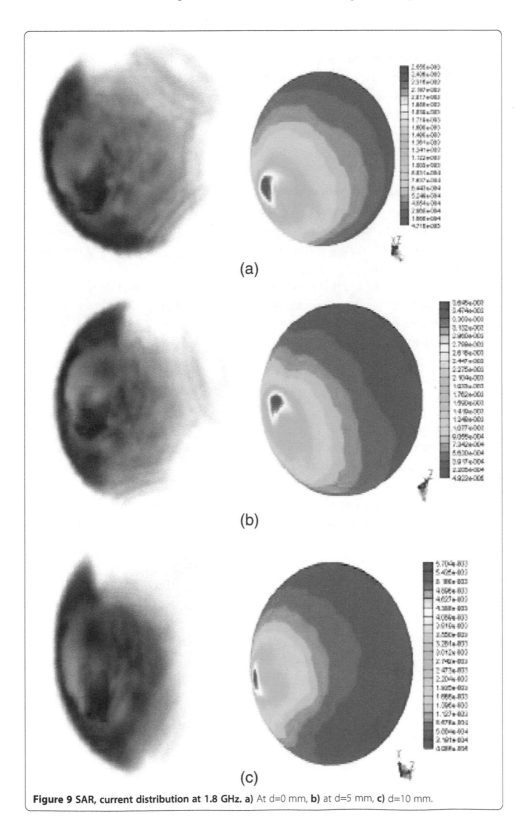

Figure 9 SAR, current distribution at 1.8 GHz. **a)** At d=0 mm, **b)** at d=5 mm, **c)** d=10 mm.

permittivity and conductivity which are also function of frequency, impacts the power coupled to tissues. The internal coupled fields can be calculated using numerical method based computational technique (FDTD), which gives information regarding realistic RF exposure.

SAR analysis and discussions

The SAR values were expressed in terms of Watts per Kilogram over 1 g and 10 g of the head tissues. Normally the distance between the head and the handset is around 10 mm, during operation. Here, the power coupled to the head tissue is noted for three different distances i.e., d = 0 mm (handset pressed to user head), d = 5 mm and d = 10 mm. Table 2 give the SAR value for Spherical head model of user in free space for 900 MHz/1800 MHz.

The results indicate that, power coupled to the human tissue gets decayed with increase in distance from handset. SAR values are well below the SAR limit which substantiates the suitability of antenna design for wireless handheld device application, when handset is placed at 10 mm from the head, which is a normal placing position of phone during operation.

From the Figures 8 and 9, it is observed that more current is distributed in the side of the head and get fluctuates towards other side and is almost null current recorded on the other side of head. Similar case is observed in 3D- SAR distribution. The red colour (hot spot) in the figure indicates higher value of power coupled, where mobile handset is placed nearer. In general, the SAR in the head tissue decreases as the distance from the head to the handset increases.

Thermal changes

Thermal effects are mainly due to RF power absorbed by human tissues. Figures 10 and 11 show the 3D- thermal distributions in human brain tissue at 900 MHz/ 1800 MHz operating frequency. Heat induced in the tissue might affect the proper functioning of cells or affect the cell metabolism [12]. However, the constant blood flow will maintain body temperature in equilibrium state. From the Figure 10 and Figure 11, it can be seen that, the brain side where a cell phone is used receives significantly higher dose of radiation when compared to other side. The variation in the thermal distribution in different human tissues is due to their conductivity and permittivity.

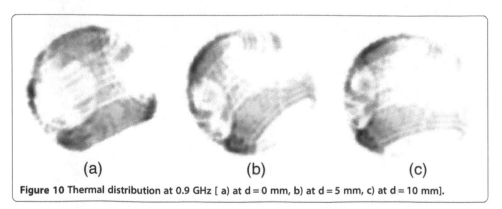

(a)   (b)   (c)

Figure 10 Thermal distribution at 0.9 GHz [a) at d = 0 mm, b) at d = 5 mm, c) at d = 10 mm].

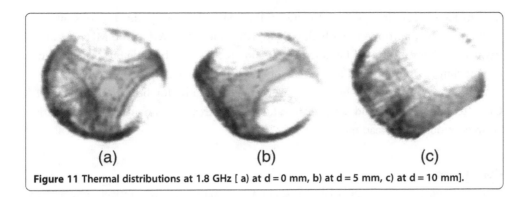

Figure 11 Thermal distributions at 1.8 GHz [a) at d = 0 mm, b) at d = 5 mm, c) at d = 10 mm].

Figure 12a shows the graphical representations of variation in coupled power due to different distance of handset interaction for 0.9GHz frequency. It may be noted that, both the 1g SAR and 10 g SAR are higher for the mobile phone antenna placed very nearer to head model and SAR value eventually decreases when the distance between antenna and head increases.

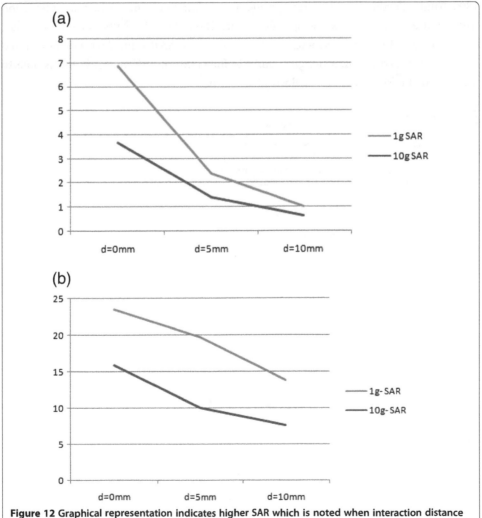

Figure 12 Graphical representation indicates higher SAR which is noted when interaction distance between mobile phone antenna and head decreases. a: Graphical representation of 1 g and 10 g SAR at 0.9 GHz. **b**: Graphical representation of 1 g and 10 g SAR at 1.8 GHz.

From Figure 12b, it is observed that, for 1800 MHz frequency, the 1 g SAR and 10d SAR are more than three times higher than SAR values observed at 900 MHz operating frequency. The values used for comparison and analysis may be little bit inaccurate due to modeling of human head as layered spherical model which is far different from real time EM exposure to real human. However in this study, for both 0.9 GHz and 1.8 GHz frequencies, 1 g and 10 g SAR values get decreased with increased separation between mobile and head model.

Conclusion

In this paper, a compact dual band E shaped antenna with comparatively low average SAR and better Bandwidth is introduced for GSM application in handheld devices. Simulations were performed for different scenarios. The antenna in free space and the handset device placed close to a user head model. The return loss was better than 25 dB at 900 MHz and 1800 MHz with bandwidth of 142 MHz and 218 MHz in the lower band and in the upper band respectively as compared to existing antennas. The 10 dB bandwidth of proposed E shaped antenna covers GSM 850/ GSM 900/ GSM 1800 bands. Further, the average specific absorption rate, due to human interaction with handset is well below the specified limit. The obtained results, including surface current distributions, S-parameters, radiation patterns, SAR values, have demonstrated that the proposed antenna design is suitable for GSM and 4G network and is able to achieve good performance for real world scenario.

Competing interests

The authors declare that they have no competing interest.

Authors' contributions

In this work, BR extended his constant guidance throughout the work, till final document verification. LR and BR together put forth the research idea and done simulation and documentation work. Both the author has read the final manuscript.

Author's information

Balamurugan Rajagopal: was born in Dindigul, Tamil Nadu, India on 1981. He is presently serving as an Assistant Director(Administration) in All India Council for Technical Education (AICTE), New Delhi on deputation from Department of Electrical and Electronics Engineering, Anna University, Regional Centre Coimbatore* where he has been serving as Assistant Professor (Power Electronics and Drives) since 2008(August) onwards. He completed B.Tech. degree in the specialization of Electronics and Instrumentation Engineering at Dr. B.R. Ambedkar National Institute of Technology(NIT), Jalandar (Punjab) in 2002 and M.E. degree (Power Electronics and Drives) at Government College of Technology, Coimbatore, Tamil Nadu in 2005. He joined Anna University, Chennai, India as Assistant Project Manager, Centre for Intellectual Property Rights and Trade Marks in February, 2006 and served until May, 2007. In June, 2007, he joined Anna University, Coimbatore as Project Manager, Centre for Intellectual Property Rights and in October, 2007, he was appointed as Assistant Professor (Faculty of Engineering and Technology, in which he continued prior to becoming to the present position of Assistant Professor (Power Electronics and Drives) in August, 2008. He also served as Asst. Controller of Examinations and Assistant Director (Centre for University Industry Collaboration) in Anna University of Technology, Coimbatore (Formerly Anna University, Coimbatore). He was granted two Erasmus Mundus Fellowships(Heritage & India4EUII), funded by European Commission to undertake Staff Mobility Programme in Univ. of Seville, Spain and Aalto University, Finland respectively in 2013. He successfully completed Staff Mobility Programme in Univ. of Seville, Spain in Oct., 2013. He is a member of IEEE and various IEEE societies (ComSoc, CIS, CSS, EDS, EMCS, IES, I&MS, MTT-S, PELS & RAS). His fields of interests are Intellectual Property Rights, Electronics, Information & Communication Technologies (E, I&CT), Mobile Phone Radiation Issues, Electrical Drives, Embedded Control Systems, Power Electronics and VLSI Designs. Note: *-Formerly Anna University, Coimbatore in 2007 and renamed as Anna University of Technology, Coimbatore in 2010. Later merged with Anna University, Chennai on 1st August, 2012 by Government of Tamil Nadu. Lalithambika Rajasekaran: was born on 1987 in Erode, Tamil Nadu, India. She is Post Graduate Engineer. She was awarded B.E. and M.E. degrees by Anna University, Chennai. She completed M.E. (Electrical Drives and Embedded Control) by securing Gold Medal with 1st Rank during 2011–2013 in the Department of Electrical and Electronics Engineering, Anna University- Regional Centre Coimbatore, Tamil Nadu and B.E. (Electronics and Communication Engineering) during 2005–2009 in Anna University, Chennai. She is a member of IEEE and various IEEE societies (ComSoc, CSS, EDS, IES, SPS, MTT-S & AP-S). Her fields of interests are Bio- Electromagnetics, Antennas for Wireless applications, Power Electronics for Renewable Energy Systems, Embedded Control Systems.

Acknowledgment

Authors would like to thank Doctors of various hospitals for their valuable explanations concerning human tissue property.

References

1. Corbett R, Lam EY (2012) "Mobile-Phone Antenna Design", IEEE Antennas and Propagation Magazine, Vol. 54, No. 4
2. Yong J (2012) "Compact Dual-Band CPW-Fed Zeroth-Order Resonant Monopole Antennas "IEEE Antennas and Wireless Propagation letters, vol. 11
3. Fuguo Z, Steven G, Anthony TS H, Abd-Alhameed RA, See CH, Tim WC B, Jianzhou L, Gao W, Jiadong X (2014) Ultra-Wideband Dual-Polarized Patch Antenna With Four Capacitively Coupled Feeds. IEEE Trans Antennas Propag 62:5
4. Hassan Tariq C, Muhammad N, Abbasi QH, Yi H, AlJa'afreh SS (2013) "Compact Low-Profile Dual-Port Single Wideband Planar Inverted-F MIMO Antenna", IEEE Antennas and Wireless Propagation Letters, VOL. 12
5. Rowley JT, Rod BW (1999) Performance of Shorted Microstrip Patch Antennas for Mobile Communications Handsets At 1800 MHz'. IEEE Trans Antennas Propag 47:5
6. Jimmy T, Yih-Chien Chen C-YW (2012) "Dual- Band Planar Inverted F Antenna for Application in ISM, HIPERLAN, UNII and WiMAX", Proceedings of APMC
7. Luyi L, Jonathan R, Richard L (2013) Tunable Multiband Handset Antenna Operating at VHF and UHF Bands. IEEE Trans Antennas Propag 61:7
8. Md Faruk A, Sujoy M, Sudhabindu R (2009) "SAR Analysis in Human Head Model Exposed to Mobile Base-Station Antenna for GSM-900 band", Loughborough Antennas & Propagation Conference
9. M. Ali, R. A. Sadler and G. J. Hayes (2002), "A Uni quely Packaged Internal Inverted-F Antenna for Bluetooth or Wireless LAN Application", IEEE antennas and wirele ss propagation letters, vol.1.
10. Qinjiang R, Kelce W (2011) Design, Modeling, And Evaluation Of A Multiband MIMO/Diversity Antenna System For Small Wireless Mobile Terminals'. IEEE Trans Components Packaging Manuf Technol 01:03
11. Simulation tool, 'General Electromagnetic Simulator', http://www.2comu.com
12. Sooman P, Juyoung J, Yeongseog L (2004) "Temperature Rise in the Human Head and Brain for Portable Handsets at 900 and 1800 MHz",4' International Conference on Microwave and Millimeter Wave Technology Proceedings
13. Mantash M, Collardey S (2013) Dual-band Wi-Fi and 4G LTE textile antenna". 7th European Conference on Antennas and Propagation (EuCAP) 8–12:422–425
14. Zuxing L, Minseok H, Jaehoon C (2012) Compact dual-band MIMO antenna for 4G USG dongle application". Microw Opt Technol Lett 54(3):744–748
15. http://en.wikipedia.org/wiki/List_of_LTE_networks // LTE network frequency range – world wide//.
16. M.E. de Cos, M.Mantash, "Dual-band coplanar waveguide feed smiling monopole antenna for Wi-FI and 4G LTE applications", IET Microwave , Antennas and Propagation, Vo. 7, Issue No. 9
17. Electromagnetic Simulation Software. Solutions for Design Engineers and EM Simulation Professionals, www.remcom.com // comparison about FEM, FDTD and FEM-FDTD//.
18. Rozlan Alias, Simulation of radiation performance for mobile phones using a hybrid FEM-TFDTD computational technique. 4th Int. Conference on Modeling, Simulation and applied optimization (ICMSAO), 2011. doi:10.11.1109/ICMSAOL2011, pp. 577–5956
19. Erdem OFLI, Chung-Huan LI (2008) Analysis and optimization of mobile phone antenna radiation performance in the presence of head and hand phantoms". Turk J Elect Engg 16:1
20. Claudio R, Fernandez (2004) FDTD simulations and measurement for cell phone with planar antennas". Ann Telecommun 59(9–10):1012–2030
21. Md Mahabub A, Md Suaibur R (2013) A Connected E-Shape and U-Shape Dual-Band Patch Antenna for Different Wireless Applications". Int J Sci Eng Res 4:1
22. Wen Piao L, Dong-Hua Y, Zong-De L (2014) Compact Dual-Band Planar Inverted-e-Shaped Antenna Using Defected Ground Structure". Int J Antennas Propagation 937423:10

14

Performance evaluation of data aggregation for cluster-based wireless sensor network

Adwitiya Sinha[*] and Daya Krishan Lobiyal

* Correspondence:
mailtoadwitiya@gmail.com
School of Computer & Systems
Sciences, Jawaharlal Nehru
University, New Delhi, India

Abstract

In wireless sensor network, data fusion is considered an essential process for preserving sensor energy. Periodic data sampling leads to enormous collection of raw facts, the transmission of which would rapidly deplete the sensor power. In this paper, we have performed data aggregation on the basis of entropy of the sensors. The entropy is computed from the proposed local and global probability models. The models provide assistance in extracting high precision data from the sensor nodes. We have also proposed an energy efficient method for clustering the nodes in the network. Initially, sensors sensing the same category of data are placed within a distinct cluster. The remaining unclustered sensors estimate their divergence with respect to the clustered neighbors and ultimately join the least-divergent cluster. The overall performance of our proposed methods is evaluated using NS-2 simulator in terms of convergence rate, aggregation cycles, average packet drops, transmission cost and network lifetime. Finally, the simulation results establish the validity and efficiency of our approach.

Keyword: Wireless sensor network; Divergence clustering; Entropy-based data aggregation; Local and global aggregation

Introduction

The wireless sensor network (WSN) [1] has started receiving huge research incentives for its omnipresence in several applications, including environmental monitoring, wildlife exploration, medical supervision and battlefield surveillance. The sensor network is formed with small electronic devices possessing self-configuring capability that are either randomly deployed or manually positioned in huge bulk [2]. It performs activities in several dimensions, for instance identifying the neighborhood, presence of targets or monitoring environmental factors (motion, temperature, humidity, sound and other physical variables). However, owing to limited battery power, the sensor networks demand energy efficient resolutions to enhance the performance of sensor network.

Energy consumption problem, being the most visible challenge, is considered central to the sensor research theme. The processing of data, memory accesses and input/output operations, all consume sensor energy. However, the major power drain occurs due to wireless communication [3]. Therefore, attempts require to be carried out to perform as much in-network processing as possible within a sensor or a group of sensors (cluster). This is achieved by performing aggregation and filtration of raw data before transmitting them to destined targets. As a result of which redundancy in the recorded sensory samples is eliminated, thereby reducing the transmission cost and network overloading. Moreover, decrease in the effective number of packet transmissions also leads to minimized chances of network congestion, thereby saving the excess energy consumption in the network. For instance, if the radio electronics requires $50nJ/bit$ and amplifier circuitry needs $10pJ/bit/m^2$ for communication, then power used in transmitting 1 bit of information to the processing center situated 1 km away, consumes 1.005×10^4 nJ per unit time (watts). However, energy used in data processing for aggregation is 5 $nJ/bit/signal$, which implies that execution of almost 2010 instructions compensates the energy used for one transmission in unit time. Therefore, it is quite recommendable to apply aggregation techniques. Previous researches have already proven the fact that in-network processing cost is much less than the communication cost [4-14].

The proliferation of sensor network has created the urge of exploring novel ideas for data aggregation. However, the aggregation schemes would require efficient clustering protocols to well-implement its functioning. Hence, in this paper we have contributed a divergence-measure based clustering protocol along with entropy based data aggregation, to the ongoing sensor network research. The remainder of this paper is organized as follows: a brief review of previous research carried out in the related field is included in section 2. Our proposed clustering technique based on divergence measure is provided in section 3. In section 4, the proposed fuzzy-entropy based aggregation scheme has been elaborated. Analysis of network diagram is presented in section 5. Section 6 shows the performance evaluation of our proposed method. Finally, the paper is concluded in section 7 along with directions for further scope.

Related work

The energy consumption in wireless sensor network has created enormous awareness among the researchers for increasing the network lifetime. The sensor network is considered to have prospective results in terms of dynamism and diversity in everyday applications. Several resource efficient protocols have been introduced by researchers in order to limit the sensor energy usage, at the same time maintaining a sufficient degree of reliability and throughput.

Several methods of data aggregation depend on the topology of the sensor network [15]. For instance, a tree-based data aggregation protocol constructs a simple topology based on a parent and child association [16]. However, large transmission delays and poor rate of aggregation makes it unsuitable for the dynamic applications. Further, we have centralized aggregation protocol [17], in which aggregation is done only at the sink (data processing center). As a result, such protocols lead to heavy workload and unnecessary packet drops. There are other clustering schemes based on static [18-20] and dynamic cluster aggregation [21-23]. In case of static environment, the clusters are formed in the initial stage and the aggregation is carried out by the cluster heads. The clusters once formed remain unchanged throughout the network lifespan. This procedure is suitable for area monitoring (recording earthquake, temperature, humidity, etc.), but not supported over wide range of applications, like- forest fire supervision, wildlife monitoring, target tracking, etc. Therefore most of the research awareness can be found in dynamic cluster aggregation schemes, where clusters are formed

dynamically and updated on sensing environmental parameters followed by aggregation at the cluster head. The clusters formed in this case, are also known as
adaptive clusters.

An energy aware algorithm has been provided in [4] for constructing an aggregation
tree prior to data transmission. The algorithm seems to reflect the influence of both
the energy and distance parameters to construct the tree. In another research [5], the
authors have performed aggregation by considering entropy of correlated data transmitted
by the source nodes. This procedure reduces the amount of redundant data forwarded to
the sink. Furthermore, the estimation of joint entropy of the correlated data set helps in
maximizing information integrity. Another interesting aggregation protocol is developed
in [6] on the basis of wavelet-entropy. Initially, multi-scale wavelet transforms are used to
spread signals in multi-scale range, after which information is aggregated using wavelet-
entropy discriminance theorem. Simulation results indicate that the proposed method is
capable to extend the lifetime of networks to a much greater degree than Low-Energy
Adaptive Clustering Hierarchy (LEACH) protocol [7]. In [8] the authors have put forward
a novel approach that focusses on data aggregation with significantly reduced aggregation
latency. Collision-free schedule is generated by a distributed algorithm for performing
data aggregation in wireless sensor network. The time latency of aggregation schedule is
minimized using greedy strategy.

In a recent research [9], an aggregation scheme called smart aggregation is developed for
continuous monitoration in sensor networks. The proposed technique maintains a tolerable
deviation (a bounded error) in the aggregated data while utilizing the spatio-temporal
correlation of data. In another subsequent work [10], data aggregation techniques are
designed on the basis of statistical information extraction. The applied methods
exhibits bounded message overhead and robustness against link failures. The
expectation–maximization (EM) algorithm is used in order to accomplish accurate
estimation of distribution parameters of sensory data. The experimental outcome
confirms reduced network communication cost even in large scale sensor networks.
In a latest publication [11], the corresponding authors have presented α-local
spatial clustering algorithm along with data aggregation mechanism. The contribution
was mainly made for environmental surveillance applications in high density sensor
networks. The aggregation algorithm constructs a dominating set by exploiting the
spatial correlation between data measured by different sensors. The dominating
set is further considered as network backbone to execute data aggregation on the
basis of information summarization of the dominator nodes. Another research in
[12] proposed cooperative information aggregation (CIA) mechanisms to handle
observation noise and communication errors initially found in the sampled data.
Moreover, the authors have designed an aggregation hard decision estimator
(AHDE) and an Aggregation Maximum-Likelihood Estimator (AMLE). Simulation
shows the effectiveness of CIA schemes to be suitably applied to environments prone to
observation noise.

In this paper, we have proposed a dynamic clustering and aggregation strategy that
aggregates data at the sensor node and cluster head as well. With the use of entropy
and information theory, we attempt to reduce the transmission and processing cost,
but maintaining the relevance of the aggregated data. For the evaluation of the
performance of our proposed strategy, we make a comparative analysis with two

well-known clustering protocols: Hybrid Energy-Efficient Distributed Clustering (HEED) [13] and an inference clustering protocol based of Belief Propagation (BP) [14]. HEED is a distributed clustering approach that operates in energy efficient manner and helps in prolonging network lifetime. It is scalable over large network sizes and performs load balancing within clusters. However, frequent computation of communications cost and broadcasting among neighbors degrades its performance. As a strong counterpart, BP clustering method offers energy effective solutions based on belief calculations with potential functions. Though BP performs better than HEED in terms of clustering the network and packet delivery performance, but long-length messages induce larger overheads in message passing. This makes transmission cost higher in case of BP. Previous simulations have shown a marginal difference in network lifetimes contributed by these protocols.

Proposed divergence measure based clustering technique

Clustering is the process of assigning a set of sensor nodes, with similar attributes, to a specified group or cluster. In our research, we have proposed a new energy efficient clustering algorithm that operates in two phases: preliminary and final clustering phase. In preliminary phase, sensor nodes sensing the same category of data are placed in a distinct cluster. In final phase, the remaining unclustered sensors estimate their divergence with respect to the clustered neighbors and ultimately join the least-divergent cluster.

Preliminary clustering phase

The formation of preliminary clusters is purely distributed and is based on the sensed data. The proposed clustering method is independent of predetermination of number of clusters, geographic positioning and distance measures. We have used a window function [24] to normalize the sensed data so as to scale the value within the range [0...1]. Let us assume, a and b be the minimum and maximum value of the environmental parameter to be monitored and $x_{avg}(t)$ be the average of the set of data sensed for the time interval t. The window function $\phi(\bullet)$ can be defined as follows:

$$
\phi\left(x_{avg}(t), a, b\right) = \begin{cases} 1 & \left(\dfrac{x_{avg}(t)}{b-a}\right) \in [0, 0.2[\\[2mm] 2 & \left(\dfrac{x_{avg}(t)}{b-a}\right) \in [0.2, 0.4[\\[2mm] 3 & \left(\dfrac{x_{avg}(t)}{b-a}\right) \in [0.4, 0.6[\\[2mm] 4 & \left(\dfrac{x_{avg}(t)}{b-a}\right) \in [0.6, 0.8[\\[2mm] 5 & \left(\dfrac{x_{avg}(t)}{b-a}\right) \in [0.8, 1.0] \\[2mm] 0 & otherwise \end{cases}
$$

$$(1)$$

The sensors use the window function to map the data into one of the formats. All the nodes that sense the same format in 1-hop distance groups together to form a preliminary cluster. In the initial phase, the node with maximum energy within the preliminary cluster is appointed as the cluster head. It maintains a duration timer to keep track of the period for which it remained cluster head. Once appointed the node functions as cluster head till its duration timer expires. On the expiration of the timer, the role of cluster head rotates to other probable nodes whose residual energy qualifies above a minimum predefined energy threshold. The head rotation performs load balancing within the clusters. Moreover, the cluster head assigns a unique cluster id to all the cluster members.

Though the idea of preliminary stage of cluster formation is simple to implement but due to some situations (boundary value or out-of-bound data sensing) few nodes in the network might still remain unclustered. This problem is solved by our final clustering phase.

Final clustering phase

The final clustering phase ensures that all the nodes in the sensor network get clustered. The process begins with an unclustered node discovering one or more clustered neighbor in its direct hop. The node then obtains the array of probabilities of the sensed data from its neighbors that are distinctly clustered. This procedure is further elaborated in the following section.

Each sensor node maintains the following information in its database, which eventually helps in calculating the divergence measure required for final clustering.

$$\Delta_n^s = \left\{ P^s = \left(p_1^s, p_2^s, p_1^s, \ldots, p_n^s \right), \; p_i^s \geq 0, \Sigma_{i=1}^n \; p_i^s = 1 \right\}$$

$$(2)$$

where p_i^s is the probability of ith data format from the sensor s and the probability sequence is denoted by P^s.

Selection of divergence method

We know that the entropy of the source can be given by the Shannon's entropy $H(P)$:

$$H(P) = -\Sigma_{i=1}^n \; p_i \ln p_i$$

$$(3)$$

where $p_i \in P^s$ and P is Host or Local Probability Model (*LPM*) of host sensor node. Moreover, the inaccuracy in data is given by:

$$H(P \parallel T) = -\Sigma_{i=1}^n \; p_i \ln t_i$$

$$(4)$$

Where $t_i \in T^s$ and T is Remote Probability Model (RPM) of remote sensor node. On subtracting equation (4) from (3), we get Kullback–Leibler directed divergence measure [25]:

$$D(P \parallel T) = H(P \parallel T) - H(P) = -\Sigma_{i=1}^n \; p_i \ln t_i + \Sigma_{i=1}^n \; p_i \ln p_i = \Sigma_{i=1}^n \; p_i \ln \frac{p_i}{t_i} \quad (5)$$

However, the divergence $D(P \parallel T)$ is not a symmetric measure, i.e. $D(P \parallel T) \neq D(T \parallel P)$ and hence it cannot be directly applied. Therefore, we consider the symmetric version of Kullback–Leibler, known as Jeffrey's (J) divergence measure [26] which can be derived as following:

$$J(P \parallel T) = D(P \parallel T) + D(T \parallel P) = \Sigma_{i=1}^{n} \quad p_i \ln\frac{p_i}{t_i} + \Sigma_{i=1}^{n} \quad t_i \ln\frac{t_i}{p_i}$$

$$J(P \parallel T) = \Sigma_{i=1}^{n} \quad p_i \ln\frac{p_i}{t_i} - \Sigma_{i=1}^{n} \quad t_i \ln\frac{p_i}{t_i} = \Sigma_{i=1}^{n} \quad (p_i - t_i)p_i \ln\frac{p_i}{t_i}$$

$$(6)$$

Application of divergence measure

Divergence measure is a metric used for defining the degree of dissimilarity between two objects. In our clustering processes, an unclustered node uses the divergence measure to analyze the extent to which it differs from each of its clustered neighbors and eventually decides to join the cluster that exhibits maximum similarity (minimum divergence). Subsequently, clusters formed by the end of final clustering phase are likely to be highly correlated. For simulation purpose, we have employed Jeffrey's divergence measure owing to its symmetric nature.

According to our strategy, every unclustered sensor node makes use of the J - divergence measure derived in equation (6) to calculate the divergence between itself and every other clustered (neighboring) sensor nodes. The unclustered sensor s will join the clustered node $\bar{s}$ such that its divergence is the least as compared to other clustered nodes (equation 7). This process of clustering recursively continues till all nodes in the network are clustered.

$$\left.\begin{array}{l} J\left(T^1 \parallel P^s\right) \\ J\left(T^2 \parallel P^s\right) \\ \vdots \\ J\left(T^z \parallel P^s\right) \end{array}\right\} = \min J(T^{\bar{s}} \parallel P^s) \ , \quad 1 \le \bar{s} \le z \tag{7}$$

where $J(T^{\bar{s}} \parallel P^s)$ denote the J - divergence measure between the $\bar{s}^{th}$ clustered node and s^{th} sensor node to be clustered.

Exceptional cases

There can be two exceptional cases while executing the final clustering phase. The first case occurs at the beginning of the phase, when no clustered neighbors are found in 1-hop vicinity. This requires the node to wait till it discovers one. The waiting period ends with the expiration of *wait timer* (initialized at the beginning of final clustering phase). The second case is confronted by the end of the final clustering phase when a node discovers itself isolated, i.e. none of its neighbors in 1-hop vicinity are clustered yet. In that case, the node declares itself as cluster head and forms cluster with its 1-hop neighbors. This process continues, till a clustered node is discovered which initiates final clustering with divergence measure. Since, most of the nodes would be clustered (to the least divergent cluster) in the final phase, only fewer nodes would confront such isolation.

Proposed data fusion algorithm using fuzzy-entropy

In the proposed work, we apply the data fusion approach for monitoring the variation in the temperature. However, generalization can be done to other environmental parameters, for instance- pressure, humidity, etc.

Fuzzification of input data

We consider five data ranges, i.e. $M = \{m_i \mid i = 5\}$ for recognizing the category of sensed data, as mentioned in equation (1). Each format m_i consists of an array of sensed data that falls within its defined range. In other words, each data sampled at regular time interval is associated one of the five data categories/formats. The average of sets of data falling in the category m_i is denoted by $\bar{x}_i$ which is further used in the fuzzification process. The temperature ranges are represented by two well-known fuzzy membership functions - Sigmoidal and Generalized-bell membership function [27]. Such fuzzification of temperature function is performed using the *FIS* Editor of *MATLAB*. The Sigmoidal and Generalized-bell membership functions are given by equations (8) and (9) respectively:

$$f_{sig}(\bar{x}_i; \omega, v) = \left[\frac{1}{1 + e^{-\omega(\bar{x}_i - v)}} \right] \tag{8}$$

$$f_{gbell}(\bar{x}_i; \alpha, \beta, \gamma) = \left[1 / \left(1 + \left| \frac{\bar{x}_i - \gamma}{\alpha} \right|^{2\beta} \right) \right] \tag{9}$$

We have selected Generalized-bell membership function to model the moderate data formats: m_2 (cold temperature), m_3 (normal temperature), m_4 (hot temperature); while Sigmoidal membership function has been chosen to model extreme data formats: m_1 (very cold temperature), m_5 (very hot temperature). The temperature is continuous parameter which requires functions that can well represent its characteristics. Hence, the choice of both the membership functions is suitable as they are best known for representing maximum variation and smoothness.

Sampling process & local probability measure

We assume that the sensors sense data for a time period of t seconds. After t seconds, a sequence $\delta(t)$ of L messages is generated:

$$\delta(t) = m_{i1}, m_{i2}, m_{i3}, ..., m_{iL} \tag{10}$$

The frequency f_i of the data range m_i is recorded. On the basis of the frequency of occurrence of each range (m_i) with respect to sensor s, local probability is computed as:

$$p_i^{(s)} = \frac{f_i}{\Sigma_{i=1}^n f_i} \tag{11}$$

such that $\Sigma_{i=1}^n p_i^{(s)} = 1$. This probability function has been designed to capture the maximum variation. Finally, the entropy is calculated locally at each sensor s as the following: [28].

$$H_r^{(s)}(M) = \Sigma_{i=1}^n \ p_i^{(s)} \log_r \left(\frac{1}{p_i^{(s)}} \right) \tag{12}$$

All the sensors send the computed entropy, i.e. $\left(sensor_{id}, H_r^{(s)}(M) \right)$ to the cluster head. The cluster head then derives an entropy threshold, on the basis of the received entropy values. In the simulation, the threshold is decided to be more than the average of entropies $\bar{H}_r(M)$. This means that if $H_r^{(s)}(M) > \bar{H}_r(M)$, then the cluster head sends an acknowledgement to sensor node s to send its data. Hence, selected sensors qualifying the threshold finally participate in the data reporting process, which ultimately results in sensor compression. On receiving the acknowledgement, sensors calculates the mathematical expectation of the array of sensed data:

$$d_{(expc)}^{(s)} = \Sigma_{i=1}^n \ p_i^{(s)} \ \bar{x}_i \tag{13}$$

Finally, the sensors send $\left(sensor\_id, d_{(expc)}^{(s)}\right)$ to the cluster head. Hence, the process of sending entropy followed by the expected data value; greatly reduces the bulk of packet transmissions within the cluster.

Global probability measure

On receiving data and entropy from selected sources the cluster head computes global probability as following:

$$p_q = \frac{\left[H_r^{(q)}(M)\right]^{-1}}{\left[\Sigma_{q=1}^{|Q|} \ H_r^{(q)}(M)\right]^{-1}} \ with \ \Sigma_{q=1}^{|Q|} \ p_q = 1 \tag{14}$$

This probability function will allow capturing the focused information, rather than considering the maximum variation in information that is achieved by the local probability model. On expanding equation (14), we get:

$$p_q = \frac{\left[\Sigma_{i=1}^n \ p_i^{(q)} \log_r\left(\frac{1}{p_i^{(q)}}\right)\right]^{-1}}{\left[\Sigma_{q=1}^{|Q|} \ \Sigma_{i=1}^n \ p_i^{(q)} \log_r\left(\frac{1}{p_i^{(q)}}\right)\right]^{-1}} = \left\{\frac{\Sigma_{i=1}^n \ p_i^{(q)} \log_r\left(\frac{1}{p_i^{(q)}}\right)}{\Sigma_{q=1}^{|Q|} \ \log_r \Pi_{i=1}^n \left[\left(1/p_i^{(q)}\right)^{p_i^{(q)}}\right]}\right\}^{-1} \ \forall q \in Q \tag{15}$$

where Q refers to the set of selected sensors that qualify the entropy threshold. Finally, the cluster head computes the expected value of the actual set of data received from the selected sensors as following:

$$d_{expc} = \Sigma_{q=1}^{|Q|} \ p_q \ \bar{x}_i \tag{16}$$

Subsequently, the cluster head sends $(cluster\_id, d_{expc})$ to the data processing node (i.e. sink). As a result of the global probability model, more accurate data is filtered and sent to the sink. Besides reducing the amount of data being sent, our method also minimizes the number of participating sensors. This interprets that our proposed approach preserves the information relevance as well as enhances the energy efficiency of the aggregation process.

Network diagram analysis

The network timeline diagram in Figure 1 shows the working slots for initial cycle of our proposed work. The network initiates with the gathering of data by individual nodes, also known as random sensing. The next stage in the cycle is the proposed preliminary clustering phase (PCP), on the completion of which data aggregation and

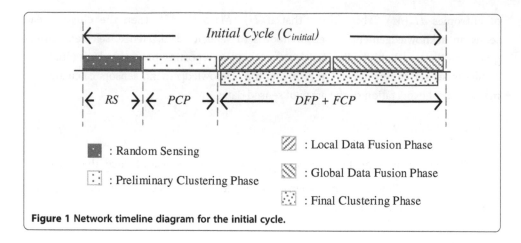

Figure 1 Network timeline diagram for the initial cycle.

final clustering phase (FCP) are executed in parallel thereby performing better time utilization. The data aggregation or data fusion phase (DFP) is further classified in local and global phases respectively. The local DFP is carried out by individual nodes with the help of local probability measure and the global DFP is performed by the cluster heads using the global probability measure. Since, the aggregation process is involved only within the cluster, the FCP can continue in parallel (outside the clusters) without collision. This efficient utilization of time ultimately results in significant energy savings. In Figure 2, the working slots for intermediate cycles are highlighted. We assume that our cluster formation procedure is static, i.e. the sensors are stationery and are all assigned to a fixed cluster at the initiation of the network that remains unchanged over the entire lifetime of the sensor network. After the clusters are formed at the network start-up, the consecutive data cycles involve random sampling (or sensing) and data fusion process (local as well as global).

Simulation and performance evaluations

The simulation of the proposed clustering and entropy-based aggregation is performed using Network Simulator (*NS*-2) [29,30]. Moreover, on the basis of the tracing data

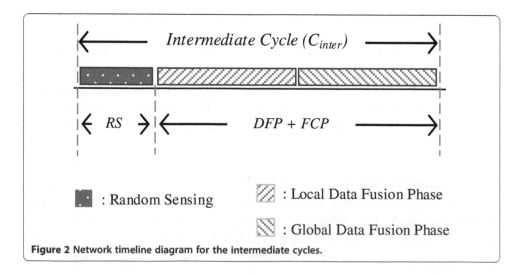

Figure 2 Network timeline diagram for the intermediate cycles.

generated in *NS*-2 and other log files, the graphical evaluation is generated using *MATLAB* [31]. In our simulation, the sensor nodes are randomly deployed over a network of dimension 1000 x 1000 square meters. Our proposed clustering method uses divergence measure to discover clusters in the network. The simulation parameters used for the experimentation are specified in Table 1.

We have used Gaussian Bell and Sigma membership functions to monitor the fuzzy environmental parameter (temperature). The simulation parameters of the membership functions are provided in Table 2 and Table 3 respectively. The trend of the membership function, over the range of temperature being monitored, is highlighted in Figure 3.

The clustered nodes keep track of the frequency of data formats sensed during the sampling period. The bar graph plotted in Figure 4 displays the variation of local probability of different data formats with respect to a randomly chosen cluster in the sensor network. Figure 4(a) represents the local entropy sent by the sensors to its CH. It is evident from the graph that node with id 5 gives highest entropy owing to the least variation of the same node in Figure 4(b). Therefore the fact that, least divergence is the implication of maximum entropy is verified.

Figure 5 provides an estimation of the number of aggregation cycles performed with 50, 100 and 150 nodes for a given amount of energy (in joules). The elevation in the trend apparently shows that the increase in number of aggregated samples is achieved at the minor cost of minimum packets transmission. Also, it is apparent that as the number of sensors rises from 50 to 150, the graph upraises specifying greater aggregation cycles. Moreover, the drift becomes smoother for 150 nodes, which implies that the performance of our protocol improves with increasing number of sensor nodes. This behavior is explained by the increase in the density of nodes ensures better exploitation of spatial property (of data sampled by different sensors).

Figure 6 shows the convergence rate of calculated entropy with absolute entropic value. It can be seen that on average the proposed algorithm performs in good conjunction with the absolute value. However, for lesser number of sensor nodes (50 nodes), the trend stagnates in the early simulation phase. The reason is reduced accuracy in sampled data

Table 1 Simulation parameters used for performance evaluation

Parameter	Value
Network dimension	1000×1000 meters^2
Number of nodes	150 nodes
Sensor radius	50 meters
Simulation time	150 seconds
Routing protocol	*DSDV*
Sampling time	5 seconds
Number of samples	16 samples
Number of data formats	5 formats
Initial energy	100 joules
Transmission power	20.500 mwatts
Reception power	40.119 mwatts
Data packet	24 bytes
Entropy packet	22 bytes
Ack packet	14 bytes

Table 2 GBELLMF parameters table

Data formats	a	b	c
m_2	2.86	2.43	12.60
m_3	4.10	3.86	24.36
m_4	2.86	2.43	35.60

because of lesser utilization of spatio-temporal correlation. With increased node deployment, the convergence improves. This proves that our theoretical aggregation model results in good performance on implementation.

The graph presented in Figure 7 shows the average transmission cost contributed by our proposed Divergence Measure based Clustering (DMC) + Entropy based Data Aggregation (EDA) along with Hybrid Energy-Efficient Distributed Clustering (HEED) and Belief Propagation (BP) [10,11]. The maximum message size of BP is 74 bytes which are forwarded frequently in the network for the purpose of updation of local belief by individual nodes. As a result of which we find degradation in the performance of BP at the beginning of simulation period. Though BP performs lesser re-clustering than HEED, but owing to the smaller size of the messages in HEED (29 bytes) it achieves eventually better results in the late simulation period. However, our proposed DMC+EDA protocol presents best results than its comparatives. The graph, however, elevates slightly during the period of 50-90 seconds to compensate for the initial cluster formation. The clusters constructed using divergence measure exhibit comparatively better stability during the course of simulation. Moreover, the packet size of our protocol is maximum 24 bytes (minimum size being 14 bytes) which reduces the transmission cost to a greater extent.

Figure 8 compares the average number of packets dropped by all the protocols respectively. As a matter of fact, HEED triggers more clustering processes than BP. Consequently, in case of HEED the nodes die out at a quicker rate. As a result, with fewer alive nodes the number of cluster heads tends to increase rapidly. This increases number of transmissions and therefore the chances of packet drops. However, due to rapid energy exhaustion the packet drop rate falls in the later simulation course. This is apparent from the HEED graph that steeps down towards the end of simulation. For BP the graph shows stability in clustering process resulting in better aggregation, lesser transmissions and reduced packet loss. But, owing to high transmission cost, BP finally deteriorates in the later simulation phase. Above all, our proposed scheme illustrates perfect combination of clustering and data aggregation over the entire simulation process. Increase in packet loss occurs at the network startup due to primary cluster formation. Once the network stabilizes, the outcome trend also becomes persistent.

Finally, in Figure 9, the results of network lifetime is plotted for our protocol in association with its comparatives for varying number of nodes, 50 (Figure 9a) and

Table 3 SIGMF parameters table

Data formats	a	c
m_1	−1.57	6.857
m_5	+1.57	41.640

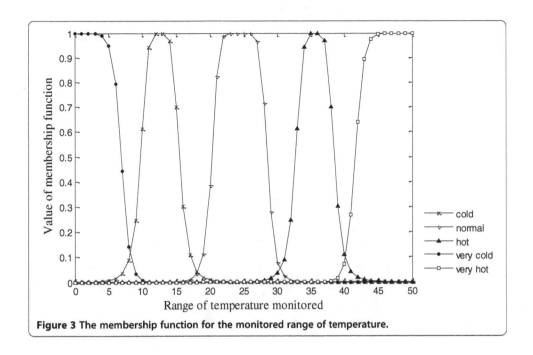

Figure 3 The membership function for the monitored range of temperature.

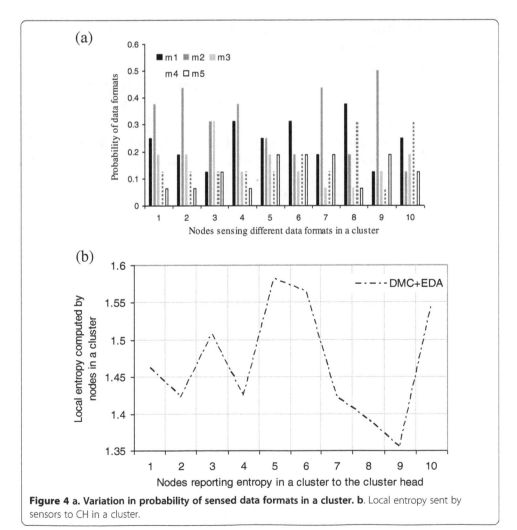

Figure 4 a. Variation in probability of sensed data formats in a cluster. b. Local entropy sent by sensors to CH in a cluster.

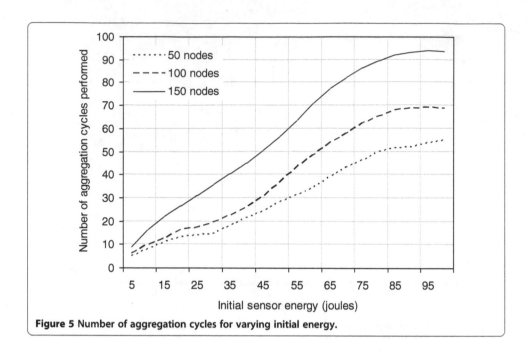

Figure 5 Number of aggregation cycles for varying initial energy.

100 (Figure 9b) respectively. The lifetime performance of the protocols is illustrated in terms of remaining number of alive nodes. Evidently, our proposed scheme achieves significant improvement during the simulation. It is worth revealing that the gain in lifetime is achieved by sending the entropy of nodes in the first phase of aggregation followed by reduced data transmission (expected value) in second phase. This results in reducing the bulk of packets transfer, thereby increasing the network lifetime commendably. Moreover, as the number of initially deployed nodes is increased to 100, HEED and BP fails to keep the network functional till the end of simulation period (Figure 9b).

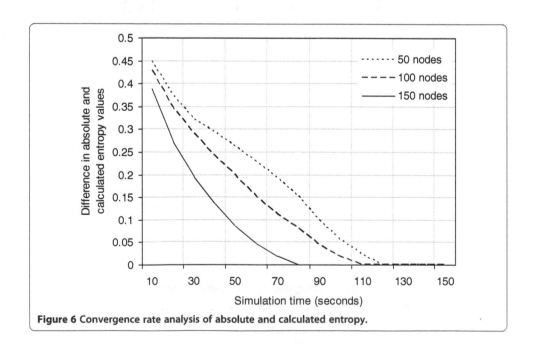

Figure 6 Convergence rate analysis of absolute and calculated entropy.

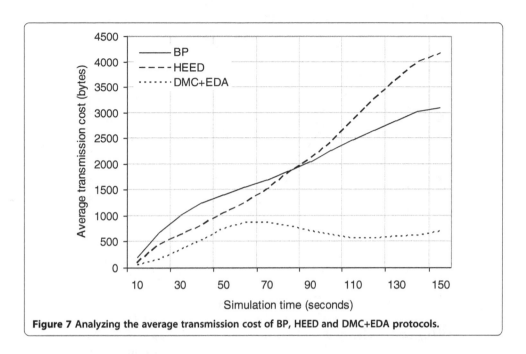

Figure 7 Analyzing the average transmission cost of BP, HEED and DMC+EDA protocols.

Hence, the above experimental results rationalize the development of our proposed clustering and aggregation strategy.

Conclusion & future research directions

In this research, we have demonstrated that our proposed clustering protocol in wireless sensor network provides significant energy savings. The clustering process is purely distributed and is based on the sensed data, regardless of geographic positioning and distance measures. We have calculated the precision of sensor data on the basis of local and global probability model. Furthermore, we have also analyzed the rate and impact

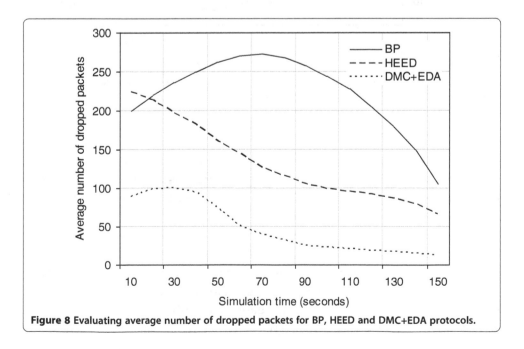

Figure 8 Evaluating average number of dropped packets for BP, HEED and DMC+EDA protocols.

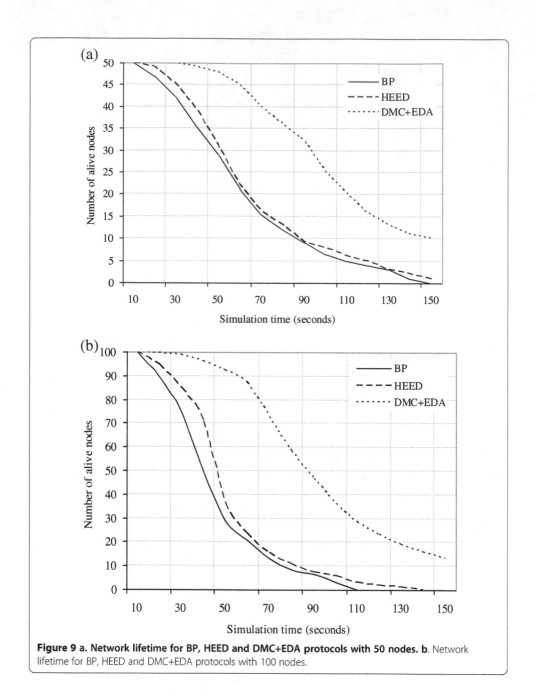

Figure 9 a. Network lifetime for BP, HEED and DMC+EDA protocols with 50 nodes. b. Network lifetime for BP, HEED and DMC+EDA protocols with 100 nodes.

of information gain, i.e. convergence rate of calculated sensor entropy towards the absolute value. We have also defined the working slots to aggregate data for the initial period with partially clustered network and for the intermediate cycles, once the whole network is clustered.

The simulations of our proposed methods have shown outperforming results. The entropy measurement facilitates the efficient selection of maximum information bearing nodes, which further makes more accurate aggregation at the cluster head. It is also clarified that our proposed data aggregation technique performs in energy efficient manner. Moreover, the energy consumption in the network has also been carried out for several aggregation cycles. Therefore, it can be concluded that entropy based fusion is relevant in terms of information integrity, network lifetime as well as energy utilization.

Thus far we have concentrated on the homogeneous sensor networks with a single powerful processing center (sink). In our future work, we would rather focus on the heterogeneous wireless sensor networks with multiple resource-rich actors for carrying out energy consuming tasks. Apart from this, we would emphasis our effort on developing novel entropy-based techniques so as to enrich the integrity of aggregated content, thereby maintaining a delay constrain on the computational efficiency.

Competing interest
Both authors declare that they have no competing interests.

Authors' contributions
The authors have performed entropy based data aggregation that is computed from the proposed local and global probability distribution models, for extracting high precision data from the sensor nodes. An energy efficient clustering method is also proposed with the help of cluster divergence measure. Experimental analysis is carried out in terms of convergence rate, aggregation cycles, average packet drops, transmission cost and network lifetime. Both authors read and approved the final manuscript.

Authors' information
Adwitiya Sinha has completed Bachelor of Computer Applications and Master of Computer Applications in 2006 and 2008. She received Master of Technology in the Computer Science and Technology in 2010 from Jawaharlal Nehru University, New Delhi, India. Presently, she is working towards her PhD in the same university. She is the recipient of Senior Research Fellowship from Council of Scientific and Industrial Research, India. Her major interest lies in energy-efficient wireless networking, mobile and ad hoc communication, data aggregation and filtration techniques. D. K. Lobiyal received his Bachelor of Technology in Computer Science from Lucknow University, India. He received Master of Technology and PhD both in Computer Science from Jawaharlal Nehru University, New Delhi, India. Presently, he is working as an Associate Professor in the School of Computer and Systems Sciences at Jawaharlal Nehru University. His areas of research interest are Wireless ad Hoc Networks, Video on Demand, and Natural Language Processing (NLP).

References
1. Akyildiz IF, Su W, Sankarasubramaniam Y, Cayirci E (2002) Wireless sensor networks: a survey. J Comp Networks 38(4):393–422, Elsevier
2. Yong-Min L, Shu-Ci W, Xiao-Hong N (2009) The architecture and characteristics of wireless sensor networks. IEEE Int Conf Comp Technol Dev 1:561–565, 13-15 November 2009
3. Potdar V, Sharif A, Chang E (2009) Wireless sensor networks: a survey. IEEE Int Conf Adv Inf Netw Appl:636–641, 26-29 May 2009
4. Eskandari Z, Yaghmaee MH, Mohajerzadeh AH (2008) Energy efficient spanning tree for data aggregation in wireless sensor networks. IEEE Proceedings of 17th International Conference on Computer Communications and Networks., pp 1–5, 3-7 August 2008
5. Galluccio L, Palazzo S, Campbell AT (2008) Efficient data aggregation in wireless sensor networks: an entropy-driven analysis. IEEE 19th International Symposium on Personal, Indoor and Mobile Radio Communications., pp 1–6, 15-18 September 2008
6. Cai W, Zhang M (2008) Data aggregation mechanism based on wavelet-entropy for wireless sensor networks. 4th IEEE International Conference on Wireless Communications, Networking and Mobile Computing, pp 1–4, 12-14 October 2008
7. Heinzelman WR, Chandrakasan A, Balakrishnan H (2000) Energy-efficient communication protocols for wireless microsensor networks. IEEE Proceedings of the 33rd Hawaii International Conference on System Sciences, pp 1–10, 4-7 January 2000
8. Yu B, Li J, Li Y (2009) Distributed data aggregation scheduling in wireless sensor networks. IEEE INFOCOM:2159–2167, 19-25 April 2009
9. Azim MA, Moad S, Bouadallah N (2010) SAG: Smart Aggregation Technique for continuous-monitoring in wireless sensor networks. IEEE International Conference on Communications, pp 1–6, 23-27 May 2010
10. Jiang H, Jin S, Wang C (2010) Parameter-based data aggregation for statistical information extraction in wireless sensor networks. IEEE Trans Vehicular Technol 59(8):3992–4001
11. Ma Y, Guo Y, Tian X, Ghanem M (2011) Distributed clustering-based aggregation algorithm for spatial correlated sensor networks. IEEE Sensors Journal 11(3):641–648
12. Tsai YR, Chang CJ (2011) Cooperative information aggregation for distributed estimation in wireless sensor networks. IEEE Trans Signal Processing 8:3876–3888
13. Younis O, Fahmy S (2004) Distributed clustering in Ad-hoc sensor networks: a hybrid, energy-efficient approach. IEEE INFOCOM:1–12, 7-11 March 2004
14. Anker T, Bickson D, Dolve D, Hod B (2008) Efficient clustering for improving network performance in wireless sensor networks. LNCS 4913/2008:221–236, Springer

15. Chitnis L, Dobra A, Ranka S (2008) Aggregation methods for large-scale sensor networks. ACM Trans Sensor Netw 4(2):1–36
16. Castelluccia C, Chan AC-F, Mykletun E, Tsudik G (2009) Efficient and provably secure aggregation of encrypted data in wireless sensor networks. ACM Trans Sensor Netw 5(3):1–36
17. Xiong N, Svensson P (2002) Multi-sensor management for information fusion: issues and approaches. Inf Fusion 3(2):163–186, Elsevier
18. Heinzelman W, Chandrakasan A, Balakrishnan H (2002) An application-specific protocol architectures for wireless microsensor networks. IEEE Trans Wireless Comm 1(4):660–670
19. Ghiasi S, Srivastava A, Yang XJ, Sarrafzadeh M (2004) Optimal energy aware clustering in sensor networks. Sensors J 2(7):258–269
20. Srinivasan SM, Azadmanesh A (2008) Data aggregation in static Adhoc networks, 3rd IEEE international conference on industrial and information systems., pp 1–6, 8-10 December 2008
21. Wang X, Li J (2009) Precision constraint data aggregation for dynamic cluster-based wireless sensor networks. 5th International Conference on Mobile Ad-hoc and Sensor Networks., pp 172–179, 14-16 December 2009
22. Zhao F, Shin J, Reich J (2002) Information-driven dynamic sensor collaboration. IEEE Signal Process Mag 19:61–72
23. Commuri S, Tadigotla V (2007) Dynamic data aggregation in wireless sensor networks, IEEE 22nd International Symposium on Intelligent Control., pp 1–6, 1-3 October 2007
24. Kong L, Chen Z, Yin F (2007) Optimum design of a window function based on the small-world networks. IEEE International Conference on Granular Computing, p 97, 2-4 November 2007
25. Eguchi S, Copus J (2006) Interpreting Kullback–Leibler Divergence with the Neyman–Pearson Lemma. J Multivar Anal 97:2034–2040, Elsevier
26. Chang H, Yao Y, Koschan A, Abidi B, Abidi M (2009) Improving face recognition via narrowband spectral range selection using Jeffrey Divergence. IEEE Trans Inf Forensics Security 4(1):111–123
27. Duch W (2004) Uncertainty of data, Fuzzy membership functions, and multi-layer perceptrons. IEEE Trans Neural Netw 20:1–12
28. Gray RM (1990) Entropy and information theory. Springer-Verlag, New York, USA
29. Fall K, Varadhan K (2009) The ns manual, the VINT project
30. Altman E, Jemenez T (2003) NS simulator for beginners. Morgan & Claypool Publishers, Florida, USA
31. Attaway S (2009) Part I: programming and problem solving using MATLAB, in: MATLAB-A Practical Approach. Elsevier, USA, pp 1–196

Permissions

List of Contributors

Yan Luo
Department of Computer Science, The University of Western Ontario, London, ON, Canada

Orland Hoeber
Department of Computer Science, Memorial University of Newfoundland, St.John's, NL, Canada

Yuanzhu Chen
Department of Computer Science, Memorial University of Newfoundland, St.John's, NL, Canada Department of Computer Science, The University of Regina, Regina, SK, Canada

Jin Hui Chong
Department of Computer Science and Mathematics, Faculty of Applied Sciences and Computing, Tunku Abdul Rahman University College, Jalan Genting Kelang, Setapak 53300 Kuala Lumpur, Malaysia

Chee Kyun Ng
Institute of Gerontology, University Putra Malaysia, UPM Serdang 43400 Selangor, Malaysia
Department of Computer and Communication Systems Engineering, Faculty of Engineering, University Putra Malaysia, UPM Serdang 43400 Selangor, Malaysia

Nor Kamariah Noordin
Department of Computer and Communication Systems Engineering, Faculty of Engineering, University Putra Malaysia, UPM Serdang 43400 Selangor, Malaysia

Borhanuddin Mohd Ali
Department of Computer and Communication Systems Engineering, Faculty of Engineering, University Putra Malaysia, UPM Serdang 43400 Selangor, Malaysia

Balamurugan Rajagopal
Anna University Regional Centre, Coimbatore 641047 TN, India

Lalithambika Rajasekaran
Anna University Regional Centre, Coimbatore 641047 TN, India

Anilkumar Kothalil Gopalakrishnan
Distributed and Parallel Computing Research Laboratory, Department of Computer Science, Faculty of Science and Technology, Assumption University, Soi 24, Ramkhamheang Road, Hua Mak, Bang Kapi, Bangkok 10240, Thailand

Jan Vanus
VSB TU Ostrava, Department of Cybernetics and Biomedical Engineering, Technical University of Ostrava, 17. listopadu 15/2172, 708 33 Ostrava, Czech Republic

Pavel Kucera
VSB TU Ostrava, Department of Cybernetics and Biomedical Engineering, Technical University of Ostrava, 17. listopadu 15/2172, 708 33 Ostrava, Czech Republic

Radek Martinek
VSB TU Ostrava, Department of Cybernetics and Biomedical Engineering, Technical University of Ostrava, 17. listopadu 15/2172, 708 33 Ostrava, Czech Republic

Jiri Koziorek
VSB TU Ostrava, Department of Cybernetics and Biomedical Engineering, Technical University of Ostrava, 17. listopadu 15/2172, 708 33 Ostrava, Czech Republic

Sebastian Feese
Wearable Computing Laboratory, ETH Zurich, Gloriastrasse 35, 8092 Zurich CH, Switzerland

Michael Joseph Burscher
Department of Psychology, University of Zurich, Binzmuehlestrasse 14, 8050 Zurich CH, Switzerland

Klaus Jonas
Department of Psychology, University of Zurich, Binzmuehlestrasse 14, 8050 Zurich CH, Switzerland

Gerhard Tröster
Wearable Computing Laboratory, ETH Zurich, Gloriastrasse 35, 8092 Zurich CH, Switzerland

Huynh Thi Thanh Binh
School of Information and Communication Technology, Hanoi University of Science and Technology, Hanoi, Vietnam

Son Hong Ngo
School of Information and Communication Technology, Hanoi University of Science and Technology, Hanoi, Vietnam

Rachid Benlamri
Department of Software Engineering, Lakehead University, 955 Oliver Rd, Thunder Bay, ON P7B 5E1, Canada

Xiaoyun Zhang
Department of Software Engineering, Lakehead University, 955 Oliver Rd, Thunder Bay, ON P7B 5E1, Canada

Anuradha Pughat
School of Information and Communication Technology, Gautam Buddha University, Greater Noida, India

Vidushi Sharma
School of Information and Communication Technology, Gautam Buddha University, Greater Noida, India

Balqies Sadoun
Department of Surveying and Geomatics Engineering, AL-Balqa' Applied University, Al-Salt, Jordan

Omar Al-Bayari
Department of Surveying and Geomatics Engineering, AL-Balqa' Applied University, Al-Salt, Jordan

Jalal Al-Azizi
Department of Surveying and Geomatics Engineering, AL-Balqa' Applied University, Al-Salt, Jordan

Samih Al Rawashdeh
Department of Surveying and Geomatics Engineering, AL-Balqa' Applied University, Al-Salt, Jordan

Admir Barolli
Faculty of Business and Technologies, Department of Information Technology, Kristal University, Autostrada Tirane - Durres, Km 3, Tirana, Albania

Shinji Sakamoto
Canadian Institute of Technology, Zayed Center, Rr. Sulejman Delvina, Tirana, Albania
Graduate School of Engineering, Fukuoka Institute of Technology (FIT), 3-30-1 Wajiro-Higashi, Higashi-Ku, Fukuoka, 811-0295 Fukuoka, Japan
Fukuoka Institute of Technology (FIT), 3-30-1 Wajiro-Higashi, Higashi-Ku, Fukuoka, 811-0295 Fukuoka, Japan
Department of Information and Communication Engineering, Fukuoka Institute of Technology (FIT), 3-30-1 Wajiro-Higashi, Higashi-Ku, Fukuoka, 811-0295 Fukuoka, Japan
Department of Languages and Informatics Systems, Technical University of Catalonia, C/Jordi Girona 1-3, 08034 Barcelona, Spain

Tetsuya Oda
Canadian Institute of Technology, Zayed Center, Rr. Sulejman Delvina, Tirana, Albania
Graduate School of Engineering, Fukuoka Institute of Technology (FIT), 3-30-1 Wajiro-Higashi, Higashi-Ku, Fukuoka, 811-0295 Fukuoka, Japan
Fukuoka Institute of Technology (FIT), 3-30-1 Wajiro-Higashi, Higashi-Ku, Fukuoka, 811-0295

Fukuoka, Japan
Department of Information and Communication Engineering, Fukuoka Institute of Technology (FIT), 3-30-1 Wajiro-Higashi, Higashi-Ku, Fukuoka, 811-0295 Fukuoka, Japan
Department of Languages and Informatics Systems, Technical University of Catalonia, C/Jordi Girona 1-3, 08034 Barcelona, Spain

Evjola Spaho
Canadian Institute of Technology, Zayed Center, Rr. Sulejman Delvina, Tirana, Albania
Graduate School of Engineering, Fukuoka Institute of Technology (FIT), 3-30-1 Wajiro-Higashi, Higashi-Ku, Fukuoka, 811-0295 Fukuoka, Japan
Fukuoka Institute of Technology (FIT), 3-30-1 Wajiro-Higashi, Higashi-Ku, Fukuoka, 811-0295 Fukuoka, Japan
Department of Information and Communication Engineering, Fukuoka Institute of Technology (FIT), 3-30-1 Wajiro-Higashi, Higashi-Ku, Fukuoka, 811-0295 Fukuoka, Japan
Department of Languages and Informatics Systems, Technical University of Catalonia, C/Jordi Girona 1-3, 08034 Barcelona, Spain

Leonard Barolli
Canadian Institute of Technology, Zayed Center, Rr. Sulejman Delvina, Tirana, Albania
Graduate School of Engineering, Fukuoka Institute of Technology (FIT), 3-30-1 Wajiro-Higashi, Higashi-Ku, Fukuoka, 811-0295 Fukuoka, Japan
Fukuoka Institute of Technology (FIT), 3-30-1 Wajiro-Higashi, Higashi-Ku, Fukuoka, 811-0295 Fukuoka, Japan
Department of Information and Communication Engineering, Fukuoka Institute of Technology (FIT), 3-30-1 Wajiro-Higashi, Higashi-Ku, Fukuoka, 811-0295 Fukuoka, Japan
Department of Languages and Informatics Systems, Technical University of Catalonia, C/Jordi Girona 1-3, 08034 Barcelona, Spain

Fatos Xhafa
Canadian Institute of Technology, Zayed Center, Rr. Sulejman Delvina, Tirana, Albania
Graduate School of Engineering, Fukuoka Institute of Technology (FIT), 3-30-1 Wajiro-Higashi, Higashi-Ku, Fukuoka, 811-0295 Fukuoka, Japan
Fukuoka Institute of Technology (FIT), 3-30-1 Wajiro-Higashi, Higashi-Ku, Fukuoka, 811-0295 Fukuoka, Japan
Department of Information and Communication Engineering, Fukuoka Institute of Technology (FIT), 3-30-1 Wajiro-Higashi, Higashi-Ku, Fukuoka, 811-0295 Fukuoka, Japan
Department of Languages and Informatics Systems, Technical University of Catalonia, C/Jordi Girona 1-3, 08034 Barcelona, Spain

Bambang AB Sarif
Electrical and Computer Engineering Department, University of British Columbia, 2332 Main Mall, Vancouver, BC V6T 1Z4, Canada

Mahsa T Pourazad
Electrical and Computer Engineering Department, University of British Columbia, 2332 Main Mall, Vancouver, BC V6T 1Z4, Canada
TELUS Communications Inc, 555 Robson St, Vancouver, British Columbia V6B 3K9, Canada

Panos Nasiopoulos
Electrical and Computer Engineering Department, University of British Columbia, 2332 Main Mall, Vancouver, BC V6T 1Z4, Canada

Victor CM Leung
Electrical and Computer Engineering Department, University of British Columbia, 2332 Main Mall, Vancouver, BC V6T 1Z4, Canada

Amr Mohamed
Computer Science and Engineering Department, Qatar University, Doha, Qatar

Balamurugan Rajagopal
Assistant Director (Administration), All India Council for Technical Education, New Delhi, India

Lalithambika Rajasekaran
Post Graduate Engineer, Anna University (Regional Centre Coimbatore), Tamil Nadu, India

Adwitiya Sinha
School of Computer & Systems Sciences, Jawaharlal Nehru University, New Delhi, India

Daya Krishan Lobiyal
School of Computer & Systems Sciences, Jawaharlal Nehru University, New Delhi, India